CONTROL AND DYNAMIC SYSTEMS

Advances in Theory and Applications

Volume 19

CONTRIBUTORS TO THIS VOLUME

W. MICHAEL BOWLES
JOHN A. CARTELLI
LEONARD CHIN
C. FARGEON
M. GAUVRIT
VYTAS B. GYLYS
DAVID F. LIANG
P. RODRIGO

CONTROL AND DYNAMIC SYSTEMS

ADVANCES IN THEORY AND APPLICATIONS

Edited by
C. T. LEONDES

School of Engineering and Applied Science
University of California
Los Angeles, California

VOLUME 19: NONLINEAR AND KALMAN FILTERING TECHNIQUES
Part 1 of 3

1983

ACADEMIC PRESS
A Subsidiary of Harcourt Brace Jovanovich, Publishers

New York London
Paris San Diego San Francisco São Paulo Sydney Tokyo Toronto

ACADEMIC PRESS RAPID MANUSCRIPT REPRODUCTION

ACADEMIC PRESS, INC.
111 Fifth Avenue, New York, New York 10003

United Kingdom Edition published by
ACADEMIC PRESS, INC. (LONDON) LTD.
24/28 Oval Road, London NW1 7DX

LIBRARY OF CONGRESS CATALOG CARD NUMBER: 64-8027

ISBN 0-12-012719-9

PRINTED IN THE UNITED STATES OF AMERICA

83 84 85 86   9 8 7 6 5 4 3 2 1

CONTENTS

Advances in Computational Efficiencies of Linear Filtering

Leonard Chin

Design of Real-Time Estimation Algorithms for Implementation in Microprocessor and Distributed Processor Systems

Vytas B. Gylys

Global Approximation for Nonlinear Filtering with Application to Spread Spectrum Ranging

W. Michael Bowles and John A. Cartelli

CONTRIBUTORS

Numbers in parentheses indicate the pages on which the authors' contributions begin.

W. Michael Bowles *(297), Space Communications Group, Hughes Aircraft Co., Systems Analysis and Design Laboratory, Los Angeles, California 90009*

John A. Cartelli *(297), Technical Staff, ESL, Sunnyvale, California*

Leonard Chin *(125), Naval Air Development Center, Warminster, Pennsylvania 18974*

C. Fargeon *(81), Department d'Etudes et de Recherches en Automatique, ONERA/CERT, Toulouse, France*

M. Gauvrit *(81), Department d'Etudes et de Recherches en Automatique, ONERA/CERT, Toulouse, France*

Vytas B. Gylys *(193), Texas Instruments, Inc., Lewisville, Texas 75067*

David F. Liang *(1), Defence Research Establishment Ottawa, Department of National Defence, Shirley's Bay, Ottawa, Canada*

P. Rodrigo *(81), Department d'Etudes et de Recherches en Automatique, ONERA/CERT, Toulouse, France*

PREFACE

The theme for Volume 19 is advances in the techniques and technology of nonlinear filters and Kalman filters. As this volume crystallized, there was so much material of basic value that it has grown to three volumes in this series; this theme, therefore, will be continued in Volumes 20 and 21. These volumes will treat the subject in three broad parts: Part 1—Advanced Topics in the Theory of Nonlinear Filters and Kalman Filters, which is the subject of the first two chapters of this volume; Part 2—Computational Techniques in Nonlinear and Linear Filters, which is the subject of the remaining three chapters of this volume and the chapters at the beginning of Volume 20; Part 3—Advanced Nonlinear Filters and Kalman Filter and Applications and Methodologies, which is the subject of the remainder of Volume 20 and all of Volume 21.

This set of volumes thus comprises the most comprehensive treatment of the theory and its many applications to date. It is in the various complex real-world application chapters that many practitioners may find these three volumes particularly useful. This would include the chapters on the many computational issues appearing in textbook literature for the first time.

The first chapter in this volume, "Exact and Approximate State Estimation Techniques for Nonlinear Dynamic Systems," by Liang, is remarkable for its unique comprehensiveness and clarity. It will undoubtedly prove to be an essential reference source on the theory for practitioners for years to come. The next chapter, "Synthesis and Performance of Bayesian Estimators," by Gauvrit, Fargeon, and Rodrigo, which emphasizes applications, is probably the single most comprehensive and modern treatment of Bayesian estimation techniques available in the textbook literature. Computational efficiencies in the various approaches to filtering techniques have not been treated at all in the textbook literature; the next chapter, by Chin, thoroughly covers this subject. This chapter will also undoubtedly be an essential reference source for many years. The implementation of filters by the use of microprocessors and distributed processor systems is an essential and very broad topic that also has not previously been treated in textbook literature. The next chapter, by Gylys, thus constitutes another unique contribution of essential value to practitioners. Finally, practical means for dealing with nonlinearities, which cannot always be avoided in practice, are also difficult to find in textbooks. The final chapter, "Global Approximation for Nonlinear Filtering with Application to Spread Spectrum Ranging," by Bowles and Cartelli, is a very substantial contribution in this area.

When the theme for this volume was decided, there seemed little doubt that it was most timely. However, because of the important contributions of the authors to this and the next two volumes, all three promise to be not only timely but of substantial lasting value.

CONTENTS OF PREVIOUS VOLUMES

Volume 4

Volume 5

Volume 6

Volume 16

Volume 17

Volume 18

Exact and Approximate State Estimation Techniques for Nonlinear Dynamic Systems

DAVID F. LIANG

Defence Research Establishment Ottawa
Department of National Defence
Shirley's Bay, Ottawa, Canada

ISBN 0-12-012719-9

I. GENERAL INTRODUCTION

A. INTRODUCTION

The optimum estimation theory is of great importance in a variety of scientific and engineering problems. The notable work by Kalman [1,2] and Kalman and Bucy [3] resulted in by far the most successful solution. They considered the non-stationary linear system from the state-space point of view with measurements corrupted by white Gaussian noise processes and obtained recursive solutions for both the continuous and the discrete cases. The original derivation was based on the derivation of the Wiener-Hopf equation, using the orthogonal projection lemma [1]. This theory has become known as Kalman-Bucy filtering, and because of the obvious computational advantages of the recursive algorithms, it has found numerous applications in the fields of missile guidance, space vehicle navigation, econometrics, seismology, meteorology, biomedicine, communications, and many others.

After the appearance of Kalman and Bucy's work, the study of linear estimation problems was further generalized to the non-white-noise problems, that is, colored or no noise in one or more of the measurements. One of the first, and in many ways one of the most complete treatments of colored noise in continuous systems, was presented by Bryson and Johansen [4]. The discrete colored noise problem was examined by Bryson and Henrikson [5]. Stubberud [6], and Stear and Stubberud [7] considered the problems for continuous systems in which each measurement has only colored noise.

However, dynamic message models and measurement models for many realistic estimation problems are inherently nonlinear. Most of the work in nonlinear filtering is very theoretical; some are no more than a philosophy of approach rather than a procedure leading to the derivation of practical estimators.

One of the main lines of attack to the nonlinear estimation problem is the probability approach pioneered by Stratonovich [8] and subsequently taken up by Kushner [9,10], Wonham [11], Bucy [12], and Mortensen [13]. The truly optimal nonlinear filters for systems corrupted with additive white noise were given by Kushner [9,14], however, their exact solutions required infinite-dimensional systems, which are practically impossible to realize except in trivially simple cases.

The problems of obtaining a good approximation to the exact solutions of the nonlinear estimation problems are therefore very important. In one group of papers [15-17] the authors attempted to obtain the numerical solution using the so-called Bayesian point of view. They assumed knowledge of a completely valid probability description of the system, so that Bayes's rule can be applied to obtain a recursive description of the a posteriori probability density function. However, in many realistic problems the mathematical model of the system contains uncertainty that cannot be previously modeled by a probability distribution function. Furthermore, the Bayesian approach has the disadvantage of imposing a rather severe computational burden for even simple systems.

Another group of methods [18-22] essentially approximates the mean and variance of the a posteriori density functions based on perturbation relative to a prescribed reference. The majority of these techniques employs the Taylor series expansion of the dynamic system and measurement nonlinearities, neglecting second- and higher-order terms. Recently Sunahara [23] proposed replacement of the nonlinear functions by quasi-linear functions via stochastic linearization. In general, methods based on the Taylor series expansion suffer from the defect of replacing global distribution properties of a function by its local derivatives aggravated by corruption of noise processes. Thus it is questionable whether the more sophisticated approximations [24] provide useful improvements relative to the widely applied first-order approximation known as the extended Kalman filter.

In the areas of nonlinear smoothing estimation, Leondes *et al.* [25] derived the exact functional differential equations for the smoothing density functions and the smoothed estimates; but their solutions are prohibitive except in trivially simple cases, and hence approximate solutions are developed for sequential nonlinear smoothing.

Other works on nonlinear smoothing were presented by Kailath and Frost [26], Lainiotis [27], and Lee [28]. However, Kelly and Anderson [29] pointed out that the algorithms for both discrete and continuous-time, linear, fixed-lag smoothing presented in [26,30,31] may be unstable and therefore impractical. To be more explicit, although the fixed-lag smoothing equations are bounded-input and bounded-output stable, realizations of these in [30,31] contain a subsystem that is unstable in the sense of Lyapunov. In [29] it was pointed out that the apparent culprit is an uncontrollable and unstable block in the smoother state equations, which can be removed without affecting the input-output characteristics.

In [32] a computationally stable smoothing algorithm was derived for linear discrete systems containing time delays, using the method of orthogonal projection. The smoother for linear discrete systems without delays can be considered as a special case of the preceding problem, with time-delay index setting to zero. The results of [32] were rederived in a simple manner in [33] using the orthogonal projection method and the device of state augmentation. However, it was pointed out in [32] that the augmentation of state vectors has the effect of increasing the dimensions of the system and thus leads to a filter that is computationally inefficient.

In the areas of distributed parameter systems (DPS), nonlinear filtering results based on purely formal approaches were presented by Tzafestas and Nightingale [34] and Lamont and Kumar [35]. Tzafestas [36,37] discussed several kinds of smoothing problems by using Kalman's limiting procedure. Curtain [38] solved the general smoothing problem in Hilbert spaces by using both the innovation theory [26] and the theory of abstract evolution operators. Approximate smoothing and filtering equations were also derived by Yu *et al.* [39] for a general class of nonlinear functional differential systems.

B. SCOPE OF THIS CHAPTER

This chapter is devoted to the derivation of nonlinear estimation algorithms for discrete and continuous nonlinear dynamic systems with and without delays, corrupted by white Gaussian noise, correlated noise, and colored noise processes.

Section II follows the presentation of [40,41] to derive discrete-time filtering and smoothing algorithms for nonlinear time-delayed systems with multichannel delayed measurement signals imbedded in additive white-noise processes. The main technique makes use of the matrix minimum principle [42] to derive the optimal values of the coefficients in the estimation algorithms under the requirement that the estimates be unbiased. The estimation algorithms directly yield the fixed-lag, fixed-point, and fixed-interval smoothing algorithms and the filtering algorithm, with proper substitution of the discrete-time indices. This is illustrated in Sections II.D and II.E, where handy sets of reference equations are presented for the filtering and the fixed-lag smoothing estimators, respectively. Results pertaining to linear problems can be directly deduced from the nonlinear estimation algorithms. They agree well with those derived in the literature using other optimization techniques. The general results presented are applicable to various special cases of nonlinear as well as linear estimation problems, for example, to the estimation problems for linear or nonlinear systems without delays and to the estimation of linear or nonlinear systems with multiple delays appearing only in the measurements.

However, all nonlinear estimation algorithms presented in this chapter require infinite-dimensional systems to be realized, which is computationally impossible except in trivially simple cases. For the estimation algorithms to be physically realizable, it is assumed that the conditional probability density functions of the estimator errors are Gaussian. Techniques are presented to show how one can exactly evaluate expectations of polynomial, exponential, product-type, and state-dependent sinusoidal nonlinearities.

Section III deals with discrete nonlinear time-delayed systems and measurements imbedded in correlated noise processes. The derivation [40,43] as well as the presentation follow those of Section II. The results presented are applied to special cases of linear discrete-time estimation problems. Linear continuous-time estimation equations are derived using Kalman's limiting procedure.

Section IV presents nonlinear estimation algorithms for nonlinear discrete delayed systems with measurements containing multiple time delays and corrupted by colored noise [40,43].

Section V presents nonlinear estimation algorithms for nonlinear distributed parameter systems [44] involving multiple time delays. The results are first derived in discrete-time form through the use of the matrix minimum principle and are then formally converted to continuous-time form using Kalman's limiting procedure.

Section VI deals with continuous-time nonlinear systems without delays corrupted with additive white and non-white-noise processes [40,45]. The basic approach makes use of the matrix minimum principle together with the Kolmogorov [46] and Kushner [9,10] equations to minimize the error variance, taken to be the estimation criterion. The filtering equations obtained for nonlinear systems with white-noise process are exact, but for non-white-noise processes the results obtained are approximate.

To assess the performance of the proposed minimum-variance filter and to compare it with various other approximate finite-dimensional filters, Liang [47] selected various types of nonlinear systems, which were simulated on a digital computer. His results clearly indicate the superiority of the proposed minimum-variance estimator over those of other filters investigated, and theoretical explanations are also given for the apparent inferior performance characteristics of the various other filters considered.

II. STATE ESTIMATION FOR DISCRETE TIME-DELAYED SYSTEMS WITH ADDITIVE WHITE NOISE

A. *INTRODUCTION*

This section is devoted to the derivation of minimum-variance filtering and smoothing algorithms for discrete nonlinear time-delayed systems with multichannel delayed measurement signals imbedded in additive white-noise processes. In general, the filtering algorithm enables one to estimate present values of the variables of interest using present data, whereas the smoothing estimator allows one to estimate past values. A typical smoothing problem is the postflight estimation of the flight path of a missile based on tracking system measurements during the entire duration of the flight. If the estimates of the missile's position and velocity at one particular flight point are desired, they can be based on all the measurements recorded, including those made before and after that particular flight point.

In Section B, the problem statement is presented. Section C presents the derivation of the nonlinear smoothing estimator. The basic approach makes use of the matrix minimum principle to derive the optimal values of the coefficients in the estimation algorithms under the requirements that the estimates be unbiased and minimize the error-variance cost function. The resulting dynamic discrete estimation algorithms are recursive in nature and directly yield the fixed-lag, fixed-interval, fixed-point smoothing and filtering algorithms. The derivation is straightforward and shows the close links between the smoothing and filtering estimation algorithms. Sections D and E provide handy sets of reference equations for the filtering and the fixed-lag smoothing estimators. Section F shows the applicability of the presented algorithms to linear estimation problems. Section G shows how one can evaluate polynomial, product-type, exponential, and state-dependent sinusoidal nonlinearities without any other approximations, under the sole assumption that the conditional probability density functions of the estimator errors are Gaussian.

B. THE PROBLEM FORMULATION

The message and measurement models for the discrete nonlinear time-delayed systems are given by

$$x(k + 1) = \sum_{i=0}^{L} f_i[x(k - \alpha_i), k - \alpha_i] + G[x(k), k]w(k), \tag{1}$$

and

$$z(k) = \sum_{j=0}^{N} h_j[x(k - \beta_j), k - \beta_j] + v(k). \tag{2}$$

Here the state x is an n vector; the measurement z is an m vector; the random input w is an r vector; the measurement noise v is an m vector; G is a nonlinear state-dependent $n \times r$ matrix; k = 0, 1, ... is the discrete-time index. The nonlinear vector-valued functions f_i and h_j are, respectively, n- and m-dimensional.

The integer quantities α_i and β_j represent time delays, which are ordered such that

$$0 = \alpha_0 < \alpha_1 < \alpha_2 < \cdots < \alpha_L$$

and

$$0 = \beta_0 < \beta_1 < \beta_2 < \cdots < \beta_N.$$

The random vectors w(k) and v(k) are independent zero-mean white Gaussian sequences for which

$$E[w(k)w^T(j)] = \psi_w(k)\delta_{kj},$$

$$E[v(k)v^T(j)] = \psi_v(k)\delta_{kj},$$

and

$$E[w(k)v^T(j)] = 0$$

for all integers k and j, where E{ } denotes the expected value, T the matrix transpose, δ_{jk} the Kronecker delta, and ψ_v and ψ_w are $m \times m$ positive-definite and $r \times r$ nonnegative-definite matrices, respectively.

The initial states $x(-\alpha_i)$ for i = 0, 1, ..., s, where $s = \max(\alpha_L, \beta_N)$ are zero-mean Gaussian random vectors, which are independent of v(k) and w(k), with a positive-definite covariance matrix

$$E\left[x(-\alpha_i)x^T(-\alpha_j)\right] = V_x(\alpha_i, \alpha_j)$$

for i, j = 0, 1, ..., s.

The smoothing problem is to obtain $\hat{x}(k - l + 1/k + 1)$, the unbiased smoothing estimate of $x(k - l + 1)$, with $0 \leq l \leq k + 1$, conditioned on the set of measurements

$$Z(k + 1) = [z(0), z(1), \ldots, z(k + 1)]$$

such that the cost function

$$J(k + 1) = \text{trace}[M(k)V_{\tilde{x}}(k - l + 1/k + 1)] \tag{3}$$

is minimized. Here $M(k)$ is some symmetric positive-definite weighting matrix and $V_{\tilde{x}}(k - l + 1/k + 1)$ is defined by

$$\begin{aligned} V_{\tilde{x}}&(k - l + 1/k + 1) \\ &= E_{k+1}\{[x(k - l + 1) - \hat{x}(k - l + 1/k + 1)] \\ &\qquad \cdot [x(k - l + 1) - \hat{x}(k - l + 1/k + 1)]^T\}, \end{aligned} \tag{4}$$

where $E_{k+1}\{\ \}$ denotes the expectation operation conditioned on $Z(k + 1)$.

Because $M(k)$ is known, it can be shown that minimizing the cost function of Eq. (3) is equivalent to minimizing the trace of $[V_{\tilde{x}}(k - l + 1/k + 1)]$ at each individual sampling point k [48].

C. THE DERIVATION OF THE NONLINEAR SMOOTHING ESTIMATOR

It is assumed that the smoothing algorithm is described by the following nonlinear difference equation:

$$\begin{aligned} \hat{x}(k - l + 1/k + 1) = \sum_{i=0}^{L} b_i[\hat{x}(k - l - \gamma_i/k), k - l - \gamma_i] \\ + K_{k+1}^{l} z(k + 1). \end{aligned} \tag{5}$$

Here, the assumption of linearity in innovations is made. The nonlinear functions $\Sigma_{i=0}^{L} b_i[\hat{x}(k - l - \gamma_i/k), k - l - \gamma_i]$ and K_{k+1}^{l} are yet to be determined.

Because the message model considered in this section consists of the sum of nonlinear functions containing time delays, it is realistic to assume that the smoothing estimate is a linear combination of the sum of nonlinear functions of $\hat{x}(k - l - \gamma_i/k)$, to account for the time-delay characteristics, and the present measurement $z(k + 1)$. Here $\hat{x}(k - l - \gamma_i/k)$ is assumed to have made optimal use of all the measurements up to $z(k)$.

The problem formulated in such a manner may therefore lead to a smoother optimal with respect to the imposed constraint, but it may not be identical to the truly optimal one.

In the meantime, it is interesting to note that even though the smoothing algorithm may be described by other dynamic equations such as

$$\hat{x}(k - l + 1/k + 1) = \sum_{i=0}^{L} b_i[\hat{x}(k - l - \gamma_i/k), k - l - \gamma_i] + K_{k+1}^{l}\tilde{z}(k + 1/k),$$

where $\tilde{z}(k + 1/k) = z(k + 1) - E_k[z(k + 1)/Z(k)]$. The resulting smoother using either Eq. (5) or the last equation would be exactly identical.

Now the estimation problem is to determine the time-varying nonlinear vector-valued function $\Sigma_{i=0}^{L} b_i[\hat{x}(k - l - \gamma_i/k), k - l - \gamma_i]$ and the gain K_{k+1}^{l} such that the trace of $V_{\tilde{x}}(k - l + 1/k + 1)$ is minimized.

Let $\tilde{x}(k - l + 1/k + 1)$ denote the smoothing error defined by

$$\tilde{x}(k - l + 1/k + 1) = x(k - l + 1) - \hat{x}(k - l + 1/k + 1). \tag{6}$$

Then one can obtain

$$\tilde{x}(k - l + 1/k + 1)$$

$$= \sum_{i=0}^{L} f_i[x(k - l - \alpha_i), k - l - \alpha_i]$$

$$+ G[x(k - l), k - l]w(k - l)$$

$$- \sum_{i=0}^{L} b_i[\hat{x}(k - l - \gamma_i/k), k - l - \gamma_i]$$

$$- K_{k+1}^{l}\left\{\sum_{j=0}^{N} h_j[x(k - \beta_j + 1), k - \beta_j + 1] + v(k + 1)\right\}.$$

For $\hat{x}(k - l + 1/k + 1)$ to be an unbiased smoothing estimate, it is necessary that

$$\sum_{i=0}^{L} b_i[\hat{x}(k - l - \gamma_i/k), k - l - \gamma_i]$$

$$= \sum_{i=0}^{L} \hat{f}_i[x(k - l - \alpha_i), k - l - \alpha_i/k]$$

$$- K_{k+1}^{l} \sum_{j=0}^{N} \hat{h}_j[x(k - \beta_j + 1), k - \beta_j + 1/k], \tag{7}$$

where

$$\hat{f}_i[x(k - l - \alpha_i), k - l - \alpha_i/k]$$

$$= E_k\{f_i[x(k - l - \alpha_i), k - l - \alpha_i]\}$$

and

$$\hat{h}_j[x(k - \beta_j + 1), k - \beta_j + 1/k]$$

$$= E_k\{h_j[x(k - \beta_j + 1), k - \beta_j + 1]\}.$$

Substituting Eq. (7) into (5), the smoothing algorithm becomes

$$\hat{x}(k - l + 1/k + 1) = \hat{x}(k - l + 1/k) + K_{k+1}^{l}\left\{z(k + 1) - \sum_{j=0}^{N} \hat{h}_j[x(k - \beta_j + 1), k - \beta_j + 1/k]\right\} \quad (8)$$

for k = 0, 1, 2, ... and $0 \leq l \leq k + 1$, where

$$\hat{x}(k - l + 1/k) = \sum_{i=0}^{L} \hat{f}_i[x(k - l - \alpha_i), k - l - \alpha_i/k]. \quad (9)$$

Substitution of Eq. (8) into (6) yields

$$\tilde{x}(k - l + 1/k + 1) = \tilde{x}(k - l + 1/k) - K_{k+1}^{l}\left\{\sum_{j=0}^{N} \tilde{h}_j[x(k - \beta_j + 1)/k] + v(k + 1)\right\},$$

where

$$\tilde{h}_j[x(k - \beta_j + 1)/k] = h_j[x(k - \beta_j + 1), k - \beta_j + 1] - \hat{h}_j[x(k - \beta_j + 1), k - \beta_j + 1/k].$$

Therefore, the smoothing error-variance equation is specified by

$$
\begin{aligned}
&V_{\tilde{x}}(k - l + 1/k + 1) \\
&\quad = V_{\tilde{x}}(k - l + 1/k) \\
&\qquad - E_k\left\{\tilde{x}(k - l + 1/k) \sum_{j=0}^{N} \tilde{h}_j^T[x(k - \beta_j + 1)/k]\right\}K_{k+1}^{lT} \\
&\qquad - K_{k+1}^{l}E_k\left\{\sum_{j=0}^{N} \tilde{h}_j[x(k - \beta_j + 1/k]\tilde{x}^T(k - l + 1/k)\right\} \\
&\qquad + K_{k+1}^{l}\Psi_v(k + 1)K_{k+1}^{lT} \\
&\qquad + K_{k+1}^{l}E_k\left\{\sum_{i=0}^{N} \sum_{j=0}^{N} \tilde{h}_i[x(k - \beta_i + 1)/k]\right. \\
&\qquad\qquad \left. \cdot\, \tilde{h}_j^T[x(k - \beta_j + 1)/k]\right\}K_{k+1}^{lT}. \qquad (10)
\end{aligned}
$$

Here K_{k+1}^{l} is the only variable available for manipulation. The necessary condition for minimizing the trace of $V_{\tilde{x}}(k - l + 1/k + 1)$ subject to the constraint of Eq. (10) is provided by the matrix minimum principle for which K_{k+1}^{l} is considered to be the control variable and is obtained from the condition

$$\nabla \operatorname{trace}[V_{\tilde{x}}(k - l + 1/k + 1)] = [0],$$

where ∇ denotes the gradient matrix operation and [0] is the null matrix.

Hence, the gain algorithm is given by

$$K_{k+1}^{l} = E_k\left\{\tilde{x}(k - l + 1/k) \sum_{j=0}^{N} \tilde{h}_j^T[x(k - \beta_j + 1)/k]\right\}$$

$$\cdot \left\{\Psi_v(k + 1) + E_k\left[\sum_{i=0}^{N} \sum_{j=0}^{N} \tilde{h}_i[x(k - \beta_i + 1)/k]\right.\right.$$

$$\left.\left.\cdot \tilde{h}_j^T[x(k - \beta_j + 1)/k]\right]\right\}^{-1} \tag{11}$$

and Eq. (10) is reduced to

$$V_{\tilde{x}}(k - l + 1/k + 1)$$

$$= V_{\tilde{x}}(k - l + 1/k)$$

$$- K_{k+1}^{l} E_k\left\{\sum_{j=0}^{N} \tilde{h}_j[x(k - \beta_j + 1)/k]\tilde{x}^T(k - l + 1/k)\right\}. \tag{12}$$

Using Eqs. (1) and (9), there is the relation

$$\tilde{x}(k - l + 1/k) = \sum_{i=0}^{N} \tilde{f}_i[x(k - l - \alpha_i)/k]$$

$$+ G[x(k - l), k - l]w(k - l),$$

where

$$\tilde{f}_i[x(k - l - \alpha_i)/k] = f_i[x(k - l - \alpha_i), k - l - \alpha_i]$$

$$- \hat{f}_i[x(k - l - \alpha_i), k - l - \alpha_i/k].$$

Then the following recursive smoothing algorithms can also be derived:

$$V_{\tilde{x}}(k - l + 1, k/k)$$

$$= E_k\left\{\sum_{i=0}^{L} \tilde{f}_i[x(k - l - \alpha_i)/k]\tilde{x}^T(k/k)\right\}, \tag{13}$$

$$V_{\tilde{x}}(k - l + 1, k - m + 1/k)$$

$$= \sum_{i=0}^{L} \sum_{j=0}^{L} E_k\left\{\tilde{f}_i[x(k - l - \alpha_i)/k]\tilde{f}_j^T[x(k - m - \alpha_j)/k]\right\}$$
$$+ E_k\left\{G[x(k - l), k - l]\Psi_w(k - l) \cdot G^T[x(k - l), k - l]\right\}\delta_{k-l,k-m}, \tag{14}$$

$$V_{\tilde{x}}(k - l, k + 1/k)$$

$$= \sum_{i=0}^{L} E_k\left\{\tilde{x}(k - l/k)\tilde{f}_i^T[x(k - \alpha_i)/k]\right\}, \tag{15}$$

and

$$V_{\tilde{x}}(k - l + 1, k - m + 1/k + 1)$$

$$= V_{\tilde{x}}(k - l + 1, k - m + 1/k)$$

$$- K_{k+1}^{l}E_k\left\{\sum_{j=0}^{N} \tilde{h}_j[x(k - \beta_j + 1)/k]\tilde{x}^T(k - m + 1/k)\right\} \tag{16}$$

for $0 \leq l, m \leq k + 1$. The algorithms derived here are listed in Table I for ease of reference.

For $k < 0$, there are no inputs to the smoother, and therefore $\hat{x}(-\alpha_i/-1)$ is set to zero for $i = 0, 1, \ldots, s$, where $s = \max(\alpha_L, \beta_N)$, which in turn leads to

$$\tilde{x}(-\alpha_i/-1) = x(-\alpha_i)$$

and

$$V_{\tilde{x}}(-\alpha_i, -\alpha_j/-1) = V_x(\alpha_i, \alpha_j)$$

for $i, j = 0, 1, \ldots, s$.

Table I. Nonlinear Estimation for Discrete Delayed Systems with Additive White Noise.

System state and measurement equations

$$x(k + 1) = \sum_{i=0}^{L} f_i[x(k - \alpha_i), k - \alpha_i] + G[x(k), k]w(k),$$

$$z(k) = \sum_{j=0}^{N} h_j[x(k - \beta_j), k - \beta_j] + v(k)$$

Estimation algorithm

$$\hat{x}(k - l + 1/k + 1)$$

$$= \hat{x}(k - l + 1/k)$$

$$+ K_{k+1}^{l}\left\{z(k + 1) - \sum_{j=0}^{N} \hat{h}_j[x(k - \beta_j + 1), k - \beta_j + 1/k]\right\},$$

$$\hat{x}(k - l + 1/k)$$

$$= \sum_{i=0}^{L} \hat{f}_i[x(k - l - \alpha_i), k - l - \alpha_i/k].$$

Gain algorithm

$$K_{k+1}^{l} = E_k\left\{\tilde{x}(k - l + 1/k) \sum_{j=0}^{N} \tilde{h}_j^T[x(k - \beta_j + 1)/k]\right\}$$

$$\cdot \left\{\Psi_v(k + 1) + E_k\left[\sum_{i=0}^{N} \sum_{j=0}^{N} \tilde{h}_i[x(k - \beta_i + 1)/k]\right.\right.$$

$$\left.\left.\cdot\ \tilde{h}_j^T[x(k - \beta_j + 1)/k]\right]\right\}^{-1}.$$

(*Table I continues*)

Table I. (Continued)

Error-variance algorithm

$$V_{\tilde{x}}(k - l + 1, k - m + 1/k)$$

$$= \sum_{i=0}^{L} \sum_{j=0}^{L} E_k\left\{\tilde{f}_i[x(k - l - \alpha_i)/k]\tilde{f}_j^T[x(k - m - \alpha_j)/k]\right\}$$

$$+ E_k\left\{G[x(k - l), k - l]\Psi_w(k - l) \cdot G^T[x(k - l), k - l]\right\}\delta_{k-l,k-m},$$

$$V_{\tilde{x}}(k - l + 1, k - m + 1/k + 1)$$

$$= V_{\tilde{x}}(k - l + 1, k - m + 1/k)$$

$$- K_{k+1}^{l} E_k\left\{\sum_{j=0}^{N} \tilde{h}_j[x(k - \beta_j + 1)/k]\tilde{x}^T(k - m + 1/k)\right\},$$

$$V_{\tilde{x}}(k - l + 1, k/k) = E_k\left\{\sum_{i=0}^{L} \tilde{f}_i[x(k - \alpha_i - l)/k]\tilde{x}^T(k/k)\right\}$$

$$V_{\tilde{x}}(k - l, k + 1/k) = \sum_{i=0}^{L} E_k\left\{\tilde{x}(k - l/k)\tilde{f}_i^T[x(k - \alpha_i)/k]\right\}.$$

Because the smoothing estimator is unbiased, the expectations that are in Eqs. (11)-(16) can be further simplified as

$$E_k\left\{\tilde{x}(k - l + 1/k) \sum_{j=0}^{N} \tilde{h}_j^T[x(k - \beta_j + 1)/k]\right\}$$

$$= E_k\left\{\tilde{x}(k - l + 1/k) \sum_{j=0}^{N} h_j^T[x(k - \beta_j + 1), k - \beta_j + 1]\right\}, \quad (17)$$

$$E_k\left\{\sum_{i,j=0}^{N} \tilde{h}_i[x(k - \beta_i + 1)/k]\tilde{h}_j^T[x(k - \beta_j + 1/k]\right\}$$

$$= E_k\left\{\sum_{i,j=0}^{N} h_i[x(k - \beta_i + 1), k - \beta_i + 1]\right.$$

$$\left.\cdot\ h_j^T[x(k - \beta_j + 1), k - \beta_j + 1]\right\}$$

$$- \sum_{i,j=0}^{N} \hat{h}_i[x(k - \beta_i + 1), k - \beta_i + 1/k]$$

$$\cdot\ \hat{h}_j^T[x(k - \beta_j + 1), k - \beta_j + 1/k], \tag{18}$$

and

$$E_k\left\{\sum_{i,j=0}^{L} \tilde{f}_i[x(k - l - \alpha_i)/k]\tilde{f}_j^T[x(k - l - \alpha_j)/k]\right\}$$

$$= E_k\left\{\sum_{i,j=0}^{L} f_i[x(k - l - \alpha_i), k - l - \alpha_i]\right.$$

$$\left.\cdot\ f_j^T[x(k - l - \alpha_j), k - l - \alpha_j]\right\}$$

$$- \sum_{i,j=0}^{L} \hat{f}_i[x(k - l - \alpha_i), k - l - \alpha_i/k]$$

$$\cdot\ \hat{f}_j^T[x(k - l - \alpha_j), k - l - \alpha_j/k]. \tag{19}$$

It should be noted that three different types of smoothing and the filtering algorithms all follow immediately from Eqs. (8), (9), (11)-(16) with substitutions as shown in the accompanying tabulation.

Algorithm	*Replacement for k + 1*	*Replacement for l*
Filtering estimation	$k + 1$	0
Fixed-lag smoothing	k	M
Fixed-point smoothing	$k + 1$	$k - M + 1$
Fixed-interval smoothing	M	$M - k$

Results presented here are expected to be computationally efficient because no augmentation of state variables is involved. Also notice that, in the case of nonlinear systems, the preceding algorithms require infinite-dimensional systems to realize the various terms involving the expectations. The problem of obtaining a good approximation to these expectations is, therefore, of practical importance. For practical realization it is assumed that the conditional probability density functions of the smoothing error $\tilde{x}$ are Gaussian; then the expectation can be obtained without any further approximation for systems with polynomial, product-type, exponential, and state-dependent sinusoidal nonlinearities. This is further elaborated in Section II.G.

D. NONLINEAR FILTERING

The nonlinear filtering algorithm can be easily obtained from Eqs. (8), (9), and (11)-(16) by setting $l = 0$. The estimation algorithm is

$$\begin{aligned}\hat{x}(k + 1/k + 1) &= \hat{x}(k + 1/k) \\ &\quad + K^0_{k+1}\left\{z(k + 1) - \sum_{j=0}^{N} \hat{h}_j[x(k - \beta_j + 1), k - \beta_j + 1/k]\right\},\end{aligned} \tag{20}$$

$$\hat{x}(k + 1/k) = \sum_{i=0}^{L} \hat{f}_i[x(k - \alpha_i), k - \alpha_i/k]. \tag{21}$$

The gain algorithm is

$$K_{k+1}^0 = E_k\left\{\tilde{x}(k + 1/k) \sum_{j=0}^{N} \tilde{h}_j^T[x(k - \beta_j + 1)/k]\right\} \cdot \left\{\Psi_v(k + 1) + E_k\left[\sum_{i=0}^{N}\sum_{j=0}^{N} \tilde{h}_i[x(k - \beta_i + 1)/k] \cdot \tilde{h}_j^T[x(k - \beta_j + 1)/k]\right]\right\}^{-1}. \tag{22}$$

The error-variance equations are

$$V_{\tilde{x}}(k + 1/k + 1) = V_{\tilde{x}}(k + 1/k) - K_{k+1}^0 E_k\left\{\sum_{j=0}^{N} \tilde{h}_j[x(k - \beta_j + 1)/k] \cdot \tilde{x}^T(k + 1/k)\right\}, \tag{23}$$

$$V_{\tilde{x}}(k + 1/k) = \sum_{i=0}^{L}\sum_{j=0}^{L} E_k\left\{\tilde{f}_i[x(k - \alpha_i)/k]\tilde{f}_j^T[x(k - \alpha_j)/k]\right\} + E_k\left\{G[x(k), k]\Psi_w(k)G^T[x(k), k]\right\}, \tag{24}$$

whereas $V_{\tilde{x}}(k - l + 1, k/k)$, $V_{\tilde{x}}(k - l + 1, k - m + 1/k)$, and $V_{\tilde{x}}(k - l + 1, k - m + 1/k + 1)$ are, respectively, identical with Eqs. (13), (14), and (16).

E. NONLINEAR FIXED-LAG SMOOTHING

By replacing k + 1 and l by k and m, respectively, where $M < k$, from Eqs. (8), (9), and (11)-(16), one obtains the following recursive nonlinear fixed-lag smoothing algorithms:

$$\hat{x}(k - M/k) = \hat{x}(k - M/k - 1) + K_k^M\left\{z(k) - \sum_{j=0}^{N} \hat{h}_j[x(k - \beta_j), k - \beta_j/k - 1]\right\}, \tag{25}$$

$$\hat{x}(k - M/k - 1) = \sum_{i=0}^{L} \hat{f}_i[x(k - M - 1 - \alpha_i), k - M - 1 - \alpha_i/k - 1], \tag{26}$$

$$K_k^M = E_{k-1}\left\{\tilde{x}(k - M/k - 1) \sum_{i=0}^{N} \tilde{h}_j^T[x(k - \beta_j)/k - 1]\right\} \cdot \left\{\Psi_v(k) + E_{k-1}\left[\sum_{i=0}^{N} \sum_{j=0}^{N} \tilde{h}_i[x(k - \beta_i)/k - 1] \cdot \tilde{h}_j^T[x(k - \beta_j)/k - 1]\right]\right\}^{-1}, \tag{27}$$

$$V_{\tilde{x}}(k - M/k) = V_{\tilde{x}}(k - M/k - 1) - K_k^M E_{k-1}\left\{\sum_{j=0}^{N} \tilde{h}_j[x(k - \beta_j)/k - 1]\tilde{x}^T(k - M/k - 1)\right\}, \tag{28}$$

and

$$V_{\tilde{x}}(k - M/k - 1)$$

$$= \sum_{i,j=0}^{L} E_{k-1}\Big\{\tilde{f}_i[x(k - M - 1 - \alpha_i)/k - 1] \cdot \tilde{f}_j^T[x(k - M - \alpha_j - 1)/k - 1)\Big\}$$
$$+ E_{k-1}\Big\{G[x(k - M - 1), k - M - 1]\Psi_w(k - M - 1) \cdot G^T[x(k - M - 1), k - M - 1]\Big\}.$$

Other error-variance equations are directly obtainable from Eqs. (12)-(15).

F. LINEAR DISCRETE-TIME ESTIMATION

The results presented in Table I are readily applicable to linear discrete estimation problems. In order to provide a better insight into the structure of the linear smoothed estimator, consider the particular case of linear systems and measurements described by

$$\sum_{i=0}^{L} f_i[x(k - \alpha_i), k - \alpha_i] = \sum_{i=0}^{L} F_i(k)x(k - \alpha_i),$$

$$\sum_{j=0}^{N} h_j[x(k - \beta_j), k - \beta_j] = \sum_{j=0}^{N} H_j(k)x(k - \beta_j),$$

and

$$G[x(k), k] = G(k).$$

Then the linear fixed-lag smoothing algorithm as obtained from Eqs. (25)-(28) is as follows:

$$\hat{x}(k - M/k) = \hat{x}(k - M/k - 1) + K_k^M\left[z(k) - \sum_{j=0}^{N} H_j(k)\hat{x}(k - \beta_j/k - 1)\right],$$

$$\hat{x}(k - M/k - 1) = \sum_{i=0}^{L} F_i(k - M - 1)\hat{x}(k - M - 1 - \alpha_i/k - 1),$$

$$K_k^M = \left[\sum_{j=0}^{N} V_{\tilde{x}}(k - M, k - \beta_j/k - 1)H_j^T(k)\right]$$

$$\cdot \left[\sum_{i,j=0}^{N} H_i(k)V_{\tilde{x}}(k - \beta_i, k - \beta_j/k - 1)\right.$$

$$\left. \cdot H_j^T(k) + \Psi_v(k)\right]^{-1},$$

and

$$V_{\tilde{x}}(k - M/k) = V_{\tilde{x}}(k - M/k - 1)$$

$$- K_k^M E_{k-1}\left[\sum_{j=0}^{N} H_j(k)V_{\tilde{x}}(k - \beta_j, k - M/k - 1)\right].$$

Also

$$V_{\tilde{x}}(k - l, k - m/k - 1)$$

$$= \sum_{i=0}^{L}\sum_{j=0}^{L} F_i(k - l - 1)$$

$$\cdot V_{\tilde{x}}(k - 1 - l - \alpha_i, k - 1 - m - \alpha_j/k - 1)F_j^T(k - m - 1)$$

$$+ G(k - 1 - l)\Psi_w(k - 1 - l)G^T(k - 1 - l)\delta_{k-l,k-m},$$

and

$$V_{\tilde{x}}(k + 1/k)$$

$$= \sum_{i=0}^{L}\sum_{j=0}^{L} F_i(k)V_{\tilde{x}}(k - \alpha_i, k - \alpha_j/k)F_j^T(k) + G(k)\Psi_w(k)G^T(k).$$

Note that the structure of this fixed-lag smoother agrees well with that of Shukla and Srinath [49], whereas for linear problems with delays appearing only in the message model, this algorithm agrees well with that of Priemer and Vacroux [32]. In the same manner, one can identify the linear fixed-point smoother for linear systems without delays with that of Biswas and Mahalanabis [50]. Similarly, the results presented in Table I are applicable to other special cases of filtering and smoothing estimation problems. For linear estimation problems, the results are expected to be computationally efficient; because no augmentation of states was involved, this is particularly significant for systems with numerous delay parameters.

Thus a unified approach to obtaining the filtering and smoothing algorithms for linear as well as nonlinear, delayed as well as nondelayed systems has been presented. The results presented in this section can be extended to continuous-time problems through a formal limiting procedure [2].

G. *EVALUATION OF EXPECTATIONS*

The purpose of this section is to indicate how polynomial, product-type, exponential, or state-dependent sinusoidal nonlinearities can be evaluated without the need of approximation under the assumption that the estimation errors are Gaussian.

1. *Polynomial or Product-Type Nonlinearities*

For the sake of completeness in presentation, it is worth mentioning that the expectations of higher-order power terms can be easily evaluated using the following lemma.

Lemma 1

Let $\{\tilde{x}(t),\ t \in \tau\}$ be a zero-mean Gaussian process. Then all odd-order moments of $\tilde{x}$ vanish, and the even-order moments can be expressed in terms of the second-order moments using the following formula [51]:

$$E\{\tilde{x}(t_1)\cdots\tilde{x}(t_n)\}$$

$$= \sum E[\tilde{x}(t_{i_1})\tilde{x}(t_{i_2})]\cdots E[\tilde{x}(t_{i_{n-1}})\tilde{x}(t_{i_n})],$$

where the sum is taken over all possible ways of dividing the n points into n/2 combinations of pairs. The number of terms in the summation is equal to $1 \cdot 3 \cdot 5 \cdots (n - 3)(n - 1)$.

It should also be noted that lemma 1 can be rewritten as

$$E[\tilde{x}(t_1)\cdots\tilde{x}(t_n)]$$

$$= E[\tilde{x}(t_1)\tilde{x}(t_2)]E[\tilde{x}(t_3)\cdots\tilde{x}(t_n)]$$

$$+ E[\tilde{x}(t_1)\tilde{x}(t_3)]E[\tilde{x}(t_2)\tilde{x}(t_4)\cdots\tilde{x}(t_n)] + \cdots$$

$$+ E[\tilde{x}(t_1)\tilde{x}(t_n)]E[\tilde{x}(t_2)\tilde{x}(t_3)\cdots\tilde{x}(t_{n-1})],$$

which implies that nth order moments can be obtained from the expectations of (n - 2)th order moments. This is a rather useful formula in the evaluation of the expectations of higher-order power terms.

2. Nonlinearity Involving State-Dependent Sinusoids

In practical application of estimation techniques, one often encounters nonlinear terms involving state-dependent sinusoids. Fortunately, the expectations of such type of nonlinear functions can be rigidly obtained.

Lemma 2

Let x_1 and x_2 be jointly normally distributed random variable. Then

$$E[\cos(x_1 + x_2)]$$
$$= \mathrm{Re}\{\exp[j(\hat{x}_1 + \hat{x}_2) - (V_{11} + V_{22} + 2V_{12})/2]\},$$

and

$$E[\sin(x_1 + x_2)]$$
$$= \mathrm{Im}\{\exp[j(\hat{x}_1 + \hat{x}_2) - (V_{11} + V_{22} + 2V_{12})/2]\}.$$

These relationships are clearly seen from the definition of the characteristic function

$$\zeta_{\hat{x}}(u) = E(\exp ju^T x) = \exp\left(ju^T\hat{x} - \frac{1}{2}u^T V_x u\right)$$

where

$$u^T = [u_1, u_2, \ldots, u_k, \ldots, u_n],$$

$$\hat{x}^T = [\hat{x}_1, \hat{x}_2, \ldots, \hat{x}_k, \ldots, \hat{x}_n],$$

$$V_x = [\mathrm{cov}(x_i, x_j)].$$

Lemma 3

If an operator $I_k(u)$ is defined such that [52]

$$I_k[\zeta_{\hat{x}}(u)] = 1/j\ \partial\zeta_{\hat{x}}(u)/\partial u_k,$$

then we could easily derive the following relationships:

(i) $I_k = \hat{x}_k + ju^T V_x e_k$, where e_k is the kth unit vector,

(ii) $I_k\zeta_{\hat{x}}(u)|_{u=e_n} = (\hat{x}_k + jV_{nk})\zeta_{\hat{x}}(e_n) = E\left\{x_k e^{jx_n}\right\}\Big|_{u=e}$,

where $\zeta_{\hat{x}}(e_n) = \exp(j\hat{x}_n - V_{nn}/2)$,

(iii) $E\left\{x_k x_l e^{jx_n}\right\} = [(\sigma_k + I_k)(\sigma_l + I_l)]\zeta_{\hat{x}}(u)|_{u=e_n}$,

(iv) $E\left\{x_1 x_2 \cdots x_m e^{jx_n}\right\}$

$$= [(\sigma_1 + I_1)(\sigma_2 + I_2)\cdots(\sigma_m + I_m)]\zeta_{\hat{x}}(u)|_{u=e_n},$$

and

(v) $E\left\{\tilde{x}_1 \tilde{x}_2 x_3 \cdots x_m e^{jnx}\right\}$

$$= \Big[\left(\sigma_1 + ju^T V_x e_1\right)\left(\sigma_2 + ju^T V_x e_2\right)$$

$$\cdot (\sigma_3 + I_3)\cdots(\sigma_m + I_m)\Big]\zeta_{\hat{x}}(u)|_{u=e_n},$$

where we have

$$\prod_{i=1}^{\text{odd number}} \sigma_i = 0.$$

Using these identity relationships, one could easily calculate the expectations of all Gaussian distributed state-dependent sinusoids and hyperbolic sinusoids. For example

$E(x_1 x_2 \cos x_3)$

$$= \operatorname{Re}\left\{[V_{12} + (\hat{x}_1 + jV_{31})(\hat{x}_2 + jV_{23})]\left[\exp\left(j\hat{x}_3 - \tfrac{1}{2}V_{33}\right)\right]\right\}$$

$$= \{[V_{12} + (\hat{x}_1\hat{x}_2 - V_{31}V_{23})] \cos \hat{x}_3$$

$$- (\hat{x}_1 V_{23} + \hat{x}_2 V_{31}) \sin \hat{x}_3\} \exp\left(-\tfrac{1}{2}V_{33}\right).$$

and

$$E(x_1 x_2 \sin x_3) = \{[V_{12} + (\hat{x}_1\hat{x}_2 - V_{31}V_{23})] \sin \hat{x}_3$$

$$+ (\hat{x}_1 V_{23} + \hat{x}_2 V_{31}) \cos \hat{x}_3\} \exp\left(-\tfrac{1}{2}V_{33}\right).$$

3. *Nonlinearity Involving Exponential Functions*

Lemma 3 can also be easily applied to state-dependent exponential nonlinear functions. For example,

$$E[\exp(+Ax_1)] = \zeta_{\hat{x}}(u)|_{u=-jAe_1} = \exp\left(+Ax_1 + \tfrac{1}{2}A^2 V_{11}\right),$$

$$E(2^{x_1}) = E\{\exp[(j)(-j\ ln\ 2)x_1]\} = \zeta_{\hat{x}}(u)|_{u=-j\,ln 2}$$

$$= 2^{x_1} \exp\left[(ln\ 2)^2 V_{11}/2\right],$$

$$E[x_2 \exp(-Ax_1)] = I_2 \zeta_{\hat{x}}(u)|_{u=jAe_1}$$

$$= (\hat{x}_2 - AV_{21})\left(\exp -A\hat{x}_1 + A^2V_{11}/2\right),$$

$$E[x_2x_3 \exp(-Ax_1)] = (I_2 + \sigma_2)(I_3 + \sigma_3)\zeta_{\hat{x}}(u)|_{u=jAe_1}$$

$$= \left(V_{23} + \hat{x}_3\hat{x}_2 - A\hat{x}_2V_{31} - A\hat{x}_3V_{21} + A^2V_{31}V_{21}\right)$$

$$\cdot \exp\left(-A\hat{x}_1 + A^2V_{11}/2\right),$$

and

$$E\left[x_2^2x_3 \exp(-Ax_1)\right] = (\hat{x}_2 - AV_{12} + \sigma_2)^2(\hat{x}_3 - AV_{13} + \sigma_3),$$

$$\exp\left(-Ax_1 + A^2V_{11}/2\right) = \left[(\hat{x}_2 - AV_{12})^2(\hat{x}_3 - AV_{13}) + V_{22}(\hat{x}_3 - AV_{13}) + 2V_{23}(\hat{x}_2 - AV_{12})\right]$$

$$\cdot \exp\left(-A\hat{x}_1 + A^2V_{11}/2\right).$$

4. *Nonlinearity Involving State-Dependent Relays*

Section II.C noted that the implementation of nonlinear filtering algorithms requires the evaluation of the expectations of nonlinear vector-valued functions f and h, as well as products of these functions and estimation errors of states. For a number of applications, f and h may simply be some form of state-dependent relay. Expectations of some of these state-dependent relays are tabulated in [53].

To evaluate expectations of various other types of nonlinear functions, one might consider the use of Taylor series expansion or Hermite series, etc.

III. STATE ESTIMATION FOR DISCRETE TIME-DELAYED SYSTEMS WITH CORRELATED NOISE

A. *INTRODUCTION*

In Section II the noise processes considered are assumed to be Gaussian white and mutually independent. However, in many practical situations, the message noise processes are correlated with measurement noise processes. Raja Rao and Mahalanabis [54] derived estimation algorithms for linear time-delayed systems imbedded in correlated noise processes; however, their results appear to have a fundamental mistake in the procedure given, which leads to self-contradictory results; this is reported in [55].

In this section, estimation algorithms are derived for nonlinear message and measurement models, with both involving multiple-channel time delays and corrupted by correlated message and measurement noise processes [40,43]. The derivation assumes that the smoothing estimator introduces new data in a linear additive fashion and makes use of the matrix minimum principle to minimize the error-variance cost functional. In Section B the problem statement is presented. Section C presents the derivation of the nonlinear smoothing algorithms. Sections D and E provide handy sets of reference equations, respectively, for the filtering and the fixed-point smoothing estimators. Section F presents the smoothing algorithms for linear discrete-time estimation problems. Section G applied Kalman's limiting procedure to derive estimation algorithms for linear continuous-time problems. The results coincide with those obtained by Kwakernaak [56].

B. THE PROBLEM STATEMENT

Consider the discrete nonlinear message model of Eq. (1) with the measurement model described by

$$z(k) = \sum_{j=0}^{N} h_j[x(k - \beta_j), k - \beta_j] + v(k), \tag{29}$$

where h_j is an m-dimensional nonlinear vector-valued function. Term v is a zero-mean white-noise sequence correlated with w with nonnegative definite covariance Ψ_{vw}. All other prior statistics are identical to those of Section II.B. The state estimation problem also follows that of Section II.B.

C. THE DERIVATION OF THE NONLINEAR SMOOTHING ESTIMATOR

With reasoning similar to that of Section II.C, it is assumed that the smoothed estimate satisfies the dynamic equation

$$\hat{x}(k - l + 1/k + 1) = \sum_{i=0}^{L} b_i[\hat{x}(k - l - \gamma_i/k), k - l - \gamma_i] + K_{k+1}^{l} z(k + 1).$$

Because $\hat{x}(k - l + 1/k + 1)$ is required to be an unbiased estimate, it can be shown that

$$\sum_{i=0}^{L} b_i[\hat{x}(k - l - \gamma_i/k), k - l - \gamma_i]$$

$$= \sum_{i=0}^{L} \hat{f}_i[x(k - l - \alpha_i), k - l - \alpha_i/k]$$

$$- K_{k+1}^{l} \sum_{j=0}^{N} \hat{h}_j[x(k - \beta_j + 1), k - \beta_j + 1/k],$$

where

$$\hat{f}_i[x(k - l - \alpha_i), k - l - \alpha_i/k]$$
$$= E_k\{f_i[x(k - l - \alpha_i), k - l - \alpha_i]\}$$

and

$$\hat{h}_j[x(k - \beta_j + 1), k - \beta_j + 1/k]$$
$$= E_k\{h_j[x(k - \beta_j + 1), k - \beta_j + 1]\}.$$

Also it can be shown that

$$\sum_{i=0}^{L} \hat{f}_i[x(k - l - \alpha_i), k - l - \alpha_i/k]$$
$$= \hat{x}(k - l + 1/k). \tag{30}$$

Then

$$\hat{x}(k - l + 1/k + 1)$$
$$= \hat{x}(k - l + 1/k)$$
$$+ K_{k+1}^{l}\left\{z(k + 1) - \sum_{j=0}^{N} \hat{h}_j[x(k - \beta_j + 1), k - \beta_j + 1/k]\right\}, \tag{31}$$

whereas the smoothing error satisfies the relation

$$\tilde{x}(k - l + 1/k + 1) = \tilde{x}(k - l + 1/k) - K_{k+1}^{l}\left\{\sum_{j=0}^{N} \tilde{h}_j[x(k - \beta_j + 1)/k] + v(k + 1)\right\}, \tag{32}$$

where it is defined that

$$\tilde{h}_j[x(k - \beta_j + 1)/k] = h_j[x(k - \beta_j + 1), k - \beta_j + 1] - \hat{h}_j[x(k - \beta_j + 1), k - \beta_j + 1/k],$$

and the matrix $V_{\tilde{x}}(k - l + 1/k + 1)$ can be determined from Eqs. (4) and (32).

In order that the cost function of Eq. (3) be minimized, the optimal value of the matrix K_{k+1}^{l} is obtained by setting the gradient of J(k + 1) equal to the null matrix. Hence,

$$K_{k+1}^{l} = E_k\left\{\tilde{x}(k - l + 1/k) \sum_{j=0}^{N} \tilde{h}_j^T[x(k - \beta_j + 1)/k]\right\}$$

$$\cdot \left\{\Psi_v(k + 1) + E_k \sum_{i,j=0}^{N} \tilde{h}_i[x(k - \beta_i + 1)/k]\right.$$

$$\left.\cdot\ \tilde{h}_j^T[x(k - \beta_j + 1)/k]\right\}^{-1}, \quad (33)$$

$$V_{\tilde{x}}(k - l + 1/k + 1) = V_{\tilde{x}}(k - l + 1/k)$$

$$- K_{k+1}^{l}E_k\left\{\sum_{j=0}^{N} \tilde{h}_j[x(k - \beta_j + 1)/k]\right.$$

$$\left.\cdot\ \tilde{x}^T(k - l + 1/k)\right\}, \quad (34)$$

and

$$V_{\tilde{x}}(k - l + 1, k - m + 1/k + 1)$$

$$= V_{\tilde{x}}(k - l + 1, k - m + 1/k)$$

$$- K_{k+1}^{l}E_k\left\{\sum_{j=0}^{N} \tilde{h}_j[x(k - \beta_j + 1)/k]\tilde{x}^T(k - m + 1/k)\right\}, \quad (35)$$

for any integers l, m with $0 \leq l,\ m \leq k + 1$.

Now there remains the problem of evaluating $V_{\tilde{x}}(k - l + 1/k)$ in Eq. (34). Even though substracting Eq. (30) from (1) would easily yield

$$\tilde{x}(k - l + 1/k) = \sum_{i=0}^{L} \tilde{f}_i[x(k - l - \alpha_i)/k]$$

$$+ G[x(k - l), k - l]w(k - l), \quad (36)$$

where it is defined that

$$\tilde{f}_i[x(k - l - \alpha_i)/k] = f_i[x(k - l - \alpha_i), k - l - \alpha_i] - \hat{f}_i[x(k - l - \alpha_i), k - l - \alpha_i/k],$$

it is seen that the error-variance equation cannot be obtained by taking the expectation of Eq. (36) multiplied by its own transpose, because the expectation of Eq. (36) multiplied by its own transpose, because the expectation of $E_k\left\{\Sigma_{i=0}^{L} \tilde{f}_i[x(k - l - \alpha_i)/k]w^T(k - l)\right\}$ cannot be explicitly evaluated.

On the other hand, following the estimation technique just presented, the unbiased estimate $\hat{x}(k - l + 1/k)$ of the state vector $x(k - l + 1)$ can also be obtained as

$$\hat{x}(k - l + 1/k) = \sum_{i=0}^{L} \hat{f}_i[x(k - l - \alpha_i), k - l - \alpha_i/k - 1] + \kappa_k^l\left\{z(k) - \sum_{j=0}^{N} \hat{h}_j[x(k - \beta_j), k - \beta_j/k - 1]\right\}. \quad (37)$$

Then the optimal value of the matrix κ_k^l can be obtained as

$$\kappa_k^l = \left\{E_{k-1}\left[\sum_{i=0}^{L}\sum_{j=0}^{N} \tilde{f}_i[x(k - l - \alpha_i)/k - 1]\tilde{h}_j^T[x(k - \beta_j)/k - 1]\right] + E_k[G[x(k - l), k - l]\Psi_{wv}(k)]\delta_{k,k-l}\right\} \cdot \left\{\Psi_v(k) + E_{k-1}\left[\sum_{i,j=0}^{N} \tilde{h}_i[x(k - \beta_i)/k - 1] \cdot \tilde{h}_j^T[x(k - \beta_j)/k - 1]\right]\right\}^{-1}, \quad (38)$$

and $V_{\tilde{x}}(k - l + 1, k - m + 1/k)$ is simply

$$V_{\tilde{x}}(k - l + 1, k - m + 1/k)$$

$$= \left\{ \sum_{i,j=0}^{L} E_{k-1}\left[\tilde{f}_i[x(k - l - \alpha_i)/k - 1]\tilde{f}_j^T[x(k - m - \alpha_j)/k - 1]\right]\right\}$$

$$+ E_k\left\{G[x(k - l), k - l]\Psi_w(k - l)G^T[x(k - m), k - m]\right\}\delta_{k-l,k-m}$$

$$- \kappa_k^l\left\{\Psi_{vw}(k - m)G^T[x(k - m), k - m]\delta_{k,k-m}\right.$$

$$+ E_{k-1}\left[\sum_{i=0}^{N} \tilde{h}_i[x(k - \beta_i)/k - 1]\right.$$

$$\left.\left.\cdot \sum_{j=0}^{L} \tilde{f}_j^T [x(k - m - \alpha_j)/k - 1]\right]\right\}, \tag{39}$$

for $0 \leq l, m \leq k + 1$, whereas $V_{\tilde{x}}(k - l + 1/k)$ can be obtained from this equation by setting $l = m$.

In addition, we have

$$V_{\tilde{x}}(k - l + 1, k + 1/k)$$

$$= \sum_{i=0}^{L} E_k\left\{\tilde{x}(k - l + 1/k)\tilde{f}_i^T[x(k - \alpha_i)/k]\right\}.$$

As stated in the tabulation in Section II.C, three different types of smoothing algorithms and the filtering algorithm all follow immediately from Eqs. (31), (33)-(35), and (37)-(39).

Also notice that, in the case of nonlinear systems, the algorithms involve infinite-dimensional systems for realization, which is practically impossible except in trivially simple cases.

In order that the smoother can be implemented in computer evaluation, it is assumed that the conditional probability density functions of the smoothing errors are Gaussian. This is very significant for systems with product-type, polynomial, exponential, and state-dependent sinusoidal nonlinearities, because in these cases the smoothing algorithms can be evaluated or physically realized without any further approximation.

Furthermore, it is readily observable that the algorithms presented here are also applicable to nonlinear systems imbedded in additive white-noise processes. For this special case, Ψ_{wv} is set to zero, and the results represent a two-stage minimum-variance nonlinear estimation algorithm. However, when the message model is represented by linear functions and $\Psi_{wv} = 0$, the results presented here are equivalent to those of Section II.C. This is further illustrated in Section III.F.

Liang and Christensen [43] noted that the classical Kalman-type recursive filters suffer from the deficiency that they cannot simultaneously optimize the steady-state and transient system responses. After a long period of operation, they tend to ignore the incoming measurement and depend more on the previous estimates (i.e., the Kalman gain matrix vanishes with time). As shown in the simulation result of [43], the two-stage estimator presented here does not have the narrow-bandwidth problem; this is due to the dynamics of its two-stage estimator, which may possibly be quite useful for the tracking, alignment, or estimation of parameters or states that are slowly changing with time.

D. *NONLINEAR FILTERING*

When l is set to zero, Eqs. (31), (33)-(34), and (37)-(39) become the filtering algorithms. Namely, the estimation algorithm

$$\hat{x}(k+1/k+1) = \hat{x}(k+1/k) + K_{k+1}^{0}\left\{z(k+1) - \sum_{j=0}^{N} \hat{h}_j[x(k-\beta_j+1), k-\beta_j+1/k]\right\}$$

$$\hat{x}(k+1/k) = \sum_{i=0}^{L} \hat{f}_i[x(k-\alpha_i), k-\alpha_i/k-1] + K_k^{0}\left\{z(k) \sum_{j=0}^{N} \hat{h}_j[x(k-\beta_j), k-\beta_j/k-1]\right\},$$

the gain algorithm

$$K_{k+1}^{0} = E_k\left\{\tilde{x}(k+1/k) \sum_{j=0}^{N} \tilde{h}_j^T[x(k-\beta_j+1)/k]\right\} \cdot \left\{\Psi_v(k+1) + E_k\left[\sum_{i,j=0}^{N} \tilde{h}_i[x(k-\beta_i+1)/k] \cdot \tilde{h}_j^T[x(k-\beta_j+1)/k]\right]\right\}^{-1},$$

$$K_k^{0} = \left\{E_{k-1}\left[\sum_{i,j=0}^{L} \tilde{f}_i[x(k-\alpha_i)/k-1]\tilde{h}_j^T[x(k-\beta_j)/k-1]\right] + \hat{G}[x(k), k]\Psi_{wv}(k)\right\} \cdot \left\{\Psi_v(k) + E_{k-1}\left[\sum_{i,j=0}^{N} \tilde{h}_i[x(k-\beta_i)/k-1] \cdot \tilde{h}_j^T[x(k-\beta_j)/k-1]\right]\right\}^{-1},$$

and the error-variance algorithm

$$V_{\tilde{x}}(k + 1/k + 1)$$

$$= V_{\tilde{x}}(k + 1/k) - K^0_{k+1}E_k\left\{\sum_{j=0}^{N} \tilde{h}_j[x(k - \beta_j + 1)/k]\tilde{x}^T(k + 1/k)\right\},$$

and

$$V_{\tilde{x}}(k + 1/k)$$

$$= \left\{\sum_{i,j=0}^{L} E_{k-1}\left[\tilde{f}_i[x(k - \alpha_i)/k - 1]\tilde{f}_j^T[x(k - \alpha_j)/k - 1]\right]\right\}$$

$$+ E_k\left\{G[x(k), k]\Psi_w(k)G^T[x(k), k]\right\}$$

$$- K_k^0\left\{\Psi_{vw}(k)\hat{G}^T[x(k), k]\right.$$

$$+ E_{k-1}\left[\sum_{i=0}^{N} \tilde{h}_i[x(k - \beta_i)/k - 1]\right.$$

$$\left.\left.\cdot \sum_{j=0}^{L} \tilde{f}_j^T[x(k - \alpha_j)/k - 1]\right]\right\}.$$

Other error-variance equations are obtainable from Eqs. (35) and (39), with proper substitution of l and M.

E. NONLINEAR FIXED-POINT SMOOTHING

When $l = k - M + 1$ (where $k + 1 > M$) is substituted into Eqs. (31), (33)-(35), and (37)-(39), then the recursive fixed-point smoother is given by

$$\hat{x}(M/k + 1) = \hat{x}(M/k)$$

$$+ K_{k+1}^{k-M+1}\left\{z(k + 1)\right.$$

$$\left.- \sum_{j=0}^{N} \hat{h}_j[x(k - \beta_j + 1), k - \beta_j + 1/k]\right\},$$

$$V_{x}(M/k+1) = V_{\tilde{x}}(M/k) - K_{k+1}^{k-M+1} E_k\left\{\sum_{j=0}^{N} \tilde{h}_j[x(k-\beta_j+1)/k]\tilde{x}^T(M/k)\right\},$$

$$K_{k+1}^{k-M+1} = E_k\left\{\tilde{x}(M/k) \sum_{j=0}^{N} \tilde{h}_j^T[x(k-\beta_j+1)/k]\right\} \cdot \left\{\Psi_v(k+1) + E_k\left[\sum_{i,j=0}^{N} \tilde{h}_i[x(k-\beta_i+1)/k] \cdot \tilde{h}_j^T[x(k-\beta_j+1)/k]\right]\right\}^{-1},$$

$$V_{\tilde{x}}(M, k-\beta_j+1/k+1) = V_{\tilde{x}}(M, k-\beta_j+1/k) - K_{k+1}^{k-M+1} E_k\left\{\sum_{i=0}^{N} \tilde{h}_i[x(k-\beta_i+1)/k] \cdot \tilde{x}^T(k-\beta_j+1/k)\right\},$$

$$V_{\tilde{x}}(M, k-\beta_j+1/k) = E_k\left\{\sum_{i=0}^{L} \tilde{x}(M/k) f_i^T[\tilde{x}(k-\beta_j-\alpha_i)/k]\right\}.$$

All other error-variance equations are obtainable from Eqs. (35) and (39).

F. LINEAR DISCRETE-TIME ESTIMATION

In this section the message and measurement models of the estimation problems are linear and discrete. It can be considered as a special case of the nonlinear discrete estimation problems, satisfying the following relations:

$$\sum_{i=0}^{L} f_i[x(k - \alpha_i), k - \alpha_i] = \sum_{i=0}^{L} F_i(k)x(k - \alpha_i),$$

$$\sum_{j=0}^{N} h_j[x(k - \beta_j), k - \beta_j] = \sum_{j=0}^{N} H_j(k)x(k - \beta_j),$$

and

$$G[x(k), k] = G(k).$$

Then the linear estimation algorithms can be obtained directly from results presented in Section III.C. They are the estimation algorithms

$$\begin{aligned}\hat{x}(k - l + 1) &= \hat{x}(k - l + 1/k) \\ &\quad + K_{k+1}^{l}\left\{z(k + 1) - \sum_{j=0}^{N} H_j(k + 1)x(k - \beta_j + 1/k)\right\},\end{aligned} \tag{40}$$

$$\begin{aligned}\hat{x}(k - l + 1/k) &= \sum_{i=0}^{L} F_i(k - l)\hat{x}(k - l - \alpha_i/k - 1) \\ &\quad + K_K^{l}\left[z(k) - \sum_{j=0}^{N} H_j(k)x(k - \beta_j/k - 1)\right],\end{aligned} \tag{41}$$

the gain algorithm

$$\begin{aligned}K_{k+1}^{l} &= \left[\sum_{j=0}^{N} V_{\tilde{x}}(k - l + 1, k - \beta_j + 1/k)H_j^T(k + 1)\right] \\ &\quad \cdot \left[\Psi_v(k + 1) + \sum_{i,j=0}^{N} H_i(k + 1)\right. \\ &\quad \left. \cdot V_{\tilde{x}}(k + 1 - \beta_i, k + 1 - \beta_j/k)H_j^T(k + 1)\right]^{-1},\end{aligned} \tag{42}$$

$$\kappa_k^l = \left[\sum_{i=0}^{L} \sum_{j=0}^{N} F_i(k - l)V_{\tilde{x}}(k - l - \alpha_i, k - \beta_j/k - 1)H_j(k) + G(k - l)\Psi_{wv}(k - l)\delta_{k,k-l} \right] \cdot \left[\Psi_v(k) + \sum_{i,j=0}^{N} H_i(k)V_{\tilde{x}}(k - \beta_i, k - \beta_j/k - 1)H_j^T(k) \right]^{-1}, \tag{43}$$

and the error-variance algorithm

$$V_{\tilde{x}}(k - l + 1, k - m + 1/k + 1) = V_{\tilde{x}}(k - l + 1, k - m + 1/k) - K_{k+1}^l \left[\sum_{j=0}^{N} H_j(k + 1)V_{\tilde{x}}(k - \beta_j + 1, k - m + 1/k) \right], \tag{44}$$

and

$$V_{\tilde{x}}(k - l + 1, k - m + 1/k) = \left[\sum_{i,j=0}^{L} F_i(k - l)V_{\tilde{x}}(k - l - \alpha_i, k - m - \alpha_j/k - 1)F_j^T(k - m) \right] + G(k - l)\Psi_w(k - l)G^T(k - l)\delta_{k-l,k-m} - \kappa_k^l \left[\Psi_{wv}(k - m)G^T(k - m)\delta_{k,k-m} + \sum_{i=0}^{N} \sum_{j=0}^{L} H_i(k)V_{\tilde{x}}(k - \beta_i, k - m - \alpha_j/k - 1)F_j^T(k - m) \right]. \tag{45}$$

The three different types of smoothing and the filtering algorithms all follow immediately from these equations with the proper choice of k and l listed in Section III.C.

Finally, using Eqs. (40) and (41), we have

$$\hat{x}(k - l + 1/k)$$

$$= \left[\sum_{i=0}^{L} F_i(k - l)\hat{x}(k - l - \alpha_i/k)\right] + G(k - l)\Psi_{wv}(k - l)$$

$$\cdot \left[\Psi_v(k) + \sum_{i,j=0}^{N} H_i(k)V_{\tilde{x}}(k - \beta_i, k - \beta_j/k - 1)H_j^T(k)\right]^{-1}$$

$$\cdot \left[z(k) - \sum_{j=0}^{N} H_j(k)\hat{x}(k - \beta_j/k - 1)\right].$$

This shows that when $\Psi_{vw} = 0$, the preceding equation is reduced to

$$\hat{x}(k - l + 1/k) = \sum_{i=0}^{L} F_i(k - l)\hat{x}(k - l - \alpha_i/k);$$

this is what we would have obtained from Section II.C. In fact, one could easily demonstrate that the results presented in this section are equivalent to those of Section II, in the special case that the message model is linear and $\Psi_{vw} = 0$. Furthermore, for linear state and measurement models without delays the results agree well with those in the literature [57].

G. LINEAR CONTINUOUS-TIME ESTIMATION

In this section, the state equation of the continuous-time systems is given by

$$\dot{x}(t) = \sum_{i=0}^{L} \overline{F}_i(t)x(t - \alpha_i) + \overline{G}(t)w(t) \tag{46}$$

and the measurement equation is given by

$$z(t) = \sum_{j=0}^{N} \overline{H}_j(t)x(t - b_j) + v(t), \tag{47}$$

where x(t) and z(t) are the n-dimensional state and m-dimensional state and m-dimensional measurement vectors; $\overline{F}_i$ and $\overline{H}_j$ (n × n)- and (m × n)-dimensional nonlinear matrix-valued functions, respectively; $\overline{G}$ an (n × r)-dimensional matrix; and a_i and b_j are the time-delay indices, which are ordered such that $a_i \geq a_{i-1}$, $b_j \geq b_{j-1}$, and $a_0 = b_0 = 0$. Also, w(t) and v(t) are zero-mean white Gaussian noise processes, with nonnegative-definite covariance $V_w(t)$ and positive-definite covariance $V_v(t)$, respectively, and

$$E[v(t)w^T(\tau)] = V_{vw}\delta(t - \tau). \tag{48}$$

However, the system model of Eqs. (46) and (47) can be easily discretized in time as

$$x(k + 1) = \sum_{i=0}^{L} F_i(k)x(k - \alpha_i) + G(k)w(k) \tag{49}$$

and

$$z(k) = \sum_{j=0}^{N} H_j(k)x(k - \beta_j) + v(k), \tag{50}$$

where

$$\overline{F}_i(t) = \begin{cases} \lim\limits_{t\to 0} \frac{1}{T}[F_i(k) - x(k)] & \text{for } i = 0, \\ \lim\limits_{t\to 0} \frac{1}{T}[F_i(k)] & \text{for } i \neq 0. \end{cases} \tag{51}$$

The covariance matrices $V_v(t)$, $V_w(t)$, and $V_{vw}(t)$ must be replaced by $T\Psi_v(k)$, $T\Psi_w(k)$, and $T\Psi_{vw}(k)$, respectively.

The continuous-time algorithms can immediately be obtained from Section III.F by simple application of Kalman's limiting procedure. Let it be defined that $\hat{x}(t, l) \equiv \hat{x}(t - l/t)$ and $V_{\tilde{x}}(t, l, m) \equiv V_{\tilde{x}}(t - l, t - m/t)$. Then subtracting both sides of Eq. (40) with $\hat{x}(k - l/k)$ and taking the limit yields

$$\frac{\partial}{\partial t} \hat{x}(t, l) + \frac{\partial}{\partial l} \hat{x}(t, l) = K_t^l \left[z(t) - \sum_{j=0}^{N} \overline{H}_j(t)\hat{x}(t, b_j) \right], \tag{52}$$

where

$$K_t^l = \sum_{j=0}^{N} V_x(t, l, b_j)\overline{H}_j^T(t)V_v^{-1}(t).$$

The boundary condition for Eq. (52) is to be obtained by manipulating Eq. (41) and using the relation of Eq. (51). Thus,

$$\frac{\partial}{\partial t} \hat{x}(t, 0) = \sum_{i=0}^{L} \overline{F}_i(t)\hat{x}(t, \alpha_i) + \kappa_t^0 \left[z(t) - \sum_{j=0}^{N} \overline{H}_j(t)\hat{x}(t, b_j) \right], \tag{53}$$

where

$$\kappa_t^l = \left[\sum_{j=0}^{N} V_{\tilde{x}}(t, l, b_j)\overline{H}_j^T(t) + \overline{G}(t)V_{wv}(t)\delta(t, t - l) \right] V_v^{-1}(t). \tag{54}$$

Subtracting $V_{\tilde{x}}(k + 1, l - 1, m)$ and $V_{\tilde{x}}(k, l - 1, m)$ from both sides of Eq. (44), it then follows that

$$\frac{\partial}{\partial l} V_{\tilde{x}}(t, l, m) + \frac{\partial}{\partial t} V_{\tilde{x}}(t, l, m) + \frac{\partial}{\partial m} V_{\tilde{x}}(t, l, m) = -K_t^l \sum_{j=0}^{N} \overline{H}_j(t)V_{\tilde{x}}(t, b_j, m). \tag{55}$$

From Eq. (45), setting $l = m = 0$ gives the expression

$$\frac{\partial}{\partial t} V_{\tilde{x}}(t, 0, 0) = \sum_{i=0}^{L} \overline{F}_i(t) V_{\tilde{x}}(t, a_i, 0) + \sum_{i=0}^{L} V_{\tilde{x}}(t, 0, a_i)\overline{F}_i^T(t) + \overline{G}(t)V_w(t)\overline{G}^T(t) - K_t^0\left[V_{vw}(t)\overline{G}^T(t) + \sum_{j=0}^{N} \overline{H}_j(t)V_{\tilde{x}}(t, b_j, 0)\right]. \tag{56}$$

Using the relations of Eqs. (40), (45), and (49), it can be established that

$$\frac{\partial}{\partial t} V_{\tilde{x}}(t, l, 0) + \frac{\partial}{\partial l} V_{\tilde{x}}(t, l, 0) = \sum_{i=0}^{L} V_{\tilde{x}}(t, l, a_i)\overline{F}_i^T(t) - K_t^l\left[\sum_{j=0}^{N} \overline{H}_j(t)V_{\tilde{x}}(t, b_j, 0) + V_{vw}(t)\overline{G}^T(t)\right], \tag{57}$$

and, similarly,

$$\frac{\partial}{\partial t} V_{\tilde{x}}(t, 0, m) + \frac{\partial}{\partial m} V_{\tilde{x}}(t, 0, m) = \sum_{i=0}^{L} \overline{F}_i(t)V_{\tilde{x}}(t, a_i, m) - \left[\sum_{j=0}^{N} V_{\tilde{x}}(t, 0, b_j)\overline{H}_j^T(t) + \overline{G}(t)V_{vw}(t)\right]K_t^{m^T}, \tag{58}$$

for $l, m \geq 0$ of interest. The initial conditions for the estimate and variance equations are $\hat{x}(t_0, l)$ and $V_{\tilde{x}}(t_0, l, m)$, where $l \geq 0$, $m \leq \max(\alpha_L, \beta_N)$. Equations (56)-(58) constitute the boundary conditions for Eq. (55). For the special case in which the noise processes are uncorrelated, the results obtained here coincide with those obtained by Kwakernaak [56].

To illustrate the use of Eqs. (52)-(58), we present the reference equations for fixed-point continuous-time smoothing estimator. They are obtained from the results of Eqs. (52)-(58) with the substitution of $t - l$ and $t - m$ by t_*:

$$\frac{\partial}{\partial t}\hat{x}(t_*/t) = \sum_{i=0}^{N} V_{\tilde{x}}(t_*, t - b_i/t)\overline{H}_i^T(t)V_v^{-1}(t)\left[z(t) - \sum_{j=0}^{N}\overline{H}_j(t)\hat{x}(t, b_j)\right],$$

$$\frac{\partial}{\partial t}V_{\tilde{x}}(t_*, t/t) = -\sum_{i,j=0}^{N} V_{\tilde{x}}(t_*, t - b_i/t)\overline{H}_i^T(t)V_v^{-1}(t)\overline{H}_j(t)V_{\tilde{x}}(t - b_j, t_*/t),$$

$$\begin{aligned}\frac{\partial}{\partial t}V_{\tilde{x}}(t_*, t/t) &= \sum_{i=0}^{L} V_{\tilde{x}}(t_*, t - a_i/t)\overline{F}^T(t) \\ &\quad - \sum_{i=0}^{N} V_{\tilde{x}}(t_*, t - b_i/t)\overline{H}_i^T(t)V_v^{-1}(t) \\ &\quad \cdot \left[\sum_{j=0}^{N}\overline{H}_j(t)V_{\tilde{x}}(t - b_j, t/t) + V_{vw}(t)\overline{G}^T(t)\right],\end{aligned}$$

and

$$\frac{\partial}{\partial t}V_{\tilde{x}}(t_*, t - m/t) + \frac{\partial}{\partial m}V_{\tilde{x}}(t_*, t - m/t) = -\sum_{i,j=0}^{N} V_{\tilde{x}}(t_*, t - b_i/t)\overline{H}_i^T(t)V_v^{-1}(t)\overline{H}_j(t)V_{\tilde{x}}(t - b_j, t - m/t),$$

where the filtering equations of Eqs. (53) and (56) remain unchanged.

IV. NONLINEAR ESTIMATION FOR DISCRETE TIME-DELAYED SYSTEMS WITH COLORED NOISE

A. *INTRODUCTION*

This section extends the technique developed in preceding sections to state estimation problems of nonlinear discrete time-delayed systems with measurements containing multiple delays imbedded in colored noise sequences.

In the past, for linear estimation problems without time delays, two methods have, in general, been employed to account for time-correlated measurement noise in a linear filter. The first method, proposed by Kalman [1], employed the state augmentation method. It involves the construction of a hypothetical shaping filter whose input is white noise and whose output is the noise process of the required correlations. Here, the dynamics of the shaping filter are included as a part of the system dynamics, and its states are estimated together with the system states. The second method was developed by Bryson and Henrikson [5]. It employs an output differencing technique, which devises a new modified measurement that subtracts the most recent past value of the measurement, weighted by the noise correlation coefficient matrix from the present measurement. As a result the modified measurement contains only white-noise processes.

Biswas and Mahalanabis [50] and Mishra and Rajamani [58], respectively, employed the state augmentation and the innovation techniques to derive estimation algorithms for linear discrete time-delayed systems involving colored noise processes.

This section derives nonlinear estimation algorithms for nonlinear discrete time-delayed systems with measurements containing multiple time delays, corrupted by colored noise [40,43]. Section B presents the statement of the problem and in Section C the nonlinear smoothing estimator is derived.

B. THE PROBLEM STATEMENT

In this section the discrete time-delayed message model is described by Eq. (1), the measurement model is modeled by

$$z(k) = \sum_{j=0}^{N} H_j(k)x(k - \beta_j) + \gamma(k), \tag{59}$$

and the measurement noise $\gamma(k)$ is a colored sequence given by

$$\gamma(k + 1) = A(k + 1, k)\gamma(k) + v(k). \tag{60}$$

Here $k = 0, 1, 2, \ldots$ is the discrete time index; the state x is an n vector; the measurement z an m vector; the state noise sequence w an r vector; the measurement noise γ an m vector; G a nonlinear state dependent $n \times r$ matrix; f_i a nonlinear n-dimensional vector-valued function; and H_j and A, respectively, $m \times n$ and $m \times m$ matrices. All initial conditions and prior statistics are the same as those of Section III.B. The smoothing estimation problem is also identical to that of Section III.B.

C. THE DERIVATION OF THE NONLINEAR SMOOTHING ESTIMATOR

Examination of Eqs. (59) and (60) indicates that a modified measurement signal $y(k + 1)$ consisting of an additive white-noise sequence can be obtained by multiplying $z(k)$ by $A(k + 1, k)$ and subtracting it from $z(k + 1)$:

$$y(k + 1) = z(k + 1) - A(k + 1, k)z(k). \tag{61}$$

Notice that subtracting a function of the previous measurement in no way affects the present measurement, and hence the estimate conditioned on Z(k + 1) is equivalent to that of Y(k + 1).

Equation (45) can be further simplified as

$$y(k+1) = \sum_{j=0}^{N} d_j[x(k-\beta_j),\ x(k-\beta_j+1)] + v(k), \qquad (62)$$

where

$$d_j[x(k-\beta_j),\ x(k-\beta_j+1)]$$
$$= H_j(k+1)x(k+1-\beta_j) - A(k+1,\ k)H_j(k)x(k-\beta_j).$$

Following the development of Section III, we obtain

$$\hat{x}(k-l+1/k+1)$$
$$= \hat{x}(k-l+1/k)$$
$$+ K_{k+1}^{l}\left\{y(k+1) - \sum_{j=0}^{N} \hat{d}_j[x(k-\beta_j),\ x(k-\beta_j+1)/k]\right\},$$

and

$$\hat{x}(k-l+1/k)$$
$$= \sum_{i=0}^{L} \hat{f}_i[x(k-l-\alpha_i),\ k-l-\alpha_i/k-1]$$
$$+ K_k^{l}\left\{y(k) - \sum_{j=0}^{N} \hat{d}_j[x(k-\beta_j-1),\ x(k-\beta_j)/k-1]\right\},$$

where

$$\hat{d}_j[x(k-\beta_j),\ x(k-\beta_j+1/k]$$
$$= H_j(k+1)\hat{x}(k+1-\beta_j/k)$$
$$- A(k+1,\ k)H_j(k)\hat{x}(k-\beta_j/k).$$

The optimal value of the matrix K_{k+1}^{l} is obtained by setting the gradient of Eq. (3) equal to the null matrix. As a result we have

$$K_{k+1}^{l} = \sum_{j=0}^{N}\Big[V_{\tilde{x}}(k - l + 1, k - \beta_j + 1/k)H_j^T(k + 1) - V_{\tilde{x}}(k - l + 1, k - \beta_j/k)H_j^T(k)A^T(k + 1), k)\Big]$$
$$\cdot \Big\{\Psi_v(k) + \sum_{i,j=0}^{N}\Big[H_i(k+1)V_{\tilde{x}}(k - \beta_i + 1, k - \beta_j + 1/k)H_j^T(k+1) + A(k + 1, k)H_i(k)V_{\tilde{x}}(k - \beta_i, k - \beta_j/k)H_j^T(k)A^T(k+1, k) - H_i(k + 1)V_{\tilde{x}}(k - \beta_i + 1, k - \beta_j/k)H_j^T(k)A^T(k + 1, k) - A(k+1, k)H_i(k)V_{\tilde{x}}(k - \beta_i, k - \beta_j + 1/k)H_j^T(k+1)\Big]\Big\}^{-1}. \tag{63}$$

Similarly, the optimal value of κ_k^{l} is derived as

$$\kappa_k^{l} = E_{k-1}\Big\{\sum_{i=0}^{L}\sum_{j=0}^{N}\tilde{f}_i[x(k - l - \alpha_i)/k - 1] \cdot \tilde{d}_j[x(k - \beta_j - 1), x(k - \beta_j)/k - 1] + \hat{G}[x(k - l), k - l]\Psi_{wv}(k - l)\delta_{k-l,k-1}\Big\}$$
$$\cdot \Big\{\Psi_v(k - 1) + E_{k-1}\Big[\sum_{i,j=0}^{N}\tilde{d}_i[x(k - \beta_i - 1), x(k - \beta_i)/k - 1] \cdot \tilde{d}_j^T[x(k - \beta_j - 1), x(k - \beta_j)/k - 1]\Big]\Big\}^{-1},$$

and

$$V_{\tilde{x}}(k - m + 1, k - l + 1/k + 1)$$
$$= V_{\tilde{x}}(k - m + 1, k - l + 1/k)$$
$$- K_{k+1}^{m} \sum_{j=0}^{N} [H_j(k + 1) V_{\tilde{x}}(k - \beta_j + 1, k - l + 1/k)$$
$$- A(k + 1, k) H_j(k) V_{\tilde{x}}(k - \beta_j, k - l + 1/k)] \tag{64}$$

Furthermore,

$$V_{\tilde{x}}(k - m + 1, k - l + 1/k)$$
$$= \sum_{i,j=0}^{L} \left\{E_k\left[\tilde{f}_i[x(k - m - \alpha_i)/k - 1]\tilde{f}_j^T[x(k - l - \alpha_j)/k - 1]\right]\right\}$$
$$+ E_k\left\{G[x(k - m), k - m]\Psi_w(k - m)\delta_{k-m,k-l}G^T[x(k - l), k - l]\right\}$$
$$- K_k^l\left\{\Psi_{vw}(k - m)\hat{G}^T[x(k - m), k - m]\delta_{k-l,k-m}\right.$$
$$+ E_{k-1}\left[\sum_{i=0}^{N}\sum_{j=0}^{L} \tilde{d}_i[x(k - \beta_j - 1), x(k - \beta_j)/k - 1]\right.$$
$$\left.\left. \cdot\ f_j^T[x(k - m - \alpha_j)/k - 1]\right]\right\} \tag{65}$$

and

$$V_{\tilde{x}}(k - m + 1, k - l/k)$$
$$= \sum_{i=0}^{L} E_k\left\{\tilde{f}_i[x(k - m - \alpha_i)/k]\tilde{x}^T(k - l/k)\right\}, \tag{66}$$

for all nonnegative integers m and l of interest. Note that $V_{\tilde{x}}(k - l + 1/k + 1)$ and $V_{\tilde{x}}(k - l + 1/k)$ can be easily obtained from Eqs. (64) and (65) with m set equal to l.

It should be noted that these estimation algorithms are very general; they can be applied to all three cases of smoothing as well as to the filtering estimation problems. In the particular case of a linear message model with single channel, and with or without time-delayed measurements, the results can be shown to agree with those of the literature [4,50], and for systems with multichannel time-delayed measurements, the results agree with those of Mishra and Rajamani [58].

V. STATE ESTIMATION FOR NONLINEAR DISTRIBUTED-PARAMETER SYSTEMS (DPS) INVOLVING MULTIPLE DELAYS

A. *INTRODUCTION*

This section is devoted to the derivation of nonlinear estimation algorithms for discrete and continuous-time nonlinear distributed-parameter systens (DPS) involving multiple delays. The discrete-time algorithm is directly derived using the matrix minimum principle to obtain the optimal value of the coefficient in the estimation algorithm. The continuous-time algorithm is obtained through the use of Kalman's limiting procedure. In the special case of a linear continuous lumped parameter system, the result is identical to Kwakernaak's equations [56], and for linear DPS the result agrees with that of Shukla and Srinath [59].

Consider a general class of nonlinear DPS described by

$$\frac{\partial}{\partial t} X(x, t) = \sum_{i=0}^{L_1} \overline{F}_{x_i}(X, x, t - a_i) + W(x, t), \tag{67}$$

$$Z(x, t) = \sum_{i=0}^{L_2} \overline{H}_{x_i}(X, x, t - b_i)$$

$$+ V(x, t), \quad x \in D, \tag{68}$$

$$X(x, t_0) = X_0(x), \quad x \in D, \tag{69}$$

and

$$\overline{B}_x(X, x, t) = 0, \quad x \in \delta D. \tag{70}$$

This system is defined for $t \geq t_0$ on a spatial domain D and a connected n-dimensional Euclidean space E^n, having δD as the boundary. Then $X(D, t) = \{X(x, t); x \in D\}$ is the N-dimensional state vector and $\overline{B}_x$, $\overline{F}_{x_i}$, and H_{x_i} are well-posed nonlinear matrix differential or integrodifferential operators; and $W(x, t)$ and $V(x, t)$ are independent zero-mean Gaussian distributed processes with covariances $\overline{Q}(x, x_1, t)$ and $\overline{R}(x, x_1, t)$, where $\overline{R}(x, x_1, t)$ is symmetric positive definite. Both a_i and b_i represent time-delay indices ordered such that $a_0 = b_0$, $a_i \geq a_{i-1}$, and $b_i \geq b_{i-1}$. The initial conditions are assumed to be zero mean with known covariances.

The problem here is to derive the unbiased estimate $\hat{X}(x, t, \theta)$ of the state $X(x, t - \theta)$, conditioned upon the set of measurements $\{Z(x, \tau)\}$ for all τ, $t_0 \leq \tau \leq t$, minimizing

$$J(\tau) = E_\tau\{\tilde{X}^T(x, \tau, \theta)M(\tau)\tilde{X}(x, \tau, \theta)\} \tag{71}$$

for $t_0 \leq \tau \leq t$, where $M(\tau)$ is an arbitrary symmetric positive-definite weighting matrix and $\tilde{X}(x, t, \theta) = X(x, t - \theta) - \hat{X}(x, t, \theta)$ denotes the estimator error.

B. DERIVATION OF DISCRETE-TIME NONLINEAR DPS ESTIMATOR

The system model of Eqs. (67)-(70) is first discretized in time as

$$x(x,\ k+1) = \sum_{i=0}^{L_1} F_{x_i}(X,\ x,\ k-\alpha_i) + W(x,\ k), \tag{72}$$

$$Z(x,\ k) = \sum_{i=0}^{L_2} H_{x_i}(X,\ x,\ k-\beta_i) + V(x,\ t), \qquad x \in D, \tag{73}$$

$$X(x,\ k_0) = X_0(x), \qquad x \in D,$$

and

$$B_x(X,\ x,\ k) = 0, \tag{74}$$

where

$$\overline{H}_{x_i}(X,\ x,\ t-b_i) = \lim_{T\to 0}\{H_{x_i}(X,\ x,\ k-\beta_i)\},$$

$$\overline{B}_x(X,\ x,\ t) = \lim_{T\to 0} B_x(X,\ x,\ k),$$

$$\overline{Q}(x,\ x_1,\ t) = \lim_{T\to 0} TQ(x,\ x_1,\ k), \quad \text{and}$$

$$\overline{R}(x,\ x_1,\ t) = \lim_{T\to 0} TR(x,\ x_1,\ k).$$

Also

$$\overline{F}_{x_i}(X,\ x,\ t-a_i) = \begin{cases} \lim_{T\to 0} \frac{1}{T}\{F_{x_i}(X,\ x,\ k-\alpha_i) - X(x,\ k)\} & \text{for } i = 0, \\ \lim_{T\to 0} \frac{1}{T} F_{x_i}(X,\ x,\ k-\alpha_i) & \text{for } i \neq 0. \end{cases} \tag{75}$$

It is first assumed that the estimator introduces new data additively and is constrained by a rather general form of dynamic equation

$$\hat{X}(x, k + 1, n) = \sum_{i=0}^{L_1} U_{x_i}(\hat{X}, x, k, n + c_i) + \int_D K_{k+1}^n(x, k + 1)Z(x^1, k + 1)dx^1 \tag{76}$$

involving the sum of nonlinear functions U_{x_i} and the product term of gain matrix K_{k+1}^n and measurement Z. The problem formulated here may therefore lead to an estimator optimum with respect to the imposed constraint but not identical to the truly optimal one.

The estimator error equation for $\tilde{X}(x, k + 1, n)$ can be obtained by substituting Eq. (73) into the difference of Eqs. (72) and (76). In order that $\hat{X}(x, k + 1, n)$ be unbiased, U_{x_i} can be shown to satisfy

$$\sum_{i=0}^{L_1} U_{x_i}(\hat{X}, x, k, n + c_i) = \left[\sum_{i=0}^{L_1} \hat{F}_{x_i}(X, x, k, n + \alpha_i)\right] - \int_D \left[K_{k+1}^n(x, k + 1) \sum_{i=0}^{L_2} \hat{H}_{x_i^1}\left(X, x^1, k, \beta_i - 1\right)\right] dx^1, \tag{77}$$

where

$$\hat{F}_{x_i}(X, x, k, n + \alpha_i) = E_k\{F_{x_i}(X, x, k - n - \alpha_i)\}$$

$$\hat{H}_{x_i^1}\left(X, x^1, k, \beta_i - 1\right) = E_k\left\{H_{x_i^1}\left(X, x^1, k - \beta_i + 1\right)\right\}.$$

Also note that

$$X(k, k, n-1) = \sum_{i=0}^{L_1} F_{x_i}(X, x, k, n+\alpha_i). \tag{78}$$

Now $V_{\tilde{x}}(x, k+1, n)$ can be obtained by substituting Eqs. (77) and (78) into the expectation of $\tilde{X}(x, k+1, n)$ multiplied by its own transpose. Therefore, the optimal value of the matrix K_{k+1}^n is obtained by setting the gradient of Eq. (71) equal to the null matrix; the results yield

$$\begin{aligned} K_{k+1}^n&(x, k+1) \\ &= \int_D \left\{ E_k\left[\tilde{X}(x, k, n-1) \sum_{i=0}^{L_2} \tilde{H}^T_{x_i^1}\left(X, x^1, k, \beta_i - 1\right)\right] \right. \\ &\quad \cdot E_k\left[\sum_{i,j=0}^{L_2} \tilde{H}_{x_i^1}\left(X, x^1, k, \beta_i - 1\right)\tilde{H}_{x_j^{11}}\left(X, x^{11}, k, \beta_j - 1\right)\right. \\ &\quad \left.\left. + R(x^1, x^{11}, k+1)\right]^* \right\} dx^1, \end{aligned} \tag{79}$$

$$\begin{aligned} \hat{X}(x, k+1, n) = \hat{X}&(x, k, n-1) \\ &+ \int_D \left\{ K_{k+1}^n(x, k+1) \right. \\ &\quad \cdot \left[Z(x^{11}, k+1) \right. \\ &\quad \left.\left. - \sum_{i=0}^{L_2} \hat{H}_{x_i^{11}}\left(X, x^{11}, k, \beta_i - 1\right)\right] \right\} dx^{11}, \end{aligned} \tag{80}$$

and

$$V_{\tilde{x}}(x, k+1, n)$$

$$= V_{\tilde{x}}(x, k, n-1)$$

$$- \int_D \left\{ K_{n+1}^{n}(x, k+1) E_k \left[\sum_{i=0}^{L_2} \tilde{H}_{x_i^{11}}\left(X, x^{11}, k, \beta_i - 1\right) \cdot \tilde{X}^T(x, k, n+1) \right] \right\} dx^{11}, \tag{81}$$

where the inverse distributed-parameter matrix operator * is defined by

$$\int_D A(x, x^1) A^*\left(x^1, x_1\right) dD^1 = I\delta(x - x_1). \tag{82}$$

It is also defined that

$$\tilde{H}_{x_i}\left(X, x^1, k, \beta_i - 1\right) = H_{x_i}\left(X, x^1, k, \beta_i - 1\right) - \hat{H}_{x_i}\left(X, x^1, k, \beta_i - 1\right) \tag{83}$$

and the boundary conditions for Eqs. (80)-(81) can be specified as

$$E_k[B_x(X, x, k, 0)] = 0 \quad \text{for} \quad x \in \delta D.$$

Defining

$$V_{\tilde{x}}(x, y, k, n, m) = E_k[\tilde{X}(x, k, n)\tilde{X}^T(y, k, m)] \tag{84}$$

for $n, m \geq t_0$ of interest, we have

$$V_{\tilde{x}}(x, y, k, n-1, m-1)$$

$$= E_k\left[\sum_{i,j=0}^{L_1} \tilde{F}_{x_i}(X, x, k, n+\alpha_i) \tilde{F}_{y_j}^T(X, y, k, m+\alpha_j) \right] + Q(x, y, k-n)\delta_{k-n,k-m} \tag{85}$$

and

$$
\begin{aligned}
&V_{\tilde{x}}(x, y, k+1, n, m) \\
&\quad = V_{\tilde{x}}(x, y, k, n-1, m-1) \\
&\quad\quad - \int_D\int_D \Bigg\{ K_{k+1}^{n}(x, k+1) \Bigg\{ R(x^{11}, y^{11}, k+1) \\
&\quad\quad\quad + \sum_{i,j=0}^{L_2} E_k\Big[\tilde{H}_{x_i^{11}}\big(X, x^{11}, k, \beta_i - 1\big) \\
&\quad\quad\quad\quad \cdot \tilde{H}_{y_j^{11}}\big(X, y^{11}, k, \beta_j - 1\big)\Big]\Bigg\} \\
&\quad\quad\quad \cdot K_{k+1}^{m^T}(y, k+1)\Bigg\} dx^{11} dy^{11},
\end{aligned}
\tag{86}
$$

where the initial conditions required are $\hat{X}(x, t_0, n)$ and $V_{\tilde{x}}(x, y, t_0, n, m)$ for all $x, y \in D$ and values of $n, m \geq t_0$ of interest.

C. *DERIVATION OF CONTINUOUS-TIME NONLINEAR DPS ESTIMATOR*

The continuous-time algorithm can be formally derived from the result of Section B using Kalman's limiting procedure.

Both sides of Eq. (80) are divided by T; then subtracting $\hat{X}(x, k, n)$ and taking the limit as $T \to 0$, the result is simply

$$
\begin{aligned}
&\frac{\partial}{\partial t}\hat{X}(x, t, n) + \frac{\partial}{\partial n}\hat{X}(x, t, n) \\
&\quad = \int_D\int_D \Bigg\{ E_t\Big[\tilde{X}(x, t, n) \sum_{i=0}^{L_2} \tilde{\tilde{H}}^T_{x^1}\big(X, x^1, t, b_i\big)\Big] \bar{R}^*(x^1, x^{11}, t) \\
&\quad\quad \cdot \Big[Z(x^{11}, t) - \sum_{i=0}^{L_2} \hat{H}_{x_i^{11}}\big(X, x^{11}, t, b_i\big)\Big]\Bigg\} dx^1 dx^{11}.
\end{aligned}
$$

Substituting Eq. (75) into the sum of Eqs. (78) and (80) yields

$$\frac{\partial}{\partial t} \hat{X}(x, t, n)$$

$$= \sum_{i=0}^{L_1} \hat{\hat{F}}_{x_i}(X, x, t, n + \alpha_i)$$

$$+ \int_D \left\{ K_{k+1}^n (x, k + 1) \right.$$

$$\left. \cdot \left[Z(x^{11}, t) - \sum_{i=0}^{L_2} \hat{\hat{H}}_{x_i^{11}}\left(X, x^{11}, t, b_i\right) \right] \right\} dx^{11},$$

where

$$K_{k+1}^n (x, k + 1)$$

$$= \int_D \left\{ E_t \left[\sum_{i=0}^{L_2} \tilde{X}(x, t, n) \tilde{\tilde{H}}^T_{x_i^1}\left(X, x^1, t, b_i\right) \right] \bar{R}^*(x^1, x^{11}, t) \right\} dx^1.$$

With $V_{\tilde{X}}(x, y, k + 1, n - 1, m) + V_{\tilde{X}}(x, y, k, n - 1, m)$ subtracted from both sides of Eq. (86) and using Eq. (79) the following continuous-time form easily follows

$$\frac{\partial}{\partial t} V_{\tilde{X}}(x, y, t, n, m) + \frac{\partial}{\partial n} V_{\tilde{X}}(x, y, t, n, m)$$

$$+ \frac{\partial}{\partial m} V_{\tilde{X}}(x, y, t, n, m)$$

$$= \int_D \int_D \int_D \left\{ \sum_{i=0}^{L_2} E_t \left[\tilde{X}(x, t, n) \tilde{\tilde{H}}^T_{x_i^1}\left(X, x^1, t, b_i\right) \right] \right.$$

$$\cdot \bar{R}^*(x^1, x^{11}, t) \bar{R}(x^{11}, y^{11}, t)$$

$$\left. \cdot K_{k+1}^{m^T}(y, k + 1) \right\} dx^1 dx^{11} dy^{11}.$$

Similarly, from manipulation of Eqs. (75), (78)-(79), (85), and (86), the following equations are obtained:

$$\frac{\partial}{\partial t} V_{\tilde{X}}(x, y, t, 0, 0)$$

$$= \sum_{i=0}^{L_1} \left\{ E_t\left[\tilde{X}(x, t, 0)\tilde{\bar{F}}^T_{y_i}(X, y, t, a_i)\right] + E_t\left[\tilde{\bar{F}}_{x_i}(X, x, t, a_i)\tilde{X}^T(y, t, 0)\right]\right\} + \bar{Q}(x, y, t)$$

$$- \sum_{i=0}^{L_2} \left\{ \int_D\int_D\int_D E_t\left[\tilde{X}(x, t, 0)\tilde{\bar{H}}^T_{x^1_i}\left(X, x^1, t, b_i\right)\right] \cdot \bar{R}^*(x^1, x^{11}, t)\bar{R}(x^{11}, y^{11}, t) \cdot K^0_{k+1}(y, k + 1)\right\} dx^1 dx^{11} dy^{11},$$

$$\frac{\partial}{\partial t} V_{\tilde{X}}(x, y, t, 0, m) + \frac{\partial}{\partial m} V_{\tilde{X}}(x, y, t, 0, m)$$

$$= E_t\left\{\sum_{i=0}^{L_1} \tilde{\bar{F}}_{x_i}(X, x, t, a_i)\tilde{X}^T(y, t, m)\right\}$$

$$- \sum_{i=0}^{L_2} \left\{ \int_D\int_D\int_D E_t\left[\tilde{X}(x, t, 0)\tilde{\bar{H}}^T_{y_i}(X, y, t, b_i)\right] \cdot \bar{R}^*(x^1, x^{11}, t)\bar{R}(x^{11}, y^{11}, t) \cdot K^{m^T}_{k+1}(y, k + 1)\right\} dx^1 dx^{11} dy^{11},$$

and

$$\frac{\partial}{\partial t} V_{\tilde{X}}(x, y, t, n, 0) + \frac{\partial}{\partial n} V_{\tilde{X}}(x, y, t, n, 0)$$

$$= E_t\left\{\tilde{X}(x, t, n) \sum_{i=0}^{L_1} \tilde{\tilde{F}}^T_{y_i}(X, y, t, a_i)\right\}$$

$$- \sum_{i=0}^{L_2} \left\{\int_D\int_D\int_D E_t\left[X(x, t, n)\tilde{\tilde{H}}^T_{x^1_i}\left(X, x^1, t, b_i\right)\right]\right.$$

$$\cdot \bar{R}^*(x^1, x^{11}, t)\bar{R}(x^{11}, y^{11}, t)$$

$$\left.\cdot K^T_{k+1}(y, k+1)\right\} dx^1 dx^{11} dy^{11},$$

with boundary conditions given by $\hat{\hat{B}}_x(X, x, t, 0) = 0$ and the initial conditions as in Section V.B.

It should be noted that for DPS with polynomial, product-type, exponential, and state-dependent sinusoidal nonlinearities, these algorithms can also be written in terms of the first two moments, under the sole assumption that the estimator errors are Gaussian. For other types of nonlinearities, the terms involving infinite-dimensional expectations must be further approximated using possibly the Taylor series expansion.

Many estimation problems for linear or nonlinear distributed lumped parameter systems, with or without time delays, can be considered as special cases. The results presented here could also be extended to DPS systems corrupted by correlated and colored noise processes. The derivation would be similar to that of Sections III and IV.

VI. EXACT AND APPROXIMATE MINIMUM-VARIANCE FILTERING FOR NONLINEAR CONTINUOUS SYSTEMS

A. *INTRODUCTION*

This section is devoted to the direct derivation of filtering estimation algorithms for nonlinear continuous dynamic systems corrupted by (1) additive white Gaussian noise, (2) correlated noise, and (3) noise-free processes.

In Section B the noise processes are assumed to be Gaussian white and the basic approach makes use of the matrix minimum principle to minimize the error-variance cost function, which is obtained from the exact conditional probability densi density function, as presented in Kushner [9,14] and Kolmogorov's equations [46]. Therefore, it is not unexpected that the exact nonlinear filtering equations derived for white-noise problems closely resemble those of Bass *et al.* [21], except that the argument of the expectations have been transformed from the state x(t) into its estimator error $\tilde{x}(t)$. Section G shows that, for filtering problems with polynomial, product-type, exponential, or state-dependent sinusoidal nonlinearities, the filtering algorithms can be fully realized without any other approximations, under the assumption that the conditional probability density functions of the estimator errors are Gaussian.

In many practical situations, nonlinear dynamic systems are imbedded in non-white-noise processes. Therefore, Sections C and D deal with more general nonlinear estimation problems; they are, respectively, imbedded in correlated noise and noise-free processes, and the colored noise problem can be considered as a special case of the noise-free estimation problem.

The estimation algorithms derived for non-white-noise processes are suboptimal, because the change in probability density functions due to the differential measurements δz is neglected. In the special case where the system and measurement models are linear, the resulting algorithms are optimal and agree well with those of the literature [4,57].

B. OPTIMAL MINIMUM-VARIANCE CONTINUOUS NONLINEAR FILTERING WITH WHITE-NOISE PROCESSES

Consider the class of nonlinear systems described by the stochastic differential equation

$$dx(t)/dt = f[x(t), t] + G[x(t), t]w(t), \tag{87}$$

with the measurement given by

$$z(t) = h[x(t), t] + v(t), \tag{88}$$

where x(t) and z(t) are the n-dimensional state and m-dimensional measurement vectors, f and h, respectively, n- and m-dimensional nonlinear vector valued functions, and G a vector-valued matrix.

The random vectors w(t) and v(t) are statistically independent zero-mean white Gaussian noise processes such that, for all $t, \tau \geq t_0$,

$$\begin{aligned} \text{cov}\{w(t), w(\tau)\} &= V_w(t)\delta(t - \tau), \\ \text{cov}\{v(t), v(\tau)\} &= V_v(t)\delta(t - \tau), \\ \text{cov}\{w(t), v(\tau)\} &= 0, \end{aligned} \tag{89}$$

where $\delta(\ )$ is the Dirac delta function and the variances $V_w(t)$ and $V_v(t)$ are nonnegative definite and positive definite, respectively.

The initial state vector $x(t_0) = x_0$ is a zero-mean Gaussian random process, independent of $w(t)$ and $v(t)$ for $t \geq t_0$, with a positive definite variance matrix

$$\mathrm{var}\{x(t_0),\ x(t_0)\} = V_x(t_0).$$

In the typical filtering problem, it is required to compute $\hat{x}(t)$, the unbiased estimate of $x(t)$ conditioned on the set of measurements

$$Z(t) = [z(s)/t_0 \leq s \leq t]$$

such that the cost function for $\tau > t_0$

$$J(\tau) = E\{[x(\tau) - \hat{x}(\tau)]^T M(\tau)[x(\tau) - \hat{x}(\tau)]/Z(\tau)\} \tag{90}$$

is minimized. Here $M(\tau)$ is an arbitrary symmetric positive-definite matrix, T the matrix transpose, and E the expectation operator conditioned upon the set of measurements $Z(\tau)$.

The filtering algorithm is assumed to satisfy the general nonlinear differential equation

$$\dot{\hat{x}}(t) = l[\hat{x}(t),\ t] + K(t)z(t), \tag{91}$$

where $l[\hat{x}(t),\ t]$ and $K(t)$ are yet unknown. Then the estimation problem is to determine the time-varying nonlinear vector-valued function $l[\hat{x}(t),\ t]$ and the gain algorithm $K(t)$ such that the cost function of Eq. (90) is minimized.

In fact, the nonlinear filtering equation may be assumed to take various forms; however, once enough information concerning $\hat{x}(t)$ and $z(t)$ is included in the estimator model, the resulting filtering algorithms would be unique. For example, other dynamic filtering equations such as

$$\dot{\hat{x}}(t) = l[\hat{x}(t), t] + K(t)\{z(t) - E[z(t)]\} \tag{92}$$

can also be assumed. Comparing the structures of Eqs. (91) and (92), it is obvious that an extra term $-K(t)E[z(t)]$ is included in Eq. (92). However, the resulting filtering algorithm using either one of the preceding estimator models would result in exactly the same nonlinear filtering algorithm.

Now let $\tilde{x}(t)$ denote the estimator error defined by

$$\tilde{x}(t) = x(t) - \hat{x}(t). \tag{93}$$

Using Eqs. (87), (88), and (91), the derivative of Eq. (93) becomes

$$\begin{aligned}\dot{\tilde{x}}(t) = {} & f[\tilde{x}(t) + \hat{x}(t), t] + G[\tilde{x}(t) + \hat{x}(t), t]w(t) \\ & - l[\hat{x}(t), t] - K(t)\{h[\tilde{x}(t) + \hat{x}(t), t] + v(t)\}.\end{aligned} \tag{94}$$

Because $\hat{x}(t)$ is required to be an unbiased estimate, the expectations of both $\tilde{x}(t)$ and $\dot{\tilde{x}}(t)$ must be zero. Hence, if the expectations of both sides of Eq. (94) are taken, it is necessary that

$$\begin{aligned}l[\hat{x}(t), t] = {} & \hat{f}[\tilde{x}(t) + \hat{x}(t), t] \\ & - K(t)\{h[\tilde{x}(t) + \hat{x}(t), t]\},\end{aligned} \tag{95}$$

where

$$\hat{f}[\tilde{x}(t) + \hat{x}(t), t] = E\{f[\tilde{x}(t) + \hat{x}(t), t]/Z(t)\},$$

$$\hat{h}[\tilde{x}(t) + \hat{x}(t), t] = E\{h[\tilde{x}(t) + \hat{x}(t), t]/Z(t)\}.$$

Then the estimator error can be shown to satisfy the relation

$$\begin{aligned}\dot{\tilde{x}}(t) = {} & f^{*}[\tilde{x}(t), \hat{x}(t), t] \\ & + G^{*}[\tilde{x}(t), \hat{x}(t), t]w^{*}(t),\end{aligned} \tag{96}$$

where

$$f^*[\tilde{x}(t), \hat{x}(t), t]$$
$$= f[\tilde{x}(t) + \hat{x}(t), t] - \hat{f}[\tilde{x}(t) + \hat{x}(t), t]$$
$$+ K(t)\{\hat{h}[\tilde{x}(t) + \hat{x}(t), t] - h[\tilde{x}(t) + \hat{x}(t), t]\}$$

and

$$G^*[\tilde{x}(t), \hat{x}(t), t]$$
$$= [G[x(t) + x(t), t], -K(t)]\begin{bmatrix} w(t) \\ v(t) \end{bmatrix}.$$

Furthermore, Eq. (88) can be rewritten as

$$z(t) = h[\tilde{x}(t) + \hat{x}(t), t] + v(t). \tag{97}$$

Now the filtering problem of Eqs. (87) and (88) has been transformed into that of Eqs. (96) and (97).

Let $\phi[\tilde{x}(t)]$ be a twice continuously differentiable function of the vector $\tilde{x}(t)$; by definition of the conditional expectation operator,

$$dE\{\phi[\tilde{x}(t)] = \int \phi[\tilde{x}(t)]dp[\tilde{x}(t), t/Z(t)]d\tilde{x}(t), \tag{98}$$

where $p[\tilde{x}(t), t/Z(t)]$ is the conditional probability density function.

Next, the change in $p[\tilde{x}(t), t/Z(t)]$ due to the dynamic equations of (96) and (97) must be computed. It can be shown [57] that

$$\delta p = p[\tilde{x}(t + \delta t), t + \delta t/Z(t), \delta z] - p[\tilde{x}(t), t/Z(t), \delta z]$$
$$+ p[\tilde{x}(t), t/Z(t), z] - p[\tilde{x}(t), t/Z(t)], \tag{99}$$

where the first two terms are simply the change due to the dynamic equation of (96) and the last two terms are due to the differential measurements δz. These two changes are given by

Kolmogorov and Kushner's equation [12,14]. Therefore,

$$\frac{dE\{\phi[\tilde{x}(t)]\}}{dt} = E\{L\phi[\tilde{x}(t)]\} + E\{\phi[\tilde{x}(t)][h[\tilde{x}(t) + \hat{x}(t), t] - \hat{h}[\tilde{x}(t) + \hat{x}(t), t]]\}V_v(t)^{-1}\{z(t) - \hat{h}[\tilde{x}(t) + \hat{x}(t), t]\}, \tag{100}$$

where

$$L\phi[\tilde{x}(t) = \sum_{i=1}^{n} f_i^*[\tilde{x}(t), \hat{x}(t), t] \frac{\partial\phi[\tilde{x}(t)]}{\partial\tilde{x}_i} + \frac{1}{2}\sum_{i,j=1}^{n}\left\{G^*[\tilde{x}(t), \hat{x}(t), t]V_{w*}(t)G^{*T}[\tilde{x}(t), \hat{x}(t), t]\right\}_{ij} \cdot \frac{\partial^2\phi[x(t)]}{\partial\tilde{x}_i\partial\tilde{x}_j}. \tag{101}$$

Then the error-variance equation is obtained from Eqs. (96), (97), (100), and (101) by setting $\phi[\tilde{x}(t)] = \tilde{x}(t)\tilde{x}^T(t)$ for which

$$\frac{dV_{\tilde{x}}(t)}{dt} = E\left\{\tilde{x}(t)f^{*T}[\tilde{x}(t), \hat{x}(t), t] + f^*[\tilde{x}(t), \hat{x}(t), t]\tilde{x}^T(t)\right\} + E\left\{G[\tilde{x}(t) + \hat{x}(t), t]V_w(t)G^T[\tilde{x}(t) + \hat{x}(t), t] + K(t)V_v(t)K^T(t)\right\} + E\left\{\tilde{x}(t)\tilde{x}^T(t)h^T[\tilde{x}(t) + \hat{x}(t), t] - V_{\tilde{x}}(t)h^T[\tilde{x}(t) + \hat{x}(t), t]\right\} \cdot V_v^{-1}(t)\{z(t) - \hat{h}[\tilde{x}(t) + \hat{x}(t), t]\}, \tag{102}$$

where it can be shown that

$$E\left\{\tilde{x}(t)f^{*T}[\tilde{x}(t),\ \hat{x}(t),\ t]\right\}$$

$$= E\{\tilde{x}(t)f^T[\tilde{x}(t) + \hat{x}(t),\ t] - \tilde{x}(t)h^T[\tilde{x}(t) + \hat{x}(t),\ t]K^T(t)\}.$$

Now the estimation problem takes the form of an optimal control problem in which $K(t)$ is the only variable available for manipulation such that the cost function of Eq. (90) is minimized.

To use the matrix minimum principle to solve this problem, a symmetric positive-definite costate matrix $P(t)$ is defined and the Hamiltonian is given by

$$H = \operatorname{trace}\left\{\dot{V}_{\tilde{x}}(t)P^T(t)\right\}.$$

Using the concept of gradient matrices, the necessary condition that the optimal $K(t)$ must satisfy is obtained as

$$K(t) = E\{\tilde{x}(t)h^T[\tilde{x}(t) + \hat{x}(t),\ t]\}V_v^{-1}. \tag{103}$$

Note that $K(t)$ is independent of the costate matrix $P(t)$ and the weighting factor $M(t)$.

Then the filtering estimate and the error-variance equation becomes

$$\begin{aligned}\dot{\hat{x}}(t) = \hat{f}[\tilde{x}(t) + \hat{x}(t),\ t] \\ &+ E\{\tilde{x}(t)h^T[\tilde{x}(t) + \hat{x}(t),\ t]\} \\ &\cdot V_v^{-1}(t)\{z(t) - \hat{h}[\tilde{x}(t) + \hat{x}(t),\ t]\},\end{aligned} \tag{104}$$

and

$$\frac{dV_x(t)}{dt} = E\{\tilde{x}(t)f^T[\tilde{x}(t) + \hat{x}(t), t] + f[\tilde{x}(t) + \hat{x}(t), t]\tilde{x}^T(t)\}$$
$$+ E\left\{G[\tilde{x}(t) + \hat{x}(t), t]V_w(t)G^T[\tilde{x}(t) + \hat{x}(t), t]\right\}$$
$$- E\{\tilde{x}(t) + h^T[\tilde{x}(t) + \hat{x}(t), t]\}V_v^{-1}(t)$$
$$\cdot E\{h[\tilde{x}(t) + \hat{x}(t), t]\tilde{x}^T(t)\}$$
$$+ E\left\{\tilde{x}(t)\tilde{x}^T(t)h^T[\tilde{x}(t) + \hat{x}(t), t]\right.$$
$$\left. - V_x(t)h^T[\tilde{x}(t) + \hat{x}(t), t]\right\}V_v^{-1}(t)$$
$$\cdot \{z(t) - \hat{h}[\tilde{x}(t) + \hat{x}(t), t]\}, \tag{105}$$

respectively.

It should be noted that before the preceding algorithms can be physically realized, a number of difficult expectations must be evaluated. These involve infinite-dimensional systems except in trivially simple cases. Also notice that the algorithms derived here closely resemble the exact equations due to Bass *et al.* [21]. The only difference is that the argument of the expectations have been transformed into $\tilde{x}(t)$. As stated earlier, such a transformation is particularly significant for filtering problems with polynomial, product-type, and state-dependent sinusoidal nonlinearities, because, in such cases, the filtering algorithms can be obtained without any further approximations, under the assumption that the probability density functions of the estimator errors are Gaussian.

Furthermore, this derivation can be extended to filtering problems with non-white-noise processes. However, in such cases, the change in $p[\tilde{x}(t), t/Z(t)]$ due to the differential measurements δz is neglected and Eq. (100) becomes simply

$$dE\{\phi[\tilde{x}(t)]\}/dt = E\{L\phi[\tilde{x}(t)]\}. \tag{106}$$

It is noteworthy to mention that, when such an approximation is made, the results obtained for the filtering problem corrupted by white-noise processes are equivalent to that of the stochastic linearization due to Sunahara [23]. In such a case the random forcing term in the error-variance equation of Eq. (105) is neglected, whereas the filtering algorithm of Eq. (104) remains unchanged.

When Eq. (106) is used in place of Eq. (100) to obtain the error-variance equation and the nonlinear functions are approximated by second-order Taylor series expansions, the resulting algorithms are commonly called modified minimum variance filters [24].

To test the performance of the proposed minimum-variance filter and to compare it with various other approximate nonlinear filters [18-21,23,24], Liang [47] selected various types of nonlinear systems, in which the stochastic filtering equations were transformed to Stratonovich's forms and then simulated on a digital computer. The simulation results obtained from the proposed filtering algorithms are compared with various other approximate nonlinear filters. The results indicate the superiority of the proposed filter over those of other filters investigated.

C. MINIMUM-VARIANCE GENERAL CONTINUOUS NONLINEAR FILTER

Consider the general nonlinear message model

$$\dot{x}(t) = f[x(t), t] + G[x(t), t]w(t) + E[x(t), t]u(t) \quad (107)$$

with measurement given by

$$z(t) = h[x(t), t] + v(t) + y(t), \quad (108)$$

where u(t) and y(t) are known input time functions, w(t) and v(t) are correlated noise processes with mean $\mu_w(t)$ and $\mu_v(t)$, respectively,

$$\operatorname{cov}\{w(t), v(\tau)\} = V_{wv}(t)\delta(t - \tau), \tag{109}$$

and all other prior statistics follow that of Section B.

Following the development of Section B and neglecting the change of $p[\tilde{x}(t), t/Z(t)]$ due to the differential measurements $\delta z(t)$, the filtering algorithm is given by

$$\begin{aligned}\dot{\hat{x}}(t) = {} & \hat{f}[\tilde{x}(t) + \hat{x}(t), t] + G[\tilde{x}(t) + \hat{x}(t), t]\mu_w(t) \\ & + \hat{E}[\tilde{x}(t) + \hat{x}(t), t]u(t) \\ & + K(t)\{z(t) - \mu_v(t) - y(t) - \hat{h}[\tilde{x}(t) + \hat{x}(t), t]\},\end{aligned} \tag{110}$$

where the gain algorithm is

$$\begin{aligned}K(t) = E\Big\{ & \tilde{x}(t)h^T[\tilde{x}(t) + \hat{x}(t), t] \\ & + G[\tilde{x}(t) + \hat{x}(t), t]V_{wv}(t)\Big\} V_v^{-1}(t)\end{aligned} \tag{111}$$

and the error-variance equation is given by

$$\begin{aligned}\dot{V}_{\tilde{x}}(t) = {} & E\{\tilde{x}(t)f^T[\tilde{x}(t) + \hat{x}(t), t] + f[\tilde{x}(t) + \hat{x}(t), t]\tilde{x}^T(t)\} \\ & + E\Big\{G[\tilde{x}(t) + \hat{x}(t), t]V_w(t)G^T[\tilde{x}(t) + \hat{x}(t), t]\Big\} \\ & - K(t)V_v(t)K^T(t).\end{aligned} \tag{112}$$

For the particular case in which f and h are linear, G and E are independent of the state variable, namely

$$f[x(t), t] = F(t)x(t),$$

$$h[x(t), t] = H(t)x(t),$$

$$G[x(t), t] = G(t),$$

$$E[x(t), t] = E(t).$$

Then Eqs. (110)-(112) are, respectively,

$$\dot{\hat{x}}(t) = F(t)\hat{x}(t) + G(t)\mu_w(t) + E(t)u(t)$$
$$+ K(t)\{z(t) - \mu_v(t) - y(t) - H(t)\hat{x}(t)\},$$

$$K(t) = V_{\tilde{x}}(t)H^T(t) + G(t)V_{wv}(t) \; V_v^{-1}(t),$$

and

$$\dot{V}_{\tilde{x}}(t) = F(t)V_{\tilde{x}}(t) + V_{\tilde{x}}(t)F^T(t)$$
$$+ G(t)V_w(t)G^T(t) - K(t)V_v(t)K^T(t).$$

These algorithms agree with the general continuous Kalman filter [48].

D. MINIMUM-VARIANCE CONTINUOUS NONLINEAR NOISE-FREE FILTERING

Consider the continuous nonlinear message model of Eq. (87) with the noise-free measurement model given by

$$z(t) = h[x(t), t], \tag{113}$$

where w(t) is zero-mean white noise with nonnegative-definite variance $V_w(t)$. Then h[x(t), t] is assumed to be continuously differentiable in t and has continuous second mixed partial derivatives with respect to the elements of x and is also considered to be of full rank, otherwise an equivalent z(t) of lower dimension could be used.

Because z(t) is noise free and $V_w(t)$ is nonnegative definite, when z(t) is differentiated, some of its elements may not contain any white noise. Therefore, each element of z(t) has to be differentiated [60] as in

$$\frac{d}{dt} z_i = \frac{\partial}{\partial t} h_i + \frac{\partial}{\partial x} h_i \frac{d}{dt} x + \frac{1}{2} \operatorname{trace}\left[G\Psi_w G^T\left(\frac{\partial^2}{\partial x_i^2} h_i\right)\right]$$

and Eq. (87) is used to substitute for the derivative of the state variable until white noise is obtained in the derivatives of each element in z(t).

The signals obtained can be arranged into two sets. In the first set,

$$z_1(t) = h_1[x(t), V_w(t), t],$$

which comprises Eq. (113) and all linearly independent derivatives of z(t) that are noise free.

In the second set,

$$z_2(t) = h_2[x(t), V_w(t), t] + N[x(t), t]w(t),$$

which comprises all derivatives of z(t) that contain linearly independent white noise.

It is assumed that the filtering estimate $\hat{x}(t)$ is given by

$$\dot{\hat{x}}(t) = l[\hat{x}(t), t] + K_1(t)z_1(t) + K_2(t)z_2(t)$$

because in place of Eq. (113) there are two set of measurements.

Here, $z_1(t)$ is considered as a known input, it does not contain any new information. Following the development of Section B, the following filtering algorithm is obtained:

$$\dot{\hat{x}}(t) = \hat{f}[\tilde{x}(t) + \hat{x}(t), t] + K_2(t)\{z_2(t) - \hat{h}_2[\tilde{x}(t) + \hat{x}(t), V_w(t), t]\},$$

where the gain algorithm is

$$K_2(t) = E\Big\{\tilde{x}(t)h_2^T[\tilde{x}(t) + \hat{x}(t), V_w(t), t] + G[\tilde{x}(t) + \hat{x}(t), t]V_w(t)N^T[\tilde{x}(t) + \hat{x}(t), t]\Big\} \cdot \Big\{E\Big[N[\tilde{x}(t) + \hat{x}(t), t]V_w(t)N^T[\tilde{x}(t) + \hat{x}(t), t]\Big]\Big\}^{-1}$$

and the error-variance equation is given as

$$\dot{V}_x(t) = E\{\tilde{x}(t)f^T[\tilde{x}(t) + \hat{x}(t), t] + f[\tilde{x}(t) + \hat{x}(t), t]\tilde{x}^T(t)\}$$
$$+ E\Big\{G[\tilde{x}(t) + \hat{x}(t), t]V_w(t)G^T[\tilde{x}(t) + \hat{x}(t), t]\Big\}$$
$$- K_2(t)E\Big\{N[\tilde{x}(t) + \hat{x}(t), t]V_w(t)$$
$$\cdot N^T[\tilde{x}(t) + \hat{x}(t), t]\Big\}K_2^T(t).$$

In the case that the vector-valued functions are linear, the results presented here agree well with those of Bryson and Johansen [4].

VII. CONCLUSIONS

A unified approach has been presented to derive nonlinear estimation algorithms for discrete and continuous nonlinear systems with and without delays, given nondelayed measurements, as well as multichannel time-delayed measurements, corrupted by white Gaussian noise, correlated noise, colored noise, as well as noise-free processes.

Nonlinear estimation algorithms for discrete nonlinear time-delayed systems with multichannel measurements corrupted by white noise, correlated noise, and colored noise processes were, respectively, derived in Sections II, III, and IV. The estimation algorithms directly yield the fixed-lag, fixed-point, and fixed-interval smoothing and the filtering algorithms, with proper substitution of the discrete-time indices. The proposed technique makes use of the concept of the gradient matrix and the minimum principle to derive the optimal values of the coefficients in the estimation algorithms under the requirements that the estimates be unbiased and the error variances minimized. The derivation is straightforward and clearly indicates the close links between three different classifications of smoothers and the filtering estimator.

The results obtained are exact and optimal with respect to the imposed constraints on the dynamic equations of the estimators, minimizing the error variances. They are expected to be computationally efficient, because no augmentation of state variables is involved. They may also be applied to various special cases of nonlinear as well as linear estimation problems; for example, the estimation problems for linear or nonlinear systems without delays, the estimation of linear or nonlinear systems with multiple delays only appearing in the measurements, and the linear estimation problems of time-delayed systems corrupted by white noise as well as nonwhite noise processes.

For linear estimation problems the results obtained are identified with published results in the literature. In the particular case of linear time-delayed systems corrupted by additive white noise, the results are stable, but the stability behavior of the nonlinear estimators has yet to be investigated.

The results presented in Sections II, III, and IV can all be extended to continuous-time systems with the application of a Kalman limiting procedure. For systems with polynomial, product-type, exponential, and state-dependent sinusoidal nonlinearities, all the nonlinear estimation algorithms presented in these sections can be fully implemented on a digital computer under the sole assumption that the probability density functions of the estimator errors be Gaussian.

In Section V a discrete-time estimation algorithm was derived for a general class of nonlinear DPS, assuming linearity in innovations and using the matrix minimum principle. The continuous-time algorithm is formal due to the applications of Kalman's limiting procedure.

In Section VI nonlinear filtering algorithms are derived for continuous nonlinear systems without delays, corrupted by white noise, correlated noise, and noise-free processes. The main technique involves applications of the matrix minimum principle together with the Kolmogorov and Kushner equations to minimize the error variance, taken to be the estimation criterion. The filtering equations obtained for nonlinear systems with white-noise processes are exact, but for non-white-noise processes the results obtained are approximate.

ACKNOWLEDGMENTS

This work was carried out with the support of the Defense Research Establishment, Ottawa (DREO), Canada. The author wishes to thank Mr. C. R. Iverson, Chief, DREO, for his encouragement.

REFERENCES

1. R. E. KALMAN, *Trans. Am. Soc. Mech. Eng. J. Basic Eng.* *82*, 34-45 (1960).

2. R. E. KALMAN, "Proceedings of the First Symposium on Engineering Applications of Random Function Theory and Probability," Wiley, New York, 1963.

3. R. E. KALMAN and R. S. Bucy, *Trans. Am. Soc. Mech. Eng.* *83*, 95-107 (1961).

4. A. E. BRYSON and D. E. JOHANSEN, *IEEE Trans. Automatic Control AC-10*, 4-10 (1965).

5. A. E. BRYSON and L. J. HENRIKSON, Phys. Tech. Report 533, Harvard University, Div. Eng. Appl., Cambridge, Mass., 1967.

6. A. R. STUBBERUD, "Optimal Filtering for Gauss-Markov Noise," Aerospace Corporation, Report No. TR-0158 (3307-01)-10, 1967.

7. E. B. STEAR and A. R. STUBBERUD, *Int. J. Control 8*, 123-130 (1968).

8. R. L. STRATONOVICH, *Theory Prob. Appl. 5*, 156-178 (1960).

9. H. J. KUSHNER, *SIAM J. Control 2*, 106-119 (1964).

10. H. J. KUSHNER, *J. Math. Anal. Appl. 8*, 332-344 (1964).

11. W. M. WONHAM, *SIAM J. Control 2*, 347-369 (1965).

12. R. S. BUCY, *IEEE Trans. Automatic Control AC-10*, 198 (1965).

13. R. E. MORTENSEN, "Optimal Control of Continuous Time Stochastic Systems," Ph.D. Dissertation, Univ. of California, Berkeley, Calif., 1966.

14. H. J. KUSHNER, *J. Differential Equations 3*, 179-190 (1967).

15. H. W. SORENSON and D. L. ALSPACH, *IFAC J. Automatica 7*, 465-479 (1971).

16. R. S. BUCY, *J. Astro. Sci. 17*, 80-94 (1969).

17. J. L. CENTER, "Practical Nonlinear Filtering Based on Generalized Least Squares Approximation of the Conditional Probability Distribution," Ph.D. Dissertation, Washington Univ., St. Louis, 1972.

18. H. COX, *IEEE Trans. Automatic Control AC-9*, 5-12 (1964).

19. H. J. KUSHNER, *IEEE Trans. Automatic Control AC-12*, 546-556 (1967).

20. D. M. DETCHMENDY and R. SRIDHAR, *Trans. Am. Soc. Mech. Eng. 88D*, 362-368 (1966).

21. R. W. BASS, V. D. NORUM, and L. SCHWARTZ, *J. Math. Anal. Appl. 16*, 152-164 (1966).

22. A. P. SAGE and W. S. EWING, *Int. J. Control 11*, 1-18 (1970).

23. Y. SUNAHARA, *Trans. Am. Soc. Mech. Eng. J. Basic Eng. 92D*, 385-393 (1970).

24. L. SCHWARTZ and E. B. STEAR, *IEEE Trans. Automatic Control AC-13*, 83-86 (1968).

25. C. T. LEONDES, J. B. PELLER, and E. B. STEAR, *IEEE Trans. System Sci. Cyb. SSC-6*, 63-71 (1970).

26. T. KAILATH and P. FROST, *IEEE Trans. Automatic Control AC-13*, 655-660 (1968).

27. D. G. LAINIOTIS, *Int. J. Control 14*, 1137-1148 (1971)

28. G. M. LEE, *IEEE Trans. Inf. Theory IT-17*, 45-49 (1971).

29. C. N. KELLY and B. D. O. ANDERSON, *J. Franklin Inst. 291*, 271-281 (1971).

30. J. S. MEDITCH, *J. Inf. Control 10*, 598-615 (1967).

31. H. E. RAUCH, *IEEE Trans. Automatic Control AC-8*, 371-372 (1963).

32. R. PRIEMER and A. G. VACROUS, *Int. J. Control 13*, 299-303 (1971).

33. M. FAROOQ and A. K. MAHALANABIS, *IEEE Trans. Automatic Control AC-16*, 104-105 (1971).

34. S. G. TZAFESTAS and J. M. NIGHTINGALE, *Proc. Inst. Elect. Eng. 116*, 1085-1093 (1969).

35. G. LAMONT and K. S. P. KUMAR, *J. Math. Anal. Appl. 38*, 588-606 (1972).

36. S. G. TZAFESTAS, *IEEE Trans. Automatic Control AC-17*, 448-458 (1972).

37. S. G. TZAFESTAS, *Int. J. Control 15*, 273-295 (1972).

38. R. F. CURTAIN, "Estimation Theory for Abstract Evolution Equations Excited by General White Noise Processes," Rep. 38, Control Theory Centre, Univ. Warwick, Warwick, England, pp. 1-51, 1975.

39. T. K. YU, J. H. SEINFELD, and W. H. RAY, *IEEE Trans. Automatic Control AC-19*, 324-333 (1974).

40. D. F. LIANG, "Nonlinear Estimation of Systems with and without Delays," Ph.D. Dissertation, University of Alberta, Canada, 1974.

41. D. F. LIANG and G. S. CHRISTENSEN, *Int. J. Control 23*, 613-625 (1976).

42. M. ATHANS, *Information Control 11*, 592-606 (1968).

43. D. F. LIANG and G. S. CHRISTENSEN, *Int. J. Control 28*, 1-10 (1978).

44. D. G. LIANG, *IEEE Trans. Automatic Control AC-23*, 502-504 (1978).

45. D. F. LIANG and G. S. CHRISTENSEN, *IFAC J. AUTOMATICA 11*, 603-612 (1975).

46. A. N. KOLMOGOROV, *Bull. Acad. Sci., USSR, Math. Ser. 5*, 3-14 (1941).

47. D. F. LIANG, in "Control and Dynamic Systems, Advances in Theory and Applications," Vol. 20, ed. C. T. Leondes, Academic Press, New York, 1981.

48. A. P. SAGE and J. L. MELSA, "Estimation Theory with Applications to Communications and Control," McGraw-Hill, New York, 1971.

49. V. SHUKLA and M. D. SRINATH, *J. Information Control 22*, 471-486 (1973).

50. K. K. BISWAS and A. K. MAHALANABIS, *IEEE Trans. Aerospace Elect. Systems AES-8*, 676-680 (1972).

51. E. PARZEN, "Stochastic Processes," Holden-Day, San Francisco, 1962.

52. W. G. ROYDS (Private communication, 1981).

53. A. GELB and W. E. VANDER VELDE, "Multiple-Input Describing Functions and Nonlinear System Design," McGraw-Hill, New York, 1968.

54. B. V. RAJA RAO and A. K. MAHALANABIS, *IEEE Trans. Automatic Control AC-16*, 267 (1971).

55. D. F. LIANG and G. S. CHRISTENSEN, *IEEE Trans. Automatic Control AC-20*, 176-177 (1975).

56. H. KWAKERNAAK, *IEEE Trans. Automatic Control AC-12*, 169-173 (1967).

57. A. H. JAZWINSKI, "Stochastic Processes and Filtering Theory," Academic Press, New York, 1970.

58. J. MISHRA and V. S. RAJAMANI, *IEEE Trans. Automatic Control AC-20*, 140-142 (1975).

59. V. SHUKLA and M. D. SRINATH, *Int. J. Control 16*, 673-687 (1972).

60. K. YONEZAWA, *IFAC J. Automatica 15*, 123-124 (1979).

Synthesis and Performance of Bayesian Estimators

M. GAUVRIT
C. FARGEON
P. RODRIGO
Departement d'Etudes et de Reserches en Automatique ONERA/CERT Toulouse, France

I. INTRODUCTION

In the filtering theory as formulated by Kalman [1], the estimation of the state of a discrete linear system driven by white Gaussian noises requires a precise knowledge of the system parameters and noise statistics. To extend the "Kalman filter theory," on-line techniques for adaptive estimation,

ISBN 0-12-012719-9

and then adaptive control using the state estimates, are necessary: (1) when the system dynamics are known and noise statistics unknown (referred to in the following as the UNS case); (2) when the system dynamics are unknown and noise statistics known (referred to as USD); or (3) when both are unknown (referred to as UDN).

In UNS, on-line methods result in the identification of the covariance matrices or in the Kalman gain matrix. Recursive schemes have been investigated by Mehra [2], and Bayesian by Alspach *et al.* [3] and Alspach [4]. In USD, parallel techniques were developed by Ho [5] and Lainiotis [6] and Sims and Lainiotis [7], and recursive by Bar Shalom [8]. In UDN, sequential estimation of both system parameters and noise statistics has been achieved by Myers and Tapley [9].

The accuracy and sensitivity of the open loop estimators have been studied by Sage and Melsa [10], Jazwinski [11], and Liporace [12], and an attractive method based on associated ordinary differential equations has been achieved by Ljung [13] for recursive algorithms in open and closed loops. Furthermore, Hawkes and Moore [14] and Baram and Sandell [15] have studied the convergence of recursive estimators with finite parameter space.

In a previous paper [16] the authors studied the asymptotic behavior of Bayesian estimates in open loop systems. The mathematical results obtained are presented here more precisely and permit conclusions to be drawn about convergence properties and asymptotic behavior of the estimates (Sections II and III and Appendix). Numerical examples are also given.

II. QUALITY OF BAYESIAN ESTIMATORS IN OPEN LOOP

The purpose of this section is to put emphasis on the evaluation with time of Bayesian estimate covariances in open loop so that valuable information can be obtained concerning the convergence and accuracy of the Bayesian estimation algorithm. A clear relationship will appear among the precision of the estimates, the number of data, the system dynamics, and the noise environment. The first subsection deals with the UNS case, the second with the USD case. A concluding remark gives an introduction to the general UDN case in which both noise statistics and system dynamics are unknown.

A. UNKNOWN NOISE STATISTICS (UNS) CASE

1. Problem Formulation

Let us consider the following discrete linear system with constant and known matrices A, D, and C and unknown noise statistics:

$$X_{k+1} = AX_k + Dw_k, \tag{1a}$$

$$z_k = CX_k + v_k. \tag{1b}$$

From Sections II to III.C plant and measurement sequences w_k and v_k will be assumed to be *independent* Gaussian white noises; in this subsection we deal with *unknown* covariances Q and R. These assumptions are expressed by the following equations:

$$E\left(w_k w_j^T\right) = \delta_{kj} Q, \tag{1c}$$

$$E\left(v_k v_j^T\right) = \delta_{kj} R, \tag{1d}$$

$$E(w_k) = E(v_k) = 0, \tag{1e}$$

$$E\left(w_k v_j^T\right) = 0 \quad \text{for all } (k, j), \tag{1f}$$

where n is the state vector dimension and r the observation vector dimension.

a. Minimum variance state estimate

When Q and R are known, the minimum variance state estimate is given by the following recursive and discrete equations (Kalman filter):

$$\hat{X}(k/k) = E\left(X_k/Z^k\right),$$

$$\text{where } Z^k = (Z_0, Z_1, \ldots, Z_k); \tag{2}$$

$$\hat{X}(k + 1/k) = A\hat{X}(k/k),$$

$$P(k + 1/k) = AP(k/k)A^T + DQD^T, \tag{3}$$

$$M(k + 1) = CP(k + 1/k)C^T + R, \tag{4}$$

$$K(k + 1) = P(k + 1/k)C^T M^{-1}(k + 1), \tag{5}$$

$$\hat{X}(k + 1/k + 1) = \hat{X}(k + 1/k) + K(k + 1)[Z_{k+1} - C\hat{X}(k + 1/k)], \tag{6}$$

$$P(k + 1/k + 1) = [I - K(k + 1)C]P(k + 1/k)[I - K(k + 1)C]^T + K(k + 1)RK^T(k + 1). \tag{7}$$

b. Bayesian adaptive filter

When the matrices Q and R are unknown, the a priori densities of (Q, R) are defined, and hence of K. As soon as measures appear, the evolution with time of the a posteriori conditional densities can be followed. To obtain the optimal estimate of X_k, Q, R, and K, the fundamental Bayes rules are used as indicated on the continuous set of values Q and R:

$$p\left(X_k, Q, R/Z^k\right) = p\left(X_k/Q, R, Z^k\right)p(Q, R/Z^k), \tag{8}$$

$$p\left(X_k, K/Z^k\right) = p\left(X_k/K, Z^k\right)p(K/Z^k). \tag{9}$$

Thus $p\left(X_k/Q,\ R,\ Z^k\right)$ leads to the Kalman filter problem as in Section II.A.1.a, and is a Gaussian density $\mathcal{N}(X(k/k),\ P(k/k))$ denoted in the following as

$$\mathcal{N}(\hat{X}_k,\ P_k)$$
$$= (+2\pi)^{-n/2}|P_k|^{-1/2}\ \exp\left[-\tfrac{1}{2}(X_k - \hat{X}_k)P_k^{-1}(X_k - \hat{X}_k)^T\right]. \tag{10}$$

Equation (6) shows that even if Q and R are unknown a Bayesian identification of the gain matrix K, i.e., of the density $p(K/Z^k)$, is sufficient to estimate the state of the system through Eq. (9). Referring to Alspach *et al.* [3] and supposing that the Kalman filter has reached steady state, we have

$$p(K/Z^k) = \left\{\lambda p_0(K)\Big/M_{max}(K)\,[\hat{M}(K)]^{(k-2/2)}\right\}$$
$$\cdot\ G(K,\ \hat{M}(K)/M_{max}(K)), \tag{11}$$

where λ is a constant and $\hat{M}(K)$ denotes the ergodic covariance defined by

$$\hat{M}(K) = (1/k)\sum_{j=1}^{k}\ [Z_k - C\hat{X}_k(k)]^2. \tag{12}$$

As shown in [3] the limit of the function $G(K,\ \hat{M}(K)/M_{max}(K))$ is the unit step function for a sufficiently large k. So, neglecting a priori effects,

$$p(K/Z^k) = \lambda'/[\hat{M}(K)]^{k/2}. \tag{13}$$

Equations (12) and (13) show that one can estimate the gain matrix K and the corresponding covariance matrix σ_k *by implementing* m *Kalman filters in parallel*, using m different values for K. An approximation of the continuous Bayesian estimate is obtained from these m discrete values as

$$\hat{K}(k) = \frac{\Sigma_{i=1}^{m} p\left(K_i/Z^k\right)K_i}{\Sigma_{i=1}^{m} p\left(K_i/Z^k\right)} \tag{14}$$

$$\sigma_K^2(k) = \frac{\Sigma_{i=1}^{m} p\left(K_i/Z^k\right)K_i^2}{\Sigma_{i=1}^{m} p\left(K_i/Z^k\right)} - [\hat{K}(k)]^2. \tag{15}$$

Note that in Eqs. (8)-(13) p is a density, and in (14, 15) a discrete probability.

From Eqs. (14) and (15) no numerical analysis of the convergence of the parallel algorithm can be derived and the asymptotic behavior of the estimate cannot be specified. Let us look now for an analytical formula giving σ_k^2 a priori. This a priori knowledge will in practice make it possible to decide whether the Bayesian structure is feasible or not, considering the particular system dynamics, and when it is best suited.

2. *Algorithm Convergence and Gain Estimate Quality*

Using the ergodicity property one derives from Eq. (13) for large k

$$p\left(\frac{K_0 + \Delta K_i}{Z^k}\right) = \frac{\lambda'}{(M_0 + \Delta M_i)^{k/2}} = \frac{\Lambda}{[1 + (\Delta M_i/M_0)]^{k/2}}, \tag{16}$$

where λ' and Λ are constants, and p( ) a density.

In Eq. (16) there appear the nominal reference values K_0 and M_0 of the gain matrix and the measurement error covariance matrix, respectively. If Q and R were known (Kalman problem), they could be obtained from the system [see Eq. (18)]. Thus

$$P_0' = AP_0A^T + DQD^T, \tag{17a}$$

$$M_0 = CP_0'C^T + R, \tag{17b}$$

$$P_0 = (I - K_0C)P_0'(I - K_0C)^T + K_0RK_0^T, \tag{17c}$$

$$K_0 = P_0'C^TM_0^{-1}. \tag{17d}$$

In (UNS) each of the m linear filters is associated with a different value K_i ($i = 1, \ldots, m$), which can be heuristically set as $K_i = K_0 + \Delta K_i$, and executes the following recurrent operations:

$$\hat{X}_i(k + 1/k) = A\hat{X}_i(k/k), \tag{18}$$

$$\hat{X}_i(k + 1/k + 1) = \hat{X}_i(k + 1/k) + K_i[Z_{k+1} - C\hat{X}_i(k + 1/k)]. \tag{19}$$

From Eqs. (18) and (19), Eqs. (20, (21), and (22) are deduced as

$$P_i' = E(X_i - \hat{X}_i')(X_i - \hat{X}_i')^T = AP_iA^T + DQD^T, \tag{20}$$

$$P_i = E(X_i - \hat{X}_i)(X_i - \hat{X}_i)^T = (I - K_iC)P_i'(I - K_iC)^T + K_iRK_i^T, \tag{21}$$

$$M_i = E(Z_i - \hat{Z}_i)(Z_i - \hat{Z}_i)^T = CP_i'C^T + R \quad (i = 1, \ldots, m), \tag{22}$$

where $X_i = X_i(k)$, $\hat{X}_i' = \hat{X}_i(k + 1/k)$, $\hat{X}_i = \hat{X}_i(k/k)$, and $\hat{Z}_i = C\hat{X}_i(k/k)$. Equations (20), (21), and (22) yield P_i, P_i', and thus M_i for a given K_i.

Let us consider ΔK_i a change in K_0. This results in the following changes in P_0, P_0', and M_0: $P_i' = P_0' + \Delta P_i'$, $P_i = P_0 + \Delta P_i$, and $M_i = M_0 + \Delta M_i$. One obtains from Eqs. (17)-(22)

$$\Delta M_i = C \Delta P_i' C^T, \tag{23}$$

$$\Delta P_i' = A \Delta P_i A^T, \tag{24}$$

$$\Delta P_i = \Delta K_i M_0 \Delta K_i^T + (I - K_i C) \Delta P_i' (I - K_i C)^T. \tag{25}$$

It is useful to note that in Eq. (25) first-order terms ΔK_i and ΔK_i^T disappear because of relation (17d).

a. Scalar case

Let A, C, and D be scalars and, without loss of generality, let us consider the following scalar systems:

$$x_k = ax_{k-1} + w_{k-1}, \qquad E(w_{k-1}) = 0, \qquad E\left(w_{k-1}^2\right) = Q,$$

$$z_k = x_k + v_k, \qquad E(v_k) = 0, \qquad E\left(v_k^2\right) = R.$$

From Eq. (25)

$$\Delta M_i = \frac{a^2 (\Delta K_i)^2 M_0}{1 - a^2 (1 - K_i)^2},$$

where $\Delta K_i = K_i - K_0$. Substituting ΔM_i in Eq. (16) we obtain for large k

$$p\left(\frac{K_i}{z^k}\right) = \frac{\Lambda}{\left\{1 + \left[a^2 (K_i - K_0)^2 / 1 - a^2 (1 - K_i)^2\right]\right\}^{k/2}}$$

$$= \frac{1}{F(a, K_i, K_0)^{k/2}}, \tag{26}$$

with

$$F(a, K_i, K_0) > 1 \quad \text{for} \quad a \neq 0 \quad \text{and} \quad K_i \neq K_0. \tag{27}$$

Relation (26) is a very attractive one: from this *rigorous* expression of the density $p\left(K_i/z^k\right)$ in the steady state, *one can prove the convergence* of the algorithm and derive the asymptotic behavior of the error covariance.

In the present scalar case the set of possible values of K_i is [0, 1], thus

$$\hat{K}_e(k) = \int_0^1 \frac{K dK}{F(a, K, K_0)^{k/2}} \bigg/ \int_0^1 \frac{dK}{F(a, K, K_0)^{k/2}}, \tag{28}$$

$$\sigma_K^2(k) = \int_0^1 \frac{[K - \hat{K}_e(k)]^2 dk}{F(a, K, K_0)^{k/2}} \bigg/ \int_0^1 \frac{dK}{F(a, K, K_0)^{k/2}}. \tag{29}$$

Similar formulas are obtained for higher-order moments.

Convergence analysis ($a \neq 0$). Relation (27) shows that the numerator and denominator of (28) tend toward zero when k tends to infinity. By developing both integrals of (28) according to Riemann series with increment ΔK, one can easily prove that

$$\hat{K}_e(k) \xrightarrow[k\to\infty]{} K_0 \quad \text{when} \quad \Delta K \to 0 \quad \text{(consistency property).}$$

In the same way, referring to Eq. (29) and equations having higher-order moments, one can conclude that all moments tend to zero when $k \to \infty$. Thus the following theorem is proved (see Appendix).

Theorem 1

Considering the scalar and exponentially stable system (1a)-(1f), Bayesian estimate (28) locally converges to the nominal value K_0 with *quadratic-mean (QM) convergence*.

Remark. Let us consider the case wehre $a = 0$. Equations (28) and (29) yield

$$\hat{K}_e(k) = 1/2, \qquad \sigma_K^2(k) = 1/12.$$

All the possible values of K are equally distributed in this case. The algorithm does not converge because $\hat{K}_e(k)$ moves to $\frac{1}{2}$.

Error-variance asymptotic behavior. At this stage the error-variance asymptotic behavior can be made precise. It is proved in the Appendix that Eq. (29) provided an a priori calculation of $\sigma_K^2(k)$ (when $a \neq 0$).

Theorem 2

Considering the same scalar system (1a)-(1f), the error variance of the gain estimate is

$$\overline{\sigma}_K^2(k) = \left[1 - a^2(1 - K_0)^2\right]/a^2k. \tag{30a}$$

Equation (30a) links the gain estimate variance to the system parameters (a, Q/R) and to the time; thus a rough knowledge of these parameters gives a priori information about the identification method precision. Furthermore, it shows that the standard deviation $\overline{\sigma}_K(k)$ decreases proportionally as the square root of the number of data k.

Bound study. From Eq. (30a) one deduces that the less stable the system (i.e., $|a|$ is nearer to 1), the better the estimate (i.e., σ_K is smaller).

When $Q/R = 0$, $K_0 = 0$ and $\overline{\sigma}_K(k) = \dfrac{(1 - a^2)^{1/2}}{|a|k^{1/2}}$,

When $Q/R \to \infty$, $K_0 = 1$ and $\overline{\sigma}_K(k) = \dfrac{1}{|a|k^{1/2}}$.

Hence, the less perturbed the system, the better the estimate. Numerical examples illustrating these results are presented in Section V.

b. n-Dimensional state vector case

Considering a scalar observation (i.e., M_0 scalar), Eq. (24) and (25) lead, for each parallel filter associated with K_i, to

$$P_i' = H\Delta P_i' H^T + M_0 A \Delta K_i \Delta K_i^T A^T,$$

where $H = A(I - K_i C)$.

Among the n components of each gain vector K_i, n - 1 are linked by relations that are independent of (Q, R) such as

$$K_{i,j} = f_j(K_{i,1}), \quad j = 2, \ldots, n, \quad i = 1, \ldots, m,$$

and hence

$$\Delta K_{i,j} = \frac{df_j}{dK_{i,1}} \Delta K_{i,1}.$$

The f_j functions are related to the state and observation matrices A, D, and C (see [1]), therefore Eq. (25) can be rewritten for each filter as

$$\Delta P_i' = H\Delta P_i' H^T + G M_0 (\Delta K_{i,1})^2,$$

where G is an $n \times n$ matrix found off-line. A relationship similar to the one in the scalar case is then obtained as

$$\Delta M_i = \mu M_0 (\Delta K_{i,1})^2$$

μ being a function of the system parameters. Hence the extension of Theorem 2 can be written as

$$\overline{\sigma}^2_{K_{i,1}} = 1/\mu k. \tag{30b}$$

The error-variance matrix asymptotic behavior is then analytically defined a priori by μ. Such an example is presented in Section V.

3. Convergence on a Finite Parameter Set

Equations (28) and (29) were the basis of the algorithm convergence study in the previous subsection. Let us now come back to Eqs. (14) and (15), that is to say, let us consider the convergence properties on a finite set of p values of a scalar Kalman gain K. At time t_k the mean value of the estimate will be according to Eqs. (14), (26), and (28),

$$\hat{K}(k) = \sum_{i=1}^{p} \frac{K_i}{[F(a, K_i, K_0)]^{k/2}} \Bigg/ \sum_{i=1}^{p} \frac{1}{[F(a, K_i, K_0)]^{k/2}},$$

where

$$F(a, K_i, K_0) = 1 + a^2 \frac{(K_i - K_0)^2}{1 - a^2(1 - K_i)^2}.$$

Let α_m be the smallest among the logarithmic set α_i defined as

$$\alpha_i = +\frac{1}{2} \log[F(a, K_i, K_0)].$$

Then

$$\hat{K}(k) = \frac{\Sigma_{i=1}^{p} K_i e^{-\alpha_i k}}{\Sigma_{i=1}^{p} e^{-\alpha_i k}}$$

or

$$\hat{K}(k) = \frac{K_m e^{-\alpha_m k}\left[1 + (K_1/K_m) e^{-(\alpha_1-\alpha_m)k} + \cdots + (K_p/K_m) e^{-(\alpha_p-\alpha_m)k}\right]}{e^{-\alpha_m k}\left(1 + e^{-(\alpha_1-\alpha_m)k} + \cdots + e^{-(\alpha_p-\alpha_m)k}\right)}, \tag{31}$$

where K_m is the Kalman gain associated with α_m. Looking now to Eq. (31) when k tends to infinity, i.e.,

$$e^{-(\alpha_i-\alpha_m)k} \xrightarrow[k\to\infty]{} 0 \qquad \text{for} \quad i \neq m,$$

then

$$\hat{K}(k) \xrightarrow[k\to\infty]{} K_m.$$

Considering the higher moments leads to the same conclusion:

$$\mathcal{M}_n(k) = \frac{\Sigma_{i=1}^{p} [K_i - \hat{K}(k)]^n e^{-\alpha_i k}}{\Sigma_{i=1}^{p} e^{-\alpha_i k}}.$$

Then for any n

$$\mathcal{M}_n(k) \xrightarrow[k\to\infty]{} 0.$$

We can now conclude this convergence analysis on a finite parameter set by the following theorem.

Theorem 3

Considering the same scalar system (1a)-(1f) defined on a finite parameter set, the Bayesian algorithm locally converges to the K_0 value nearest that of the set with quadratic-mean convergence. (This result is an extension of [15].)

B. UNKNOWN SYSTEM DYNAMICS (USD) CASE

1. Synthetized Problem Formulation

Let $\theta = (\theta_1, \ldots, \theta_n)$ denote the vector of unknown parameters in matrix A (SISO system)

$$A = \begin{bmatrix} 0 & 1 & \cdots & \\ \vdots & \vdots & \ddots & \\ & & \cdot & 1 \\ \theta_1 & \theta_2 & \cdots & \theta_n \end{bmatrix}$$

The system is defined by Eqs. (1a)-(1f), but here Q and R are known. To compute an optimal estimate $\hat{\theta}(k)$ at time t_k, it is sufficient to estimate the a posteriori probability density $p(\theta/Z^k)$. Then for each component such as θ_1, for example,

$$\hat{\theta}_1(k) = \int \theta_1 p\left(\theta_1, \theta_2, \ldots, \theta_n/Z^k\right) d\theta_1 d\theta_2 \cdots d\theta_n, \tag{32}$$

where $Z^k = (Z_0, Z_1, \ldots, Z_k)$.

A recursive equation associated with an inherent parallel implementation is obtained in the following way:

$$p\left(\theta_j/Z^k\right) = \Lambda p\left(Z_k/\theta_j,\ Z^{k-1}\right)p\left(\theta_j/Z^{k-1}\right), \tag{33}$$

where Λ is the required constant to make $p\left(\theta_j/Z^k\right)$ a density and $\theta_j = (\theta_{1j}, \ldots, \theta_{nj})$. Knowing the noise statistics, $p\left(Z_k/\ _j,\ Z^{k-1}\right)$ is a Gaussian distribution

$$p\left(Z_k/\theta_j,\ Z^{k-1}\right) = (2\pi)^{-n/2} \cdot M_j(k)^{-1/2} \cdot \exp\left[-\overline{Z}_j^2(k)/2M_j(k)\right]. \tag{34}$$

Here $M_j(k)$ is the measurement error conditional covariance and $\overline{Z}_j(k) = Z_k - CA(\theta_j)\hat{Z}(k - 1/k - 1)$.

2. *Algorithm Convergence and θ-Estimate Quality*

Now $\Delta\theta$ denotes a *small* change in θ and θ_0 corresponds to the true (unknown) parameter values. Let $\theta = \theta_0 + \Delta\theta$ or $A = A_0 + \Delta A$. Supposing that the filter has reached steady state (i.e., k large enough), Eqs. (33) and (34) lead to

$$p\left(\theta_0 + \Delta\theta/Z^k\right) = \Lambda/(M_0 + \Delta M)^{k/2} = \Lambda'/[1 + (\Delta M/M_0)]^{k/2}. \tag{35}$$

As in Section I.A, one has to estimate ΔM. For a given θ, the Kalman filter equations are written as

$$\hat{X}(k/k - 1) = (A_0 + \Delta A)\hat{X}(k - 1/k - 1), \tag{36a}$$

$$\hat{X}(k - 1/k - 1) = \hat{X}(k - 1/k - 2) + (K_0 + \Delta K)[Z_{k-1} - C\hat{X}(k - 1/k - 2)], \tag{36b}$$

with

$$\Delta K = f(\Delta A) \tag{36c}$$

and f a known function of the nominal system parameters and of the (known) noise statistics. The a priori estimate error covariance matrix becomes $(P_0' + \Delta P')$

$$P_0' + \Delta P' = E\left\{[X_k - \hat{X}(k/k - 1)][X_k - \hat{X}(k/k - 1]^T\right\}.$$

The term between { } is written as a function of $X_{k-1} - X(k - 1/k - 2)$ and the stationarity property of second-order moments is applied Introducing the following quantities:

$$L = E\left(X_k X_k^T\right),$$

$$L' = E[\hat{X}(k/k)\hat{X}^T(k/k)],$$

$$L'' = E[\hat{X}(k/k - 1)\hat{X}^T(k/k - 1)],$$

$$N = E\left[\hat{X}(k/k - 1)(X_k - \hat{X}(k/k - 1)^T)\right],$$

one obtains

$$\begin{aligned} P_0' + \Delta P' = {} & [A - (A_0 + \Delta A)(K_0 + \Delta K)C](P_0' + \Delta P') \\ & \cdot [A - (A_0 + \Delta A)(K_0 + \Delta K)C]^T \\ & + DQD^T + (A_0 + \Delta A)(K_0 + \Delta K)R(K_0 + \Delta K)^T(A_0 + \Delta A)^T \\ & + \Delta AL''\Delta A^T - [A_0 - (A_0 + \Delta A)(K_0 + \Delta K)C]N^T\Delta A^T \\ & - \Delta AN[A_0 - (A_0 + \Delta A)(K_0 + \Delta K)C]^T. \end{aligned} \tag{37}$$

The following relations give a *first-order definition* of L, L', L", and N:

$$L = A_0LA_0^T + DQD^T, \tag{38}$$

$$L' = L - P_0, \tag{39}$$

$$L'' = A_0L'A_0^T, \tag{40}$$

$$\begin{aligned} N = {} & A_0N(I - K_0C)^TA_0^T - A_0L''\Delta A^T \\ & - A_0K_0M_0(\Delta AK_0 + A_0\Delta K)^T. \end{aligned} \tag{41}$$

Referring to Eq. (37), first-order terms disappear and neglecting the third and higher orders, we obtain

$$\Delta P' = (A_0 \Delta K + \Delta A K_0) M_0 (A_0 \Delta K + \Delta A K_0)^T$$
$$+ A_0 (I - K_0 C) \Delta P' (I - K_0 C)^T A_0^T + \Delta A L'' \Delta A^T$$
$$- A_0 (I - K_0 C) N^T A^T - AN(I - K_0 C)^T A_0^T, \tag{42}$$

$$\Delta M = C \Delta P' C^T. \tag{43}$$

Equations (38)-(43) make possible the determination of ΔM corresponding to a *small* change $\Delta\theta$ in θ_0. These computations can be carried out off-line by solving implicit linear matrix equations of the type $X = AXA^T + B$ and yield

$$\Delta M / M_0 = \Delta\theta G_{\theta_0}^{-1} \Delta\theta^T, \tag{44}$$

where G_{θ_0} is a matrix function of matrix A_0 and of the ratio Q/R. Then from Eqs. (44) and (35) we obtain the following expressions for the estimate vector and its covariance matrix at time t_k:

$$\hat{\theta}_{ie}(k) = \frac{\displaystyle\int_\theta \frac{\theta_i \, d\theta}{\left[1 + (\theta - \theta_0) G_{\theta_0}^{-1} (\theta - \theta_0)^T\right]^{k/2}}}{\displaystyle\int_\theta \frac{d\theta}{\left[1 + (\theta - \theta_0) G_{\theta_0}^{-1} (\theta - \theta_0)^T\right]^{k/2}}}, \tag{45a}$$

$$\sigma_{\theta_i}^2(k) = \frac{\displaystyle\int_\theta \frac{(\theta_i - \hat{\theta}_{ie}(k))^2 \, d\theta}{\left[1 + (\theta - \theta_0) G_{\theta_0}^{-1} (\theta - \theta_0)^T\right]^{k/2}}}{\displaystyle\int_\theta \frac{d\theta}{\left[1 + (\theta - \theta_0) G_{\theta_0}^{-1} (\theta - \theta_0)^T\right]^{k/2}}}. \tag{45b}$$

Mathematical developments similar to those of Section I lead to the algorithm convergence and to the error covariance matrix P_θ asymptotic behavior (see the Appendix).

Theorem 4

Considering the exponentially stable system (1a)-(1f), the Bayesian estimate of the parametric vector QM converges to its nominal value θ_0 when $G_{\theta_0}^{-1}$ is a strictly positive matrix. Furthermore its covariance matrix P_θ is given by

$$P_\theta = G_{\theta_0}/k \tag{46}$$

a. Scalar case

Considering the scalar system previously defined in Section II.A.2.a but keeping in mind that here (Q, R) are known and that the nominal value a_0 of a is unknown, one obtains through Eqs. (36)-(43),

$$\begin{aligned}
\Delta K &= \frac{2a_0K_0^2(1 - K_0)}{(Q/R) + a_0^2K_0^2}\,\Delta a,\\
M_0 &= R/(1 - K_0),\\
P_0 &= RK_0,\\
\overline{\sigma}_a^2 &= \frac{1}{k}\,\frac{s_4}{K_0^2}\,\frac{1}{(s_1 + s_2)^2 + s_3},
\end{aligned} \tag{47}$$

where

$$s_1 = \frac{2a_0^2K_0(1 - K_0)}{(Q/R) + a_0^2K_0},$$

$$s_2 = \frac{1}{1 - a_0^2(1 - K_0)},$$

$$s_3 = \frac{a_0^2}{1 - a_0^2}\,s_4s_2^2,$$

and

$$s_4 = 1 - a_0^2(1 - K_0)^2.$$

The convergence study is then straightforward.

b. Concluding remark introducing UDN case

When both the noise covariances and system dynamics are unknown, ΔA and ΔK are *independent*; Eqs. (36)-(43) are nevertheless fully valuable [except (36c)]. Results in the scalar case are

$$\bar{\sigma}_a^2 = \frac{\left(1 - a_0^2\right)\left[1 - a_0^2(1 - K_0)^2\right]}{a_0^2 K_0^2 k}, \tag{48a}$$

$$\bar{\sigma}_K^2 = \frac{1 - a_0^4(1 - K_0)^2}{a_0^4 k}, \tag{48b}$$

$$\bar{r} = \frac{|\bar{\sigma}_{aK}|}{|\bar{\sigma}_a|\ |\bar{\sigma}_K|} = \frac{\left(1 - a_0^2\right)^{1/2}}{\left[1 - a_0^4(1 - K_0)^2\right]^{1/2}}. \tag{48c}$$

So the UDN case is heuristically subsumed in the UNS and USD cases. Theorem 4 is then fully valuable.

III. ASYMPTOTIC BEHAVIOR OF BAYESIAN ESTIMATORS IN CLOSED LOOP

Let us consider a single-input/single-output linear system in closed loop:

$$X_{k+1} = AX_k + BU_k + Dw_k, \tag{49a}$$

$$Z_k = CX_k + v_k, \tag{49b}$$

$$U_k = -G_e\hat{X}_e(k/k). \tag{50}$$

It is useful to note here that, if A and B are known, Eq. (50) gives the optimal control when $G_e = f(A, B, C)$ (the minimum output variance control, for example).

A. USD CASE

Referring to the set of hypotheses of Section II.B.1, the state estimate $\hat{X}(k/k)$ can be obtained with m Kalman linear filters operating in a parallel structure with different values of matrix A (i.e., of the unknown vector θ in A) on the continuous set Θ.

Each filter i ($\theta_i \in \Theta$) operates according

$$\hat{X}_i(k + 1/k) = A_i\hat{X}_i(k/k) + BU(k), \tag{51a}$$

$$\hat{X}_i(k + 1/k + 1) = \hat{X}_i(k + 1/k) + K_i[Z_{k+1} - C\hat{X}_i(k + 1/k)], \tag{51b}$$

$$K_i = f(A_i). \tag{51c}$$

The estimate at time t_k is then

$$\hat{X}_e(k/k) = \int_\Theta p\left(\theta_i/Z^k\right)\hat{X}_i(k/k)\,d\theta_i. \tag{52}$$

Because we are interested in the asymptotic behavior of the estimate in closed loop, a *small* change ΔA in A_0 is considered. Hence the filter equations become

$$\hat{X}_i(k + 1/k) = (A_0 + \Delta A)\hat{X}_i(k/k) + BU(k),$$

$$\hat{X}_i(k + 1/k + 1) = \hat{X}_i(k + 1/k) + (K_0 + \Delta K)[Z_{k+1} - C\hat{X}(k + 1/k)],$$

$$\Delta K_i = f(\Delta A_i).$$

Referring to Section II.B, one has

$$\Delta\theta P_\theta^{-1}\Delta\theta^T = k\Delta M/M_0 \quad \text{for large } k,$$

P_θ being the covariance matrix of the parameter estimate errors. The aim is now to evaluate P_θ when applying U_k.

The equation giving $\Delta P'$ from ΔA and ΔK is the same as Eq. (42) because in the expression $X(k) - \hat{X}(k/k-1)$ the control U_k does not appear, although the control does modify L" and N, as will be shown.

Using first-order approximations we obtain

$$N = (A_0 - BG_e)N(I - K_0C)^T A_0^T - (A_0 - BG_e)L''\Delta A^T$$
$$- (A_0 - BG_e)K_0M_0(\Delta AK_0 + A_0\Delta K)^T, \tag{53}$$

$$L'' = (A_0 - BG_e)L''(A_0 - BG_e)^T$$
$$+ (A_0 - BG_e)K_0M_0K_0^T(A_0 - BG_e)^T. \tag{54}$$

Substituting L" into Eq. (53) we obtain N, which is then substituted into Eq. (42); $\Delta P'$ is then given as a function of $\Delta\theta$, which leads to

$$\Delta M/M_0 = M_0^{-1}C\Delta P'C^T = \Delta\theta G_{\theta_0}^{-1}\Delta\theta^T.$$

Theorem 5

Considering the exponentially stable system (49) driven by (50) with a constant gain matrix G_e, the Bayesian estimate of θ QM converges to its nominal value θ_0 when $G_{\theta_0}^{-1}$ is a strictly positive real matrix. Then the covariance matrix asymptotic behavior is

$$P_\theta = G_{\theta_0}/k.$$

The computation of the asymptotic behavior of the error-covariance matrix is carried out by resolving the implicit linear matrices in Eqs. (42), (53), and (54).

To point out the importance of these relations, consider the following *scalar* case:

$$x_k = a_0x_{k-1} + bu_{k-1} + w_{k-1},$$

when a_0 is unknown and b is known, and

$$y_k = x_k + v_k.$$

Assuming that the ratio Q/R is large enough,

$$K_0 \simeq 1, \qquad \Delta K << \Delta A, \tag{55a}$$

$$\Delta M = \Delta P' = (M_0 + L'')\Delta a^2, \tag{55b}$$

$$L'' = (a_0 - bg_e)^2 M_0 / \left[1 - (a_0 - bg_e)^2\right], \tag{55c}$$

$$\overline{\sigma}_a^2 = \left[1 - (a_0 - bg_e)^2\right] / k. \tag{55d}$$

In this particular scalar case, the highest value of σ_a is obtained when $g_e = a_0/b$, which corresponds to the optimal quadratic linear control. The farther away from this optimum the control gain is, the better the parameter estimate (at the bounds of stability, i.e., when $g_e = \pm(1 + a_0)/b$, σ_a tends to zero. This approximate result (set for large Q/R) will introduce the study of duality, which will be given in Section IV.

B. *UDN HYPOTHESIS*

Assuming that ΔA and ΔK are independent, $G_{\theta_0}^{-1}$ is still obtained from Eqs. (42), (53), and (54), but now θ is a vector including the system parameters (unknown coefficients in A) and the gain matrix. The Bayesian algorithm convergence is then studied through the same Theorem 5, which remains fully valuable.

In the scalar case ($A = a_0$, $B = b$, $C = 1$) the solution is easily carried out as

$$|P_\theta^{-1}| = k^2 |G_{\theta_0}^{-1}| = \frac{a_0^2 K_0^2 \alpha^2 k^2}{\left[1 - a_0^2(1 - K_0)^2\right](1 - \alpha^2)\left[1 - a_0\alpha(1 - K_0)^2\right]}, \tag{56a}$$

$$\bar{\sigma}_a^2 = \frac{(1 - \alpha^2)[1 - a_0\alpha(1 - K_0)]^2}{K_0^2\alpha^2 k}, \qquad \alpha \neq 0, \tag{56b}$$

$$\bar{\sigma}_K^2 = \frac{1 - a_0^2\alpha^2(1 - K_0)^2}{a_0^2\alpha^2 k}, \qquad \alpha \neq 0, \tag{56c}$$

$$\bar{r} = \frac{|\bar{\sigma}_{aK}|}{|\bar{\sigma}_a|\ |\bar{\sigma}_K|} = \frac{(1 - \alpha^2)^{1/2}}{\left[1 - a_0^2\alpha^2(1 - K_0)^2\right]^{1/2}}. \tag{56d}$$

Here

$$\alpha = a_0 - bg_e, \qquad K_0 = f(Q_0/R_0, a_0). \tag{56e}$$

Equation (56) shows that convergence can be achieved for any value of g_e but $g_e = a_0/b$ (i.e., $\alpha = 0$). For this particular value, which minimizes a variance cost function, the estimates $\hat{a}(k)$ and $\hat{K}(k)$ do not converge to their true values; nevertheless we can conclude with the help of Eqs. (42), (53), and (54) that the product $\widehat{aK}(k)$ (i.e., the estimate of the true product a_0K_0) can be identified and converges according to

$$\bar{\sigma}_{ak}^2(k) = \left[1 - a_0^2(1 - K_0)^2\right]/k. \tag{57}$$

A numerical example given in the fifth section verifies the main theoretical results pointed out in Sections III.A and B.

C. SYSTEMS WITH CORRELATED NOISES

In this section we place emphasis on closed-loop systems using the certainty equivalence property. Our basic case, as defined in the Introduction, will be USD (UNS and UDN would be easily studied in a similar way), where unknown coefficients belong to the matrices A_0 and D_0.

The state-form model is then

$$X_k = A_0 X_{k-1} + BU_{k-1} + D_0 w_{k-1}, \tag{58a}$$

$$Z_k = CX_k + w_k, \tag{58b}$$

where

$$E\left(w_k w_j^T\right) = \delta_{kj} \cdot R \qquad (R \text{ known}), \tag{58c}$$

$$E(w_k) = 0, \tag{58d}$$

$$U_k = -G_e \hat{X}_e(k/k). \tag{58e}$$

Such a state form is derived from the well-known ARMAX model, as used in the canonical theory of "self-tuning regulators," for example,

$$\mathscr{A}(q^{-1}) Z(k) = q^{-1} \mathscr{B}(q^{-1}) U(k) + \mathscr{D}(q^{-1}) w(k), \tag{59}$$

where q^{-1} denotes the backward shift operator [12].

Our aim is to show how the general Bayesian theory developed in this and Section II allows us to draw conclusions regarding local convergence and to predict the asymptotic behavior of the estimates. System (58) can be rewritten as

$$X_k = (A_0 - D_0 C) X_{k-1} + D_0 Z_{k-1} + BU_{k-1}, \tag{60a}$$

$$Z_k = CX_k + w_k. \tag{60b}$$

Let us note

$$\tilde{A}_0 = A_0 - BG_e, \tag{61}$$

$$\tilde{A}_0^* = A_0 - BG_e - D_0 C. \tag{62}$$

Referring to the previous study (Section III.A), we can write, in the present case of correlated state and measurement noises, the a priori error-covariance matrix of parameter estimates $(P_0' + \Delta P')$, which is of interest in evaluating the asymptotic expected behavior of θ_0 estimates:

$$P'_0 + \Delta P' = L - S - S^T - V, \tag{63}$$

where $L = E\left[X_k \cdot X_k^T\right]$; $S = E\left[X_k \cdot \hat{X}^T(k/k-1)\right]$; and $V = E[\hat{X}(k/k-1) \cdot \hat{X}^T(k/k-1)]$.

In order to calculate these expressions, we consider small variations $\Delta\theta_0$ (i.e., ΔA_0 and ΔD_0) around the nominal value; developments similar to those of Section III.A lead to

$$L = \tilde{A}_0 L \tilde{A}_0^T + R D_0 D_0^T, \tag{64}$$

$$S = \tilde{A}_0 S\left(\tilde{A}_0^* + \Delta\tilde{A}_0^*\right)^T + \tilde{A}_0 L C^T (D_0 + \Delta D_0) + R D_0 (D_0 + \Delta D_0)^T, \tag{65}$$

$$V = \left(\tilde{A}_0^* + \Delta\tilde{A}_0^*\right) V \left(\tilde{A}_0^* + \Delta\tilde{A}_0^*\right)^T + \left(\tilde{A}_0^* + \Delta\tilde{A}_0^*\right) S^T C^T (D_0 + \Delta D_0)^T + (D_0 + \Delta D_0) C S \left(\tilde{A}_0^* + \Delta\tilde{A}_0^*\right)^T + (D_0 + \Delta D_0)(R + CLC^T)(D_0 + \Delta D_0)^T, \tag{66}$$

and

$$\Delta M_0 = C \Delta P' C^T = \Delta\theta_0 G_{\theta_0}^{-1} \Delta\theta_0^T. \tag{67}$$

So Theorem 5 is once more fully valuable when applied to system (58) or (59), but the local convergence and the asymptotic behavior of the covariance of θ estimates are now conditioned to the positive realness of $G_{\theta_0}^{-1}$ solution of (off-line calculated) implicit relations (63)-(67).

Let us consider a scalar open-looped system to illustrate the amount of information one can expect from this method:

$$x_k = a_0 x_{k-1} + d_0 w_{k-1}, \tag{68a}$$

$$z_k = x_k + w_k, \qquad E\left(w_j^2\right) = R. \tag{68b}$$

Or, in the ARMAX formulation,

$$\mathscr{A}_0(q^{-1}) \cdot z_k = \mathscr{D}_0(q^{-1})w_k, \tag{69}$$

where

$$\mathscr{A}_0(q^{-1}) = 1 - a_0 q^{-1}, \qquad \mathscr{D}_0(q^{-1}) = 1 + (d_0 - a_0)q^{-1}.$$

From (63)-(67) we obtain

$$|G_{\theta_0}^{-1}| = \frac{d_0^2 R^2}{\left(1 - a_0^2\right)\left(1 - a_0^2 + a_0 d_0\right)^2 \left[1 - (a_0 - d_0)^2\right]}. \tag{70}$$

This yields, to local convergence conditions,

$$|a_0| < 1, \qquad |a_0 - d_0| < 1, \qquad d_0 \neq 0. \tag{71}$$

Applying the ODE method (as shown in [13]) to the ARMAX model (69), the same local convergence requirement would be found [i.e., $1/\mathscr{D}_0(q^{-1})$ strictly positive real, which leads to (71)], but we obtain further results on the expected covariances when Eq. (71) is fulfilled:

$$\bar{\sigma}_a^2(k) = \frac{\left(1 - a_0^2 + a_0 d_0\right)^2 \left[1 - (a_0 - d_0)^2\right]}{k d_0^2}, \tag{72}$$

$$\bar{\sigma}_d^2(k) = \frac{\left(1 + a_0^2 - a_0 d_0\right)\left(1 + a_0 d_0 - a_0^2\right)}{k}, \tag{73}$$

$$\bar{r}_{ad} = \frac{|\bar{\sigma}_{\bar{a}d}|}{|\bar{\sigma}_a|\ |\bar{\sigma}_d|} = \frac{|a_0|\ \left[1 - (a_0 - d_0)^2\right]^{1/2}}{\left[1 - a_0^2(a_0 - d_0)^2\right]^{1/2}}. \tag{74}$$

Furthermore, when $d_0 = 0$, Eqs. (63)-(67) lead to

$$\bar{\sigma}_d^2(k) = \left[1 - a_0^2\right]/k, \tag{73b}$$

$$\lim_{k\to\infty} \hat{a}(k) = (a_M + a_m)/2. \tag{75}$$

This means that d_0 remains identifiable, but a_0 does not and its estimate tends toward the half-sum of a_M and a_m, the bounds of the chosen finite variation set of parameter a. The consistency property of the a_0 estimate is then lost.

So, on the one hand, Ljung's method gives local *and global* convergence conditions but no knowledge of the covariance expected values, whereas the Bayesian gives local convergence conditions *and* an a priori knowledge of the expected precision of the estimates on a finite parameter set in the neighborhood of the true values.

IV. DUALITY BETWEEN ROBUST CONTROL AND BAYESIAN IDENTIFICATION

We shall introduce the problem by considering the discrete linear scalar system studied in Section III.A and leading to Eqs. (55):

$$x_k = a_0 x_{k-1} + u_{k-1} + w_{k-1},$$

$$z_k = x_k + v_k. \tag{76}$$

Noise statistics Q and R are assumed to be known and b = 1. When a_0 is exactly known, a feedback control such as

$$u_k = -g_e \hat{x}(k/k) \tag{77}$$

makes it possible to minimize a quadratic criterion provided that g_e is a suitable function of a_0, and the state estimate is obtained through a standard Kalman filter. Let us now suppose that a_0 is not exactly known.

A. *BAYESIAN IDENTIFICATION QUALITY VERSUS ROBUST CONTROL*

Let us consider the same case with some approximate knowledge of the parameter a_0, where a Bayesian parallel set provides a state and a parametric estimate. The inherent property of such a parallel structure (i.e., every Kalman filter in the set deals with a wrong value $a_i = a_0 + \Delta a_i$) allows us to apply the previous result of Section III concerning the asymptotic behavior of the estimates, especially formulas (55) and the convergence theorem.

Let P_0' denote the steady-state value of the state estimate covariance when a_0 is exactly known (Kalman classical filter) and P' the same in the present case of rough knowledge. Then we can write

$$P' = P_0' + \partial_1 \Delta a + \partial_2 \Delta a^2, \tag{78a}$$

$$\Delta P' = \Delta M = M_0 \Delta a^2 / k\sigma_a^2. \tag{78b}$$

Equation (78b) is directly deduced from the general formulas and from Eq. (55b) and σ_a^2 is the parametric estimate variance.

Equations (78) are the basis of the study of duality between robust estimation and Bayesian identification. As a matter of fact one can note that

$$\partial_1 = \partial P'/\partial a = 0 \qquad \text{for any value } a_i,$$

$$\partial_2 = \partial^2 P'/\partial a^2,$$

which is small if σ_a^2 is large. This can be set in the following terms.

Property 1

The feedback gain value g_e^*, in Eq. (78), which *minimizes* the variation of state-predicted estimate covariances (as far as we are concerned with asymptotic behavior) is the same one that leads to a *maximum* value of the closed-loop parametric estimate covariance.

This fundamental property means that the better the state estimation is [in the sense, $\min(\partial^2 P'/\partial a^2)$] the worse the Bayesian identification of the corresponding parameter a. In such a sense, *the robustness of state estimation and the Bayesian parametric identification quality can be said to be dual.*

In the present linear scalar case, an exact resolution of the implicit equations of Section III is available; the parametric estimate covariance is then at time t_k,

$$\sigma_a^2 = \frac{(1 - \alpha^2)[1 - a_0\alpha(1 - K_0)]\left[1 - a_0^2\left(1 - K_0^2\right)\right]}{k\left\{a_0^2\gamma^2(1-\alpha^2)[1-a_0\alpha(1-K_0)]+K_0^2[1+a_0\alpha(1-K_0)]+2a_0K_0\gamma(1-\alpha^2)\right\}}. \tag{79}$$

Introducing

$$\gamma \triangleq \left(\frac{\Delta K}{\Delta a}\right)_{a=a_0} = \frac{2a_0K_0(1 - K_0)^2}{1 - a_0^2(1 - K_0)^2},$$

$\alpha = (a_0 - g_e)$ is the control mode and $\mu_0 = a_0(1 - K_0)$ is the estimation mode, both being obtained by solving the classical characteristic equation.

For a given value of a_0 and (Q_0, R_0), we can draw the variation versus α, or g_e, of the quality of the Bayesian estimate $\hat{a}_{(k/k)}$ that is to say, of $\sigma_a^2 = f(\alpha)$ given by Eq. (79).

Let α_M denote, according to Property 1, *the optimal control mode*, where σ_a^2 reaches its largest values

$$\alpha_M = \text{Arg}\left[\left(\frac{d\sigma_a^2}{dg_e}\right)_{a_0, Q_0, R_0} = 0\right],$$

$$= \text{Arg}[h(\mu_0, \alpha) = 0] \qquad \text{for} \quad 1 \leq \alpha_M \leq 1.$$

This yields

$$h(\mu_0, \alpha) = 2\mu_0^3\alpha^4 - \mu_0^2\left(1 - \mu_0^2\right)\alpha^3 - \mu_0\left(1 + 3\mu_0^2\right)\alpha^2$$
$$+ \left(1 - \mu_0^2\right)\alpha + \mu_0 + \mu_0^3.$$

The attractive property of $h(\mu_0, \alpha)$ is that for any value μ_0 belonging to (-1, +1) [note that for any asymptotically stable system, $\mu_0 = a_0(1 - K_0)$ always belongs to this interval], the optimal control mode α_M is very close to the opposite of μ_0 (third-order residual). The following second property can then be set.

Property 2

At any moment of the Bayesian identification in the scalar ARMAX case, the maximal variance of the parametric estimate is reached when the control mode is opposite that of the estimation. And according to Property 1, this value of the control mode α_M is associated with the best state-estimate robustness. So we can write

$$\alpha_M = \text{Arg}\left[\left(\frac{d\sigma_a^2}{dg_e}\right)_{a_0, K_0} = 0\right] = -\mu_0, \tag{80}$$

where

$$\alpha_M = a_0 - g_e^*, \qquad \mu_0 = a_0(1 - K_0).$$

B. *CONCLUDING REMARK*

A command such as g^* is not suitable for minimizing any *quadratic* criterion of the general frame $x_i^2 + \lambda u_i^2$, $\lambda > 0$) because α_M is the opposite of μ_0. This single-boundary case can occur: When K_0 is equal to unity (i.e., when the noise covariance is null or when Q/R is large), then the optimal control that minimizes a minimum variance *quadratic* criterion ($\lambda = 0$) is dual of the robust estimation process.

This remark essentially means that the research engaged in the duality concept will have to define its own optimality criterion. The focus on quadratic criterion is, in the authors' minds, a wrong way to attempt to achieve precise duality, essentially because such criteria do not intrinsically account for the parametric identification process.

V. NUMERICAL EXAMPLES

The algorithms given in Sections II and III are tested on an inherent parallel structure with ($m = 10$) parallel paths. Examples given here consider scalar systems (as defined in Section II.A.2.a) or two-dimensional ones [as defined by the general matrix formulas (1a)-(1f)].

A. *OPEN-LOOP SYSTEMS*

To start, Fig. 1 gives the simulation results of a *scalar system* where $a = 0.7$ is assumed to be known and $(Q/R)_0$ unknown (i.e., UNS case; see Section I). We test here formulas (14), (15), and (30a) leading to $\hat{K}_e(k)$ $\sigma_K(k)$, and $\overline{\sigma}_K(k)$, respectively. Conclusions derived from Eqs. (28)-(30a) about the bound study are also illustrated here.

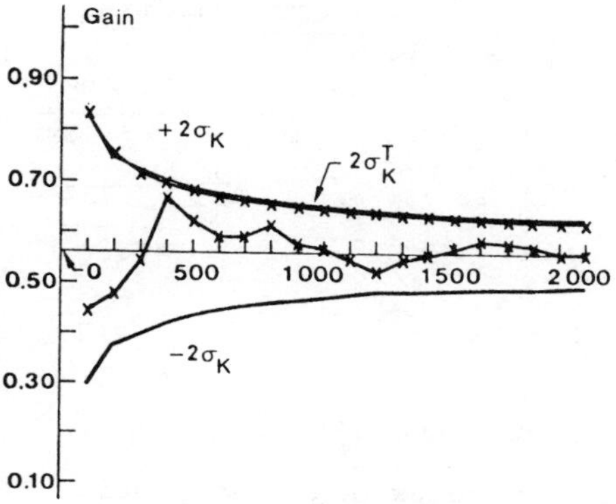

Fig. 1. Scalar UNS case: $(Q/R)_0 = 1$, $a = 0.7$.

Figure 2 represents the following *two-dimensional UNS* example:

$$A = \begin{bmatrix} 0 & 1 \\ -0.95 & 1.9 \end{bmatrix}, \qquad B = \begin{bmatrix} -1 \\ 1 \end{bmatrix}, \qquad C = [0 \quad 1].$$

The relationship between K_2 and K_1 has been computed off-line; Eqs. (14), (15), and (30b) are tested and verified. The two-dimensional implicit matrix Eqs. (23)-(25) were used to calculate μ appearing in Eq. (30b).

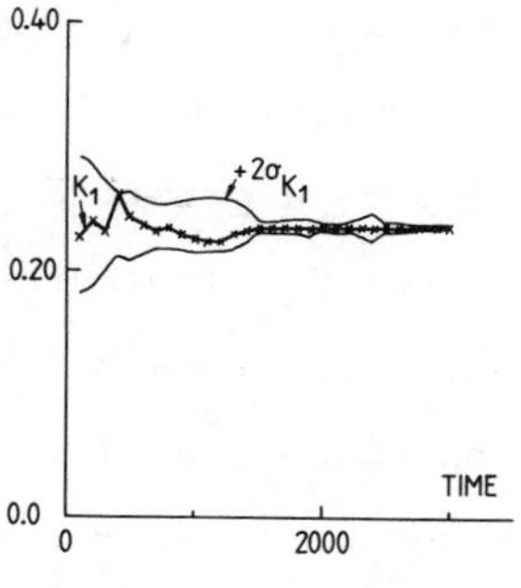

Fig. 2. Two-dimensional UNS case: $(Q/R)_0 = 5$.

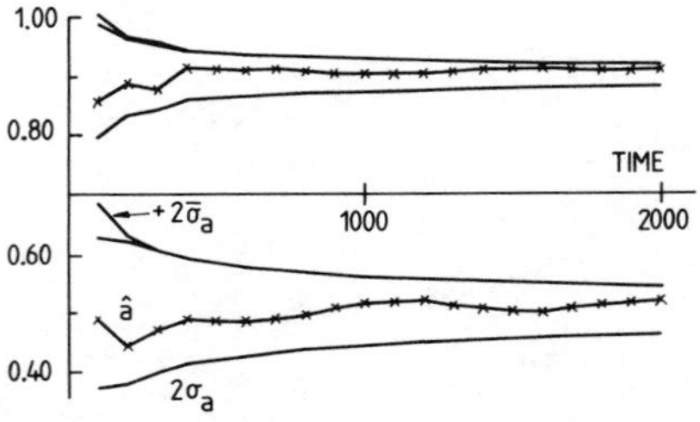

Fig. 3. Scalar USD case: $(Q/R) = 0.1$, $a_0 = 0.5/0.9$.

Figure 3 deals with the *USD scalar case.* The noise statistics are assumed to be known (see Section II.B.2.a). Equation (47) makes possible the computation of the a priori convergence $\bar{\sigma}_a$, which is shown to be an excellent approximation of σ_a after 500 data inputs (this number depends on Q/R as demonstrated in the text).

Figure 4 introduces a *two-dimensional USD* example that makes possible the verification of Eqs. (37)-(46) related to the general USD study:

$$X_{k+1} = \begin{bmatrix} 0 & 1 & & 1 \\ -0.5 & 1 & X_k + & -1 \end{bmatrix} w_k,$$

$$Z_k = CX_k + v_k, \qquad C = [0,\ 1].$$

The two unknown parameters are then $a_0 = -0.5$ and $b_0 = 1$; Q/R is known (Q/R = 1). The implicit matrix relations in Eqs. (37)-(46) allow us to compute a priori $\bar{\sigma}_a$ and $\bar{\sigma}_b$ and, furthermore, the correlation factor $\bar{r}_{ab}$ (compared with σ_a, σ_b, r_{ab}).

According to our concluding remark (in Section II), the *UDN case* is then illustrated on a scalar case as shown in Fig. 5. This case corresponds to $(Q/R)_0 = 10$ and $a_0 = 0.9$ and will be our reference when comparing the open-loop and closed-loop qualities of the estimates.

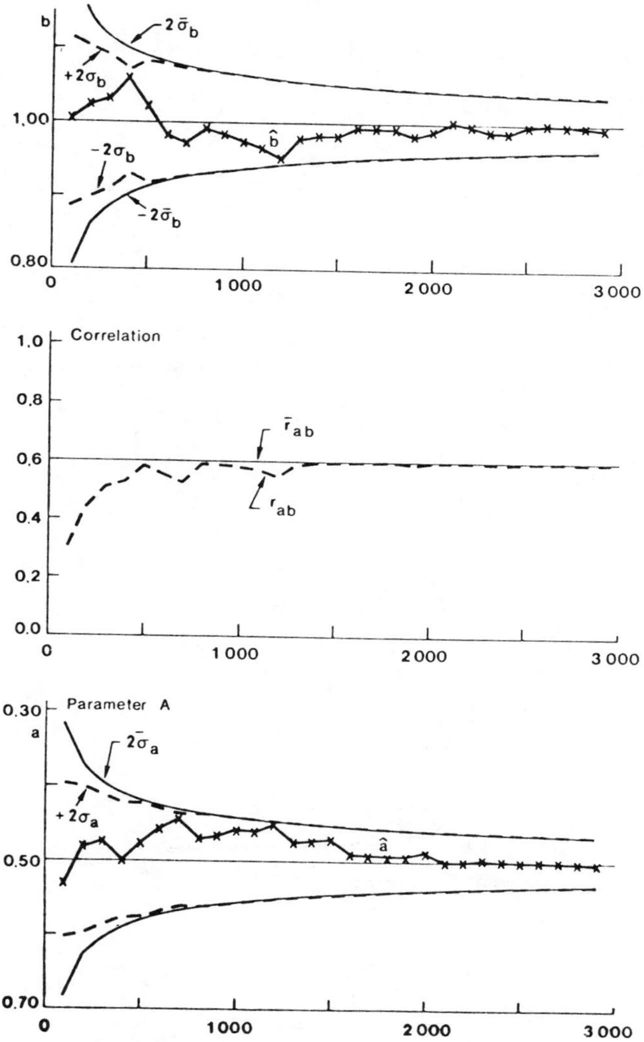

Fig. 4. Two-dimensional USD case: $(Q/R) = 1$, $a_0 = -0.5$, $b_0 = 1$.

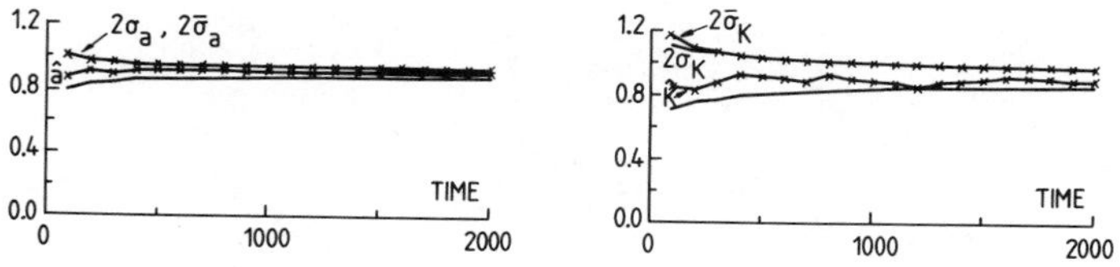

Fig. 5. Scalar UDN case: $(Q/R)_0 = 10$, $a_0 = 0.9$.

B. CLOSED-LOOP SYSTEMS

The last two sets of figures (Figs. 6 and 7) refer to the most general UDN hypothesis (see Section III.B) applied to a scalar system.

Figure 6 verifies Eqs. (56a)-(56e); when compared with the open-loop case (see Fig. 5) it clearly points out the lack of identification due to control when no dual properties are taken into account. The theoretical a priori estimates of σ_a and σ_k (denoted as $\bar{\sigma}_a$ and $\bar{\sigma}_k$) appear to be excellent approximations, the correlation r between a and κ is also given in its calculated (r) and predicted ($\bar{r}$) values.

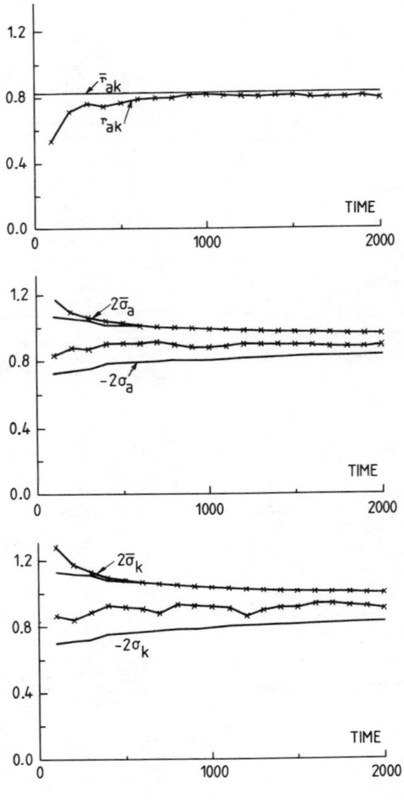

Fig. 6. Same as Fig. 5 but $u_k = -0.3\hat{x}_{k/k}$.

Figure 7 corresponds to the optimal control ($u_k = -a_0/b_0 \cdot \hat{x}_{k/k}$). As shown in the theory, a and K are here not identified; but according to Eq. (57) the product has been. Its standard deviation σ_{aK} is given as is its a priori prediction $\overline{\sigma}_{aK}$.

The theoretical results of Sections II and III are then fully verified, convergence theorems regarding open and closed loops of the Bayesian algorithms have been proved. Emphasis

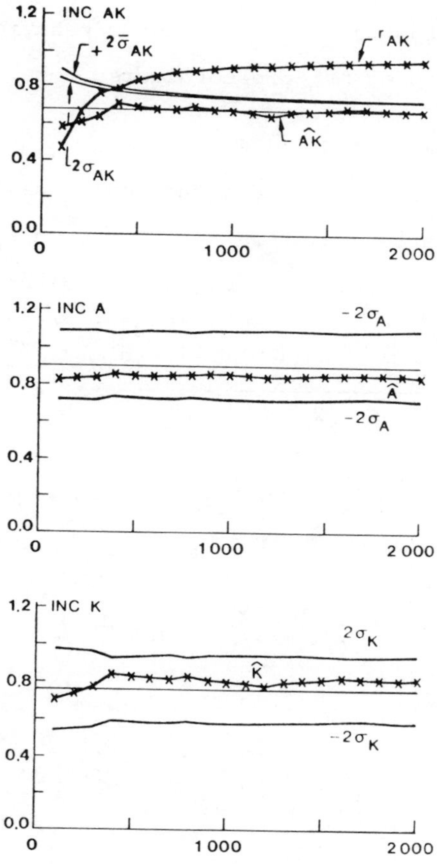

Fig. 7. Same as Fig. 6 but $u = -0.9x_{k/k}$ (optimal control).

was put on the asymptotic behavior of the estimates. For a fixed number of data and a given precision, *one can decide beforehand* if Bayesian methods are suitable for the estimation problem under consideration. Furthermore, the prediction of estimate covariances is of prime importance in dual stochastic control.

APPENDIX

The mathematical developments leading from Eqs. (27)-(29) to Eq. (30) (which leads to conclusions about the estimate convergence and the variance asymptotic behavior, and then to the fundamental theorems) are considered here.

A.1. STUDY OF THE SCALAR CASE

As a first step we consider the scalar case where $K_0 = 1$, which corresponds to a high ratio Q/R. Then $\hat{K}_e(k)$ for large k can be written, according to Eqs. (27)-(29) as

$$\hat{K}_e(k) = \frac{\int_0^1 K[1 - a^2(1 - K)^2]^{k/2}\, dK}{\int_0^1 [1 - a^2(1 - K^2]^{k/2}\, dK}. \tag{A.1}$$

Now let $n = k/2$, and by changing variables, $u/(2n)^{1/2} = a(1 - K)$, one obtains, for $a \neq 0$,

$$\hat{K}_e(n) = \int_0^{a(2n)^{1/2}} \left(1 - \frac{u}{a(2n)^{1/2}}\right)\left(1 - \frac{u^2}{2n}\right)^n du \Bigg/ \int_0^{a(2n)^{1/2}} \left(1 - \frac{u^2}{2n}\right)^n du. \tag{A.2}$$

Lemma 1

$$\lim_{n\to\infty} \int_0^{n^{1/2}} \left(1 - \frac{u^2}{2n}\right)^n du = \int_0^{\infty} e^{-u^2/2} du. \tag{A.3}$$

When n tends to infinity, for each point u $[1 - (u^2/2n)]^n$ has a limit $e^{-u^2/2}$. In spite of that, Eq. (A.3) cannot be directly written because the integration interval depends on n.

Proof

(a) The following inequalities are true for $0 \leq \alpha \leq n$:

$$1 - \frac{\alpha}{n} \leq e^{-\alpha/n}, \qquad 1 + \frac{\alpha}{n} \leq e^{\alpha/n}, \qquad 1 - \frac{\alpha^2}{n} \leq \left(1 - \frac{\alpha^2}{n^2}\right)^n.$$

(b) From the three preceding inequalities we deduce

$$\left(1 - \frac{\alpha^2}{n}\right) e^{-\alpha} \leq \left(1 - \frac{\alpha}{n}\right)^n \leq e^{-\alpha}$$

and

$$0 \leq e^{-\alpha} - \left(1 - \frac{\alpha}{n}\right)^n \leq \frac{\alpha^2\, e^{-\alpha}}{n}. \tag{A.4}$$

Considering the upper limit in (A.4) when n tends to infinity as

$$\sup_\alpha \left|\frac{\alpha^2\, e^{-\alpha}}{n}\right| = \frac{4\, e^{-2}}{n} \xrightarrow[n\to\infty]{} 0 \qquad \text{for} \quad 0 < \alpha < \infty.$$

Therefore the sequence $\{v_n\}$ defined by

$$v_n = \begin{cases} [1 - (\alpha/n)]^n & \text{for} \quad 0 \leq \alpha \leq n, \\ 0 & \text{for} \quad \alpha \geq n, \end{cases}$$

tends uniformly to $e^{-\alpha}$ on the interval $0 \leq \alpha \leq \infty$.

(c) If $\alpha = u^2/2$, the integration of (A.4) leads to

$$0 \leq \int_0^{n^{1/2}} e^{-u^2/2} du - \int_0^{n^{1/2}} \left(1 - \frac{u^2}{2n}\right)^n du \leq \int_0^{n^{1/2}} \frac{u^4\, e^{-u^2/2}}{4n} du. \tag{A.5}$$

Furthermore,

$$0 \leq \int_0^{n^{1/2}} \frac{u^4\, e^{-u^2/2}}{4n} du < \frac{1}{n} \int_0^{\infty} \frac{u^4\, e^{-u^2/2}}{4} du = \frac{\lambda}{n},$$

where λ is a constant. Then we conclude from (A.5) that

$$\lim_{n\to\infty} \int_0^{n^{1/2}} \left(1 - \frac{u^2}{2n}\right)^n du = \int_0^{\infty} e^{-u^2/2} du = \left(\frac{\pi}{2}\right)^{1/2}. \tag{A.6}$$

Similar demonstrations allow us to proceed as follows:

$$\lim_{n\to\infty} \int_0^{n^{1/2}} u^{2p}\left(1 - \frac{u^2}{2n}\right)^n du = \int_0^{\infty} u^{2p} e^{-u^2/2} du = \frac{(2p)!}{2^p p!}\left(\frac{\pi}{2}\right)^{1/2}$$

$$\lim_{n\to\infty} \int_0^{n^{1/2}} \left[u^{2p}\ du\ 1 + \frac{u^2}{2n}^{n}\right] = \int_0^{\infty} u^{2p} e^{-u^2/2} du = \frac{(2p)!}{2^p p!}\left(\frac{\pi}{2}\right)^{1/2}. \tag{A.7}$$

The proof of the Lemma is then achieved. Now (A.2) can be written as

$$\hat{K}_e(n) = 1 - \frac{n}{2(n+1)a(2n)^{1/2}}\left[1 - (1 - a^2)^{n+1}\right] \Big/ \int_0^{a(2n)^{1/2}} \left(1 - \frac{u^2}{2n}\right)^n du. \tag{A.8}$$

Using (A.6) for large k,

$$\hat{K}_e(k) \approx 1 - \frac{2^{1/2}}{a\pi^{1/2}k^{1/2}} \tag{A.9}$$

and

$$\lim_{k\to\infty} \hat{K}_e(k) = 1.$$

The mean convergence is proved (but this was still done) and furthermore important information on the asymptotic behavior of the estimate is obtained by (A.9) and hence the algorithm accuracy with time and according to a. Still, with the same assumption $K_0 = 1$, one has

$$\sigma_K^2(k) = \frac{\int_0^1 [K - \hat{K}_e(k)]^2 [1 - a^2(1 - K)^2]^{k/2} dK}{\int_0^1 [1 - a^2(1 - K)^2]^{k/2} dK}.$$

In a similar way, changing variables $u/(2n)^{1/2} = a(1 - K)$, $n = k/2$ and using Eqs. (A.7) and (A.8) we obtain

$$\sigma_K^2(k) \approx 1/a^2k \quad \text{for} \quad a \neq 0, \quad k \text{ large.} \tag{A.10}$$

A.II. STUDY OF THE GENERAL SCALAR CASE ($K_0 \neq 1$)

Let us now consider the general scalar case $K_0 \neq 1$. The mean convergence has been proved in the text, so Eqs. (28) and (29) are rewritten as

$$\sigma_K^2(k) = \frac{\int_0^1 (K - K_0)^2 F(a, K, K_0)^{-k/2} dK}{\int_0^1 F(a, K, K_0)^{-k/2} dK},$$

$$= \frac{\int_0^1 N(K_0, K, k)dK}{\int_0^1 D(K_0, K, k)dK}. \tag{A.11}$$

In order to use relationship (A.8) and to confirm convergence, we first state another lemma.

Lemma 2

Given any positive ε and any ΔK as small as required, one can find $\mu_1(\Delta K, \varepsilon)$ such that

$$\frac{I_1}{J_1} = \frac{\int_{(E)} N(K_0, K, k)dK}{\int_{K_0-\Delta K}^{K_0+\Delta K} N(K_0, K, k)dK} < \varepsilon \qquad \text{for} \quad k > \mu_1(\Delta K, \varepsilon), \tag{A.12}$$

where $(E) = [0, 1] - [K_0 - \Delta K, K_0 + \Delta K]$.

This essentially means that the numerator of $\sigma_K^2(k)$ is, for a sufficiently large k, equivalent to J_1:

$$\int_0^1 N(K_0, K, k)\,dK = \int_{(E)} N dK + \int_{K_0-\Delta K}^{K_0+\Delta K} N dK$$

$$= \int_{K_0-\Delta K}^{K_0+\Delta K} N dK \left[1 + \frac{\int_E N dK}{\int_{K_0-\Delta K}^{K_0+\Delta K} N dK} \right],$$

and through Eq. (A.12),

$$\int_0^1 N dK \approx J_1 \qquad [\forall k > \mu_1(K, \varepsilon)].$$

In a similar manner we shall prove the following lemma.

Lemma 3

Given any positive ε and any ΔK as small as required, one can find $\mu_2(\Delta K, \varepsilon)$ such that

$$\frac{I_2}{J_2} = \frac{\int_{(E)} D(K_0, K, k)\,dk}{\int_{K_0-\Delta K}^{K_0+\Delta K} D(K_0, K, k)\,dk} < \varepsilon \qquad [\forall k > \mu_2(\Delta K, \varepsilon)]. \tag{A.13}$$

For Eqs. (A.12) and (A.13) we then deduce that

$$\sigma_K^2(k) \approx J_1/J_2 \qquad \text{for} \quad k > \max(\mu_1, \mu_2).$$

Proof of Lemma 3. It is straightforward to see that $\forall K \in (E)$

$$N(K_0, K, k) < \frac{(K - K_0)^2}{[(1 + a^2(\Delta K)^2]^{k/2}}. \tag{A.14}$$

So

$$I_1 < \frac{K_C}{[1 + a^2(\Delta K)^2]^{k/2}}, \qquad \text{where} \quad K_C = \frac{(1 - K_0)^3 - K_0^3}{3}. \tag{A.15}$$

Equation (A.15) gives a majorant of I, so we now find a minorant of J_1. By changing variable $t = \alpha_0(K - K_0)k^{1/2}$, where $\alpha_0^2 = \left[a^2/1 - a^2(1 - K_0)^2\right]$, one obtains

$$J_1 = \frac{1}{\alpha_0^3 k^{3/2}} \int_{-\alpha_0 \Delta K k^{1/2}}^{\alpha_0 \Delta K k^{1/2}} \frac{t^2 dt}{[1 + (t^2/k)]^{k/2}}. \tag{A.16}$$

So through Eqs. (A.4) and (A.8) one can conclude: for sufficiently large $\Delta K k^{1/2}$ there exists a β such as

$$J_1 > \beta/k^{3/2}. \tag{A.17}$$

In particular when k is large we have $J_1 \approx (2\pi)^{1/2}/\alpha_0^3 k^{3/2}$ and $J_2 \approx (2\pi)^{1/2}/\alpha_0 k^{1/2}$. Now Eqs. (A.17) and (A.15) are used to prove Eq. (A.12) such that

$$I_1/J_1 < K_C k^{3/2}/\beta[1 + a^2(\Delta k)^2]^{k/2}. \tag{A.18}$$

For increasing k, the denominator in Eq. (A.18) increases faster than the numerator, so I_1/J_1 tends to zero. Equation (A.12) is then proved provided that

$$K_C k^{3/2}/\beta[1 + a^2(\Delta K)^2]^{k/2} < \varepsilon. \tag{A.19}$$

This inequality defines the relation $\mu_1(\Delta K, \varepsilon)$ used in the lemma. The proof of the lemma is achieved when Eq. (A.13) is determined; this can be conducted in a similarly rigorous manner.

Now, considering the asymptotic behavior $\sigma_K^2(k)$ we shall write

$$\sigma_K^2(k) \approx J_1/J_2 \qquad \forall k > \max(\mu_1, \mu_2), \qquad \Delta K << K_0.$$

Changing variables as

$$\frac{u}{k^{1/2}} = \frac{a\Delta K}{\left[1 - a^2(1 - K_0)^2\right]^{1/2}}$$

and once more using relation (A.8), it is straightforward to calculate the asymptotic equivalent of $\sigma_K^2(k)$ denoted as $\bar{\sigma}_K^2(k)$:

$$\bar{\sigma}_K^2(k) = \frac{1 - a^2(1 - K_0)^2}{a^2 k}. \tag{A.20}$$

So Eq. (30) is now clearly proved. These calculations are easily extended to Eq. (46) in the general matrix formulation, which will now be discussed.

A.III. STUDY OF THE MATRIX CASE

Let us consider a matrix system. We shall deal with the quadratic form $u^T P^{-1} u$, where u is an n-dimensional vector and P^{-1} is a definitive strictly positive square matrix. Lemma 1 can be rewritten as follows.

Lemma 3

$$\lim_{n\to\infty} J_n = \int_0^{n^{1/2}} \left(1 - \frac{u^T P^{-1} u}{2n}\right)^n du = \int_0^{\infty} e^{-u^T P^{-1} u/2} du. \tag{A.21}$$

The proof will easily be achieved by changing [in Eqs. (A.4)-(A.10)] the scalar u^2 in the positive quadratic form $(u^T P^{-1} u)$, which is equal to zero if and only if $u = 0$. Furthermore, Lemma 3 can easily be proved by the analogy between the positive scalar

$$F(a, K, K_0) = 1 + \frac{a^2(K - K_0)^2}{1 - a^2(1 - K)^2}$$

as in Eqs. (28), (29), and (A.11), and $F(\theta, \theta_0) = 1 + (\theta - \theta_0) \cdot G_{\theta_0}^{-1}(\theta - \theta_0)^T$, as in Eqs. (45), where $G_{\theta_0}^{-1}$ is a strictly positive real matrix and $(\theta - \theta_0)^T$ is a column vector. Equation (46) is then proved, and theorems 4 and 5 follow.

ACKNOWLEDGMENT

This work was supported by DGRST No. 78 2119 and DRET No. 78293 contracts. Grateful acknowledgments to the *International Journal of Control* for permission to reproduce [17].

REFERENCES

1. R. E. KALMAN, *Trans. Am. Soc. Mech. Eng. J. Basic Eng. 82*, 34-45 (1960).

2. R. K. MEHRA, *IEEE Trans. Automatic Control AC-15*, 175-184 (1970).

3. D. L. ALSPACH, L. L. SCHARF, and A. ABIRI, *Int. J. Control 19*, 265-287 (1974).

4. D. L. ALSPACH, *Computer and Elect. Eng. 1*, 83-94 (1973).

5. Y. C. HO, *IEEE Trans. Automatic Control AC-9*, 334-339 (1964).

6. D. G. LAINIOTIS, *IEEE Trans. Automatic Control AC-16*, 160-170 (1971).

7. F. L. SIMS, and D. G. LAINIOTIS, *IEEE Trans. Automatic Control AC-14*, 215-217 (1969).

8. Y. BAR SHALOM, *IEEE Trans. Automatic Control Ac-17*, (1972).

9. K. A. MYERS, and D. B. TAPLEY, *IEEE Trans. Automatic Control AC-21*, 520-523 (1976).

10. P. SAGE, and J. L. MELSA, "Estimation Theory with Applications to Communications and Control," McGraw-Hill, New York, 1971.

11. A. H. JAZWINSKI, "Stochastic Processes and Filtering Theory," Academic Press, New York (1970).

12. L. A. LIPORACE, *IEEE Trans. Inf. Theory IT-17*, 665-668 (1971).

13. L. LJUNG, *IEEE Trans. Automatic Control AC-22-4*, 551-575 (1977).

14. R. M. HAWKES, and J. B. MOORE, *Proc. IEEE 64*, 1143-1150 (1976).

15. Y. BARAM, and N. R. SANDELL, *IEEE Trans. Automatic Control AC-23* (1978).

16. C. FARGEON, M. GAUVRIT, and P. RODRIGO, *IFAC, Helsinki 3*, 2139 (1978).

17. M. GAUVRIT, C. FARGEON, and P. RODRIGO, *Int. J. Control 33*, No. 5, 811-837 (1981).

Advances in Computational Efficiencies of Linear Filtering

LEONARD CHIN

Naval Air Development Center
Warminster, Pennsylvania

THE PURPOSE

A broad overview of various discrete-time linear filtering techniques including the square root and variations of square root, factorized, Chandrasekhar, partitioning, and decentralized algorithms as well as the basic Covariance and Information filters are presented. The purpose of this chapter is to examine and compare computer burdens of these well-known filtering algorithms from a practical operation point of view.

ISBN 0-12-012719-9

I. INTRODUCTION

The intriguing problem of estimation (prediction, filtering, and smoothing) has attracted many mathematicians, scientists, and engineers throughout history -- beginning with the Babylonians, who applied a form of mathematics similar to the Fourier series to interpret observations and make decisions. Recent history has shown that Euler, Lagrange, Laplace, Bernoulli, and others contributed to the advancement of estimation theories in many ways. However, the solution to a class of estimation problems that dealt with finding the best value of an unknown parameter corrupted by noise (additive) was given by Gauss and Legendre, who separately but concurrently formulated the method of least squares, in which the fundamental concepts of redundant measurement data, observability, dynamic modeling, etc., were introduced. These concepts have provided foundations for many new developments in estimation theories known today. Readers interested in antiquity should consult Neugebauer [1] and Sorenson [2].

Modern history has recoreded that Fisher [3] was one of the original investigators in the formulation of statistical estimation methods. However, the development of the *linear, minimum, mean-square-error* estimator, which is most familiar to engineers today, was not completed until the 1940s, when the Wiener-Hopf equation was first established by Kolmogorov [4] and Wiener [5]. Unfortunately the filter design using the Wiener-Hopf equation proved to be impractical, owing to difficulties in obtaining explicit solutions. Swerling [6] as well as Carlton and Follin [7] circumvented these difficulties by obtaining the least square estimates in a recursive manner.

This new development is believed to be the starting point of the so-called "Kalman filtering." The main contribution of Kalman and Bucy [8,9] was the transformation of the Wiener-Hopf integral equation into an equivalent nonlinear differential equation, the solution of which yields the covariance matrix, which contains all necessary information for the design of the optimal filter. Hence, by demanding a numerical rather than an analytical solution of the Wiener-Hopf equation, they successfully developed a recursive filter that can be conveniently realized in real time by a digital computer. In practical applications, the on-line computer used to implement the filter equations is usually limited in speed and memory. Frequently, it is not possible to program the ideal (theoretical filter) equations, because the truly optimal filter must model *all* error sources of the system. The solution to this problem (excessively large dimension) is usually to design suboptimal filters, in which certain states in the system have to be ignored or simplified. Another implementation problem associated with all digital computers is the numerical accuracy, which is seriously affected by the inherent finite nature of the computer. For example, in the case of the Kalman-Bucy algorithm, the covariance matrix contains all information needed for the filter synthesis (hence, it is called the covariance filter). For this reason, it is critical that the correctness of this matrix be preserved at all times. However, because of the matrix subtractions involved in each computing cycle, nonpositive elements in the covariance matrix could result from truncation and round-off errors. Chin [10] reported that this computational instability could lead to filter divergence.

To preserve the correctness of the covariance matrix (hence preventing filter divergence), a number of methods called "square root covariance algorithms" have been introduced [11-20]. In a parallel effort to preserve the correctness of the information matrix (inverse of covariance matrix) in the "information filter," the square root information filters have also been developed [21-23]. Although these algorithms generally yield improved numerical stability, the number of computational steps is usually greater than that of the standard Kalman filter. For this reason, engineers do have a certain degree of reluctance to employ the square root algorithms. An attempt to improve this situation was made by Bierman [24] who used factorization techniques [25,26] not involving square root computations.

In the early 1970s, a different approach was explored for the design of recursive filters that avoids the utilization of the matrix Riccati equation. Kailath [27] showed that, for a certain class of special applications, the so-called X - Y function of Chandrasekhar could be used to gain two magnitudes of computational improvement over the usual Riccati-type algorithms. Independently, Linquist [28,29] and Lainiotis [30] derived Chandrasekhar algorithms for discrete-time-invariant and continuous-time-varying systems, respectively. However, there is no guarantee that these algorithms will provide computational stability. Other intrinsic aspects of Chandrasekhar filters were discussed by Brammer [31].

Advancement in the design of a practical filter and smoother was done to seek *entirely new* algorithms that not only provide computational stability but also minimize computer burdens. This new approach has been taken by Lainiotis [32-37] who introduced partitioning estimation concepts that are radically different from those of the Kalman type. The partitioning approach constitutes essentially an adaptive framework, which yields fundamentally new estimation algorithms in naturally decoupled, parallel-processing realization; and most important of all, it is computationally attractive.

Another new attempt to economize computational steps as well as to ensure filter stability is the surely locally unbiased (SLU) decentralized approach. The basic concept is to decompose a large system into small subsystems in such a manner that the filter for the overall system will be optimized. This method is also attractive because it is believed that computation of several low-order subsystems is more efficient than the computation of one aggregated high-order system. Also the decentralized filter has a special property that provides asymptotic stability.

The purpose of the chapter is to examine, from computational aspects, advantages and disadvantages of various *discrete-time linear* filtering algorithms previously mentioned. To facilitate the discussion, a linear system model as well as notations and conventions are defined in Section II. Prior to the investigation of computer burdens, an overview of filtering algorithms selected for this study is presented in Section III. The main contribution of this chapter -- a survey of filtering computational efficiencies -- is given in Section IV, in which computer time and memory requirements for the Kalman (covariance and information filters), square root, factorized, Chandrasekhar, partitioning, and decentralized algorithms are summarized. Finally, conclusions as well as recommendation are given in Section V.

II. SYSTEM MODEL, NOTATIONS, AND CONVENTIONS

The linear filtering problem treated in this chapter is stated using the following discrete-time model:

$$x(k + 1) = \Phi(k + 1, k)x(k) + u(k), \quad (1)$$

$$z(k) = H(k)x(k) + v(k). \quad (2)$$

For a given set of measurements

$$\lambda_k = z(l), z(l + 1), \ldots, z(k),$$

it is desired to find the optimal (in the sense of mean-square-error) filtered estimate $\hat{x}(k/k, l)$ of $x(k)$. It is assumed that $u(k)$ and $v(k)$ are uncorrelated zero-mean Gaussian noise with covariances $Q(k)$ and $R(k)$, respectively. Other notations and conventions are given in the accompanying tabulation.

Symbol[a]	*Definition*
$x(k)$	*system state vector at discrete time index k*
$x(l)$	*initial system state vector (Gaussian distributed)*
$\hat{x}(l)$	*the mean value of* $x(l)$
$\hat{x}_n(l)$	nominal *initial system state vector*
$\hat{x}_r(l)$	remainder *initial system state vector*
$\hat{x}(k/k, l)$	*optimal filtered estimate of* $x(k)$
$\hat{x}_n(k/k, l)$	nominal *optimal filtered estimate of* $x(k)$
$\hat{x}_r(k/k, l)$	remainder *optimal filtered estimate of* $x(k)$
$x_i(k)$	*ith subsystem state vector*
$\hat{x}_i(k + 1/k)$	*optimal state estimate of the ith subsystem*
$x(t)$	*system state vector (continuous-time)*

(Tabulation continues)

Tabulation (Continued)

Symbol[a]	Definition
$\hat{x}(t)$	optimal filtered estimate of $x(t)$
$\nu(k)$	innovation sequence
$\Phi(k+1, k)$	system state transition matrix
$z(k)$	measurement vector at discrete time index k
$z_i(k)$	ith subsystem measurement vector
$z_u(k)$	measurement vectors of the "data equation"
$z_x(k)$	measurement vectors of the "data equation"
$\Phi_{ii}(k+1, k)$	ith subsystem state transition matrix
$h^T(k)$	linearized measurement operator (vector)
$H(k)$	linearized measurement operator (vector)
$\overline{H}_i(k)$	ith subsystem measurement matrix
$\hat{H}_i(k)$	coupling measurement matrix bit, ith and other systems
$H_L(k)$	linearized measurement matrix
$F(t)$	fundamental matrix
$F[\hat{x}(t), t]$	linearized fundamental matrix
$u(k)$	system noise vector
$\overline{u}_i(k)$	ith subsystem noise vector
$Q(k)$	system noise covariance matrix
$R_u(k)$	square root of $Q(k)$
$Q_i(k)$	ith subsystem noise covariance matrix
$v(k)$	measurement noise vector
$\overline{v}_i(k)$	ith subsystem measurement noise vector
$R(k)$	measurement noise covariance matrix
$R_i(k)$	ith subsystem measurement noise covariance matrix

Tabulation (Continued)

Symbol[a]	Definition
$r(k)$	*scalar measurement noise variance*
$P(l, l)$	*a priori state error covariance matrix*
$P_x(0)$	*a priori state error covariance matrix*
$P_n(l)$	nominal *a priori state error covariance matrix*
$P_r(l)$	remainder *a priori state error covariance matrix*
$P(k/k, l)$	*state error covariance matrix*
$P_n(k/k, l)$	nominal *state error covariance matrix*
$P_r(k/k, l)$	remainder *state error covariance matrix*
$P_i(k/k)$	*ith subsystem state error covariance matrix*
$P^{-1}(k/k, l)$	*information matrix*
$S^{-1}(k/k, l)$	*square root of information matrix*
$R_x(k/k, l)$	*square root of information matrix*
$S(k/k)$	*square root of covariance matrix*
$R_{ux}(k + 1)$	*square root of cross-covariance between variables of "data equations"*
$\hat{V}(k)$	*lower-triangular square root of measurement noise covariance matrix*
$\hat{U}(k)$	*lower-triangular square root of systems noise covariance matrix*
Z	$Z = S^T H$
$W(k/k)$	*antisymmetric matrix chosen to maintain $S(k, k)$ in lower triangular form*
T, $\hat{T}(k)$ and $T(k + 1)$	*transformation matrix whose columns are composed of eigen vectors of the covariance matrix P*
$D(k)$, $\overline{D}(k)$	*diagonal matrix whose diagonal elements are eigenvalues of the state error covariance matrix*
$U(k)$, $\overline{U}(k)$	*unit upper-triangular matrix*

Tabulation (Continued)

Symbol[a]	*Definition*
$d(k/k)$	*transformed state vector*, $d(k/k) = P^{-1}(k/k,l)x(k/k)$
$K(k)$	*Kalman filter gain matrix*
$K_n(k, l)$	nominal *Kalman filter gain matrix*
$K_i(k)$	*ith subsystem filter gain matrix*
L_{ij}	*coupling matrix between ith and jth subsystems*
$O_n(k, l)$	*observation matrix*
$b(k/k)$	*transformed optimum state vector*
$e(k)$	*residual error of least squares fit*
N_x. N_u	*dimensions of x-data equation and u-data equation*

[a] *Conventions: (1) Superscript T is used to denote transpose of vectors and matrices; $[\ ]^{-T}$ is used to denote the transpose of the inverse of a matrix. (2) Matrices are denoted by upper case letters. Vectors are denoted by lower case letters except for k, l, m, and n, which are integers, and t denotes time. (3) Vectors are assumed to be columns unless otherwise denoted by superscript T. (4) Unless otherwise specified, the dimension of the state vector is n and the dimension of the measurement vector is m, $n \geq m$.*

III. ALGORITHM DESCRIPTIONS

A. *COVARIANCE FILTERS*

1. *Standard Kalman Filter*

The "standard" form of the Kalman filter refers to the estimator first given by Kalman [8], from which the discrete optimal filter was derived and subsequently documented in many books [38-44]. The filter algorithm is usually given in two sets of equations--one for extrapolating, the other one for updating.

Extrapolation

$$\hat{x}(k + 1/k, l) = \Phi(k + 1, k)\hat{x}(k/k, l), \tag{3}$$

$$P(k + 1/k, l) = \Phi(k, k)P(k/k, l)\Phi^T(k, k) + Q(k) \tag{4}$$

Updating

$$\hat{x}(k + 1/k + 1, l) = \hat{x}(k + 1/k, l) + K(k + 1, l)[z(k + 1) - H(k + 1)\hat{x}(k + 1/k, l)], \tag{5}$$

$$K(k + 1, l) = P(k + 1/k, l)H^T(k + 1) \cdot [H(k + 1)P(k + 1/k, l)H^T(k + 1) + R(k + 1)]^{-1}, \tag{6}$$

$$P(k + 1/k + 1, l) = [I - K(k + 1, l)H(k + 1)]P(k + 1/k, l). \tag{7}$$

Note that Eq. (7) is correct only if the gain $K(k + 1, l)$ is optimum.

2. Stabilized Kalman Filter

The stabilized filter (sometimes called the Joseph algorithm [45]) is less sensitive to computer round-off errors. Another benefit is that it yields correct $P(k + 1/k + 1, l)$ even if $K(k + 1, l)$ is nonoptimum. The updating covariance matrix is given by

$$P(k + 1/k + 1, l) = [I - K(k + 1, l)H(k + 1)]P(k + 1/k, l) \cdot [I - K(k + 1, l)H(k + 1)]^T + K(k + 1, l)R(k + 1)K^T(k + 1, l). \tag{8}$$

Other updating and extrapolating equations are the same as Eqs. (3)-(6). Initial conditions for the *standard* as well as the stabilized filters are defined as

$$E[x(l)] = \hat{x}(l/l), \tag{9}$$

$$E\{[\hat{x}(l) - x(l/l)][\hat{x}(l) - \hat{x}(l/l)]^T\} = P(l, l). \tag{10}$$

3. *Extended Kalman Filter*

Extended Kalman filtering is a popular technique for treating nonlinearities in the design of *minimum variance* estimators. Other methods of the same type (Taylor series expansion) are iterated extended Kalman filtering, Gaussian second-order filtering, and linearized Kalman filtering [39].

Because most physical nonlinear systems can be represented by *differential* equations and because measurements are usually available at discrete time, it is proper as well as convenient (for series expansion) to describe system and measurement models as

$$\dot{x}(t) = f[x(t), t] + u(t), \tag{11}$$

$$z(k) = h[x(t_k)] + v(k), \tag{12}$$

in which u(t) and v(k) are uncorrelated zero-mean Gaussian noise with

$$E[u(t)u^T(t)] = Q(t), \tag{13}$$

$$E[v(k)v^T(k)] = R(k); \tag{14}$$

also the initial vector $x(l)$ is Gaussian with mean and covariance given by Eqs. (9) and (10).

Define

$$F[\hat{x}(t), t] = \partial f[x(t), t]/\partial x(t)\,|_{x(t)=\hat{x}(t)}, \tag{15}$$

$$H_L(k) = \partial h[x(t_k)]/\partial x(t_k)\,|_{x(t_k)=\hat{x}(t_k)}. \tag{16}$$

The extrapolation equations are given by

$$dx(t)/dt = f[x(t), t)], \tag{17}$$

$$dP(t)/dt = F[\hat{x}(t), t]P(t) + P(t)F^T[\hat{x}(t), t] + Q(t). \tag{18}$$

$$\hat{x}(k+1/k+1,\ l) = \hat{x}(k+1/k,\ l) + K(k+1,\ l)\{z(k+1) - h[\hat{x}(k+1/k,\ l)]\}, \tag{19}$$

$$P(k+1/k+1,\ l) = [I - K(k+1)H_L(k+1)]P(k+1/k,\ l), \tag{20}$$

$$K(k+1,\ l) = P(k+1/k,\ l)H_L(k+1) \cdot \left[H_L(k+1)P(k+1/k,\ l)H_L^T(k+1) + R(k+1)\right]^{-1}. \tag{21}$$

Other forms of variation (Gaussian second order, etc.) are given in Reference [46].

B. SQUARE ROOT COVARIANCE FILTERS

1. Potter

The first square root algorithm was introduced by Potter [11] for a restricted application of zero system noise and measurements that are scalar quantities, i.e., Eqs. (1) and (2) become

$$x(k+1) = \Phi(k+1,\ k)x(k), \tag{22}$$

$$z(k) = h^T(k)x(k) + v(k), \tag{23}$$

where $h(k)$ is a vector and the variance of the measurement noise $r(k)$ is a scalar value. This method, as well as other methods discussed in the following text, consists of defining a square root matrix S such that

$$P(k/k,\ l) \triangleq S(k/k,\ l)S^T(k/k,\ l). \tag{24}$$

The factorization of covariance square roots is generally not unique. However, this lack of uniqueness is not serious because a unique square root factorization can always be obtained by using the Cholesky decomposition technique [46] (sometimes referred to as the Banachiewicz and Dwyer algorithm), which factors any positive semidefinite symmetric matrix into the product of a lower triangular matrix and its transpose. The description of this algorithm can be found in Reference [47] as well as in many other sources.

Define

$$y(k+1, l) \triangleq S^T(k+1/k, l)h(k+1). \tag{25}$$

Consider the case in which $Q(k) = 0$; then the extrapolation equation for $S(k+1/k, l)$ is given by

$$S(k+1/k, l) = \Phi(k+1, k)S(k/k, l). \tag{26}$$

The extrapolating as well as updating of the state vector is the same as Eqs. (3) and (5), respectively. Other update equations are

$$S(k+1/k+1, l) = S(k+1/k, l)[I + \alpha(k+1, l)y(k+1, l)y^T(k+1, l)], \tag{27}$$

$$K(k+1, l) = \frac{S(k+1/k, l)S^T(k+1/k, l)h(k+1)}{h^T(k+1)S(k+1/k, l)S^T(k+1/k, l)h(k+1) + r(k+1)}, \tag{28}$$

in which $\alpha(k+1, l)$ is given by

$$\alpha = \frac{-1 \pm \{1 - [y^Ty/(y^Ty + r)]\}^{1/2}}{y^Ty}. \tag{29}$$

In Eq. (29), the time index for α, y, and r is the same, hence it is omitted for clarity. When there is no ambiguity, simplified notations such as Eq. (29) will be used in subsequent discussions.

2. Bellantoni and Dodge

This square root filter is an extension of the Potter algorithm by considering vector measurements (simultaneous) with correlated component errors. This method requires diagonalization of an n × n matrix, i.e.,

$$D \triangleq \begin{bmatrix} s_1 & & & \\ & s_2 & & \\ & & \ddots & \\ & & & s_n \end{bmatrix} = T^T(S^TH^TRHS)T, \tag{30}$$

where $s_1, s_2, \ldots, s_n$ are eigenvalues of the covariance matrix and T is the transformation matrix consisting of eigenvectors in its columns. The extrapolation equations are the same as the Potter filter; the update equations were derived in Reference [12] as

$$S(k+1/k+1, l) = S(k+1/k, l)\{I + T[(I+D)^{-1/2} - I]T^T\}, \tag{31}$$

$$K(k+1, l) = S(k+1/k, l)B(I + B^TB)^{-1}(R^{1/2})^{-1}, \tag{32}$$

where

$$B = S^T(k+1/k, l)H^T(k+1)(R^{1/2})^{-1}. \tag{33}$$

The extrapolating and updating of the system state vector are always the same as Eqs. (3) and (5). As such subsequent discussions will concentrate on the covariance and gain matrices.

3. Andrews; Tapley and Choe; Morf, Levy, and Kaileth (Continuous-Time Case)

(Note: Although this chapter is mainly concerned with the discrete-time case, it is felt, however, that a brief discussion of the continuous-time case should be given here for completeness.)

Consider the system model given by

$$x(t) = F(t)x(t) + G(t)u(t), \tag{34}$$

$$z(t) = H(t)x(t) + v(t), \tag{35}$$

where u(t) and v(t) are zero-mean noncorrelated white Gaussian noise with unity covariances. Let P(t) be the covariance of the error of the state estimate; P(t) obeys the following Riccati equations:

$$\dot{P}(t) = F(t)P(t) + P(t)F^T(t) + G(t)G^T(t) - P(t)H^T(t)H(t)P(t), \tag{36}$$

with initial condition

$$P(0) = P_0. \tag{37}$$

The Andrews algorithm [13] was the first square root filter application considering the existence of system noise. Similar to the Bellantoni and Dodge algorithm, it also processes vector measurements. However, it does not require any matrix diagonalization. The extrapolation of the square root covariance is given as

$$S(t) = F(k)S(t) + \left[W(t) + \frac{1}{2} G(t)Z(t)G^T(t)\right]S^{-T}(t), \tag{38}$$

in which Q(t) is the covariance of the system noise and W(t) a skew symmetric matrix that maintains S(t) in the lower triangular form.

It should be pointed out that the solution of Eq. (38) requires that the inverse of $S^T(t)$ be computed at each integration step; this requires a large number of multiplications, which is undesirable. Therefore, Tapley and Choe [48] restructured the problem and let the skew symmetric matrix W(t) be chosen in such a way that inversion of $S^T(t)$ is not needed.

$$[S(t) - F(t)S(t)]S^T(t) = \frac{1}{2} Q(t) + W(t). \tag{39}$$

Furthermore, to maintain S(t) in a lower triangular form, the definitions

$$E(t) \triangleq F(t)S(t), \tag{40}$$

$$\overline{C}(t) \triangleq S(t) - E(t), \tag{41}$$

$$\overline{W}(t) \triangleq W(t) + \frac{1}{2} Q(t), \tag{42}$$

will be used to rewrite Eq. (39) as

$$\overline{C}(t)S^T(t) = \overline{W}(t), \tag{43}$$

which is the desired result.

However, because the skew symmetric matrix W(t) can be chosen arbitrarily, Morf *et al.* [49] provided another method for computing the lower-triangular S(t) matrix that is simpler than the method just described.

Let S(t) be nonsingular and define

$$P(t) \triangleq S(t)S(t)^T. \tag{44}$$

Equation (36) can be written as

$$\dot{P}(t) = \dot{S}(t)S^T(t) + S(t)\dot{S}^T(t), \tag{45}$$

$$\dot{P}(t) = \left(F - \frac{1}{2} SS^TH^TH\right)SS^T + \frac{1}{2} GG^TS^{-T}S^T$$
$$+ SS^T\left(F^T - \frac{1}{2} H^THSS^T\right) + \frac{1}{2} SS^{-1}GG^T. \tag{46}$$

Multiplying Eq. (45) on the left by S^{-1} and on the right by S^{-T} yields

$$S^{-1}S + \dot{S}^TS^{-T} = L, \tag{47}$$

where

$$L \triangleq \overline{F}\overline{F}^T + \overline{G}\overline{G}^T - \overline{H}^T\overline{H}, \tag{48}$$

$$\overline{F} = S^{-1}FS, \tag{49}$$

$$\overline{G} = S^{-1}G, \tag{50}$$

$$\overline{H} = HS. \tag{51}$$

Because S is lower triangular, $S^{-1}\dot{S}$ is the lower-triangular part of L, hence

$$\dot{S} = S\bar{L}, \tag{52}$$

where $\bar{L}$ is the "lower-triangular part" operator.

Because Eq. (52) does not involve an explicit skew symmetric matrix, it seems to be simpler to compute than the other two square root methods previously discussed.

4. Schmidt

Instead of using Eq. (34) to extrapolate the square root covariance matrix, Schmidt [14] introduced a method that facilitates digital computations. This algorithm requires finding an orthogonal transformation matrix T, dimension $(n + m) \times (n + m)$, such that $T^T T = I$ (where n is the dimension of the state vector and m of the measurement vector).

Consider the expression

$$\left[\Phi(k+1, k) S(k/k, l) \;\vdots\; [Q(k)]^{1/2}\right] T^T T \left[\begin{array}{c} S^T(k/k, l)\Phi^T(k+1, k) \\ \hline Q(k)^{1/2} \end{array}\right], \tag{53}$$

which can be written as

$$\Phi(k+1, k) S(k/k, l) S^T(k/k, l) \Phi(k+1, k) + Q(k). \tag{54}$$

Expression (54) is the right side of Eq. (4). Hence expression (53) must be the left side of Eq. (4). Therefore the following relationship is established for the extrapolation of $S(k/k, l)$:

$$\begin{array}{l} n\,\{ \\ m\,\{ \end{array} \left[\begin{array}{c} S^T(k+1/k, l) \\ \hline \underbrace{0}_{n} \end{array}\right] = T\left[\begin{array}{c} S^T(k/k, l)\Phi^T(k+1, k) \\ \hline \underbrace{(Q^{1/2}(k+1))^T}_{n} \end{array}\right] \begin{array}{l} \}\, n \\ \}\, m \end{array}. \tag{55}$$

To express $S^T(k + 1/k, l)$ uniquely in terms of $S^T(k/k, l)$, $\Phi(k + 1, k)$, and $Q^{1/2}(k + 1)$, matrix T must be constructed such that Eq. (55) will be in triangular form. This can be done by using the Gram-Schmidt process or the Householder transformation.

Reference [16] provides descriptions of the Gram-Schmidt and Householder transformations. A more extensive treatment of this subject is found in Chapter 5 of Reference [47].

5. Carlson

The essence of Carlson's technique is to preserve the square root covariance matrix in triangular form during the extrapolation interval as well as the update time. In addition, Carlson recognized that the transition matrix is often block-triangular. This fact can be exploited to reduce computation steps further. To preserve $S(k + 1/k, l)$ in triangular form during extrapolation, two methods are suggested. One is basically the same as Eq. (55), the other is called the root sum square (RSS), which computes the covariance matrix using Eq. (4), then $P(k + 1/k, l)$ is factored (Cholesky decomposition) to triangular square root matrices $S(k + 1/k, l) \cdot S^T(k + 1/k, l)$. To make certain that $S(k + 1/k + 1, l)$ is in triangular form during update, the Potter algorithm is modified by demanding that

$$\bar{A} \triangleq \left(I - \frac{yy^T}{y^Ty + r}\right)^{1/2} \tag{56}$$

be upper triangular, i.e., for scalar measurements

$$P(k + 1/k + 1, l) = P(k + 1/k, l) - K(k + 1)h^T(k + 1)P(k + 1/k, l), \tag{57}$$

which can be written as

$$P(k + 1/k + 1, l) = S(k + 1/k, l)S^T(k + 1/k, l) - \frac{Syy^TS^T}{y^Ty + r}, \tag{58}$$

and factored into

$$P(k + 1/k + 1, l) = S\left(I - \frac{yy^T}{y^Ty + r}\right)S^T. \tag{59}$$

Hence

$$S(k + 1/k + 1, l) = S(k + 1/k, l)\overline{A}(k + 1), \tag{60}$$

in which $\overline{A}(k + 1)$ must be chosen such that $S(k + 1/k + 1, l)$ is *also* upper triangular. A method that can be used to select and compute the $A(k + 1)$ matrix is given in Reference [20].

C. INFORMATION FILTERS

The covariance filter discussed in Section III.A is the Kalman-Bucy filter in its original form (the filter equations are derived from the *covariance* matrix). The information filter discussed in this section is basically of the same type. However, the filter equations are derived from the inverse of the covariance matrix, which is closely related to the information matrix [40, p. 241]. The motivation for taking this approach is to avoid computation difficulties in the case where the initial state error covariance $P(l, l)$ is unknown and assumed to be infinity.

The development of information filter equations is straightforward. This is done by applying the matrix inversion lemma

$$(\Gamma + \Pi^T\Sigma)^{-1} = \Gamma^{-1} - \Gamma^{-1}\Pi^T(I + \Sigma\Gamma^{-1}\Pi^T)^{-1}\Sigma\Gamma^{-1} \tag{61}$$

to the covariance matrix

$$P(k+1/k, l) = \Phi(k+1, k)P(k/k, l)\Phi^T(k+1, k) + Q(k) \quad (62)$$

by identifying

$$\Gamma = \Phi P \Phi^T, \qquad \Pi^T = Q, \quad \text{and} \quad \Sigma = I. \quad (63)$$

The propagation of the information matrix is shown [50] to be

$$P^{-1}(k+1/k, l) = F(k) - F(k)[F(k) + Q^{-1}(k)]^{-1}F(k), \quad (64)$$

where

$$F(k) \triangleq [\Phi^T(k+1, k)]^{-1}P^{-1}(k/k, l)\Phi^{-1}(k+1, k). \quad (65)$$

The update of the inverse covariance matrix from $P^{-1}(k/k-1, l)$ to $P^{-1}(k/k, l)$ is given by

$$P^{-1}(k/k, l) = P^{-1}(k/k-1, l) + H^T(k)R^{-1}(k)H(k). \quad (66)$$

By defining the state of the information filter as

$$\hat{d}(k/k) \triangleq P^{-1}(k/k, l)\hat{x}(k/k), \quad (67)$$

$$\hat{d}(k+1/k) \triangleq P^{-1}(k+1/k, l)\hat{x}(k+1/k). \quad (68)$$

It can be easily shown that the propagation of $\hat{d}(k+1/k)$ is

$$\hat{d}(k+1/k) = [I - P^{-1}(k+1/k, l)Q(k)]\Phi^{-T}(k+1/k)\hat{d}(k/k), \quad (69)$$

and the update of $\hat{d}(k/k)$ is

$$\hat{d}(k) = \hat{d}(k/k-1) + H^T(k)R^{-1}(k)z(k). \quad (70)$$

It will be shown in the next section that the information filter is more efficient than the covariance filter as far as update is concerned. However, regarding propagation, the covariance filter requires fewer computations.

Because of computational error, the use of Eqs. (64) and (66) may lead to nonnegative definiteness of $P^{-1}(k+1/k, l)$. Once again this difficulty can be avoided by applying the square root concept, which will be discussed next.

D. *SQUARE ROOT INFORMATION FILTERS*

1. *Dyer and McReynolds*

An efficient square root solution to the least square problem using the Householder algorithm was demonstrated by Golub [51], Businger and Golub [52], and Jordan [53]. Hanson and Lawson [54] extended the theory to include rank deficient systems and adapted the Householder algorithm to solve sequential least squares problems. Dyer and McReynolds developed the square root information filter based on Householder's matrix triangularization procedure and Cox's [55] sequential estimation algorithm (dynamic programming formulation).

Recall that in Section III.B a square root matrix S was defined [Eq. (24)] as

$$P(k/k, l) \triangleq S(k/k, l)S^T(k/k, l).$$

For the development of the square root information filter (SRIF), it is consistent to define

$$P^{-1}(k/k, l) \triangleq S^{-T}(k/k, l)S^{-1}(k/k, l), \tag{71}$$

$$b(k) \triangleq S^{-1}(k/k, l)\hat{x}(k/k). \tag{72}$$

The update of the inverse covariance square root is given by

$$\begin{matrix} n\,\{ \\ m\,\{ \end{matrix}\begin{bmatrix} S^{-1}(k/k, l) \\ \hline \underbrace{0}_{n} \end{bmatrix} = T\begin{bmatrix} S^{-1}(k/k - 1, l) \\ \hline V^{-1}(k)H(k) \end{bmatrix}, \tag{73}$$

where T is the orthogonal transformation matrix defined previously. The update of b(k/k) is given by

$$\begin{matrix} n\,\{ \\ m\,\{ \end{matrix}\begin{bmatrix} b(k/k) \\ \hline e(k) \end{bmatrix} = T\begin{bmatrix} b(k/k^{-1}) \\ \hline V^{-1}(k)z(k) \end{bmatrix}, \tag{74}$$

where e(k) is the residual error after processing the measurement. The propagation of the inverse covariance is given by

$$\left[\begin{array}{c|c} E(k+1/k) & G(k+1/k) \\ \hline 0 & S^{-1}(k+1/k,\ l) \end{array}\right] = T\left[\begin{array}{c|c} U^{-1}(k) & 0 \\ \hline S^{-1}(k/k,\ l)\Phi^{-1}(k/k) & S^{-1}(k/k,\ l)\Phi^{-1}(k/k) \end{array}\right], \tag{75}$$

where

$$G(k+1/k) \triangleq [R(k+1) + Z^T(k+1/k)Z(k+1/k)]^{1/2}. \tag{76}$$

The propagation of b(k + 1/k) is given by

$$\begin{array}{l} 1\ \{ \\ n\ \{ \end{array}\left[\begin{array}{c} a(k+1) \\ \hline b(k+1/k) \end{array}\right] = T\left[\begin{array}{c} 0 \\ \hline b(k/k) \end{array}\right], \tag{77}$$

where

$$a^{-1}(k) = C^T(k)C(k) + Q^{-1}(k), \tag{78}$$

$$C(k) = S^{-1}(k/k,\ l)\Phi^{-1}(k/k). \tag{79}$$

A different form of propagating $S^{-1}(k + 1/k,\ l)$ and $b(k + 1/k)$ is also available

$$S^{-1}(k+1/k,\ l) = \left\{I - \left[1 + (a(k)Q^{-1}(k))^{1/2}\right]^{-1} C(k)a(k)C^T(k)\right\} \cdot S^{-1}(k/k,\ l)\Phi^{-1}(k/k), \tag{80}$$

$$b(k+1/k) = \left\{I - a(k)\left[1 + (a(k)Q^{-1}(k))^{1/2}\right]^{-1} C(k)C^T(k)\right\} b(k/k). \tag{81}$$

2. *Bierman (G. J.)*

It should be apparent from the previous section that, although the Dyer-McReynolds SRIF is attractive, it relies heavily on the Householder transformation as well as relying on the concept of dynamic programming, which seems to be a little too abstract and difficult to understand. For this reason. Bierman [22] introduced the recursive least square approach intended to simplify the basic structure of SRIF. In essence, Bierman's square root data processing method utilized the so-called "data equation" and the sum-of-squares performance functional to develop equations that propagate the state estimate and its error covariance. Equations (1) and (2) are considered as "measurement equations" and Eqs. (82) and (83) are considered to be a priori "data equations" associated with Eqs. (1) and (2), respectively:

$$z_u(k) = R_u(k)u(k) + w_u(k), \tag{82}$$

$$z_x(k) = R_x(k)X(k) + w_x(k), \tag{83}$$

where w_u and w_x are assumed to be zero-mean, independent random processes with unity covariances. Define

$$Q(k) \triangleq R_u^T(k)R_u(k),$$

$$P_x(0) \triangleq R_x^{-T}(0)R_x^{-1}(0).$$

By selecting the performance functional to be

$$J(k+1) = \|R_x(0)x(0) - z_x(0)\|^2 + \sum_{i=0}^{k} \Big(\|H(i)x(i) - z(i)\|^2 + \|R_u(i)u(i) - z_u(i)\|^2\Big), \tag{84}$$

the problem is then to minimize $J(k+1)$ with respect to $x(i)$ and $u(i)$ for $i = 0, 1, 2, \ldots, k$ such that the solution yields the optimal estimate of $x(k)$.

Bierman [47] has shown that the following "information arrays" contain all necessary information needed for state and covariance update as well as propagation. The actual data processing requires a transformation and update (mapping) given by Eq. (85) and Eq. (86), respectively

$$\hat{T}(k)\left[\begin{array}{c|c} R_x(k) & z_x(k) \\ \hline H(k) & (k) \end{array}\right] = \left[\begin{array}{c|c} R_x(k) & \hat{z}_x(k) \\ \hline \underbrace{0}_{N_u} & \underbrace{e(k)}_{1} \end{array}\right] \begin{array}{l} \} \, N_u \\ \} \, N_x \end{array}, \tag{85}$$

$$T(k+1)\left[\begin{array}{c|c|c} \overbrace{R_u(k)}^{N_u} & \overbrace{0}^{N_x} & \overbrace{z_u(k)}^{1} \\ \hline -\hat{R}_x(k)\Phi^{-1}(k+1) & \hat{R}_x(k)\Phi^{-1}(k+1) & \hat{z}_x(k) \end{array}\right] \begin{array}{l} \} \, N_u \\ \} \, N_x \end{array}$$

$$= \left[\begin{array}{c|c|c} R_u(k+1) & R_{ux}(k+1) & z_u(k+1) \\ \hline 0 & R_x(k+1) & z_x(k+1) \end{array}\right], \tag{86}$$

in which N_x and N_u are dimensions of x(k) and u(k), respectively, e(k) is the error in the least squares fit, and T(k) and T(k + 1) are products of N_u elementary Householder transformations. Definitions of other symbols are given in Section II.

The update estimate and covariance are

$$x(k+1) = R_x^{-1}(k+1)z_x(k+1), \tag{87}$$

$$P_x(k+1) = R_x^{-1}(k+1)R_x^{-T}(k+1). \tag{88}$$

The propagation of state vector requires solution of $\hat{u}(k)$ and $\hat{x}(k+1)$ $\left(\text{i.e., } u(k) \text{ and } x(k+1) \text{ form an augmented data equation } \left[\frac{u(k)}{x(k+1)}\right]\right)$.

$$R_u(k+1)u(k) + R_{ux}(k+1)x(k+1) = z_u(k+1) - w_u(k), \quad (89)$$

$$R_x(k+1)x(k+1) = z_x(k+1) - w_x(k), \quad (90)$$

which can be solved using the Gaussian elimination method.

E. FACTORIZED FILTERS

During the 1970s a number of authors [25,26,47,56-61] have contributed improvements to the Kalman filtering computation efficiency by suggesting square-root-free triangular factorizations. Essentially, this approach is based on the rank one modification of the Cholesky method. For example, Agee and Turner [56] have proved that for a positive-definite covariance matrix P such that $P = UDU^T$, in which U is a unit upper triangular matrix and D is a diagonal matrix with elements d_1, d_2, ..., d_n, where n is the dimension of P, there exists an update P(k) matrix such that

$$P(k) = \overline{U}(k)\overline{D}(k)\overline{U}^T(k) = U(k)D(k)U^T(k) + cv(k)v^T(k), \quad (91)$$

where c is a scalar and v(k) a vector of n-dimension. If P(k) is positive definite, then $\overline{U}(k)$ and $\overline{D}(k)$ can be computed as follows.

For j = n, n - 1, ..., 2, recursively compute $d_j(k)$ and $u_{ij}(k)$, which are elements of $\overline{D}(k)$ and $\overline{U}(k)$,

$$d_j(k+1) = d_j(k) + c_j v_j^2(k), \quad (92)$$

$$v_i(k) \leftarrow v_i(k) - v_j(k)u_{ij}(k), \quad i = 1, \ldots, j-1, \quad (93)$$

$$u_{ij}(k+1) = u_{ij}(k) + c_j v_j(k) v_i(k)/d_j(k+1), \quad i = 1, \ldots, j-1, \quad (94)$$

$$c_{j-1} = c_j d_j(k)/d_j(k+1). \quad (95)$$

The notation $\leftarrow$ is used for "replacement" in the FORTRAN implementation. Detailed proof is given in Reference [47] (p. 45). This method of calculating $\overline{D}(k)$ and $\overline{U}(k)$ is generally valid for both covariance filters as well as information filter updates. To illustrate the usefulness of this factorized approach, consider the covariance update (Kalman filter)

$$P(k + 1/k + 1, l) = P(k + 1/k, l) - P(k + 1/k, l)H^T(k)H(k) \cdot P(k + 1/k, l)H^T(k)H(k)P(k + 1/k, l). \tag{96}$$

By assuming that scalar measurement (96) can be factored into

$$U(k + 1/k + 1)D(k + 1/k + 1)U^T(k + 1/k + 1) = U(k + 1/k)[D(k + 1/k) - (1/a)V(k + 1/k)V^T(k + 1/k)]U^T(k + 1/k), \tag{97}$$

where

$$V(k + 1/k) = D(k + 1/k)U^T(k + 1/k)H^T(k + 1), \tag{98}$$

and the scalar a is given by

$$a = H(k + 1)P(k + 1/k)H^T(k + 1) + R(k + 1). \tag{99}$$

Using Eq. (91) let

$$\overline{U}(k + 1/k)\overline{D}(k + 1/k)\overline{U}^T(k + 1/k) = [D(k + 1/k) - (1/a)V(k + 1/k)V^T(k + 1/k)]. \tag{100}$$

Then Eq. (97) can be written as

$$U(k + 1/k + 1)D(k + 1/k + 1)U^T(k + 1/k + 1) = [U(k + 1/k)\overline{U}(k + 1/k)]\overline{D}(k + 1/k)[U(k + 1/k)U(k + 1/k)]^T. \tag{101}$$

Because $U(k + 1/k)$ and $\overline{U}(k + 1/k)$ are unit upper triangular, Eq. (101) yields

$$U(k + 1/k + 1) = U(k + 1/k)\overline{U}(k + 1/k), \tag{102}$$

$$D(k + 1/k + 1) = \overline{D}(k + 1/k). \tag{103}$$

The preceding results show that the problem of factoring the filter update covariance has been reduced to the task of factoring a symmetric matrix $[D(k + 1/k)(1/a)V(k + 1/k)V^T(k + 1/k)]$ to $\overline{U}(k + 1/k)$ and $\overline{D}(k + 1/k)$.

Now consider the covariance propagation

$$P(k + 1/k) = \Phi(k + 1, k)P(k/k)\Phi^T(k + 1, k) + Q(k). \tag{104}$$

It is required to find $[U(k + 1/k)D(k + 1/k)U^T(k + 1/k)]$ such that it is equal to the right-hand side of Eq. (104). Without loss of generality let $Q(k)$ be a diagonal matrix and let

$$G(k + 1/k) \triangleq [\Phi(k + 1, k)U(k/k) \mid I], \tag{105}$$

$$\tilde{D}(k + 1/k) \triangleq \left[\begin{array}{c|c} D(k/k) & 0 \\ \hline 0 & Q(k) \end{array}\right]. \tag{106}$$

Then it can be shown that

$$G(k + 1/k)\tilde{D}(k + 1/k)G^T(k + 1/k)$$
$$= \Phi(k + 1, k)U(k/k)D(k/k)U^T(k/k)\Phi^T(k + 1, k) + Q(k), \quad (107$$

which is the desired result. Equation (105) can be efficiently computed using the modified Gram-Schmidt method, the Householder transformation, or the Givens transformation.

F. CHANDRASEKHAR FILTERS

An approach used to minimize the computer burden was introduced by Kailath [27] who considered a special case of continuous-time stationary process and showed that differential equations of the Chandrasekhar type, instead of the matrix Riccati differential equation, can be used to compute the filter gain. This development was immediately followed by Linquist [28] who treated the same problem by means of the backward innovation process. Morf *et al.* [62,63] and Linquist [29] have solved the discrete-time stationary process problem; Friedlander *et al.* [64] have treated the discrete-time nonstationary process problem by introducing a way of classifying stochastic processes in terms of an "index of nonstationarity." It was shown that Chandrasekhar equations can be derived from the extended Levinson-Whittle-Wiggins-Robinson algorithms for stationary time series; Lainiotis [30] provided generalized algorithms for the continuous-time nonstationary and stationary processes.

Approaching from the square root algorithm viewpoint (i.e., propagation of the square root of $dP(t)/dt$ instead of the square root of $P(t)$), Morf *et al.* [65] derived the continuous-time Chandrasekhar filter equations, which are identical to results given in Reference [30] in which the "partitioning formulas" of Lainiotis were used.

For the purpose of comparing digital computational efficiency, only the discrete-time Chandrasekhar algorithm is described in this chapter because it was pointed out in Reference [65] that the number of computing operations is approximately equal for various versions of Chandrasekhar filters.

By considering constant matrices Φ, H, P_0, Q, and R associated with a system model given in Eqs. (1) and (2), Reference [29] presented the following results, from which the optimal filter gain matrix K(k) can be determined in the following manner:

$$K(k) = \Phi A(k)[HA(k) + R]^{-1}, \qquad (108)$$

where

$$A(k) = A(k-1) - A'(k-1)C^{-1}(k-1)A'^{-1}(k-1)H^T, \tag{109}$$

$$A'(k) = \Phi A'(k-1)\Phi A(k-1)[HA(k-1) + R]^{-1}HA'(k-1), \tag{110}$$

$$C(k) = C(k-1) - A'^T(k-1)H^T(HA(k-1) + R)^{-1}HA'(k-1), \tag{111}$$

with initial considerations

$$A(0) = P_0H^T, \tag{112}$$

$$A'(1) = \Phi P_0H^T, \tag{113}$$

$$C(0) = HP_0H^T + R. \tag{114}$$

Note that $A(k)$ and $A'(k)$ are $n \times m$ matrices and $C(k)$ is a symmetric $m \times m$ matrix. Thus, to solve for $A(k)$ only $2nm + [m(m+1)]/2$ equations are needed, in contrast to the conventional Kalman algorithm in which n^2 equations are required to compute the filter gain. If $m \ll n$, which is true in many practical situations, the number of equations to be solved in each step is of order n versus n^2. Because only the inverse of $C(k)$ is needed in Eq. (109), Eq. (111) may be replaced by

$$\begin{aligned} \mathbf{C}^{-1}(\mathbf{k}) = {} & C^{-1}(k-1) \\ & + C^{-1}(k-1)A'^T(k-1)H^T(HA(k) + R)^{-1} \\ & \cdot HA'(k-1)C^{-1}(k-1), \end{aligned} \tag{115}$$

which can be obtained by applying the matrix inversion lemma to Eq. (111).

The preceding results were also extended to the continuous-time case by Linquist [28] and were shown to be exactly corresponding to the equations derived by Kailath [27].

G. *PARTITIONING FILTERS*

In a radically different approach to filtering and estimation in general, Lainiotis [32-38,66-81] developed the partitioning algorithms, which are fundamentally new techniques never explored before. The partitioning approach yields new results for linear as well as nonlinear estimation in naturally decoupled, computationally attractive, and fast parallel-processing realizations. The partitioned filter contains the Kalman filter as a special case and it constitutes the natural framework for efficient change of initial conditions *without recourse to reprocessing the data.* This special property will lead to efficient computations. Several partitioning algorithms for discrete-time linear systems are given in the following discussions.

1. *General Partitioned Algorithm (GPA)*

In the filtering problem stated in Section II, the solution provided by the partitioning approach consists of decomposing the initial state vector $x(l)$ to the sum of two independent vectors

$$x(l) = x_n + x_r, \tag{116}$$

where x_r is an unknown model parameter vector to be adapted (References [32,33,67]). Let $\hat{x}_n$ and P_n be the mean and the covariance of x_n, respectively (the choice of $\hat{x}_n$ and P_n is arbitrary). Because x_n and x_r are assumed to be independent, the following initial conditions relationship hold:

$$\hat{x}(l/l) = \hat{x}_n(l) + \hat{x}_r(l), \tag{117}$$

$$P(l, l) = P_n(l) + P_r(l). \tag{118}$$

The optimal filtered estimate and the corresponding error-covariance matrix $P(k, l)$ are given by

$$\hat{x}(k/k, l) = \hat{x}_n(k/k, l) + \hat{x}_r(k/k, l), \tag{119}$$

$$P(k, l) = P_n(k, l) + P_r(k, l) \quad \text{for} \quad k \geq l, \tag{120}$$

where $\hat{x}_n(k/k, l)$ and $P_n(k, l)$ are computed using the standard Kalman filter equations with initial conditions $\hat{x}(l/l, l) = \hat{x}_n$ and $P(l, l) = P(l)$. The remainder estimate $\hat{x}_r(k/k, l)$ and the corresponding error-covariance matrix are given by

$$\hat{x}_r(k/k, l) = \Phi_n(k, l)\hat{x}_r(l/k, l), \tag{121}$$

$$P_r(k/l) = \Phi_n(k, l)P_r(l/k)\Phi_n^T(k, l), \tag{122}$$

where $\hat{x}_r(l/k, l)$ and $P_r(l/k)$ are the smoothed estimate of the partial initial state $x_r(l)$ and its covariance matrix, respectively. They are given by

$$\hat{x}_r(l/k, l) = P_r(l/k)[M_n(k, l) + P_r^{-1}(l)\hat{x}_r(l)], \tag{123}$$

$$P_r(l/k) = [P_r(l)O_n(k, l) + I]^{-1}P_r(l), \tag{124}$$

where

$$\begin{aligned} M_n(k, l) = {} & M_n(k - 1, l) \\ & + \Phi_n^T(k - 1, l)\Phi^T(k, k - 1)H^T(k) \\ & \cdot P_{\tilde{z}_n}^{-1}(k/k - 1, l), \end{aligned} \tag{125}$$

$$\begin{aligned} \tilde{z}_n(k, l)O_n(k, l) = {} & O_n(k - 1, l)\Phi_m^T(k - 1, l)\Phi^T(k, k - 1)H^T(k) \\ & \cdot P_{\tilde{z}_n}^{-1}(k/k, l)H(k)\Phi(k, k - 1)\Phi_n(k - 1, l), \end{aligned} \tag{126}$$

$$\Phi_m(k, k - 1) = [I - K_n(k, l)H(k)]\Phi(k, k - 1), \tag{127}$$

$$\tilde{z}_n(k, l) = z(k) - H(k)\Phi(k, k - 1)\hat{x}_n(k - 1/k - 1, l), \tag{128}$$

$$P_{\tilde{z}_n}(k/k-1, l) = H(k)P_n(k/k-1, l)H^T(k) + R(k), \quad (129)$$

$$K_n(k, l) = P_n(k/k-1, l)H^T(k)P_{\tilde{z}_n}^{-1}(k/k-1, l). \quad (130)$$

The GPA previously given [Eqs. (119)-(130)] constitutes a family of realizations of the optimal linear filter, one for each initial-state-vector partitioning. For example, the Kalman filter is a member of this family for nominal initial conditions equal to actual initial conditions, namely $\hat{x}_r = 0$ and $P_r(l) = [0]$. Unlike the Kalman filter, GPA is applicable to all initial conditions including $P(l, l) = \infty$. With the freedom of choosing nominal initial conditions, GPA is closely related to the Chandrasekhar realization of the Kalman filter algorithm. Specifically, the computational advantages of the Chandrasekhar algorithm depends on the low-rank property of the actual initial conditions.

The basic approach of GPA is to decompose the initial state vector to the sum of *two statistically independent* Gaussian random vectors [Eq. (116)]. The natural extension of this concept is to consider the decomposition of the initial state to the sum of an arbitrary number of jointly Gaussian random vectors, which may be *statistically dependent*. Indeed this concept has been developed by Lainiotis and Andrisani [80] into the so-called "multipartitioning" algorithm, which can be used for, among other applications, efficient parameter identifications and filtered state estimate of off-diagonal terms in the initial-state covariance matrix.

2. Lambda Algorithm

The lambda algorithm has a decoupled structure that results from partitioning of the total data interval into nonoverlapping subintervals. Elemental filtering solutions are first computed in each subinterval with arbitrarily chosen nominal initial conditions. Then the overall solution is obtained by connecting the elemental piecewise solutions via GPA. Thus the desired estimation results over the entire interval have been decomposed into a set of completely decoupled elemental solutions that can be computed in either a serial or parallel-processing mode.

Let the data interval consist of measurements $\lambda_n = \{z(0), z(1), \ldots, z(n)\}$, where $z(k) \triangleq z(t_k)$ and $t_0 \leq t_k \leq t_n$. Given data interval $\{t_0, t_n\}$ to be divided into nonoverlapping subintervals $\{t_i, t_j\}$, the lambda algorithm is given by

$$\hat{x}(j, 0) = \hat{x}_n(j, i) + \hat{x}_r(j, 0), \tag{131}$$

$$P(j, 0) = P_n(j, i) + P_r(j, 0), \tag{132}$$

where

$$\hat{x}(j, 0) \triangleq \hat{x}(t_j/t_j, t_0), \tag{133}$$

$$P(j, 0) \triangleq P(t_j, t_0) \tag{134}$$

are the optimal estimate and its covariance matrix at t_j with initial conditions $x(t_0/t_0)$ and $P(t_0, t_0)$ at t_0. The nominal quantities

$$\hat{x}_n(j, i) \triangleq \hat{x}_n(t_j/t_j, t_i), \tag{135}$$

$$P_n(j, i) \triangleq P_n(t_j, t_i) \tag{136}$$

are the nominal estimate of the corresponding nominal covariance at t_j obtained using the standard Kalman filtering equations with initial conditions at t_i given by

$$\hat{x}_n(i, i) \triangleq x_n(t_i), \tag{137}$$

$$P_n(i, i) = P_n(t_i). \tag{138}$$

The remainder initial conditions are given by

$$\hat{x}_r(i, 0) \triangleq \hat{x}(i, 0) - \hat{x}_n(i, i), \tag{139}$$

$$P_r(i, 0) \triangleq P(i, 0) - P_n(i, i). \tag{140}$$

The remainder smoothed estimate $x_r(j, 0)$ and its covariance matrix $P_r(j, 0)$ are given by Eqs. (121)-(130) with the following proper identifications: $t_k = t_j$, $t_l = t_i$, $\hat{x}_r(l) = \hat{x}_r(i, 0)$, and $P_r(l) = P_r(i, 0)$.

To show the recursive nature of the lambda algorith, Eqs. (131) and (132) and the present version of Eqs. (123) and (124) may be combined to yield

$$\hat{x}(j, 0) = \hat{x}_n(j, i) + \Phi_n(j, i)[P_r(i, 0)O_n(j, i) + I] \cdot [P_r(i, 0)M_n(j, i) + \hat{x}_r(i, 0)], \tag{141}$$

$$P(j, 0) = P_n(j, i) + \Phi_n(j, i)[P_r(i, 0)O_n(j, i) + I] \cdot P_r(i, 0)\Phi_n^T(j, i), \tag{142}$$

where $O_n(j, i) \triangleq O_n(t_j, t_i)$ and $M_n(j, i) \triangleq M_n(t_j, t_i)$ are obtained from Eqs. (125)-(127) for the subinterval $\{t_i, t_j\}$. The recursive operations are repeated for each subinterval until $t_j = t_n$.

3. Delta Algorithm

The delta algorithm was developed on the basis of "doubling" the length of the partitioning interval of the lambda algorithm. This development was motivated by applications of the partitioned filter to time-invariant models, in which the number of iterations needed to reach steady state depends on the time constants of the model.

The "doubling" algorithm, known to be faster than the Chandrasekhar algorithm, is given [72] by the following recursive equations:

$$P(2^{n+1}\Delta) = P_n(2^n\Delta) + \Phi_0(2^n\Delta)\left[P(2^n\Delta)O_n(2^n\Delta)\right]^{-1} P_n(2^n\Delta)\Phi_n^T(2^n\Delta), \tag{143}$$

where $P_n(\ )$, $\Phi_n(\ )$, and $O_n(\ )$ are given by $P_n(2^{n+1})$,

$$P_n(2^{n+1}\Delta) = P_n(2^n\Delta) + \Phi_n(2^n\Delta)\left[P_n(2^n\ )O_n(2^n\ ) + I\right]^{-1} P_n(2^n\Delta)\Phi_n^T(2^n\Delta), \tag{144}$$

$$\Phi_n(2^{n+1}\Delta) = \Phi_n(2^n\Delta)\left[P_n(2^n\Delta)O_n(2^n\Delta) + I\right]^{-1}\Phi_n(2^n\Delta), \tag{145}$$

$$O_n(2^n\Delta) = O_n(2^n\Delta) + \Phi_n^T(2^n\Delta)\left[P_n(2^n\Delta)O_n(2^n\Delta) + I\right] \cdot P_n(2^n\Delta)\Phi_n(2^n\Delta) \quad \text{for} \quad n = 0, 1, 2, 3, \ldots . \tag{146}$$

Therefore matrix inversions that are required to obtain the Riccati solution at the end of a time interval that is twice as long as the interval in the previous iteration results in *doubling*.

4. Per-Sample Partitioning

Per-sample partitioning is another extension of the basic lambda algorithm, in which partitioning is done at *every sample* with zero nominal initial conditions, i.e., $\hat{x}_n(k) = 0$ and $P_n(k) = 0$ for $k = 1, 2, \ldots, N$. This ultimate partitioning of the data interval at every sampling instant yields completely decoupled linear estimation from sample to sample, thus resulting in a simple recursive algorithm, which is given [35,37,68] by the following recursive equations:

$$\hat{x}(k+1,0) = \hat{x}_n(k+1,k) + \Phi_n(k+1,l)[P(k,0)O_n(k+1,k)+I]^{-1} \cdot [P(k,0)M_n(k+1,k)+\hat{x}(k,0)], \tag{147}$$

$$P(k+1,0) = P_n(k+1,k) + \Phi_n(k+1,k)[P(k,0)O_n(k+1,k)+I]^{-1} \cdot P(k,0)\Phi_n^T(k+1,k), \tag{148}$$

where

$$M_n(k+1,k) = \Phi^T(k+1,k)H^T(k+1)A(k+1)z(k+1), \tag{149}$$

$$O_n(k+1,k) = \Phi^T(k+1,k)H^T(k+1)A(k+1)H(k+1) \cdot \Phi(k+1,k); \tag{150}$$

and the per-sample nominal filter equations are as follows

$$\hat{x}_n(k+1,k) = k_n(k+1,k)z(k+1), \tag{151}$$

$$P_n(k+1,k) = [I - k_n(k+1,k)H(k+1)]Q(k), \tag{152}$$

$$K_n(k+1,k) = Q(k)H^T(k+1)A(k+1), \tag{153}$$

where

$$A(k+1) \equiv [H(k+1)Q(k)H^T(k+1) + R(k+1)]^{-1}. \tag{154}$$

The per-sample partitioning filter is memoryless, as can be seen from Eqs. (149)-(154), because all memory has been transferred to the basic partition filter Eq. (147). It may be observed that computation of the nominal filter gain $K_n(k+1,k)$ is accomplished using Eq. (153) and Eq. (154), without repeated use of the Riccati equation as is required in the Kalman filter computation.

It also may be observed that all other quantities, M_n, O_n, $\mathbf{x}_n$, P_n, and Φ_n, are completely determined *nonrecursively* by Eqs. (149)-(154), using only the model quantities and the data at the current time $(t_k + 1)$.

The remarkable nature of the per-sample partitioned filter and its computational advantages can be seen further by considering the case of time-invariant models. For time-invariant models, the recursive algorithm is exactly as given in Eqs. (147)-(154), except that now all relevant quantities are time-invariant. Specifically, the per-sample partitioned filter is now given [35,37,68] as

$$\begin{aligned} \hat{x}(k + l, 0) &= \hat{x}_n(k + 1, k) \\ &\quad + \Phi_n[P(k, 0)O_n + I]^{-1} \\ &\quad \cdot [P(k, 0)M_n(k + 1, k) + \hat{\hat{x}}(k, 0)], \end{aligned} \tag{155}$$

where

$$M_n(k + 1, k) = \Phi^T H^T A z(k + 1), \tag{156}$$

$$O_n = \Phi_n^T H^T A H \Phi_n, \tag{157}$$

$$\hat{x}_n(k + 1, k) = k_n z(k + 1), \tag{158}$$

$$P_n = [I - k_n H]Q, \tag{159}$$

$$K_n = QH^T A, \tag{160}$$

and

$$A \equiv [HQH^T + R]^{-1}. \tag{161}$$

To appreciate fully how interesting the preceding version of the partitioned filter is, it must be noted that both the Kalman filter realization and the Chandrasekhar realization of the optimal linear estimate result in filter algorithms that are time varying even for time-invariant models. Namely, both the Kalman and Chandrasekhar realizations are time-varying filters in the transient stage even for time-invariant models, yet it is seen that the preceding per-sample partitioning realization of the optimal filter for time-invariant models is a completely time-invariant one even from the first iteration. This transformation of a basically time-varying filter (at least at the transient stage) into an effectively time-invariant one is due to partitioning and the zero initialization at each sampling instant, which lead to completely decoupled and memoryless nominal filters.

It is noted further then, in view of the time invariance of all the relevant quantities, namely O_n, K_n, Φ_n, and P_n, that they only need to be computed once and stored for subsequent use.

H. DECENTRALIZED FILTERS

During the 1970s a novel approach used for state estimation of large-scale systems has been *decentralization*. As a result, a number of decentralized filters have been developed. Two of which, addressing the general problem (interconnections exist in all subsystems as well as in the measurement), are the so-called surely locally unbiased (SLU) [82-87] and the sequentially partitioned algorithm (SPA) filters. The attractive features of these algorithms are filter stability and computation efficiency. These properties for the continuous-time SLU formulation have been demonstrated by Sanders *et al.* [86]. The discussion of the discrete-time decentralized filters is given by Kerr and Chin [88]. For self-contained purposes, a brief summary of these algorithms is now given.

1. The Surely Locally Unbiased Filter

Consider the following collection $\{S_i,\ i = 1, 2, \ldots, N\}$ of N interconnected subsystems:

$$x_i(k + 1) = \Phi_{ii}(k + 1, k)x_i(k) + L_{ii} \sum_{j=1, i\neq j}^{N} L_{ij}x_j(k) + u_i(k). \tag{162}$$

With measurement at S_i,

$$z_i(k) = \overline{H}_i(k)x_i(k) + \hat{H}_i(k) \sum_{j=1, i\neq j}^{N} L_{ij}x_j(k) + v_i(k), \tag{163}$$

where $\hat{H}_i(k)$ is a matrix of rank $p_i < q_i$ and has the physical interpretation that the local decision maker at S_i can observe all subsystem interactions, and $\overline{H}_i(k)$ is the local state observation matrix. The problem is to find N decentralized filter gains of the specific SLU class to minimize a global cost function. The approach is, first, to decouple into N local minimization of the constituent cost functions for the N local subsystems, then apply the discrete-time matrix minimum principle to solve for the gain of each local subsystem. This procedure yields recursive computations.

The optimal state estimate is given by

$$\hat{x}_i(k + 1/k) = \Phi_{ii}(k + 1, k)\hat{x}_i(k/k - 1) + L'_{ii}(z'_{i1} - \overline{H}'_{i1}\hat{x}_i) + K'_{i2}(z'_{i2} - \overline{H}'_{i2}\hat{x}_i), \tag{164}$$

where

$$\begin{matrix} p_i \; \{ \\ q_i \; \{ \end{matrix} \begin{bmatrix} z_{i1} \\ --- \\ z_{i2} \end{bmatrix} \triangleq u_2^{-1} z_i, \qquad p_i < q_i, \tag{165}$$

$p_i \times q_i$ is the dimension of the ith local measurement,

$$u_2^{-1}\hat{H}_i u_1 \triangleq \begin{bmatrix} Ip_i \\ --- \\ 0 \end{bmatrix} \} q_i, \tag{166}$$

$$L_{ii}u_1 \triangleq L'_{ii}, \tag{167}$$

$$u_1^{-1}L_i \triangleq L'_i, \tag{168}$$

$$u_1^{-1}L_i \triangleq v_i \triangleq \begin{bmatrix} v_{i1} \\ --- \\ v_{i2} \end{bmatrix}, \tag{169}$$

$$u_2^{-1}\overline{H}_i \triangleq \overline{H}'_i \triangleq \begin{bmatrix} \overline{H}'_{i1} \\ --- \\ \overline{H}'_{i2} \end{bmatrix} \begin{matrix} \} p_i \\ \\ \} q_i - p_i \end{matrix}, \tag{170}$$

$$u_2^{-1}R_i u_2^{-T} \triangleq R'_i \triangleq \left[\begin{array}{c|c} R'_{i1} & R'_{i3} \\ \hline R'_{i3} & R'_{i2} \end{array}\right] \} q_i - p_i, \tag{171}$$

$$K_i u_2 \triangleq K'_i \triangleq \left[K'_{i1} \mid K'_{i2}\right], \tag{172}$$

$$\begin{aligned} K'_{i2}(k) = &\Big\{\Phi_{ii}(k+1, k)P_i(k/k-1)\overline{H}'^T_{i2}(k) \\ &- L'_{ii}(k)\Big[\overline{H}'_{ii}(k)P_i(k/k-1)\overline{H}'^T_{i2}(k) + R'_{i3}(k)\Big]\Big\} \\ &\cdot \Big[\overline{H}'_{i2}(k)P_i(k/k-1)\overline{H}'^T_{i2}(k) + R'_{i2}(k)\Big]^{-1}, \end{aligned} \tag{173}$$

$$\begin{aligned} P_i(k+1/k) = &[\Phi_{ii}(k+1, k) - L'_{ii}(k)\overline{H}'_{i1}(k)P_i(k/k-1)] \\ &\cdot [\Phi_{ii}(k+1, k) - L_{ii}(k)\overline{H}'_{i1}]^T \\ &- \Big\{[\Phi_{ii}(k+1, k) - L'_{ii}(k)\overline{H}'_{i1}(k)] \\ &\quad \cdot P_i(k/k-1)\overline{H}'^T_{i2}(k) - L'_{ii}(k)R'_{i3}(k)\Big\} \\ &\cdot \Big[\overline{H}'_{i2}(k)P_i(k/k-1)\overline{H}'^T_{i2}(k) + R_{i2}(k)\Big]^{-1} \end{aligned}$$

$$\cdot \Big\{ [\Phi_{ii}(k+1, k) - L'_{ii}(k)\overline{H}'_{i1}(k)] \cdot P_i(k/k-1)\overline{H}'^{T}_{i2}(k) - L'_{ii}(k)R'_{i3}(k) \Big\}^T + \Big[\overline{Q}_i(k) + L'_{ii}(k)R'_{i1}(k)L^T_{ii}(k) \Big], \tag{174}$$

$$\overline{Q}_i(k) \triangleq Q_i(k) - L'_{ii}(k)R'_{i1}(k)L'^{T}_{ii}(k). \tag{175}$$

Equation (174) describes how the variance in estimation error evolves in discrete time. The SLU filter treats the interaction input to each local subsystem as if it were just a zero-mean, Gaussian white noise but of the appropriately adjusted covariance.

Although it is necessary to find $u_1(k)$ and $u_2(k)$ at each measurement, calculation of their inverses is not needed because they are imbedded in the decentralized filtering algorithm.

2. *The Sequentially Partitioned Algorithm*

Another formulation of the decentralized filter is given by Shah [89]. The so-called SPA filter can be summarized by the following discussion. Consider the following subsystem and measurement equations:

$$x_i(k+1) = \overline{\Phi}_{ii}(k+1, k)x_i(k) + \sum_{j=1, j\neq i}^{N} \overline{\Phi}_{ij}(k+1, k)x_j(k) + w_i(k), \tag{176}$$

$$z_i(k) = \overline{H}_i(k)x_i(k) + \hat{H}_i(k)L_i(k)x(k) + v_i(k), \tag{177}$$

$$= \overline{H}_i(k)x_i(k) + H_i(k) \sum_{j=1, j\neq i}^{N} L_{ij}(k)x_j(k) + v_i(k) \tag{178}$$

for i - 1, 2, ..., N. The estimation error is defined in the usual manner, that is,

$$e_i(k/k) \triangleq x_i(k) - \hat{x}_i(k/k), \tag{179}$$

where

$$\hat{x}_i(k/k) = E\{x_i(k)/Z(k)\}, \tag{180}$$

in which Z(k) is the measurement set. By combining Eqs. (176) and (179), the ith subsystem may be written as

$$x_i(k+1) = \overline{\Phi}_{ii}(k+1, k)x_i(k) + \sum_{j=1, j\neq i}^{N} \overline{\Phi}_{ij}(k+1, k)\hat{x}_j(k) + w_i^*(k), \tag{181}$$

and the measurement equation for the ith subsystem is represented by

$$z_{ii}(k) = \overline{H}_i(k)x_i(k) + \hat{H}_i(k) \sum_{j=1, j\neq i}^{N} L_{ij}(k)\hat{x}_j(k/k-1) + v_i^*(k), \tag{182}$$

where

$$w_i^*(k) \triangleq w_i(k) + \sum_{j=1, j\neq i}^{N} \overline{\Phi}_{ij}(k+1, k)e_j(k/k), \tag{183}$$

$$v_i^*(k) \triangleq v_i(k) + \sum_{j=1, j\neq i}^{N} L_{ij}(k)e_j(k/k-1). \tag{184}$$

Assume that e_j, w_i^*, and v_i^* can be treated as Gaussian white noise, then the standard Kalman filter algorithm can be applied to each subsystem with the following appropriately modified covariances:

$$Q_{ii}^*(k) \triangleq E\left[w_i^*(k)w_i^{*T}(k)\right], \tag{185}$$

$$Q^*_{ii}(k) = Q_{ii}(k) + \sum_{j=1, j\neq i}^{N} \overline{\Phi}_{ij}(k+1, k) P_j(k/k) \overline{\Phi}^T_{ij}(k+1, k), \quad (186)$$

$$R^*_{ii}(k) \triangleq E\left[v^*_i(k) v^{*T}_i(k)\right], \quad (187)$$

$$R^*_{ii}(k) = R_{ii}(k) + \hat{H}_i(k)\left[\sum_{j=1, j\neq i}^{N} L_{ij}(k) P_j(k/k-1) L^T_{ij}(k)\right]\hat{H}^T_i(k). \quad (188)$$

The result of applying the Kalman filtering technique yields the following subsystem state propagation and state update:

$$\hat{x}_i(k+1/k) = \Phi_{ii}(k+1, k)\hat{x}_i(k/k) + \sum_{j=1, j\neq i}^{N} \overline{\Phi}_{ij}(k+1, k)\hat{x}_j(k/k), \quad (189)$$

or

$$\hat{x}_i(k+1/k) = \overline{\Phi}_{ii}(k+1, k)\hat{x}_i(k/k) + \sum_{j=1, j\neq i}^{N} \hat{x}_j(k+1/k), \quad (190)$$

$$\hat{x}_i(k+1/k+1) = \hat{x}_i(k+1/k) + \overline{K}_i(k+1)\left[z_{ii}(k+1) - \overline{H}_i(k+1)\hat{x}_i(k+1/k) - \hat{H}_i(k+1) \sum_{j=1, j\neq i}^{N} L_{ij}(k+1) \cdot \hat{x}_j(k+1/k)\right], \quad (191)$$

in which the filter gain $\overline{K}_i(k+1)$ is computed in the usual (Kalman filtering) manner, that is,

$$\overline{K}_i(k+1) = P_{ii}(k+1/k)\overline{H}_i^T(k+1) \cdot \left[\overline{H}_i(k+1)P_{ii}(k+1/k)\overline{H}_i^T(k+1) + R_{ii}^*(k+1)\right]^{-1}, \tag{192}$$

and the covariance propagation and update are given by

$$P_{ii}(k+1/k) = \Phi_{ii}(k+1/k)P_{ii}(k/k)\Phi_{ii}^T(k+1/k) + Q_{ii}^*(k), \tag{193}$$

$$\begin{aligned} P_{ii}(k+1/k+1) = {} & [I - \overline{K}_i(k+1)\overline{H}_i(k+1)]P_{ii}(k+1/k) \\ & \cdot [I - \overline{K}_i(k+1)\overline{H}_i(k+1)]^T \\ & + \overline{K}_i(k+1)R_{ii}^*(k+1)\overline{K}_i(k+1). \end{aligned} \tag{194}$$

IV. COMPUTER BURDENS

Discussions of computer burdens of various algorithms described in the previous section can be found in open literature (e.g., [14-24]) in which considerable data were provided pertaining to the computation efficiency of covariance and information filters, and their square root variations, as well as the Chandrasekhar and factorized filters. However, computer burdens of the partitioning and decentralized filters have been documented only in closed literature (e.g., [90,91]). The purpose of this section is to provide an assessment of computer time and memory requirements of these relatively new approaches as well as other conventional algorithms.

It is well known that a precise quantitative statement of computer central processing unit (cpu) time and memory storage requirements are difficult to obtain, because the exact number of counts depends on the manner in which the filter equations are programmed and the particular computer used to process the data. For these reasons, only an approximate assessment is given here. For example, the logic time [15] has been excluded. Also, the transition matrix and the measurement matrix are assumed to be given, because the number of operations required to compute these matrices is heavily dependent on the nature of the problem. Furthermore, in the process of assessing operation counts, no distinction is made between multiplication and division. Although the cpu time required to perform a division is longer than multiplication, this assumption affects the results in a minimal manner because the number of divisions in a filtering cycle is very small compared to the number of multiplications. Because multiplication requires much more cpu time than addition and subtraction, hence, for first-order-magnitude approximation, it is reasonable to regard computer time as directly proportional to the number of multiplications (including divisions and extracting square roots) needed to complete the filtering cycle. In general, computer time and memory requirements are given in terms of n and m, where n is the dimension of the state vector and m of the measurement vector. In the case of decentralized filtering, n_i and q_i are used to represent dimensions of the state vector and measurement vector, respectively. In the case of sequential processing of vector measurements or scalar measurements, other symbols will be used. For example, Bierman's equations for SQIF and the factorized filters belong to this category. Naturally, cautions must be taken when a comparison is made between sequential- or scalar-processing technique and vector-processing technique.

All matrix inversions are assumed to be performed via the Cholesky factorization routine, which requires only $[(1/2)n^3 + (3/2)n^2 + nq]$ operations (q is the number of multiplications required to extract the square root of a scalar) and $[(1/2)n^2 + (1/2)n]$ memory locations. The number of operations required for the calculation of eigenvalues and eigenvectors are difficult to assess because of the iterative process involved. Thus a variational parameter is allowed in the operation counts.

Following the simplified approach together with the preceding assumptions, the number of predominant operations (multiplication) and memories required for various algorithms are assessed, and results are presented in the Appendix (Tables I-XII). In addition, Table XIII is provided to show recent trends in computer operation speeds, so that cpu time for different machines can be derived for each algorithm.

A separate table for the Extended Kalman filter is not being made because the standard Kalman filter includes the Extended Kalman filter, in which a set of nonlinear differential equations must be integrated in order to propagate states between measurements. For this reason, up to 90% of cpu time required per filter cycle is spent in integrating differential equations. The remaining 10% of cpu time would be spent on performing the computation sequence of the stantard Kalman filter. The square root covariance filter of Andrews, Tapley and Choe, Morf, Levy, and Kailath are close enough (as far as computer operations are concerned) to be considered as one class; therefore, only one table is provided under the heading of "Andrews' square root filter."

Computation details of the three derivatives of the general partitioned algorithm -- lambda, delta, and per-sample partitioning -- as well as their square root formulations are documented in [92]. In general, computer burdens of these derivatives are considerably less than those required by the general formulation. Particularly attractive is the per-sample partitioning algorithm, which is memoryless and performs without the repeated use of the Riccati equation.

V. CONCLUSION

The question of how to attain computational efficiency has puzzled many engineers despite the fact that many attempts have been made to present guidelines as to which algorithm is the best (most efficient). The answer is still imprecise because it depends on factors such as operational computer parameters (instruction set, word length, cpu time, etc.), programming methods (single or double precision, linear or multidimension arrays, exploitation of symmetric and sparse matrices, etc.), the size and complexity (cross-coupling) of the transition matrix, and methods of processing measurement data (simultaneous, subgroup, sequential, decentralized, etc.).

The purpose of this chapter is to provide an order-magnitude approximation on computational requirements of various filtering algorithms without making any specific recommendations as to which one is the "best." Results are given in tabulated form (Tables I-XII). In using these tables, caution must be exercised (especially when comparisons are made among algorithms) because they are not -- and cannot be -- compiled on a uniform basis. For example, Bierman's SRIF and factorized filters are designed for the processing of sequential measurement data of a zero-order dynamic system; the partitioning filter is designed to deal with unknown parameters as well as state estimation, hence this algorithm is efficient in the sense that a separate adaptive routine is not needed. The decentralized filter is most appropriate for large-scale but decomposed subsystems application; it is efficient in the sense that computer operations are fewer for a set of subsystems than those required for the aggregate system. Therefore, users of these algorithms are advised to perform cost-effectiveness trade-off studies according to given situations -- before deciding which algorithm to be selected. It is hoped that this chapter does provide sufficient information for such trade-off studies.

APPENDIX

The entire class of zero-order systems with scalar sequential measurements has been treated in great detail by Bierman [47], who includes tables summarizing operation counts of SRIF and factorized filters as well as counts of the Householder transformation. Hence these tables are not duplicated here.

Table I. Computational Requirements of the Standard Kalman Filter

Step	Computation sequence	Operations	Storage
1	$\hat{x}(k/k, l)$		n
2	$P(k/k, l)$		n^2
3	$\Phi(k+1, k)$		n^2
4	$\Phi(k+1, k)P(k/k, l)$	n^3	Store in 2
5	$\Phi(k+1, k)P(k/k, l) \cdot \Phi(k+1, k)$	n^3	Store in 4
6	$Q(k)$		n^2
7	$P(k+1/k, l) = \Phi(k+1, k)P(k/k, l) \cdot \Phi^T(k+1, k) + Q(k)$		Store in 5
8	$\hat{x}(k+1/k, l) = \Phi(k+1, k)\hat{x}(k/k, l)$	n^2	Store in 1
9	$H(k+1)$		mn
10	$P(k+1/k, l)H^T(k+1)$	mn^2	Store in 7
11	$R(k+1)$		m^2
12	$H(k+1)P(k+1/k, l)H^T(k+1) + R(k+1)$	m^2n	m^2
13	$[H(k+1)P(k+1/k, l) \cdot H^T(k+1) + R(k+1)]^{-1}$	$\frac{1}{2}(m^3 + 3m^2) + mq$	
14	$K(k+1, l) = P(k+1/k, l)H^T(k+1) \cdot [H(k+1)P(k+1/k, l) \cdot H^T(k+1) + R(k+1)]^{-1}$	m^2n	mn
15	$z(k+1)$		m
16	$\hat{x}(k+1/k+1, l) = \hat{x}(k+1/k, l) + K(k+1, l) \cdot [z(k+1) - H(k+1) \cdot \hat{x}(k+1/k, l)]$	mn	Store in 8
17	$P(k+1/k+1, l) = P(k+1, l) - K(k+1, l) \cdot [P(k+1/k, l)H^T(k+1)]^T$	mn^2	Store in 10
	Total	$2n^3 + n^2 + 2mn^2 + 2m^2n + mn + (1/2)m^3 + (3/2)m^2 + mq$	$3n^2 + n + 2mn + 2m^2 + m$

Table II. Computational Requirements of the Stabilized Kalman Filter

Step	Computation sequence	Operations	Storage
1	$\hat{x}(k/k, l)$		n
2	$P(k/k, l)$		n^2
3	$\Phi(k+1, k)$		n^2
4	$\Phi(k+1, k)P(k/k, l)$	n^3	Store in 2
5	$\Phi(k+1, k)P(k/k, l)\Phi^T(k+1, k)$	n^3	Store in 4
6	$Q(k)$		n^2
7	$P(k+1/k, l) = \Phi(k+1, k)P(k/k, l) \cdot \Phi^T(k+1, k) + Q(k)$		Store in 5
8	$\hat{x}(k+1/k, l) = \Phi(k+1, k)\hat{x}(k/k, l)$	n^2	Store in 1
9	$H(k+1)$		mn
10	$P(k+1/k, l)H^T(k+1)$	mn^2	Store in 7
11	$R(k+1)$		m^2
12	$H(k+1)P(k+1/k, l)H^T(k+1) + R(k+1)$	m^2n	m^2
13	$[H(k+1)P(k+1/k, l)H^T(k+1) + R(k+1)]^{-1}$	$\frac{1}{2}(m^3 + 3m^2) + mq$	Store in 12
14	$K(k+1, l) = P(k+1/k, l)H^T(k+1) \cdot [H(k+1)P(k+1/k, l) \cdot H^T(k+1) + R(k+1)]^{-1}$	m^2	mn
15	$z(k+1)$		m
16	$\hat{x}(k+1/k+1, l) = \hat{x}(k+1/k, l) + K(k+1, l) \cdot [z(k+1) - H(k+1) \cdot \hat{x}(k+1/k, l)]$	mn	Store in 8
17	$I - K(k+1, l)H(k+1)$	n^2m	Store in 10
18	$[I - K(k+1, l)H(k+1)] \cdot P(k+1/k, l)$	n^3	Store in 3
19	$[I - K(k+1, l)H(k+1)] \cdot P(k+1/k, l) \cdot [I - K(k+1, l)H(k+1)]^T$	n^3	Store in 17
20	$K(k+1, l)R(k+1)$	m^2n	Store in 18

(Table II continues)

Table II (Continued)

Step	Computation sequence	Operations	Storage
21	$P(k+1/k+1, l) = [I - K(k+1, l)H(k+1)] \cdot P(k+1/k, l) \cdot [I - K(k+1, l)H(k+1)]^T + K(k+1, l)R(k+1) \cdot K^T(k+1, l)$	n^2m	Store in 19
	Total	$4n^3 + n^2 + 3mn^2 + 3m^2n + mn + (1/2)m^3 + (3/2)m^2 + mq$	$3n^2 + n + 2mn + 2m^2 + m$

Table III. Computational Requirements of the Potter Square Root Filter

Step	Computation sequence	Operations	Storage
1	$\hat{x}(k/k, l)$		n
2	$S(k/k, l)$		n^2
3	$\Phi(k+l, k)$		n^2
4	$\hat{x}(k+1/k, l) = \Phi(k+1, k)\hat{x}(k/k, l)$	n^2	Store in 1
5	$S(k+1/k, l) = \Phi(k+1, k)S(k/k, l)$	n^3	Store in 2
6	$h(k+1)$		n
7	$y(k+1, l) = S^T(k+1/k, l)h(k+1)$	n^2	n
8	$S(k+1/k, l)y(k+1, l)$	n^2	n
9	$r(k+1)$		1
10	$y^T(k+1, l)y(k+1, l)$	n	1
11	$K(k+1, l) = S(k+1/k, l)y(k+1, l)/[y^T(k+1, l)y(k+1, l) + r(k+1)]$	n	Store in 8
12	$z(k+1)$		1
13	$h^T(k+1)\hat{x}(k+1/k, l)$	n	1

(Table III continues)

Table III (Continued)

Step	Computation sequence	Operations	Storage
14	$\hat{x}(k+1/k+1, l) = \hat{x}(k+1/k, l) + K(k+1, l) \cdot [z(k+1) - h^T(k+1) \cdot \hat{x}(k+1/k, l)]$	n	Store in 4
15	$1 - y^T(k+1, l)y(k+1, l)/ [y^T(k+1, l)y(k+1, l) + r(k+1)]$	1	Store in 12
16	$-1 \pm \{1 - y^T(k+1, l) \cdot y(k+1, l)/ [y^T(k+1, l)y(k+1, l) + r(k+1)]\}^{1/2}$	q	Store in 15
17	α = [Step 16]/[Step 10]	1	Store in 13
18	$y(k+1, l)y^T(k+1, l)$	n	Store in 6
19	$\alpha y(k+1, l)y^T(k+1, l)$	n	Store in 18
20	$S(k+1/k+1, l) = S(k+1/k, l) \cdot [I - \alpha y(k+1, l) \cdot y^T(k+1, l)]$	n^2	Store in 5
	Total	$n^3 + 4n^2 + 6n + q + 2$	$2n^2 + 4n + 4$

Table IV. Computational Requirement of the Bellantoni and Dodge Square Root Filter

Step	Computation sequence	Operations	Storage
1	$\hat{x}(k/k, l)$		n
2	$S(k/k, l)$		n^2
3	$\Phi(k+1, k)$		n^2
4	$\hat{x}(k+1/k, l) = \Phi(k+1, k)\hat{x}(k/k, l)$	n^2	Store in 1
5	$S(k+1/k, l) = \Phi(k+1, k)S(k/k, l)$	n^3	n^2
6	$R^{-1/2}(k+1)$		m^2
7	$H(k+1)$		mn

(Table IV continues)

Table IV (Continued)

Step	Computation sequence	Operations	Storage
8	$R^{-1/2}(k+1)H(k+1)$	m^2n	mn
9	$z(k+1)$		m
10	$z(k+1) - H(k+1)\hat{x}(k/k, l)$	mn	Store in 9
11	$B^T(k+1) = R^{-1/2}(k+1)H(k+1) \cdot S(k+1/k, l)$	n^2m	Store in 7
12	$I + B^T(k+1)B(k+1)$	m^2n	Store in 3
13	$[I + B^T(k+1)B(k+1)]^{-1}$	$(1/2)(n^3 + 3m^2) + mq$	Store in 12
14	$R^{-1/2}(k+1)$[Step 10]	m^2	Store in 4
15	[Step 13][Step 14]	m^2	Store in 10
16	$[B(k+1)]$[Step 15]	mn	Store in 8
17	$\hat{x}(k+1/k+1, l) = \hat{x}(k+1/k, l) + S(k+1/k, l)$[Step 16]	n^2	Store in 4
18	$B(k+1)B^T(k+1)$	mn^2	Store in 12
19	D, diagonal matrix consisting eigenvalues	μ^a	Store in 15
20	T, transformation matrix consisting eigenvectors		Store in 16
21	$(I+D)^{-1/2} - I$	mq	Store in 20
22	$[(I+D)^{-1/2} - I]T^T$	mn	Store in 11
23	T[Step 22] $+ I$	mn^2	Store in 18
24	$S(k+1/k+1, l) = S(k+1/k, l)$[Step 23]	n^3	Store in 2
	Total	$2n^3 + 2n^2 + 3n^2m + 2m^2n + 3mn + (7/2)m^2 + (1/2)m^3 + 2mq + \mu$	$3n^2 + n + 2nm + m + m^2$

[a] Variable number of operations depending on computer being used as well as method being used to compute eigenvalues and eigenvectors.

Table V. Computational Requirements of the Andrews Square Root Filter

Step	Computation sequence	Operations	Storage
1	$\hat{x}(k/k, l)$		n
2	$S(k/k, l)$		n^2
3	$\Phi(k+1, k)$		n^2
4	$\hat{x}(k+1/k, l) = \Phi(k+1, k)\hat{x}(k/k, l)$	n^2	Store in 1
5	$S(k+1/k, l) = \Phi(k+1, k)S(k/k, l)$	n^3	n^2
6	$H(k+1)$		nn
7	$R(k+1)$		$(m^2/2) + (m/2)$
8	$R^{1/2}(k+1)$		$(m^2/2) + (m/2)$
9	$\overline{H}(k+1) = H(k+1)S(k+1/k, l)$	n^2m	Store in 2
10	$UU^T = R + \overline{H}^T\overline{H}$	$(nm^2/2) + (nm/2)$	Store in 3
11	U, U^{-1}	$(m^3/3) + m^2 - (m/3) + mq$	Store in 10
12	$z(k+1)$		m
13	$z(k+1) - H(k+1)\hat{x}(k+1/k, l)$	mn	Store in 12
14	U^{-1}[Step 13]	$(m^2/2) + (m/2)$	Store in 13
15	$\overline{H}U^{-T}$	$(nm^2/2) + (nm/2)$	Store in 6
16	$[U + R^{1/2}]^{-1}$	$(m^3/6) + (m^2/2) + (m/3)$	Store in 7
17	$S(k+1/k, l)$[Step 15]	n^2m	Store in 11
18	[Step 16]$\overline{H}^T$	$(nm^2/2) + (nm/2)$	Store in 15
19	$\hat{x}(k+1/k+1, l) = \hat{x}(k+1/k, l)$ + [Step 17][Step 14]	nm	Store in 4
20	$S(k+1/k+1, l) = S(k+1, l) \cdot [I - (\text{Step 15})(\text{Step 16})\overline{H}^T]$	n^2m	Store in 9
	Total	$n^3 + n^2 + 3n^2m + (3/2)nm^2 + (7/2)nm + (1/2)m^3 + 2m^2 + (1/2)m + mq$	$3n^2 + n + mn + m^2 + 2m$

Table VI. Computational Requirements of the Schmidt Square Root Filter

Step	Computation sequence	Operations	Storage
1	$\hat{x}(k/k, l)$		n
2	$S(k/k, l)$		n^2
3	$\Phi(k+1, k)$		n^2
4	$\hat{x}(k+1/k, l) = \Phi(k+1, k)\hat{x}(k/k, l)$	n^2	Store in 1
5	$Q^{1/2}(k+1)$		n^2
6	$A = [\Phi(k+1, k) \cdot S(k/k, l) \mid Q^{1/2}(k+1)]$	n^3	$2n^2$
7	A^Te (e is an arbitraryn-column vector)		$2n$
8	AA^Te		n
9	AA^Tee^T		Store in 3
10	$T = I - AA^Tee^T/$[first element of AA^Te vector]		Store in 9
11	$\bar{A} = TA$		Store in 6
12	[first element of AA^Te vector]$^{1/2}$		1
13	First column of $S(k+1/k, l) = AA^Te/$[Step 12]		Store in 8
14	To complete the $S(k+1/k, l)$ matrix, Steps 7-13 will be iterated $(n-1)$ times. Because the dimensions of A and T are effectively reduced by one at each iteration, the number of operations for:	7 and 8 $\sum_{i=1}^{n}(n+m)(n+1-i)$ 9 and 10 $\sum_{i=1}^{n}(n-i)$ 11 $\sum_{i=1}^{n-1}(n+m)(n-i)^2$ 12 and 13 $\sum_{i=1}^{n}(n-i)$	
15	$h(k+1)$		n

(Table VI continues)

Table VI (Continued)

Step	Computation sequence	Operations	Storage
16	$y(k+1, l) = S^T(k+1/k, l)h(k+1)$	n^2	Store in 13
17	$S(k+1/k, l)y(k+1, l)$	n^2	n
18	$r(k+1)$		1
19	$y^T(k+1, l)y(k+1, l)$	n	1
20	$K(k+1, l) = S(k+1/k, l)y(k+1, l)/ y^T(k+1, l)y(k+1, l) + r(k+1)$	n	Store in 17
21	$z(k+1)$		1
22	$h^T(k+1)\hat{x}(k+1/k, l)$	n	1
23	$\hat{x}(k+1/k+1, l) = \hat{x}(k+1/k, l) + K(k+1, l) \cdot [z(k+1) - h^T(k+1)\hat{x}(k+1/k, l)]$	n	Store in 4
24	$1 - y^T(k+1, l)y(k+1, l)/ [y^T(k+1, l)y(k+1, l) + r(k+1)]$	1	Store in 21
25	$-1 \pm \{1 - y^T(k+1, l) \cdot y(k+1, l)/ [y^T(k+1, l)y(k+1, l) + r(k+1)]\}^{1/2}$	q	Store in 24
26	$\alpha =$ [Step 25]/[Step 19]	1	Store in 22
27	$y(k+1, l)y^T(k+1, l)$	n	Store in 15
28	$\alpha y(k+1, l)y^T(k+1, l)$	n	Store in 27
29	$S(k+1/k+1, l) = S(k+1/k, l) \cdot [1 - \alpha y(k+1, l) \cdot y^T(k+1, l)]$	n^2	Store in 2
	Total	$n^3 + 3n^2 + 6n + q + 2 + 2\sum_{i=1}^{n}(n-i) + \sum_{i=1}^{n}(n+m)(n+1-i) + \sum_{i=1}^{n}(n+m)(n-i)^2$	$5n^2 + 6n + 5$

Table VII. Computational Requirements of the Carlson Square Root Filter

Step	Computation sequence	Operations	Storage
1	$\hat{x}(k/k, l)$		n
2	$S(k/k, l)$		n^2
3	$\Phi(k+1, k)$		n^2
4	$\hat{x}(k+1/k, l) = \Phi(k+1, k)\hat{x}(k/k, l)$	n^2	Store in 1
5	$Q(k+1)$		n^2
6	$\Phi(k+1, k)S(k/k, l)$	n^3	Store in 2
7	$\Phi(k+1, k)S(k/k, l)S^T(k/k, l) \cdot \Phi^T(k+1, k)$	n^3	
8	$S(k+1/k, l) = [\Phi(k+1, k)S^T(k/k, l) \cdot \Phi(k+1, k) + Q(k+1)]^{1/2}$	$\sum_{i=1}^{n-2}(n-1-i) + \sum_{i=1}^{n-1}(n-i) + (n-2) + (n-1)q$	
9	$h(k+1)$		n
10	$y(k+1, l) = S^T(k+1/k, l)h(k+1)$	n^2	n
11	$S(k+1/k, l)y(k+1, l)$	n^2	n
12	$r(k+1)$		1
13	$y^T(k+1, l)y(k+1, l)$	n	1
14	$K(k+1, l) = S(k+1/k, l)y(k+1, l)/[y^T(k+1, l)y(k+1, l) + r(k+1)]$	n	Store in 11
15	$z(k+1)$		1
16	$h^T(k+1)\hat{x}(k+1/k, l)$	n	1
17	$\hat{x}(k+1/k+1, l) = \hat{x}(k+1/k, l) + K(k+1, l) \cdot [z(k+1) - h^T(k+1) \cdot \hat{x}(k+1/k, l)]$	n	Store in 4
18	$y(k+1, l)y^T(k+1, l)$	n	Store in 9
19	$I - [y(k+1, l)y^T(k+1, l)]/[y^T(k+1, l)y(k+1, l) + r(k+1)]$	n	Store in 3

(Table VII continues)

Table VII (Continued)

Step	Computation sequence	Operations	Storage
20	$\{I - [y(k+1, l)y^T(k+1, l)]/[y^T(k+1, l)y(k+1, l) + r(k+1)]\}^{1/2}$	Same as Step 8	Store in 19
21	$S(k+1/k+1, l) = S(k+1/k, l)$ [Step 20]	$\sum_{i=1}^{n} i[n-(i-1)]$	Store in 7
	Total	$2n^3 + 3n^2 + 6n + 2\sum_{i=1}^{n-2}(n-1-i) + 2(n-2) + 2(n-1)q + 2\sum_{i=1}^{n-1}(n-i) + \sum_{i=1}^{n} i[n-(i-1)]$	$3n^2 + 4n + 4$

Table VIII. Computational Requirements of the Information Filter

Step	Computation sequence	Operations	Storage
1	$\hat{a}(k/k, l)$		n
2	$P^{-1}(k/k, l)$		n^2
3	$\Phi^{-1}(k+1, k)$		n^2
4	$Q^{-1}(k)$		n^2
5	$Q(k)$		n^2
6	$P^{-1}(k/k, l)\Phi^{-1}(k+1, k)$	n^3	Store in 2
7	$F(k) = \Phi^{-T}(k+1, k)P^{-1}(k/k, l) \cdot \Phi^{-1}(k+1, k)$	n^3	Store in 6
8	$[F(k) + Q^{-1}(k)]^{-1}$	$(1/2)(n^3 + 3n^2) + nq$	Store in 7
9	$F(k)[F(k) + Q^{-1}(k)]^{-1}$	n^3	Store in 8
10	$P^{-1}(k+1/k, l) = F(k) - F(k) \cdot [F(k) + A^{-1}(k)]^{-1}F(k)$	n^3	Store in 9

(Table VIII continues)

Table VIII (Continued)

Step	Computation sequence	Operations	Storage
11	$P^{-1}(k+1/k, l)Q(k)$	n^3	Store in 5
12	$\Phi^{-T}(k+1, k)\hat{d}(k/k, l)$	n^2	Store in 1
13	$\hat{d}(k+1/k, l) = [I - P^{-1}(k+1/k, l)Q(k)] \cdot \Phi^{-T}(k+1, k)\hat{d}(k/k, l)$	n^2	Store in 12
14	$H(k+1)$		nm
15	$z(k+1)$		m
16	$R^{-1}(k+1)$		m^2
17	$H^T(k+1)R^{-1}(k+1)$	nm^2	Store in 14
18	$\hat{d}(k+1/k+1, l) = \hat{d}(k+1/k, l) + H^T(k+1)R^{-1}(k+1)z(k+1)$	m^2	Store in 13
19	$P^{-1}(k+1/k+1, l) = P^{-1}(k+1/k, l) + H^T(k+1)R^{-1}(k+1)H(k+1)$	nm^2	Store in 10
	Total	$(11/2)n^3 + (7/2)n^2 + 2nm^2 + m^2 + nq$	$4n^2 + n + nm$

Table IX. Computational Requirements of the Chandrasekhar Filter

Step	Computation sequence	Operations	Storage
1	$\hat{x}(k/k)$		n
2	$\Phi(k+1, k)$		n^2
3	$\Phi(k+1, k)\hat{x}(k/k)$	n^2	Store in 1
4	$A(k-1)$		nm
5	$A'(k-2)$		nm
6	$C^{-1}(k-2)$		m^2
7	H		mn
8	R		m^2
9	$(HA(k-1)+R)^{-1}$	$(1/2)(m^3 + 3m^2) + mq$	m^2
10	Eq. (115)	$2m^3 + 3m^2n + mn^2$	Store in 6
11	Eq. (110)	$2m^2n + 4mn^2$	Store in 5
12	Eq. (109)	$m^2n + 2mn^2$	Store in 4

(Table IX continues)

Table IX (Continued)

Step	Computation sequence	Operations	Storage
13	Eq. (108)	$n^2m + m^2n$	nm
14	$\hat{x}(k+1/k+1) = \hat{x}(k+1/k) + K(k+1) \cdot [z(k+1) - H\hat{x}(k+1)]$	mn	Store in 3
	Total	$2m^3 + 7nm^2 + n^2(1+8m) + mn + (1/2)(m^3 + 3m^2) + mq$	$2m^2 + n^2 + n(1+4m)$

Table X. Computational Requirements of the General Partitioning Filter (in addition to the "nominal" Kalman filter computation)

Step	Computation sequence	Operations	Storage
1	$x_n(k-1/k-1, l)$		n
2	$\Phi(k, k-1)$		n^2
3	$H(k)$		mn
4	Eq. (128)	mn^2	m
5	$P_n(k/k-1, l)$		n^2
6	$R(K)$		m^2
7	Eq. (129)	m^2n	n^2
8	$P_{z_n}^{-1}(k/k-1, l)$		m^2
9	Eq. (130)	n^2m	nm
10	Eq. (127)	n^2m	n^2
11	$O_n(k-1, l)$		n^2
12	Eq. (126)	$2n^3 + 3n^2m + 2nm^2$	n^2
13	$P_r(l)$		n^2
14	$P_r(l)O_n(k, l)$	n^3	n^2
15	$(P_r(l)O_n(k, l) + I)^{-1}$	$(1/2)(n^3 + 3n^2) + nq$	Store in 14
16	Eq. (124)	n^3	Store in 15
17	$M(k-1, l)$		nm
18	Eq. (125)	$n^3 + n^2m + nm^2$	Store in 17

(Table X continues)

Table X (Continued)

Step	Computation sequence	Operations	Storage
19	$P_r^{-1}(l)$		n^2
20	$\hat{x}_r(l)$		n
21	Eq. (123)	$n^2m + n^3$	Store in 20
22	Eq. (121)	n^2	Store in 1
23	Eq. (122)	$2n^3$	n^2
	Total	$8n^3 + n^2(8m + 1) + 4m^2n + (1/2)(n^3 + 3n^2) + nq$	$10n^2 + 2n + 2m^2 + m + 3mn$

Table XIA. Computational Requirements of the SLU Filter

Step	Computation sequence	Operations	Storage
1	$x_i(k/k - 1)$		n_i
2	$P_i(k/k - 1)$		n_i^2
3	$\Phi_{ii}(k + 1, k)$		n_i^2
4	$\hat{H}_i(k)$		$q_i \times p_i$
5	$U_2^{-1}(k)\hat{H}_i(k)U_1(k)$	See Table XIB	Store in 4
6	$\dot{L}_{ii}(k)$		$n_i \times p_i$
7	$\dot{L}_{ii}(k)U_1(k)$	$n_ip_i^2$	Store in 6
8	$L_i(k)$		$p_i \times m$
9	$U_1^{-1}(k)L_i(k)$	p_i^2n	Store in 8
10	$\overline{H}_i(k)$		$q_i \times n_i$
11	$U_2^{-1}(k)\overline{H}_i(k)$	$q_i^2n_i$	Store in 10
12	$z_i(k)$		q_i
13	$U_2^{-1}(k)z_i(k)$	q_i^2	Store in 12
14	$R_i(k)$		q_i^2
15	$U_2^{-1}(k)R_i(k)U_2^{-T}(k)$	q_i^3	Store in 14

(Table XIA continues)

Table XIA (Continued)

Step	Computation sequence	Operations	Storage
16	Eq. (174)	$2n_i^3 + n_i^2(3q_i - p_i) + n_i(q_i - p_i)(2q_i - p_i) + n_ip_i^2 + (q_i - p_i)^3$	Store in 2
17	Eq. (173)	$2n_i^2(q_i - p_i) + 2n_i(q_i - p_i) + q_i + (q_i - p_i)^3$	$n_i \times (q_i - p_i)$
18	Eq. (164)	$n_i^2 + 2n_iq_i$	Store in 1
	Total	$2n_i^3 + q_i^3 + 2(q_i - p_i)^3 + n_i^2[1 + 5q_i - 3p_i] + p_i^2(3n_i + n) + q_i^2(i + 3n_i) + q_i - 3n_ip_iq_i + 2n_i(2q_i - p_i)$	$2n_i^2 + n_i + q_ip_i + p_in + 2q_in_i$

$n \triangleq$ aggregate system dimension $p_i \triangleq$ interactive measurement dimension

$n_i \triangleq$ local system dimension $q_i \triangleq$ local measurement dimension

Table XIB. Step 5 of the SLU Filter Computation Sequence (Reference [91])

Machine	Execution time (sec)
IBM 370/195 (Argonne National Laboratory)	1.0
IBM 360/75 (University of Illinois)	9.7
IBM 360/65 (AMES Laboratory)	17.0
IBM 370/165 (University of Toronto)	2.6
IBM 370/168 Mod 3 (Stanford University)	2.3
Burroughs 6700 (University of California, San Diego)	82.0
CDC 6600 (Kirtland Airforce Base)	4.4
CDC Cyber 175 (NASA Langley Research Center)	1.2
CDC 7600 (National Center for Atmospheric Research)	0.87
CDC 7600 (Lawrence Livermore Laboratory)	1.2
CDC 6400 (Northeastern University)	15.0
CDC 6400/6500 (Purdue University)	17.0
CDC 6600/6400 (University of Texas)	5.2

(Table XIB continues)

Table XIB (Continued)

Machine	Execution time (sec)
Honeywell 6070 (Bell Laboratories)	9.6
Univac 1110 (University of Wisconsin)	7.7
DEC KA - PDP - 10 (Yale University)	79.0
AMDAHL 470V/6 (University of Michigan)	2.1

Table XII. Computational Requirements of the SPA Filter

Step	Computation sequence	Operations	Storage
1	$\hat{x}_i(k/k)$		n_i
2	$P_{ii}(k/k)$		n_i^2
3	$\overline{\Phi}_{ii}(k+1, k)$		n_i^2
4	$\overline{\Phi}_{ii}(k+1, k)\hat{x}_i(k/k)$	n_i^2	Store in 1
5	Eq. (186)	$N(2n_i^3)$	n_i^2
6	Eq. (193)	$4n_i^3$	Store in 2
7	Eq. (188)	$q_i^3 + (n_i^2 q_i + n_i q_i^2)N$	q_i^2
8	Eq. (192)	$n_i^2 q_i + 2n_i q_i^2 + q_i^2$	$n_i \times q_i$
9	Eq. (191)	$q_i + 2n_i q_i + (n_i^2 + n_i^2 q_i)N$	Store in 4
10	Eq. (194)	$2n_i^3$	Store in 2
	Total	$2n_i^3(N+3) + n_i^2(1 + 2q_i + N + q_i N) + n_i(q_i^2 N + 2q_i^2 + 2q_i) + q_i^3 + q_i^2 + q_i$	$3n_i^2 + n_i + q_i^2 + n_i q_i$

$N \triangleq$ number of subsystems

$n_i \triangleq$ local system dimension

$q_i \triangleq$ local measurement dimension

Table XIII. Trends in Speed of Computer Operations

Operation	1968 (μsec)	1974 (μsec)	1980 (μsec)
Load	2	1	0.66
Multiply	10	6	2.86
Divide	15	7	5.61
Add	3	2	1.54
Store	2	2	0.44
Increment index register	2	1	0.33

REFERENCES

1. O. NEUGEBAUER, "The Exact Sciences in Antiquity," Princeton Univ. Press., Princeton, New Jersey, 1952.
2. H. W. SORENSON, *IEEE Spectrum 7*, 63-68 (July 1970).
3. R. A. FISHER, "Contributions to Mathematical Statistics," Wiley, New York, 1950.
4. A. N. KOLMOGOROV, *Bull. Acad. Sci., USSR, Math. Ser. 5*, 3-14 (1941).
5. N. WIENER, "The Extrapolation, Interpolation and Smoothing of Stationary Time Series," Wiley, New York, 1949.
6. P. SWERLING, *J. Astron. Sci. 6*, 46-52 (1959).
7. A. G. CARLTON and J. W. FOLLIN, *NATO AGARD. 21* (1956).
8. R. E. KALMAN, *J. Basic Eng. Trans. ASME 82*, 35-45 (1960).
9. R. E. KALMAN and R. S. BUCY, *J. Basic Eng. Trans. ASME 83D*, 95-108 (1961).
10. L. CHIN, "Control and Dynamic Systems," (C. T. Leondes, ed.), Academic Press, New York, 1979.
11. R. H. BATTIN, "Astronautical Guidance," McGraw-Hill, New York, 1964.
12. J. G. BELLANTONI and K. W. DODGE, *AIAA J. 5*(7), 1309-1314 (July 1976).
13. A. ANDREWS, *AIAA J. 6*(6), 1165-1166 (June 1968).

14. S. F. SCHMIDT, *NATO AGARD. 139*, 65-86 (Feb. 1970).

15. J. M. Mendel, *IEEE Trans. Autom. Cont. AC-16*(6), 748-758 (Dec. 1971).

16. P. G. KAMINSKI, A. E. BRYSON, and S. F. SCHMIDT, *IEEE Trans. Autom. Cont. AC-16*(6), 727-736 (Dec. 1971).

17. I. A. GURA and A. B. BIERMAN, *Automatica 7*, 299-313 (1971).

18. J. S. MEDITCH, *Proc. 10th Ann. Allerton Conf. Ckt. Syst. Theory, Univ. Ill.*, 68-75 (Oct. 1972).

19. G. J. BIERMAN, *IEEE Trans. Aero. and Elect. Syst. AES-9*(1), 29 (Jan. 1973).

20. N. A. CARLSON, *AIAA J. 11*(9), 1259-1265 (Sept. 1973).

21. G. J. BIERMAN, *Int. J. Cont. 20*(3), 465-477 (1974).

22. G. J. BIERMAN, *Automatica 10*, 147-158 (1974).

23. G. J. BIERMAN, *J. Optimization Theory Appl. 16*(1 and 2), 165-178 (July 1975).

24. G. J. BIERMAN, *Automatica 12*, 375-382 (1976).

25. R. FLETCHER and M. J. D. POWELL, *Math. Comp. 28*(128), 1067-1087 (Oct. 1974).

26. P. E. GILL, G. H. GOLUB, W. MURRAY, and M. A. SAUNDERS, *Math. Comp. 28*(126), 505-535 (Apr. 1974).

27. T. KAILATH, "Some New Algorithms for Recursive Estimation in Constant Linear Systems," *IEEE Trans. Inf. Theory IT-19*, 750-760 (Nov. 1973)

28. A. LINQUIST, *SIAM J. Cont. 12*, 747-754 (Nov. 1974).

29. A. LINQUIST, *SIAM J. Cont. 12*, 736-746 (Nov. 1974).

30. D. G. LAINIOTIS, *IEEE Trans. Autom. Cont.*, 728-732 (Oct. 1976).

31. R. G. BRAMMER, *IEEE Trans. Inf. Theory 21*, 334-336 (May 1975).

32. D. G. LAINIOTIS, *Proc. IEEE 65*(8), 1126-1143 (1976).

33. D. G. LAINIOTIS, *J. Inf. Sci. 10*(4), 243-278 (June 1976).

34. D. G. LAINIOTIS, *J. Inf. Sci. 7*(3), 317-340 (Nov. 1974).

35. D. G. LAINIOTIS, *IEEE Trans. Autom. Cont. 20*(3), 256-257 (Apr. 1975).

36. D. G. LAINIOTIS, *IEEE Trans. Autom. Contr 20*(4), 255-256 (Aug. 1975).

37. D. G. LAINIOTIS, *Inf. Sci 17*, 177-193 (Jan. 1979).

38. A. H. JAZWINSKI, "Stochastic Processes and Filtering Theory, Academic Press, New York, 1970.

39. A. GELB (ed.), "Applied Optimal Estimation," MIT Press, Cambridge, Massachusetts, 1974.

40. P. S. MAYBECK, "Stochastic Models, Estimation and Control Control," Academic Press, New York, 1979.

41. A. P. SAGE and J. L. MELSA, "Estimation Theory with Applications to Communications and Control," McGraw-Hill, New York, 1971.

42. J. L. MELSA and D. L. COHN, "Decision and Estimation Theory," McGraw-Hill, New York, 1978.

43. B. D. O. ANDERSON and J. B. MOORE, "Optimal Filtering," Prentice-Hall, Englewood Cliffs, New Jersey, 1979.

44. J. S. MEDITCH, "Stochastic Optimal and Linear Estimation and Control," McGraw-Hill, New York, 1969.

45. R. S. BUCY and P. D. JOSEPH, "Filtering for Stochastic Processes with Applications to Guidance," Wiley, New York, 1968.

46. V. N. FADEEVA, "Computational Methods of Linear Algebra," Dover, New York, 1959.

47. G. J. BIERMAN, "Factorization Methods for Discrete Sequential Estimation," Academic Press, New York, 1977.

48. B. D. TAPLEY and C. Y. CHOE, *IEEE Trans. Autom. Cont. AC-21*, 122-123 (Feb. 1976).

49. E. A. BATISTA and E. COSMIDIS, *Proc. 1979 Conf. Model. and Sim., ISA, Pittsburgh PA*, 171-175 (1979).

50. A. S. HOUSEHOLDER, "The Theory of Matrices in Numerical Analysis," Ginn (Blaisdell), Boston, Massachusetts, 1964.

51. G. H. GOLUB, *Numer. Math. 7*, 206-216 (1965).

52. P. BUSINGER and G. H. GOLUB, *Numer. Math 7*, 269-276 (1965).

53. T. JORDAN, *Math. Comput. 20*, 325-328 (1966).

54. R. J. HANSON and C. L. LAWSON, *Math. Comput 23*, 787-812 (1969).

55. H. C. COX, *Proc. JACC*, 376-381 (1964).

56. W. S. AGEE and R. H. TURNER, "Triangular Decomposition of a Positive Definite Matrix Plus a Symmetric Dyad with Application to Kalman Filtering," White Sands Missile Range Tech. Rept. No. 38, 1972.

57. G. J. BIERMAN and C. L. THORNTON, *Automatica 13*, 23-35 (1977).

58. W. M. GENTLEMAN, *J. Inst. Math. Appl. 12*, 329-336 (1973).

59. P. E. GILL, W. MURRAY, and M. A. SAUNDERS, *Math. Comp. 29*(32), 1051-1077 (1975).

60. C. L. THORNTON and G. J. BIERMAN, *Proc. IEEE Cont. Dec. Conf., Houston, Texas*, 489-498 (1975).

61. R. H. WAMPLER, *J. Am. Stat. Assoc. 65*(330), 549-565 (1970).

62. M. MORF, G. S. SIDHU, and T. KAILATH, *IEEE Trans. Autom. Cont. AC-19*, 315-323 (Aug. 1974).

63. M. MORF and T. KAILATH, *IEEE Trans. Autom. Cont. AC-20*(4), 487-497 (Aug. 1975).

64. B. FRIEDLANDER, T. KAILATH, M. MORF, and L. LJUNG, *IEEE Trans. Autom. Cont. AC-23*(4), 653-658 (Aug. 1978).

65. M. MORF, B. LEVY, and T. KAILATH, *IEEE Trans. Autom. Cont. AC-23*(5), 907-911 (Oct. 1978).

66. D. G. LAINIOTIS, *IEEE Trans. Autom. Cont. AC16*(2), 160-170 (Apr. 1971).

67. D. G. LAINIOTIS, *Proc. IEEE 64*(8), 1182-1198 (1976).

68. D. G. LAINIOTIS, *J. Inf. Sci. 7*(3), 203-235 (Nov. 1974).

69. D. G. LAINIOTIS, *Int. J. Cont. 14*(6), 1137-1148 (Dec. 1971).

70. D. G. LAINIOTIS (ed.), "Estimation Theory," Amer. Elsevier, New York, 1974.

71. D. G. LAINIOTIS, *IEEE Trans. Autom. Cont. AC-21*(5), 677-688 (Oct. 1976).

72. D. G. LAINIOTIS, *IEEE Trans. Autom. Cont. AC-21*(5), 728-732 (Oct. 1976).

73. S. K. PARK and D. G. LAINIOTIS, *Int. J. Cont. 16*(6), 1029-1040 (Dec. 1972).

74. D. G. LAINIOTIS, S. K. PARK, and R. KRISHNAIAH, *IEEE Trans. Autom. Cont. AC-16*(2), 197-198 (Apr. 1971).

75. D. G. LAINIOTIS and K. S. GOVINDARAJ, *Proc. IEEE Conf. Dec. Cont., New York* (Dec. 1975).

76. D. G. LAINIOTIS and K. S. GOVINDARAJ, *Proc. IEEE Conf. Dec. Cont., New York* (Dec. 1975).

77. D. G. LAINIOTIS, *Proc. IEEE Conf. Dec. Cont., New York* (Dec. 1975).

78. D. G. LAINIOTIS, *Proc. IEEE Conf. Dec. Cont., New York* (Dec. 1975).

79. D. G. LAINIOTIS, *J. Comp. Elect. Engin. 2*(6), 389-396 (Nov. 1975).

80. D. G. LAINIOTIS and D. ANDRISANI, II, *IEEE Trans. Autom. Cont. AC-24*(6), 937-944 (Dec. 1979).

81. B. J. EULRICH, D. ANDRISANI, and D. G. LAINIOTIS, *IEEE Trans. Autom. Cont. AC-25*(3), 521-528 (June 1980).

82. C. W. SANDERS, E. C. TACKER, and T. D. LINTON, "Decentralized Estimation via Constrained Filters," Tech. Rept. ECE-73-1, Univ. of Wisconsin Press, Madison, 1973.

83. C. W. SANDERS, *Proc. 4th Symp. Nonlinear Est. Theory and Appl., San Diego, CA* (1973).

84. C. W. SANDERS, *Proc. 1974 IEEE Conf. on Dec. and Cont., Phoenix, AZ* (1974).

85. C. W. SANDERS, E. C. TACKER, and T. D. LINTON, *IEEE Trans. Autom. Cont. AC-19*(3), 259-262 (1974).

86. C. W. SANDERS and E. C. TACKER, *Int. J. Cont. 23*(2), 197-206 (1976).

87. C. W. SANDERS, E. C. TACKER, T. D. LINTON, and R. Y. S. LING, *IEEE Trans. Autom. Cont. AC-23*(2), 255-261 (Apr. 1978).

88. T. KERR and L. CHIN, "Advances in the Theory and Technology of Applications of Nonlinear Filter and Kalman Filters," AGARDograph AG-256, pp. 3-1 to 3-39, Noordhoff, Leiden, 1982.

89. M. SHAH, "Suboptimal Filtering Theory for Interacting Control Systems," Ph.D. Dissertation, Cambridge University, Cambridge, England, 1971.

90. T. H. KERR, "Stability Conditions for the RELNAV Community as a Decentralized Estimator," Intermetrics Rept. No. IR-480, March 1980.

91. B. S. GARBOW, "Matrix Eigensystem Routines — EISPACK Guide Extension," Lecture Notes in Computer Science, Vol. 51, Springer-Verlag, Berlin and New York, 1977.

92. E. COSMIDES, "Analysis of Estimation Algorithms," Ph.D. Dissertation, State University of New York at Buffalo, 1981.

Design of Real-Time Estimation Algorithms for Implementation in Microprocessor and Distributed Processor Systems

VYTAS B. GYLYS

*Texas Instruments Inc.
Lewisville, Texas*

ISBN 0-12-012719-9

I. INTRODUCTION

A. *TECHNOLOGICAL PERSPECTIVE*

During the last decade, adoption of microprocessors and distributed systems of micros as hardware for implementation of real-time estimation schemes has proliferated the use of Kalman filters in new and, until recently, undreamed of applications. The new hardware technology and improved theoretical and implementational understanding of Kalman filters have made many of these applications technically feasible. Because the dramatic decrease in the cost of hardware, Kalman filters -- even applications for which a few years ago only a very crude estimator would have been considered -- have become economically attractive. In many newly emergin real-time control systems built on the methodology of artificial intelligence, Kalman filters will continue to play a central role. The new artificial intelligence techniques will help the system "see" and perhaps, to some extent, interpret its own environment. However, the need for a mechanism that would estimate the state of the system will continue to persist. In fact, such future systems will place even higher technical demands on estimation, partly because of the increasing availability of smart sensors (designs of which also exploit the microprocessor and special chip technologies) and an expanding variety of measurements from such sensors.

We complement the preceding philosophical remarks by referring to R. K. Smyth [1], who notes that the advent of microprocessors has started sweeping changes in avionics, one of the main application areas of real-time estimation. He identifies the disciplines and technologies that, according to him, will most likely influence the next generation of systems. They include modular and distributed avionics architectures, modern control (especially state estimation) theory, acceptance of high level programming languages in development of real-time software, radically reduced cost and size of airborne data processing equipment, and newly emerging software design and management techniques.

Successful integration of such diverse factors requires a multidisciplinary approach if the potential synergism is to be exploited. This requires that each specialist member of a multidisciplinary design team understand the other disciplines affecting his aspect of design. As an example, consider a control specialist who is a member of the team entrusted with the design of a real-time estimation scheme. Such a person should be capable of not only performing his traditional functions (such as selecting an appropriate system model and the right estimation algorithms) but also of stating the functional requirements for sensors (whose measurements the estimation scheme is to use) or specifying the mechanization of estimation algorithms in the form of real-time software. Current digital technology makes designing smart sensors, capable of aiding the estimation process, a practically attainable goal. (These are the sensors capable of producing not only the basic estimation measurements but also some system identification data. For example, having such extra information continuously furnished to the estimator may preempt the problem of determining the parameters of noise statistics under severe timing constraints.) In the same vein, understanding the possibilities offered by recent ideas in operating system theory and software engineering may facilitate the transformation of the mathematical model of an estimation scheme (i.e., of estimation algorithms) into robustly working real-time software. This latter aspect of real-time estimator development is the main topic of this chapter.

B. IMPLEMENTAL DESIGN

Development of Kalman filters (or, more generally, of recursive estimators) for real-time applications roughly involves three aspects of design: system modeling, algorithm design, and implemental design. System modeling, although critically important, is very dependent on the problem at hand, so it is not discussed in this chapter. In a wide sense, algorithm design addresses not only the design of kernel estimation algorithms but also the design of complementary procedures such as one whose function is to detect and then respond to detected nonwhite noise in measurements. Algorithm design is extensively covered in current literature. The same cannot be said, however, about the implemental design, i.e., about the process of mapping the algorithms into a system of software procedures that when executed on some target equipment will interact correctly with the environment and among themselves and also will satisfy the real-time constraints of the problem. One possible reason for this paucity of attention in literature to implemental design of real-time estimators is that it cannot be discussed in a mathematically concise way. The other reason, which is probably more fundamental, is that implemental design has been viewed as a domain of programmers.

C. SCOPE AND OBJECTIVES

This chapter addresses estimation and control system specialists who mainly are experts in system modeling and algorithm design but who also would like to learn more about transforming their designs into working real-time schemes. A control specialist must often depend on system programmers or on software engineers who also are members of the design team for advice and contributions. Because the design team is often led by the control specialist, it is important that he know how to communicate with his software counterparts and state the requirements for implemental design. Thus one objective of this chapter is to help a control specialist acquire the technical background for performing these functions.

The level of this chapter is introductory: we assume that the reader knows little about the design of real-time software, especially about its processing environment. Hence, in the following text, we do not discuss a wide spectrum of design possibilities in general but rather concentrate on a few approaches that have been experimentally proved to work, explaining them sometimes in detail. We feel that this will enhance the tutorial value of the exposition. One aspect of implemental design that is stressed is the real-time process control environment for estimation algorithms. However, this is not intended to be a general exposition of real-time operating systems, so here again we take a narrow path through the labyrinth of issues concerned with operating system and software engineering design.

We further narrow the scope of discussion to real-time estimator design for implementation on distributed microprocessor systems, although we use the term "microprocessor" generically: it refers to almost any small computer. However, this restrictive assumption about hardware has implications on the class of control systems considered.

D. BOUNDEDLY LOADABLE SYSTEMS

Currently, distributed systems of small computers are used mainly for small to medium size control systems. Examples of such systems built around estimators are navigation, guidance, and flight control systems, as well as various types of artificial intelligence systems in which the dynamics of system state can be modeled stochastically and must be estimated. We refer to such systems as *boundedly loadable*; i.e., they are a priori designed to take a certain maximum loading, perhaps in the form of fixed maximal rates for measurement inputting and processing. We do this for two reasons: (a) typically, such control systems do not require sophisticated resource allocation algorithms so they are easier to understand; and (b) they are the systems most likely to be implemented on the computers of the type considered here.

As a contrast we could also have considered estimator design for large-scale control systems that are smart enough to select intelligently any additional loading past a near-saturation point so as not to overload themselves and at the same time perform their mission in some optimal way. For convenience we shall call them *nonsaturable* systems. Various large-scale air traffic control and defense systems, discussed in literature during the 60s and 70s, are examples of the latter type of control systems. Although many such systems use estimators as kernel algorithms, they would not (even nowadays) be implemented on distributed systems of small computers. More likely, multiprocessor architectures, augmented with special (such as parallel) processors, would be applied to such a problem. They would also require the use of complex processing resource allocation algorithms and thus of a very different philosophy of real-time processing control from the one presented in the following text. The use of sophisticated resource allocation probably would make centralized processing control preferable. Such processing control schemes are not only more difficult to understand but also much more difficult to validate. Instead, we shall describe what could be characterized as a fixed allocation, decentralized processing control scheme, i.e., decentralized over the processing elements of a distributed system.

The total state of a nonsaturable system is partly defined in terms of the states of N objects currently handled (processed) by the system. For example, if each object represents a tracked aircraft, the state of an object may consist of the description of its position, velocity, and some other parameters. As the number of handled objects increases and as a nonsaturable system approaches its saturation point, the system must decide (typically on the basis of some risk function) which present objects could be deleted at a minimum risk to create processing capacity for newly incoming and possibly more critical objects. Often the estimation procedure for all N objects is nearly identical. In such a situation the use of large-scale computers with parallel or vector pipeline arithmetic units is attractive. This leads to estimators that differ in structure and mechanization from those considered in this chapter, for such large-scale computers can be best exploited if all N parallel estimation processes are centrally controlled.

In contrast, a boundedly loadable system is a priori designed to handle no more than B objects, where B is a fixed small positive integer. Simple, fixed allocation, decentralized real-time process control schemes are effective for boundedly loadable estimation systems.

E. OUTLINE

Typical microprocessor system architectures under consideration consist of small generic building blocks, such as microcomputers, stand-alone direct access memory units, and digital interface units, the latter needed for communications among microcomputers or with the "outside" world. These building blocks are interconnected by means of bus systems and direct access global memory units. Smyth [1] mentions the DAIS and the Draper Laboratory fault-tolerant multiprocessor as prototypes of such new architectures. We shall loosely refer to such architectures, formed from "small" building blocks, as "distributed microprocessor systems." Consequently, we begin (in Section II) by examining the implications of microprocessor use on algorithm design and implementation. Then (in Section III) we proceed to the problem of controlling in real-time the computational processes resulting from the software organization outlined in Section II. Next (in Section IV) we review current practices of Kalman filter design for real-time applications without paying too much attention to the complications imposed by the hardware under consideration. Then (in Section V) we address the problems arising from hardware limitations and timing constraints. That section illustrates techniques for overcoming many of these limitations by decomposing the filter algorithms into concurrently executable procedures. A summary follows in Section VII. Three appendixes follow at the end: Appendix I is a summary of the standard Kalman filtering equations; Appendix II is a review of the so-called U-D factorization algorithms for a Kalman filter; and Appendix III is an outline of a simple estimation problem from GPS navigation, which is referred to as an illustration in text.

In specification of computational algorithms we use ":=" instead of "=" to connect the left- and right-hand sides of assignment statements. The algorithms are stated in a self-explanatory, informal programming language.

II. PROGRAMMING FOR REAL-TIME DISTRIBUTED SYSTEMS

A. *HARDWARE ARCHITECTURE*

For the development of the main theme we need a generic model of hardware architecture. Thus, we view distributed systems considered here as built from constituent computers by interconnecting these computers either through shared, directly accessed global memory units or through data links (buses). These links may vary in speed, parallelism, and length. Obviously some distributed systems use both types of interconnections, i.e., direct access global memory units as well as buses.

For our purposes a constituent processing element of any distributed system under consideration is assumed to be a small computer, not necessarily a "microcomputer" in the strict sense of the term, which consists of a CPU (an instruction/arithmetic processing unit) and interconnection ports/devices. It usually has some local (or private) memory and may also have special devices, such as a floating-point arithmetic unit, connected to it. In the following text such a constituent computer of a distributed system, regardless of whether it is a microcomputer or a computer of some different type, is called a *processing element* (PE). As a special case, the entire distributed system may consist of a single PE. If a PE accesses both global and local memories, then its instruction address space must possess facilities to address both types of memories.

Another building block needed for the assumed model of distributed systems is a global data memory unit. "Data" refers here to the read-write and random access properties of such memory, whereas "global" emphasizes that such a memory unit is accessible from at least two processing elements. In contrast, a processing element may have two types of local memory: *local data memory* for storing the problem data, which does not have to be communicated to other processing elements, and *local program memory* of the read-only type for storing the instructions of programs residing in that processing element. In our model of a distributed system, executable instructions of a program are always assumed to be stored in the local memory of a processing element.

As an aside, many ideas presented in the following text apply to hardware architectures more general than the one just introduced. For example, we could have considered hierarchical distributed systems in which some processing elements themselves are distributed systems, or distributed systems each processing element of which is a multiprocessor system by itself, consisting of several CPUs interconnected by common access memory modules. But the generic model introduced earlier, which is simpler and less centralized than the architectures mentioned in this paragraph, can be effectively used with a relatively simple real-time operating system. Furthermore, it is sufficient for the applications considered here, so it will be assumed in the following text.

B. PROCESSES EXECUTED IN A DISTRIBUTED SYSTEM

The notion of a (computational) process is fundamental to the modern theory of operating systems and is discussed in recent texts on operating systems and system programming (e.g., [2-5]. It is also used extensively in the following text to explain our models of real-time software and real-time process control. The term "process" will describe the behavior or, say, the dynamics of a computer program that is "residing" in a computer regardless of whether at the moment this program is executing or is in a dormant state.

Freeman [3, p. 108] further elaborates the concept of a process by noting that (the notion of) a program usually specifies a single and isolated sequence of actions; hence, if we admit the possibility that the execution of a program may be interrupted intermittently by the operating system to lend the system resources to other (perhaps more urgent) work, it becomes necessary to supplement such an interruptable program with information that will enable the operating system to resume the execution of the program after each interrupt. This leads to the notion of program "in execution," which at any particular moment is not necessarily actively executed. Thus, in a system, a process may be viewed to be a program (which specifies a sequence of data processing actions) supplemented with state information (which fully describes the current state of the program).

Thus a single process is just a generalization, or an abstraction, of a processor moving through the text of a computer program. However, one additional idea is implied: there exists a controlling mechanism (an operating system) that is keeping track of the state of the processing resources (hardware, data, and programs) being used by or reserved for the executing programs. Keeping track of the state becomes important if the execution of a program can be temporarily interrupted by the operating system in favor of another waiting program.

Analogous to finite automata theory, it is convenient to characterize a process by describing the *process states* that such a process may attain and by defining the rules that govern transitions among these states. When a program is in execution or is considered by the operating system to be scheduled and executed, we say that the process created by that program is in an *active state*; otherwise the process is said to be in an *inactive state*. Typically, there is only one inactive state.

The concept of a process is a powerful tool for understanding, modeling, and designing a computer system in which several programs reside in memory simultaneously so that the central processor of the computer (which in our case is a processing element of the distributed system) keeps switching among them according to some scheme or schedule. In such a situation, processes created by these programs are said to be executing *concurrently*, i.e., interleaved in time. The resulting processing environment is called *multiprogrammed processing*. This is the processing model that we assume for estimation schemes executed on a distributed system, or even on a single processing element.

When a distributed system is operating, several processes may be executed concurrently. Concurrent execution of processes can occur in several ways. On a single processing element of a distributed system, for example, processes may be executed interleaved in time by dividing the time line into segments and alternating the processes among segments such that the process that initiates execution at the start of a segment is interrupted at its end, at which time the use of the processor is passed to another process. Thus concurrent processes may occur under multiprogramming, even on a single processor. Another form of concurrent process execution in a distributed system arises when processes are executed *simultaneously* and possibly asynchronously in several processing elements of the system.

The hardware facilities needed for data communications among two communicating concurrent processes depend on where these processes are executed. If they are executed in interleaved time fashion within the same processing element, the local data memory unit of that processing element, provided that such a unit exists, may be used for communications among processes; otherwise a global data memory unit, accessible from that processing element, is needed. On the other hand, if two communicating concurrent processes are executed on different processsing elements, then the following two (not necessarily mutually exclusive) possibilites exist: either a mutually accessible global memory unit is available or data links (buses) interconnecting the system are needed.

The designer of a real-time control system is responsible for structuring algorithms so that they result in computational processes that properly cooperate among themselves in real time; i.e., they are appropriately synchronized and can correctly communicate (exchange) data. Selection of an appropriate programming language and access to convenient real-time process management utilities (the latter to be furnished by the real-time operating system) will make the designer's work easier. Still, in order to be assured about the implementability of design, he must conceptually understand the logical consequences of process synchronization and communication requirements and must be capable of translating these requirements into his design. The purpose of Section III is to introduce process management concepts and techniques that have proved themselves in implementation of real-time estimation schemes.

C. SOFTWARE MODEL

Work-load partitioning, algorithm scheduling, and memory sizing are critical tasks in the design of real-time control (in our case, estimation) systems for implementation under hardware constraints. These tasks are started early in the development cycle, usually during preproposal investigations, and are reiterated many times thereafter until a design that satisfies requirement specifications emerges. The capability to transform algorithms into working real-time software is the key to success in this endeavor. This process of implemental design is greatly helped by having a suitable model of software architecture. As will become evident in Section III, such a model is also needed for design of a real-time operating system.

The software model introduced next is intended for a boundedly loadable system that is to be implemented on a distributed system of small computers or even on a single microprocessor. This model assumes that some extended form of FORTRAN is used as the programming language. It will be mentioned in the following text how a software model for an ALGOL related language, such as ADA, would differ from the model to be introduced next.

MODEL

(a) The entire real-time applications software used to implement a control scheme is partitioned into a set of programs and data structures.

(b) Each program contains a *main procedure* and may also contain *subprograms* (subordinate or lower-level procedures).

(c) Each program can create precisely one real-time process (which may remain inactive), so there is *one-to-one correspondence between programs and processes*. (This assumption is not too restrictive for boundedly loadable systems implemented on small computers. Besides, the resulting implementation can be more easily understood and tested than that of a system with no restrictions on the extent of reentrance. Here a program unit is said to be *reentrant* if it may be shared or executed concurrently by several processes at a time.)

(d) Subprograms of the following two types are admissible: *private subprograms* -- such a subprogram belongs to a single program and, by assumption (c), to a single process because it may be invoked only from that program; and *shared subprograms* -- such a subprogram may be invoked from several programs and used by the processes generated by these programs. Shared subprograms must be implemented as reentrant procedures, but only as reentrant procedures of a priori known maximum concurrency.

(e) *Fixed allocation* of programs to a processing element is used: at design time each program is assigned to a single processing element and is never "split" among several processing elements. In the event that software redundancy can be tolerated, the present assumption does not forbid assigning replicas of a program (or of a subprogram) to processing elements, or even to a single processing element.

(f) With assumptions (c) and (d), data sets of applications programs can be hierarchically divided into three globality levels: *interprocess (interprogram) communication* data sets; *intraprocess (intraprogram) communication* data sets; and *local* data sets. For example, when FORTRAN (possibly extended to handle limited reentrance) is used as a programming language, interprocess and intraprocess communication data sets are implemented as labeled COMMON blocks and local data sets as locally declared data with special provisions made for handling local variables in reentrant procedures. Furthermore, variables and constants are always placed into separate data sets. To distinguish between two types of constants (i.e., between physical constants, such as the speed of light or the equatorial radius of a reference ellipsoid and design parameters, such as the length of a state vector, which may change as the design progresses, but become constants by the time it is completed) they are put into separate data sets.

Although the use of an ALGOL-like programming language, such as ADA [6], instead of FORTRAN would hardly perturb the model just described, it would affect the format and structure of the source program. First, the nested block structure of an ALGOL-like language facilitates the hierarchical nesting of procedures (private to a program) and the corresponding nesting of data sets according to the globality (scope) of data access. Furthermore, ADA provides basic language constructs for defining and implementing process control and synchronization mechanisms, such as the mechanism for synchronized communications among concurrent processes discussed in Section III. (For more information on this subject, refer to the discussion of multitasking in [6].)

D. *IMPLICATIONS ON ALGORITHM DESIGN*

Adoption of distributed microprocessor systems as hardware has far-reaching implications on algorithm design. To meet the real-time response constraints while not exceeding the throughput capacity of individual processing elements, the entire estimation procedure must be partitioned into concurrently executable and interacting processes. The main implications of the resulting work-load partitioning are that some algorithms will be decomposed into a set of concurrently executable smaller algorithms, the functional performance of which may not be as good as that of the original algorithm.

In the second part of this chapter we shall review several common decomposition schemes for a Kalman filter. It will suffice to mention at this point that for a recursive estimator, such as a Kalman filter, the covariance processing and the computation of Kalman gains are time-consuming procedures on a microprocessor and so may become prohibitively expensive if the microprocessor has no hardware-implemented floating arithmetic and if, consequently, all floating-point computing must be performed in interpretive form. On the other hand, there may exist a requirement, or just a need, to process the incoming measurements at a rate that would exceed the processing capacity of a processing element, i.e., that would "bust" its time line. As explained in the second part of this chapter, this problem has several solutions, each of which results in suboptimal performance.

According to our previous characterization of distributed microprocessor systems, it would seem that such a system could be incremented in small steps by adding to it, on the basis of need, processing elements, global data memory units, and other special boxes. Besides, hardware costs are relatively low. Then what are the reasons for having to struggle with an austere hardware budget? The answer to this question is that in estimation applications considered here severe constraints are typically imposed on the power consumption, volume, and weight of equipment. Besides, if the equipment under consideration is to be manufactured in large quantities, even small savings in cost per unit count. Another reason is the "smallness" of individual processing elements. For example, a single element may not have sufficient throughput capacity to accommodate a Kalman filter with a minimally acceptable rate of measurement processing. On the other hand, we may not want to split the filter algorithm between two processing elements for reasons such as the complexity or degraded performance of the modified algorith.

E. PARTITIONING OF WORK LOAD

During a design cycle the processing work load resulting from algorithms is several times repartitioned into concurrent processes until a satisfactory partitioning is obtained. We say that a work-load partitioning is acceptable if it (a) satisfies the overall hardware budget, (b) does not overload individual processing elements, (c) yields minimally required or better execution rates to time-critical algorithms, (d) does not appreciably degrade the functional performance of algorithms through their decomposition, (e) does not excessively complicate the overall structure of real-time software, and (f) does not cause too much real-time processing overhead through introduced concurrencies.

It is difficult to satisfy this long list of requirements without some compromises. However, the first four are essential to the implementability and the performance of design.

Work-load partitioning is a critical design issue in distributed real-time processing. Thus when the interest in such processing began to emerge, attempts were made to formulate the principles and derive the algorithms for optimal work-load partitioning. Samples of work from that period are [7] and [8]. Later design experience showed that it is best to take a heuristic approach roughly based on the following principles:

(a) Distribute the work load over the processing elements (PEs) to minimize the level of communications among the processes executed on different PEs, thus minimizing the inter-PE data traffic and the use of global data memory while not overloading individual PEs.

(b) Decompose the work load assigned to a PE into processes so that the tasks that must run at about the same rate and can be executed at about the same time are assigned to the same process and thus are implemented as part of the same program.

(c) Guarantee that all time-critical algorithms (in their original or in a decomposed form) will be executed at acceptable rates.

Ideally, hardware requirements should be stipulated as a by-product of completed work-load partitioning, but in practice this is seldom the case.

It should be evident from the foregoing that the quantitative prediction of processor and memory loading must be obtained for each candidate partitioning before it can be evaluated. This is one reason why software timing and sizing, as pointed out previously, are so critical in design of real-time computing systems.

F. PREDICTION OF PROCESSOR AND MEMORY LOADINGS

Real-time system designers often refer to the task concerned with the prediction of processor and memory loadings as *software timing and sizing* (ST&S). This task produces input data for work-load partitioning and also evaluates candidate partitioning schemes. It is therefore reiterated several times during the development cycle of a real-time system.

Load prediction requires much clerical effort (compilation and tabulation of input data, performance of arithmetic, and generation of reports). Hence, these tasks must be computerized. After this has been done, the effort is essentially reduced to the derivation of execution timing and memory occupancy estimates for individual modules of the currently tentative software model. Once the ST&S data base has been established by entering in it the initial timing and sizing estimates for individual modules, it needs only to be updated as better estimates become available.

Even the modeling of execution timing and memory occupancy for individual modules can be expedited by means of automated data processing techniques. As an example, the following methods have been found to be useful:

(a) extend the compiler of the programming language to enable it, as a by-product of compilation, (i) to segment the source code into blocks, each block ending with a branch operation, then (ii) to time each block while using an inputted timing model of the target machine, and (iii) to estimate the memory requirements of each module of executable code and of each data set defined in the source code;

(b) use an instruction-level simulator to derive a timing model of each program, based on the a priori inputted probabilities or on the experimentally observed frequencies of various execution paths.

With the information provided by (i) and (ii) of method (a), one can quickly time the most critical execution paths and compute the memory requirements of software design.

Method (b) produces a probabilistic model of processor loading and data memory occupancy, so its ourputs in a sense complement those of method (a).

After either (a) or (b) has been accomplished the first time, the obtained processor timing and memory sizing data can be entered in the software model data base. Thereafter, as the design progresses toward maturity, the processor and memory loading predictions need only to be iteratively refined.

These techniques presuppose the availability of some source code. Often the source code of key algorithms becomes available early during the development cycle and can be used to bootstrap the timing and sizing process by means of the previously described techniques. Typically, these algorithms are programmed early in the high-level language of the ultimate real-time code for performance analysis simulations on a large computer in non-real-time mode.

In the event that the source code of key algorithms is not available when the timing and sizing process must be bootstrapped, one may resort to mathematical timing and sizing models of key algorithms. For a Kalman filter or a similar estimator, such a model is formulated in terms of the state vector and measurement vector lengths; it predicts the timing in terms of basic arithmetic operation counts and the memory occupancy in terms of memory needed to store the principal vectors and matrices. References [9], [10], and [11] contain such loading prediction models for the estimation algorithms considered later.

G. DATA IDENTIFICATION

Experience in implemental design of real-time estimation systems has taught a bitter lesson about the identification of time- and source-dependent data. Implicit identification techniques, based on the order in which data arrives (or is generated) or dependent on the location where it is placed, are often favored by novice designers. But they are dangerous: some data may arrive late or never; some sources may intermittently fail to send data; the implicit identification of data by position in an array may be perturbed by the deletion or addition of sources. Also, implicit identification techniques lead to awkward software designs that cannot be modified easily.

Explicit identification of data and events and recording of their reference times constitute a safer approach. Explicit identification also leads to a more flexible implementation in the sense that the meaning of real-time data no longer depends on the time when it becomes available and on the memory location where it can be found.

Technically, explicit identification means that every data group (or record of an even) that is time dependent is time tagged by its reference time. Similarly, every source-dependent data group is tagged with the identification (ID) of its source. For example, suppose that a real-time Kalman filter, used for target tracking, operates on range and range-rate measurements of tracked targets. Then every simultaneous batch of range and range-rate measurements is time-tagged, say, with the estimated time at which the radar signal is reflected from the target or with the observed time at which the signal is returned. Furthermore, as new targets are detected and go into tracking, they are assigned explicit and unique target IDs.

To facilitate the time tagging of real-time data and events, a clock is needed. Such a clock, which will be called the *system control clock*, is usually hardware implemented and is driven by an oscillator. The time of this clock must be available to all processing elements of a distributed system. In Section III.C we outline how the system control clock can be used to synchronize processes over the entire distributed system. Such a clock is needed even in a uniprocessor (not necessarily multiprogrammed) real-time system. Computational processes retrieve the time of this clock by calling a special subprogram.

H. SOFTWARE DEVELOPMENT METHODOLOGY AND TOOLS

During the 1970s a great deal of progress was scored in the areas of software engineering and software development management. Some of the events contributing to this progress were the emergence of a robust programming style, known as *structured programming*, of software development management techniques such as the *chief programmer's team*, and of computer-aided software development and software management tools such as interactive program development terminals, data base management systems, or programming languages amenable to structured programming and concurrent processing.

These techniques and tools are useful in the development of real-time software for the multiprogrammed processing environment, but they are well covered in the literature and thus are not addressed here. The only thing we want to note is that the software development for the applications and for the processing environment considered here requires a hierarchical sequence of simulations.

One starts with high-level functional simulations of key algorithms in order to validate their performance and to determine the required processing rates. These high-level simulations are usually put together and performed by the person responsible for algorithm design. Typically they are performed off-line (i.e., not in real time) on a large-scale computer system. The insights obtained from such simulations facilitate the timing and sizing of software and the partitioning of work load for real-time implementation.

As the design process progresses and as the designer begins to think about the implementation of algorithms for the real-time processing environment, he starts (guided by the feedback from the performance analysis, the tentative work-load partitioning scheme, and the results of software timing and sizing) to modify and restructure them. In this effort he continues to use the off-line simulator as a testbed. If this iterative process of design refinement is continued long enough, the modeled real-time software and algorithms begin to look increasingly similar to the ultimate product. At the same time, the level of simulations progressively goes down as more details are modeled, simulated, and investigated.

Ultimately, the off-line simulation process reaches a point of diminishing returns, primarily because of the difficulties in creating sufficiently realistic simulation scenarios, needed for complete validation of design, and in modeling with fidelity interactions among concurrent processes. Also at this time, partly tested real-time software for the target hardware usually becomes available. This availability can be speeded up by copying pertinent portions of off-line simulation software and then embedding the copied software into the prepared control structure of real-time software.

The next step is to switch to on-line (or real-time) simulations in which the actual real-time hardware and software are driven by *special test equipment*. To serve its purpose, such test equipment must

(a) be capable of generating (or acquiring) at real-time rates the measurements and other system inputs that would be highly similar, if not identical, to the actual measurements (inputs) of the target operational system and

(b) possess built-in facilities for collecting and reporting performance data.

For comparison, it is desirable that the performance analysis reports generated in simulations on the special test equipment be designed to look similar in form and content to the performance reports generated in off-line simulations. Finally, for testing various failure modes, the special test equipment must be capable of generating a wide range of extreme measurements and inputs. Examples of such special test equipment are briefly mentioned in [12] and [13].

III. CONTROL OF REAL-TIME PROCESSES

A. *INTRODUCTION*

The modern theory of operating systems, based on the concepts of *process (task)* and of *process management*, furnishes powerful tools for understanding and designing not only the operating systems but also the applications software executed under the control of an operating system. (In the following text the term "applications software," in contrast to "system software," will refer to those parts of real-time software that implement control or estimation algorithms; analogous meanings will also apply to "applications program" and "applications process.") In real-time multiprogrammed computing the applications processes are more intertwined with process state control than in non-real-time environment. Hence, the designer of such applications software needs to understand certain aspects of process management to be able to come up with a working implemental design. In contrast, a casual non-real-time scientific programmer, who programs in a high-level programming language, rarely needs to know much about the operating system beyond specifying his job to the operating system, getting it into the computer, and writing input and output statements. Thus he can perform his functions almost without any understanding of the actual environment in which his program is executed.

Understanding of the following aspects of process management, we think, is essential to a designer of a real-time multiprogrammed control system: resource allocation, process synchronization, process scheduling, and interprocess communications. Hence, the purpose of this section is to serve as a review of these as well as other related aspects of process management. We shall henceforth use the term "real-time executive," or its abbreviated form "RT executive," to refer to a real-time operating system. Also we shall use the terms "process management" and "process control" synonymously.

B. FUNDAMENTAL ISSUES OF PROCESS MANAGEMENT

In the description of a software model for a distributed system, we assumed multiprogramming as the program execution environment in the processing elements (PEs) of such a system. We also noted that concurrent processes executed within a processing element, or in several different processing elements, communicate among themselves through exchange of problem and control data. Next we review fundamental issues of process management in the multiprogrammed multiprocessing environment to establish a perspective for the design approach described in the latter parts of this section.

These fundamental issues, well known in operating system theory, are *mutual exclusion*, *synchronization*, *deadlocks* and their prevention, and interprocess *communications*. *Critical regions* and *communication primitives* are presented as techniques for implementing mutual exclusion and synchronization. There are two additional issues of process management, allocation of memory resources and allocation of processor time (or scheduling), that will be addressed in Sections III.C-E. Because of the limitation of space, this exposition of fundamental issues is more concise that it ought to be. The issues are discussed only to the extent needed to make the reader aware of their existence and criticality. For a more detailed exposition, the reader is referred to recent texts on operating systems and system programming such as [2-5] or [14]. References [3] and [4] are readable, elementary expositions of the topic, written mainly for aspiring system programmers; [5] and [14] are more detailed but still elementary texts, less advanced than [2].

1. Critical Regions

Consider a computer program, say $PROG_j$, and the process P_j created by execution of this program. A *critical region* (CR) of program $PROG_j$ is an executable segment of instructions in $PROG_j$, the executions of which may produce unpredictable and varying results if the values of some variables referenced from within this CR are changed by another process, say P_k, while P_j is executing the CR. Here P_k is assumed to be a process concurrent with P_j. Such unpredictable results may occur if (a) we do not know anything about the relative speeds of processes P_j and P_k and (b) we do not program $PROG_j$ and $PROG_k$ to prevent the unpredictable results.

If program segments CR_j and CR_k are critical regions in concurrently executed programs $PROG_j$ and $PROG_k$, respectively, then two mutually exclusive possibilities exist: either CR_j and CR_k are critical with respect to each other (because each of them accesses the same data) or else CR_j and CR_k are mutually not critical (because each of them operates on different data). In the latter case, each of these two critical regions is critical with respect to other program segments. Hence, to be precise about a critical region, one must also specify the data set with respect to which the CR is critical. In the preceding paragraph we could have done it by writing $CR_j(D)$ and $CR_k(D)$, where D would have referred to a mutually accessed data set.

The next example illustrates the use of critical regions in a Kalman filter.

EXAMPLE: Unpredictable results in a parallel-mechanized Kalman filter. Suppose that:

(a) process P_s propagates the state vector $\underline{s}$, predicts the measurement vector $\underline{m}$, stores (perhaps occasionally) in a buffer the data needed for computation of linearized state-to-measurement transformations H, computes residuals, retrieves Kalman gains K computed by process P_c, and applies them to update $\underline{s}$;

(b) process P_c propagates the state error covariance matrix P, retrieves the data for computation of H, computes Kalman gains K, and updates P.

Two segments in program $PROG_s$ are critical regions: one, say, $CR_{s1}(H)$, contains the code for storing in a record (from which P_c reads) the data for computation of H; the other, say, $CR_{s2}(K)$, copies (from the array into which P_c writes) for its own use the Kalman gains K computed by P_c. Similarly, there are two corresponding segments in program $PROG_c$, which also are critical regions: one [denoted by $CR_{c1}(H)$] retrieves the data for computation of H; the other [to be denoted by $CR_{c2}(K)$] stores the computed Kalman gains. If the relative speeds of processes P_s and P_c are unpredictable (even if they are executed concurrently on the same processing element) and if no precautions are made to synchronize or otherwise regulate P_s and P_c in accessing mutually accessed data, then the results are unpredictable.

Section E is a review of interprocess communication techniques for preventing such unpredictable outcomes. The preceding illustrations lead to the first fundamental issue of process management, *mutual exclusion* of communicating processes, which we discuss next.

2. *Mutual Exclusion*

Mutual exclusion of interdependent processes (of each process with respect to a mutually related critical region in its own generating program) means that no more than one process can be in its critical region at a given time. We say that a *process is in a critical region* if it has already started the execution of the first executable instruction of this region but has not yet completed the execution of the last. Thus the statement "the time when process P is in a critical region CR" refers to the entire time interval during which the previously defined conditions hold, i.e., to the time interval spanned by the following two events: "P has entered CR" (P has started the execution of the first instruction of CR) and "P has left CR" (P has completed the execution of the last instruction).

We assumed in the preceding the *principle of indivisibility of instruction execution*. According to this principle execution of an instruction, such as storing a quantity into a memory location or reading one from it, is an indivisible operation in the sense that the action performed by such an instruction cannot be interrupted after its execution has been started and before it is completed. By programming a short uninterruptable procedure we can generalize this concept to an "indivisible macrooperation." In Section E we discuss the use of such indivisible macrooperations (or procedures) in construction of *communication primitives*. These will be uninterruptable segments of code, sometimes implemented as uninterruptable subprograms, designed to protect entries to and handle exits from critical regions.

3. Synchronization

Synchronization of a process P_i with some other process P_j, where $i \neq j$, or with several other processes means ensuring that P_i will not proceed past some given point without an explicit signal, which P_i itself cannot generate because of the lack of information about process P_j. Hence this information must be explicitly or implicitly provided to P_i from outside, i.e., by P_j, by other processes, or by the real-time executive. Note that strictly sequential processing on a single processor does not require any synchronization information.

A real-time executive passes synchronization information implicitly by scheduling processes for execution. Explicit exchange of synchronization information among concurrent processes generally requires the use of critical regions serviced by appropriate communication primitives.

4. Deadlocks

Two processes are said to be *deadlocked* if neither can continue until the other continues. A system deadlock occurs when all processes in the system become deadlocked.

Two concurrent processes P_1 and P_2, communicating through the execution of critical regions CR_1 and CR_2, respectively, may become deadlocked if the critical regions are improperly implemented, for example, if P_1 hangs up after entering CR_1 when it finds out that P_2 meanwhile has entered CR_2, and vice versa.

As pointed out in literature on operating system concepts (e.g., [3, p. 157]), the occurrence of a deadlock is defined by the *simultaneous* coexistence of the following conditions.

(a) Processes claim exclusive control of the resources that they need for execution.

(b) Processes hold resources already allocated to them while awaiting additionally needed resources.

(c) Resources cannot be forcibly removed from the processes holding them until these processes no longer need them.

(d) There exists a circular chain of processes such that each process in the chain holds some resources requested by the next process in the chain.

Although there is often little probability of a deadlock in a typical multiprogrammed system designed without any safeguards against deadlocks, it is imperative that any real-time system be designed so that deadlocks in such a system cannot occur, i.e., so the preceding four conditions can never be satisfied simultaneously. In applications considered here we can attain this objective by proper design of communication primitives and by requiring that no process by design be allowed to stay in a critical region longer than some a priori set length of time.

C. DECENTRALIZED REAL-TIME EXECUTIVE WITH FIXED RESOURCE ALLOCATION

Next we characterize (as an illustration) a class of RT executives, several variations of which were successfully used in Phase I GPS (Global Positioning System) navigation user equipment sets designed by Texas Instruments (References [12],

[13], and [15] describe the navigation filters used in these sets). The main features of this class of RT executives are as follows.

(a) *Decentralized control* -- each processing element (PE) has its own autonomously functioning RT executive that supports multiprogrammed execution of concurrent processes in the PE.

(b) *Fixed allocation* -- there is fixed allocation of PEs to programs and of memory to global data sets, with the assumption that the software model defined in Section II.C is used (one implication of which is one-to-one correspondence between programs and processes).

(c) *Synchronization of processes* -- processes executed in the distributed system and data communications among these processes are synchronized by means of periodic, systemwide interrupts. For this purpose, the time line is decomposed into consecutive intervals of fixed length Δt and an interrupt is broadcast systemwide at the end of each interval. Such intervals are often called *fundamental time frames* (FTFs). The jth processing element PE_j may be set up to respond only to every (n_j)th interrupt and to ignore the others. Typically, n_j is chosen so that $(n_j)\Delta t$ equals the period of the highest-rate, periodically executed process in PE_j.

(d) *Restricted reentrance* -- because (according to the software model outlined in Section II.C) there is one-to-one correspondence between the programs and the processes created by these programs, subprograms concurrently shared by at least two processes are implemented either as uninterruptable procedures (if they are executed fast) or as reentrant procedures of a priori maximum reentrance.

(e) *Scheduling* -- three types of processes are admissible and characterized according to the way they are scheduled.

(1) *Cyclic (C-) processes* -- such a process is executed at a fixed rate, with the stipulated execution rate guaranteed to be met.

(2) *Deadline (D-) processes* -- each time such a process is scheduled, the deadline of its execution completion is specified; the RT executive tries to meet but does not guarantee this deadline.

(3) *Background (B-) processes* -- such a process is allocated all the processing time of a PE that remains after (or between) execution of foreground and deadline processes; at any time at most a single active background process is allowed in a PE.

Scheduling of processes is further discussed in Section D.

(f) *Interprocess communications* -- depending on the nature of interaction between two processes, only the first or both of the following interprocess communication types are permitted without further reservations than those stated.

(1) Critical regions (sections), protected/controlled by the WAIT and SIGNAL communication primitives, may be used to implement data communications among any two concurrent processes.

(2) Data buffers, whose access is controlled by a SET/RESET flag, may be used to implement certain types of one-way communications between two cyclic processes, scheduled at about the same rate, whose executions are usually not interleaved in split fashion; i.e., if A and B are two such processes, then when process

A starts execution, it usually completes this execution before B can start its next execution.

Interprocess communications are further discussed in greater detail in Section E.

D. *PROCESS SCHEDULING AND PROCESS STATE CONTROL*

1. *Scheduling Philosophy and Requirements*

Process scheduling allocates the processor time to processes and thus determines when processes will be executed. Because scheduling also influences the structuring of algorithms into concurrent processes, it is an important issue of real-time design. Under the decentralized process control scheme introduced in this section, all processes assigned to a processing element, with one exception, are scheduled independently of processes executed on other processing elements. The exception applies to cyclically scheduled processes, which may be synchronized systemwide by means of systemwide timer interrupts.

Scheduling can be best explained through process states and process state control. This is the approach we take in the present section. However, we proceed with the discussion of process state control only to the extent needed to define selected scheduling strategies for the decentralized, fixed allocation scheme introduced in the preceding section. Coffman [2] and [16] discusses process scheduling on an advanced (abstract) level; in References [3], [5], and [14] the authors deal with it on a more elementary (less mathematical) level. In References [17], [18], [20], and [21] the narrow viewpoint on real-time scheduling taken in the present chapter is supplemented.

As previously noted, process scheduling may be best introduced by defining the states that a process of a specified type may attain and then by defining the rules governing state transitions. We do this, but in an informal fashion. Implementational design of a scheduler for a real-time executive is a task that is usually delegated to system programmers; thus a control specialist is seldom concerned with its details. He primarily needs to understand, in addition to the information conveyed by the state transition graphs, the scheduling priorities of processes and the facilities provided by the real-time executive for defining a process and for changing process states.

Many strategies are possible for setting scheduling priorities. In the literature (e.g., [3]), priority disciplines are often divided into two major classes.

(a) *Static priorities* -- such a priority is set a priori in the sense that it cannot change while the process to which it applies is in an active state.

(b) *Dynamic priorities* -- such a priority may change while the process to which it applies is in an active state.

In contrast to non-real-time systems, scheduling of real-time processes requires some use of dynamic priorities or perhaps a mixture of static and dynamic priorities. This becomes clearer if one recalls that in a general non-real-time system, (a) very little is known about the incoming jobs (processes); (b) incoming jobs are imprecisely characterized as they come into the system; and (c) the optimality criteria, such as maximizing the throughput without much regard for the turnaround time of individual jobs, make sense. Besides, the techniques for implementing schedulers operating on fixed priorities are more easily understood. These observations explain why static priorities are so widely used in general, non-real-time processing.

The main objective of scheduling in the real-time applications considered here is to meet the response-time constraints required for specified performance while minimizing the cost of hardware or while staying within the allocated hardware budget. Designing a real-time scheduler operating with fixed priorities is not difficult if the available hardware resources are comfortably adequate. For example, Jordan [19] discusses a simple scheme for doing it by means of an a priori fixed multiharmonic scheduling pattern. We could proceed similarly, because nearly all processing load in the applications considered here is owing to the algorithms that must be periodically reexecuted. We called these cyclic algorithms. Usually it is not difficult to (a) identify a cyclic algorithm with the shortest period, say T_0; (b) define a harmonic hierarchy of h periods ΔT_0, ΔT_1, ΔT_2, ..., ΔT_h such that $\Delta T_k = 2\Delta T_{k-1}$ for k = 1, ..., h; and (c) assign every cyclic algorithm to a period class. Jordan then uses this technique as a basis for constructing a multiharmonic scheduling pattern. But such an approach, based on the estimates of algorithm maximum execution times, underutilizes the available processor resources.

A more flexible approach is to classify all procedures and/or algorithms into three categories: (a) those with periodic rates that cannot be slipped because of the enormous penalty that would have to be paid otherwise (in estimation work these typically are the procedures that logically control the estimation scheme but are not the estimation algorithms themselves); (b) those having period boundaries that represent the desired but not absolutely required completion deadlines (in estimation work these are the estimation algorithms); and (c) noncyclic procedures/algorithms that must be executed only occasionally, owing to special conditions that may arise, and that typically have no strict deadline (for example, a filter initialization procedure). This leads to the three types of processes (cyclic, deadline, and background) introduced in Section C.

2. *Process Types, Their States and State Transitions*

Nearly all real-time estimation schemes of the type considered here can be realized by means of these three types of processes (cyclic, deadline, and background). Hence we next characterize these processes in greater detail than previously and, by means of the state graphs shown in Fig. 1, define their states and the rules governing state transitions.

(a) *Cyclic (C-) processes* -- at the beginning of each new cycle (scheduling/execution period) of an active cyclic process, the RT executive automatically puts this process into the ready state so that the process can always be executed within each cycle, with the events representing the starting time and the completion time of an execution instance not separated by the boundary of a period. In other words, these two events are always located within the time interval spanning a single scheduling/execution period. As indicated in Fig. 1, a cyclic process, after it becomes activated by another process or by the RT executive, remains active until it becomes explicitly deactivated (which is not shown in the state transition diagram) by a process or by the RT executive.

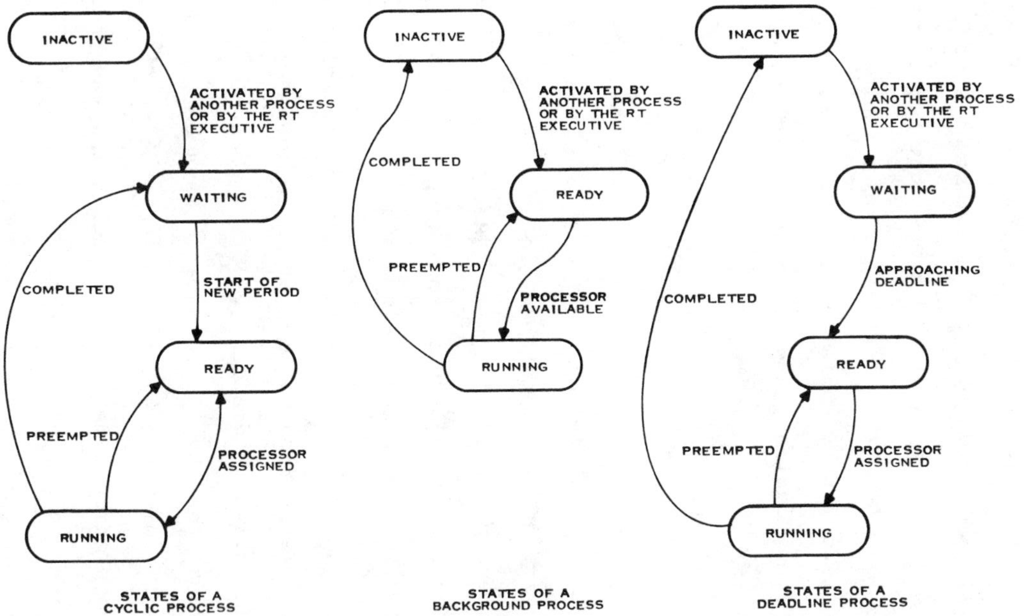

Fig. 1. State transitions of three process types. To not clutter up the diagram, it is not shown here (although assumed) that a process of any of the above three types may be deactivated from any of its active states.

(b) *Deadline (D-) process* -- such a process must be activated by another process or by the RT executive. With each activation, one needs to specify the completion deadline. The scheduler of RT executive does its best to meet the specified deadline or at least to minimize slipping the deadline. After the completion of each execution, a deadline process automatically returns to the inactive state.

(c) *Background (B-) processes* -- at most one active background process at a time is allowed in a processing element of a distributed system. Such a process is then given all processor time that remains after all currently active cyclic and deadline processes have been serviced. After each complete execution pass, a background process automatically returns to the inactive state.

It is further assumed that a process of any of the preceding three types, regardless of its current state, can be forcefully deactivated by invoking a special utility subprogram furnished by the RT executive. This provision facilitates sudden reconfigurations of algorithms in real time, which may be important in handling of emergency situations or of sudden changes in the operational environment.

Complete specification of scheduling requires definition of priority rules for selecting a process (from the processes waiting in various *ready queues*) to be executed next on the processing element under consideration.

3. Priority Rules

Symbolically denote the priority of process x by Pr(x). For processes x and y, write Pr(x) > Pr(y) if x has a higher priority than y; Pr(x) $\geq$ Pr(y) if the priority of x is higher than or equal to that of y, etc. The following priority scheme seems to be reasonable for scheduling on a processing element processes of the three types introduced earlier. Suppose that C, D, and B represent three processes of the cyclic, deadline, and background types, respectively, all in the ready state; then always

$$\Pr(C) > \Pr(D) > \Pr(B).$$

For any two ready cyclic processes, C_1 and C_2, with periods of lengths $\Delta t(C_1)$ and $\Delta t(C_2)$, respectively,

$$\Pr(C_1) \geq \Pr(C_2) \quad \text{if} \quad \Delta t(C_1) \leq \Delta t(C_2),$$

with

$$\Pr(C_1) = \Pr(C_2) \quad \text{only if} \quad \Delta t(C_1) = \Delta t(C_2).$$

For any two ready deadline processes D_1 and D_2,

$$\Pr(D_1) \geq \Pr(D_2)$$

$$\text{if} \quad F[\Delta t_P(D_1), \Delta t_D(D_1)] \leq F[\Delta t_P(D_2), \Delta t_D(D_2)]$$

with

$$\Pr(D_1) = \Pr(D_2)$$

only if

$$F[\Delta t_P(D_1), \; t_D(D_1)] = F[\Delta t_P(D_2), \Delta t_D(D_2)].$$

Here, (i) F is a real-valued priority function that is monotonically nondecreasing in each of its arguments [e.g., $F(r, x) = ar + bx$, where a and b are nonnegative constants; if $a > 0$ and $b > 0$, then $F(r, x)$ is strictly increasing both in r and in x]; (ii) $\Delta t_P(x)$ is the processor time needed to complete the current execution of process x; (iii) $\Delta t_D(x)$ is the time remaining until the current deadline of process x.

Because at most one active background process is allowed at a time in a processing element, no resolution of priorities among the background processes assigned to the same processing element is needed. Priority ties among deadline processes can be resolved randomly, i.e., arbitrarily. However, it is best to specify a priori how to resolve the priority ties among a set of cyclic processes with periods of identical lengths, for the order in which these processes will be executed may affect the results.

4. *Overall Synchronization of Processes*

Suppose that the distributed system under consideration contains n_{PE} processing elements (PEs). For reasons of simplicity, we assumed decentralized executive control over these n_{PE} PEs. Unless appropriate measures are taken, the scheduling of processes executed not only in different PEs but even within the same PE will remain unsynchronized. Actually, two (although related) kinds of synchronization are implied here: synchronization of actions among processes, which can be attained by means of interrupts and interprocess data communications, and synchronization of processing with the outside world. The latter type of synchronization is accomplished through the monitoring of progression of time, of incoming measurements, or of other signals (such as external interrupts) received from outside.

One technique for implementing synchronization is to introduce systemwide timer interrupts, driven by an oscillator, for dividing the computational time line of each PE into time intervals of length Δt. In Section C such intervals were called fundamental time frames (FTFs); the timer interrupts separating FTFs were called FTF interrupts. The length of an FTF depends on the estimation problem and can be chosen to represent the fastest working rhythm in the system or in its measurement acquisition process. For example, in the estimation problem of GPS navigation (outlined in Appendix C), FTFs were chosen to be 20 msec long, because 20 msec cycles represent the basic transmission rhythm of GPS satellites; the length of an estimation cycle varies, but typically is from 1 to several seconds long.

To enable the applications processes in a processing element to read the time (actually, to count the FTF interrupts), the local real-time executive of such a PE must furnish a noninterruptable function subprogram, each call to which returns to the caller the current count of completed FTF interrupts. Applications processes, especially the measurement acquisition process, can use this time information to time-tag their outputs.

The synchronization method based on FTF interrupts, previously introduced, can be applied to synchronize the scheduling of cyclic processes over the entire distributed system. This can be done by extending the scheduling scheme credited to Jordan [19] in the next-to-last paragraph of Subsection 1 of this section. With the notation introduced in that subsection, the wanted extension is as follows.

(a) Let the lengths of fundamental time frames (FTFs) be expressible as $\Delta t = \Delta T_0/2^{k'}$ for some fixed nonnegative integer k', with ΔT_0 now representing the periods (cycle lengths) of the highest rate cyclic process in the entire system.

(b) Synchronize all processes possessing the periods of length ΔT_0 with FTFs by requiring that the cycle boundaries of such processes be always aligned with FTF boundaries.

(c) Let the period of any cyclic process in the system be expressible as $\Delta T_k = \Delta T_0 2^k$ for some nonnegative integer k.

(d) If $k > 0$, then synchronize any cyclic process possessing the periods of length ΔT_k with all cyclic processes possessing the periods of length ΔT_j, where $j < k$, such that the cycle boundaries of the former are always aligned with those of the latter.

5. *Executive Service Routines and Program/Process Status Tables*

Each time the processing element returns the execution control to its RT executive, a subsystem of this executive, called a *scheduler*, decides which process presently posted on one of the ready queues will be executed next. (A ready queue can be thought of as a list of all processes of the same type that are in the ready state.) To make this decision, the scheduler follows the selection logic implied by the priority scheme adopted previously. Applications parts of real-time software interface with these process management facilities via a set of subprograms, which sometimes are called *executive service routines*. Each executive service routine is an uninterruptable procedure, the execution of which requires a negligible amount of processor time. It is invocable from applications processes and operates on data stored in program/process status tables. Functionally, executive service routines can be divided into two types: those that define/redefine a process for a program listed in the *program/process status tables* (PPS), and those that change the state of a process.

By a previous assumption concerning the processing environment, each program of applications part of real-time software realizes at most one process at a time. Thus the program/process status tables may be visualized as a two-dimensional array, each row of which represents a program and each column of which describes an attribute of programs or of processes generated by these programs. The entries in a row of PPS tables characterize a program and specify the state and other attributes of the process defined for this program. It is not required that a process always be defined for a program. If a program has no defined process at some time, it may be visualized as being inactive at that time, which is not equivalent to a possibly inactive but defined process.

The function of an executive service routine that defines/redefines a process for a specified program is to enter the characteristics of the process to be defined in an appropriate row of the PPS tables. Initially a newly defined/redefined process is always declared to be inactive.

The executive service routines designed for definition/redefinition of processes enable applications processes to change the nature of the process associated with a program by changing the process type, execution rate (if the latter is applicable to process type), priority, or other attributes. For example, a program that at some given time realizes a cyclic process may at some later time be redefined to realize a deadline process (provided that the program logic allows doing it), or it may at some later time be redefined as a cyclic process with a changed period and a changed priority.

One could consider an alternative approach in which process types are defined and fixed prior to real-time operations, say, perhaps at process construction or program load time. Such a rigid approach would inconvenience a control system specialist because at the start of design he often is not sure himself how his algorithms should be synchronized and under what scheduling rules they should be executed. At least the capability to define the process at cold start offers him a design convenience. Furthermore, the capability to redefine in real time the process for a program enables the real-time system to reconfigure its mode of processing after a partial failure of equipment or after a drastic change in operational environment.

Executive service routines that change the states of a defined process will not be described here in detail. It is only important to note that for each process type a procedure must be furnished for every state transition defined in the process state transition graph.

E. INTERPROCESS COMMUNICATIONS AND SYNCHRONIZATION

1. Introduction

To perform common tasks concurrent processes need to communicate through data. In this section we discuss the interprocess communication problem, as well as the related process synchronization problem, by taking a restrictive approach similar to our previous handling of other aspects of real-time executive design. For a more complete treatment of the subject, the interested reader should refer to a text on system programming or on operating systems, such as [2], [3], [4], [5], or [14].

A unit of data exchanged at a specific time is often called a *message*. In the applications considered here, a typical message is an array of homogeneous data (such as a Kalman gain vector/matrix), or a record of heterogeneous data (such as a Kalman gain vector, plus an identification tag of the measurement to which the gain vector corresponds), or just a flag indicating the occurrence of an event.

It is easier to understand the interprocess communication problem if, with each message type, one can associate an area in global data memory reserved for storing a single or several instances of that message. One often uses the terms "buffer" or "communication buffer" when referring to such a dedicated memory area. Typically, a message contains two types of data: *communicated* (or *applications*) data and *protocol data*. The function of protocol data is to control the accessing of the buffer by the communicating processes.

We say that messages of some arbitrary type implement *one-way communication* between two or more processes if each unit message is entirely produced (written) by a single *writer process* and may be consumed (read) by one or several *reader processes*. In such a case, the buffer for storing messages contains the communicated data produced only by a single writer process even though several processes may be involved in generation and exchange of protocol data.

2. *Assumptions and Design Principles*

Next, we introduce the following restrictive assumptions as interprocess communication design principles.

(a) *One-way communications* -- only one-way communications are admissible, which implies that any buffer may contain applications data produced only by a single writer process.

(b) *Restriction on the length of stay in a critical region* -- no process remains in a critical region longer than for an a priori prescribed maximum length of time such as a a few msec. (Recall that a process is assumed to be non-interruptable during the time interval spanned between entering and leaving such a region.)

(c) *Limited waiting for the reading of data* -- if a reader process during its execution reaches a point where it tries to retrieve interprocess communication data from a buffer but cannot do it because the buffer is locked out by a writer process that presently is writing into that buffer or because the buffer contains no new data that the reader process has not yet read (consumed), the reader process (perhaps after waiting at most for some predetermined length of time) proceeds to process other tasks without this time having retrieved the data.

(d) *Limited waiting for the writing of data* -- if a writer process during its execution reaches a point where it wants to write interprocess communication data into a buffer but cannot do it because a reader process is presently accessing that buffer or because the buffer is full and is not supposed to be overwritten, the writer process (perhaps after waiting at most for some predetermined length of time) proceeds to process other tasks without this time having written the data.

Principle (c) implies that on occasions (when no fresh data can be obtained) old data, such as old Kalman gains, will be repeatedly reused. Similarly, (d) implies that sometimes the passing of produced data will be skipped. The important idea here is that the processing logic must be designed not to fall apart if the situation described in (c) or in (d) arises. Only the overall system performance is allowed to degrade somewhat. Also, in view of (b), principles (c) and (d) are superfluous if all interprocess communications occur via critical regions.

Adherence to the preceding principles for design of interprocess communications eliminates the possibility of deadlocks, for then the four necessary and sufficient conditions for a deadlock (e.g., [3], p. 157) cannot simultaneously be met.

3. *Communication Mechanisms and Their Implementations*

Next we turn to specific designs of communication mechanisms, examining the capability of each to attain mutual exclusion of communication processes. In the following discussion we examine the following interprocess communication techniques: time-separated communications under the control of a single flag; communications via a multiple buffer with or without a critical region; and noninterruptable communications via a critical region under the protection of Dijkstra's P and V semaphores or, perhaps, of more general communication control primitives.

It was noted in the discussion of mutual exclusion (Section B.2) that implementation of communication control mechanisms, which we called *communication primitives*, requires special *indivisible operations*. An operation was said to be indivisible if its execution, including the accessing of memory during its execution, cannot be interrupted. An indivisible operation may be implemented on several different levels: it may be a single machine language instruction such as a *test-and-set instruction*, an uninterruptable sequence of machine language instructions resulting from the compilation of a single or several high-level language statements, a single subroutine, or a pair of subroutines and a program segment between such a pair.

As an aside, the following two uninterruptable test-and-set instructions are useful in construction of communication primitives. The first tests whether its operand flag (the contents of a memory location) is nonzero; if it is, then this instruction sets the flag to zero and skips the next instruction; else it proceeds to the next instruction with the zero value of the operand flag unchanged. The second instruction type complements the first in the following sense: it tests whether the operand flag is zero; if it is, then the instruction changes the value of the flag to 1 and skips the next instruction; if not, it goes to the next instruction.

4. *Time-Separated Communications under the Control of a Flag*

Use of a single flag to control one-way communications between a writer process W and a reader process R is the simplest of all three communication techniques presented here. It attains mutual exclusion without a deadlock of processes because of the restrictions that it imposes on the participating processes.

To define one possible implementation of this communication method, let BUFFER be the name of the communication buffer and CFLAG be the name of the variable representing the access control flag. The write procedure, executed by the writer process, is as follows.

```
write:  begin
 wait:  if CFLAG = 0 then goto alpha;
           else goto beta;
```

```
alpha:  write BUFFER;
        CFLAG := 1;
        end
 beta:  (the next executable statement).
```

With the same variable names the read procedure executed by a reader process is as follows.

```
 read:  begin
 wait:  if CFLAG = 1 then goto alpha;
           else goto beta;
alpha:  read from BUFFER;
        CFLAG := 0;
        end
 beta:  (the next executable statement).
```

Despite their structural simplicity, the preceding write and read procedures should to be used only with caution, for they may prevent new data from being enetered into the communication buffer until its previous contents have been read. On the other hand, this simple technique enforces mutual exclusion of communicating processes without assuming anything about their relative speeds. It is useful when the writer and reader processes are cyclically executed at about the same rate because information will then rarely be lost. In such a case it is convenient, although not absolutely necessary, to have the writer process precede the reader process in each cycle.

An alternative approach would be to replace "goto beta" in one or both ("write" and "read") procedures with a "goto wait." Changing to "goto wait" in both procedures would eliminate the possibility of losing information but may occasionally cause excessive waiting for a turn to read or write in a system without appropriate process scheduling and processor allocation schemes.

5. Communications via Multiple Buffers

A *multiple buffer* of multiplicity M contains M data areas (each called a buffer) of identical structure and size. Such buffers usually are (more precisely, their accessing is) *circularly arranged* in the sense that the writer process, after writing into the Mth buffer, next writes into the first buffer; similarly, the reader process, after reading from the Mth buffer, switches to the first. Hence such a storage scheme is often called a *circular buffer*. One frequently used special form of a multiple buffer is the so-called double buffer. In the presence of fluctuations in execution rates of two communicating processes, communications via a multiple buffer, owing to extra storage capacity, are less likely to lose information (or cause waiting for a turn to read or write) than communications based on the method described in the preceding subsection. Mutual exclusion without deadlocks is now attained by not allowing the reader process and the writer process simultaneously to access the same buffer. One-way communications through a multiple buffer (including the design of communication mechanisms) is a generalization of the single buffer techniques described in the preceding subsection.

6. Uninterruptable Communications via Protected Critical Regions

If one cannot or is not willing to make any assumptions about the relative speeds or execution times of communicating processes and cannot afford occasional loss of information (or occasionally excessive waiting times) as with the preceding two techniques, then the following technique constitutes a general approach for controlling the access to a global data set by two or several concurrent processes, which always works (although we shall later qualify "always").

(a) With each global data set D, accessed by at least two processes, associate an integer valued access control flag S.

(b) Allow each process, P_i, communicating through D, to access D only from within critical regions, $CR_i(S)$, each protected (enclosed) by a pair of *communication (synchronization) primitives* operating on S. Let these two synchronization primitives, one at the entry point to a critical region and the other at its exit point, be integral parts of the critical region.

(c) Make the process that enters a critical region *uninterruptable* from the moment it starts to execute the first instruction of the entry point primitive until it completes the execution of the last instruction in the companion exit-point primitive.

Thus a pair of corresponding communication primitives is a mechanism operating on S that, after having been started, is executed to completion without interruption and which can be executed by only a single process at a time. Flag S is an integer valued quantity that may be operated on only by a synchronization primitive or by a special procedure (the latter could be part of cold-start initialization) designed to initialize S.

It can be shown that the following primitives, derived from Dijkstra's P and V synchronization semaphores, handle mutual exclusion and synchronization for a pair of communicating processes in multiprogrammed multiprocessor systems of the type considered here (using the notation given in [3, p. 129], all operations in the following material enclosed within a pair of brackets are assumed to be *uninterruptable*).

```
WAIT(S):    [S := S - 1; if S < 0 then
            place the process that called WAIT on a wait
            queue Qs and release the processor to another
            process; else let the calling process enter
            the critical region.]
SIGNAL(S):  [S := S + 1; if S ≤ 0 then remove a process
            from Qs and change its state to "ready" for
            processor allocation.]
```

For such a pair of synchronization primitives, one can define an initialization function INIT(x, v) that initializes semaphore x to value v. Thus if S is initialized to 1 by executing INIT(S,1), the write process W and the read process R can use the following procedures to communicate via the data written into (read from) the data set D. Each time process W wants to write into D it executes a code segment of the form

```
begin
   WAIT(S);
   write into D;       A critical region
   SIGNAL(S);          for process W
end
```

Similarly, each time process R wants to read from data set D it must execute a code segment, such as

```
begin
   WAIT(S);            A critical region
   read from D;        for process R
   SIGNAL(S);
end
```

It is assumed that the global variable S is known as a semaphore to both of the preceding code segments. For a discussion of other and more general uses of the synchronization primitives WAIT and SIGNAL (for example, for extensions to more than a pair of communicating processes), as well as for definitions of other synchronization primitives, the interested reader is referred to Chapter 4 of [3].

We had asserted previously that the communications control mechanism based on protected critical regions is sufficient for the processing environment assumed here. The key to that is the assumptions (design principles) stated in Subsection 2 of this section, especially the second assumption, according to which a process is not supposed to remain in a critical region longer than some a priori defined length of time. Adherence to this principle prevents deadlocks. This principle must be enforced at design time (at execution time a process is uninterruptable when it is inside a critical region and so cannot be forced out of it) by exercising care about the executable code that is placed inside critical regions. In applications considered here, only the code segments requiring a limited amount of processor time and needed for writing data into a communication buffer (or for copying it from such a buffer) are allowed within a critical region.

Since the communications via critical regions protected by semaphores appear to be simpler to use than the single or multiple buffer techniques described in the preceding two subsections, the question arises why not always to use such protected critical regions? In many control systems, especially in those possessing appropriate hardware and programming language features (refer to the next paragraph), it is the right thing to do. Still in some systems, excessive use of protected critical regions may be computationally too expensive. Often a mixed approach constitutes the best solution. For example, a mixed approach had been chosen in certain GPS user's navigation systems known to us (Appendix III summarizes the estimation problem of GPS navigation), the applications software of which is programmed in FORTRAN. In one of these systems, the relatively high rate GPS measurements are cyclically passed from the receiver control process to the navigation filter by means of the single buffer techniques discussed in Subsection 4; the Kalman gains are passed at a moderately average rate (but not very regularly) by the process generating them to a concurrently executed user process by means of a double buffer; the orbital parameters of GPS transmitters are assembled at a relatively low rate and passed irregularly to the navigation filter via a protected critical region.

Finally, we want to say a few words about the implementation of communication (or synchronization) primitives. The form in which they are implemented depends on the programming language used. If assembler language or a high-level language such as FORTRAN is used, these primitives should be implemented as an integral part of the real-time executive service facilities in the form of uninterruptable subprograms. If a programming language such as ADA [6], which is designed for multiprogrammed task execution, is used, then these or similar primitives are furnished as facilities built into the programming language.

IV. ALGORITHMIC AND PROCEDURAL ISSUES IN DESIGN OF REAL-TIME ESTIMATORS

A. *INTRODUCTION*

In the first part of this chapter we examined computer implementation aspects of real-time control system design. In the course of doing it we described software architecture for the real-time estimators to be implemented on a distributed system of small computers. The ideas on implemental design presented up to this point applied not only to real-time estimators but, more genrally, to a variety of real-time control and communication systems.

In the second part, i.e., in Sections IV and V, we focus our attention on real-time estimators. We do it in two steps. This section reviews selected issues pertaining to the design of computational algorithms and procedural logic for Kalman filters, although nearly all ideas will also apply to other types of recursive real-time estimators. Then Section V illustrates filter mechanizations resulting from several known work-load partitioning schemes. Typically, we end up with a scheme requiring multiprogrammed processing environment. Concepts and techniques discussed in Sections II and III can then be applied to complete the implemental design of estimator software.

It is difficult to be objective and sufficiently broad in selection of algorithm and procedure design issues; what is important to one person is often determined by his background and interests, and may appear to be insignificant to another. In our selection we were guided mainly by what we viewed as being critical to the real-time estimators of the type considered here. These critical factors are (a) modeling of the estimation problem, (b) design of algorithms for implementing the covariance/gain filtering portion of the estimator, (c) system identification techniques in real time, (d) increasing the robustness of the estimation process against the perturbations such as bursts of high amplitude noise due to environmental disturbances, sensor failures, or sudden and drastic changes in the system model.

It is difficult to exaggerate the importance of modeling of the dynamics and observations of the system whose states we want to estimate. But modeling is outside the scope of this chapter and so we shall not discuss it here.

One possible approach to reduction of real-time computational load is mentioned next in passing. Considerable savings in loading can often be attained for almost (or better, for completely) time invariant linear systems through the use of precomputed gains K and the state error covarainces P. In many estimation problems for such systems (especially under the dominating process noise) only a few pairs of (P, K) often yield nearly optimal performance. With this approach, covariances P are not needed for the measurement updating of estimates and must be stored only if they are used for some purpose.

B. FILTER ALGORITHMS

In a Kalman filter, the algorithms that perform covariance and gain processing constitute a critical kernel of real-time estimation software. They are critical primarily for two reasons: (a) they may potentially destabilize the estimation process or prevent it from converging, and (b) they may require an excessive amount of processing time and memory.

Covariance and gain (C/G) processing (filtering) algorithms perform the following functions: time propagation of state error covariance matrix P, computation of Kalman gains, and measurement updating of P. The current practice is to structure an estimation scheme so that the measurements in an estimation cycle are processed sequentially one by one and the Kalman gains are computed and state error covariances updated for each measurement separately. Such a scheme is called sequential processing of measurements.

Appendix I summarizes the original form of C/G processing algorithms for a linear Kalman filter with discrete measurements. Unfortunately, the covariance update operation in the original form of Kalman filter algorithms [Eq. (7) in Appendix I] is computationally unstable. Roundoff errors may eventually make the state error covariance matrix acquire negative characteristic roots and thus lose its positive definiteness. Hence, the criticality of numerical stability requirement in applications considered here motivates the use of square root filtering algorithms for covariance/gain processing.

Several variations of square root filtering are known. The version that has been defined and refined largely by Bierman is summarized in Appendix II. (References [11] and [10] contain descriptions of what we shall refer to as Bierman's method. In the first of these references the author also discusses applications of square root filtering techniques to information matrix estimation.) There is some controversy in literature about which particular form of square root filtering should be used. Carlson [22] describes what could be viewed as a partial alternative to Bierman's method. Our selection of Bierman's method has been motivated mainly by years of satisfactiry experience with it in applications to navigation problems. In any case, saving just a few percent of processing time should not be the decisive criterion for using one set of algorithms instead of another. For a "neutral" over-view of available options in square-root filtering, the interested reader is referred to Chapter 7 of [9] in which the author also summarizes comparative timing data for better known variants.

One benefit derived from the use of numerically stable covariance and gain processing algorithms is the feasibility to implement them and to make them perform in signle (or reduced) precision floating-point arithmetic except for computations of some dot products. In a microprocessor this often saves not only memory but also processing time because of the relative disparity in the speeds of single- and double-precision floating-point operations. This disparity in processing speeds becomes especially large if the microprocessor does not have floating point arithmetic implemented in hardware form.

C. *SYSTEM IDENTIFICATION*

1. *Identification Problems in Real Time*

We use the term "system identification" in a restricted sense to indicate acquisition of knowledge about the distributional properties of the stochastic processes representing the process and measurement noise sources in a Kalman filter.

In practice one usually assumes that each noise source is represented by a stochastic process from some particular class of processes. In such a case the identification problem is reduced to determination of the parameters that define a particular process in the assumed class. Two distributional parameters that are usually of interest are the mean and the covariances of the stochastic process. These quantities may not be time invariant, so their values may have to be updated repeatedly. As the system model of a Kalman filter in

Appendix I indicates, each noise source is typically modeled as a white, zero-mean Gaussian process with unknown variances or covariances.

Should there be any suspicion that the stochastic process representing a noise source has a nonzero mean of unknown but significant value, the unknown mean should be included in the system model as a state variable and estimated. Thus the unknown parameter whose value is most often sought is the variance (for a scalar-valued noise process) or the covariance matrix (for a vector-valued noise process). In cases of sequentially correlated noise, one also must effectively estimate the autocorrelation of the process in order to whiten the noise.

2. *Identification Methods for a Kalman Filter*

In the presence of colored noise (as is pointed out in Chapter 11 of [23]), retention of optimality properties of the filter is usually possible, although at the expense of increased complexity. Illustrated in that reference are a few special cases (such as a situation in which the measurement noise process is Markov) and techniques for handling them, which save the optimality properties of filter without increasing the dimensions of the state vector. Another approach is to replace the filter with one that is less complex by means of model order reduction. References [23] and [9] are probably the best introduction to the subject.

Methods for identifying the unknown covariances of noise processes can be roughly divided into (a) adaptive (i.e., estimation time) methods, (b) heuristic on-line methods, and (c) a priori modeling methods. Occasionally several methods are combined.

3. Adaptive Identification Methods

In Kalman filtering the term "adaptive estimation" usually refers to on-line estimation techniques that include estimation of unknown distributional parameters in noise models. Many adaptive estimation schemes have been investigated, and the results of this research are reported in literature, e.g., refer to Brewer [24] or to Ohap and Stubberud [25].

Unfortunately, these on-line system identification techniques nontrivially increase the processing load in almost all cases and so may become prohibitively expensive with respect to processing time. For example, any measurement bias (i.e., nonzero mean of measurement noise) in principle can be estimated by modeling it as a component of the system state vector; but the computational load owing to the processing Kalman gains and covariances in a filter is roughly proportional to Kn^3 operations, where n is the length of the state vector and K is a scaling factor that depends on a particular algorithm used.

The adaptive techniques become even more computationally expensive when the noise random process under consideration is nonstationary or sequentially correlated. Then it is not enough to estimate the unknown distributional parameters once, say as the start of the estimation process, and then to continue using the obtained parameter estimates throughout the remaining part of the estimation process; but there is a need, then, to continue the estimation of changing distributional parameters throughout the estimation process. Furthermore, in some applications such as missile dynamics during powered flight, the noise characteristics may change so rapidly that even with almost unlimited processing resources available it would be impossible to input at a sufficiently high rate the measurements needed for system identification.

4. *Heuristic On-line and A Priori Modeling Methods*

Current microprocessor and, in particular, special chip technologies, aided by modern methodology of software design and implementation, have made a heuristic approach to system identification feasible. This approach utilizes the following two ideas.

First, with some planning one can design the sensors and other measurement input ports (or at least the digital controllers of these devices) for real-time estimation so as to make them produce extra information in addition to the "regular" measurements specified in the system model. Usually such extra information can be obtained at little additional cost as a by-product of regular estimation measurements. This information (coming as extra measurements of noise and system model parameters) is intended to help the estimation process (a) promptly detect a change in the characteristics of a noise process or, more generally, in system model and (b) accurately approximate the values of process and measurement noise covariances.

Second, real-time test equipment (capable of creating a wide range of possible operational environments and producing close-to-real-life measurements plus their extras) can be utilized to calibrate the noise parameters as a function of the received extra inputs for quick computation of covariances or of changes in system model.

Next we illustrate applications of the heuristic modeling techniques previously outlined to two estimation problems in GPS navigation. (In Appendix III we define a simple version of the estimation problem for GPS navigation.) Several models of GPS navigation equipment have been or are being developed. A typical set of GPS user's equipment is built around a system of microprocessors and utilizes a specially designed receiver for obtaining pseudorange and delta pseudorange measurements at a high repetition rate. The receiver passes these measurements to a microprocessor based estimation system. The latter recursively produces a primary navigation solution (i.e., estimates the state vector) from which other navigation quantities of interest can be derived as by-products.

EXAMPLE 1. One type of GPS navigation equipment was developed as part of test instrumentation for a long-range missile [13]. Analysis of the process noise showed that all dynamics related elements of a process noise covariance matrix were expressible in terms of a single parameter, the acceleration variance. During a short powered flight each of the three engines of the missile undergoes an acceleration peak and an acceleration valley; after the missile goes into the coasting flight, nearly all acceleration is because of gravitational attraction, which thereafter changes very slowly. Several adaptive process noise covariance identification techniques have been tried. They responded too slowly and were too expensive computationally. Thereafter, it was decided to instrument the system so as to provide the estimator with a discrete warning (completion) signal before (after) each event that drastically affected the acceleration (e.g., liftoff or a change in engine). Special real-time test equipment -- producing not only realistic GPS pseudorange and delta pseudorange measurements throughout a test mission but also the previously described discrete event warning (completion) signals -- was then used to select experimentally the best possible acceleration variance for each segment of test mission.

EXAMPLE 2. This example deals with GPS navigation equipment for a medium-dynamics user [26]. The GPS receiver of this navigation equipment is designed to produce, in addition to GPS satellite pseudorange and delta pseudorange measurements, several parameters for computing the measurement noise variances; also the velocity variance from which all dynamics related process noise covariances can be directly computed.

D. INCREASING THE ROBUSTNESS OF AN ESTIMATION PROCESS

The objective of robust inference is retention of performance when the distributional assumptions are violated or when some measurements are bad (outliers). What is nice about "off-line" statistical analysis is that if one method of inference leads to suspicious results, the statistician can always try another one on the original data. In real-time estimation, however, we do not enjoy this luxury: data is processed at about its arrival rate; if the on-line analysis of data fails, it may be physically impossible or too expensive to repeat the experiment. This strongly motivates increasing the robustness of an on-line estimation process. Proper preprocessing and screening of measurements contribute to it. Thus when designing a real-time estimation scheme one should always examine whether the considered application requires special procedures for (a) screening the measurements against isolated outliers, (b) detecting the leading and trailing edges of high-amplitude noise bursts, (c) detecting the onset of and then taking appropriate measures against nonwhiteness in measurement noise, and (d) censoring (imposing bounds on) measurements. One should also examine whether any special procedures are required for detecting the onset of a drastic change in the system model and for taking appropriate measures against detected changes.

One area that should be examined for each application is whether it is necessary to have procedures for monitoring the estimates and for altering them in case their values exceed predetermined bounds. This simple heuristic technique, known as *censored estimation*, may save the stability of the estimation process during short, undetected bursts of exceedingly severe measurement noise such as intermittent jamming. It may also be helpful during the periods following sudden, radical changes in the system model until appropriate adjustments of the model can be made.

A highly readable account that complements the discussion of algorithm and procedure design issues in the present section is to be found in Reference [27]. Its discussion of the balancing of covariance matrices for filter convergence and stability is especially noteworthy.

V. DECOMPOSITION OF A KALMAN FILTER INTO CONCURRENT PROCESSES

A. *MOTIVATION AND OVERVIEW*

Sections II and III outlined software engineering techniques for decomposing a real-time control problem into concurrent processes. In applications considered here such decomposition may enable an estimation scheme to satisfy the real-time constraints of the problem on a distributed system of small computers. Specified limitations on weight, volume, power consumption, or cost of equipment often do not allow extending a distributed system through addition of extra processing elements. Thus trying to satisfy the real-time constraints by incrementing the equipment is often unacceptable. In such a situation, decomposing the work load into concurrent processes is the only recourse. In this section we illustrate this approach by means of several schemes for decomposing Kalman filters. Such decomposition of a Kalman filter (or of any recursive estimator) into concurrently executable procedures often constitutes part of what is known as *filter mechanization*, a term we primarily reserve for filter structuring.

In the following text we first introduce two basic structural formulations, *direct* and *indirect*, of a Kalman filter. Each can be used as a basis for decompositions presented subsequently. Next, to establish rationale and common reference for discussion of decompositions we review the processing tasks comprising a single estimation cycle of a sequentially structured filter. Finally, we examine several schemes for decomposing the computations of such a filter to concurrent processes.

B. *DIRECT/INDIRECT FORMULATIONS AND FEEDFORWARD/FEEDBACK MODES OF USE*

1. *Direct and Indirect Mechanizations*

Two alternate approaches for formulating a Kalman filter are known. In the first, called *direct* (or *total state*) formulation, the state vector $\underline{s}$, which describes the total state of the system, is directly estimated; i.e., in each estimation cycle, $\underline{s}$ is first time-propagated and then measurement-updated. In the second approach, called *indirect* (or *state error*) formulation, a Kalman filter estimates not the system total state vector $\underline{s}$ but the error $\delta\underline{s}$ in $\underline{s}$. Thus, if an indirectly formulated filter is used, each estimation cycle involves three major steps: time propagation of $\underline{s}$, estimation of error $\delta\underline{s}$ in $\underline{s}$, and updating of the propagated value of $\underline{s}$ by subtracting from it the estimate of $\delta\underline{s}$. For the estimation cycle with reference time t_k, the last step can be symbolically written as

$$\underline{\hat{s}}(k|k) = \underline{\hat{s}}(k|k-1) - \delta\underline{\hat{s}}(k|k).$$

2. *Feedforward and Feedback Modes of Use*

There are two basic modes, illustrated in Fig. 2, for using a Kalman filter (or any recursive estimator) in a control system: feedforward use and feedback use.

A recursive estimator, used in feedback mode, feeds some of its estimates back into subsystems from which it is receiving measurements. Feedback mechanization is widely used in integrated navigation systems, i.e., in navigation systems built around a recursive estimator that operates on measurements from several different types of sensors or measurement subsystems. Consider, for example, an integrated navigation

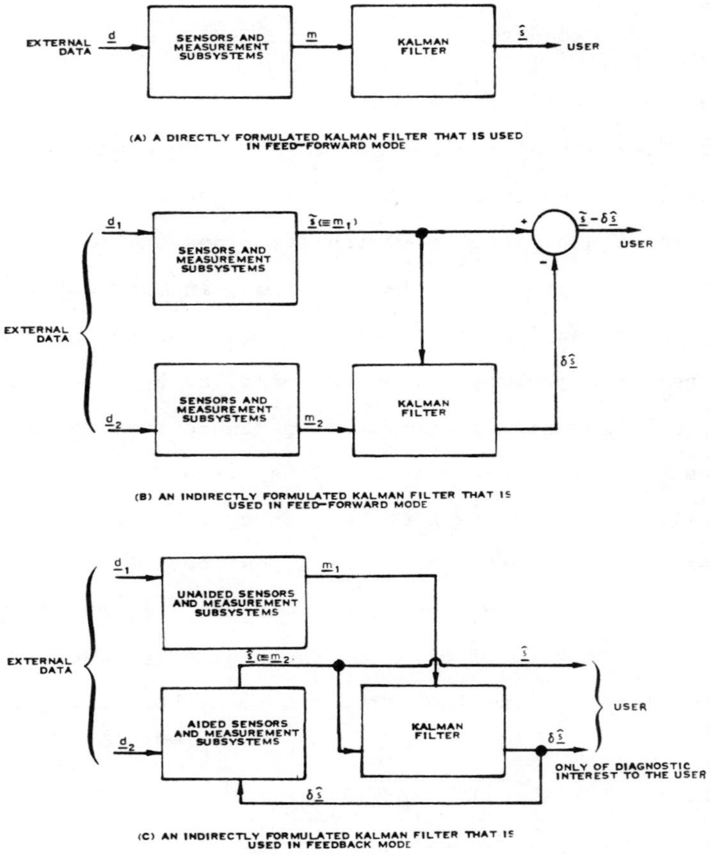

Fig. 2. Three formulation and use mode combinations of a Kalman filter.

system operating on two types of measurements: (a) position, velocity, and acceleration outputs of an inertial measurement subsystem; and (b) pseudorange and delta pseudorange measurements of GPS satellites. A loop that feeds back the estimation outputs into the inertial measurement subsystem could be used to recalibrate the inertial subsystem while the GPS measurements are being received and when they produce excellent navigation data. Another feedback loop could be used for feeding aiding data to the GPS sensor (a special receiver) for quick reacquisition of lost GPS space vehicles (SVs). (Estimates of SV ranges and their time derivatives are the quantities that aid acquisition of a new SV or reacquisition of an SV whose track had been lost.) With feedback mechanization it is often more convenient (although not mandatory) to use an indirectly mechanized Kalman filter. Part c of Fig. 2 graphically summarizes the previously described filter mechanization with the "aided sensors and measurement subsystems" box representing both the inertial measurement subsystem and the GPS receiver and with the "unaided sensors and measurement subsystems" box standing for other possible (unidentified) measurement sources, such as an altimeter.

In the example of the preceding paragraph if the user of equipment were interested only in accurate estimates of navigation quantities (such as position or velocity) and if he were indifferent to the calibration of the inertial measurement subsystem, he could have the filter mechanized in feedforward fashion, as illustrated in Part b of Fig. 2. In the latter case, the filter estimates errors in the navigational outputs of the inertial measurement subsystem (IMS), which, in Part b of Fig. 2, is the box outputting $\underline{m}_1$. Estimates of these errors are then subtracted from the navigational outputs of the IMS. Note that now (a) the outputs of the IMS can be used by the Kalman filter for time propagation of the navigation state vector $\underline{s}$ and (b) the GPS receiver, the outputs of which are represented by $\underline{m}_2$, is not being aided (which is not a realistic assumption) by the Kalman filter. Similar to the feedback mechanization it is often more convenient (as indicated in Part b of Fig. 2) with the feedforward mechanization to use indirect formulation of a Kalman filter.

Care must be exercised in the design of a recursive estimator used in feedback fashion. A feedback loop may become unstable, which sometimes will manifest itself through sequentially correlated (nonwhite) measurement noise.

3. *Pros and Cons of Indirect Formulation*

In many applications of the type considered here (such as navigation systems) an indirectly formulated Kalman filter, designed to estimate low-frequency errors, can be executed at a considerably lower rate than the rate at which a direct filter would have to be run to perform comparably. This is because a linear model is often adequate for representation of low-frequency error dynamics. In contrast, indirect formulation of a parallely structured filter usually costs more in processor time overhead than does direct formulation because the error estimates in such a filter generally must be time-propagated to match their reference times with those of the state vector at each update of the latter.

C. *REVIEW OF PROCESSING TASKS IN A SEQUENTIALLY STRUCTURED KALMAN FILTER*

1. *Sequentially Structured Filter*

Before discussing parallely structured estimators we briefly review the processing tasks comprising a single estimation cycle of a sequentially structured Kalman filter. We assume that such a filter processes measurements sequentially as scalars and that it is indirectly formulated. The standard Kalman filter equations summarized in Appendix I, then, suggest decomposition of work at time t_k into the following tasks.

1. Time propagation of state vector $\underline{s}$ from t_{k-1} to t_k; i.e., computation of $\hat{\underline{s}}(k)^- \triangleq \hat{\underline{s}}(k|k-1)$.
2. Time propagation of state error covariance matrix P; i.e., computation of $P(k)^- \triangleq P(k|k-1)$.
3. Setting up of the measurement processing loop, which (depending on the type of filter mechanization) may include activities such as the clearing of state error estimate vector $\delta\underline{s}$, the saving of state data, etc.
4. Measurement processing loop: each pass through it processes a scalar measurement $m_i(k)$ $(i = 1, 2 \ldots, n_m)$ and requires execution of the following tasks.
   a. Setting up of indices and logic for the ith pass through the loop.
   b. Preprocessing of $m_i(k)$, which may include its conversion and prefiltering.
   c. Computation of linear (or linearized) state-to-measurement transformation vector $\underline{h}(k)$, predicted value of $m_i(k)$, and measurement residual.
   d. Screening of measurement $m_i(k)$ for acceptance/rejection by means of residual analysis.
   e. Measurement updating of state error covariance matrix P [such that the update $P(k)^+ \triangleq P(k|k)$ is completed in the last pass through the measurement loop] and computation of Kalman gain vector $\underline{k}_i(k)$ for $m_i(k)$.
   f. Updating of the estimate of state error $\delta\underline{s}(k)$ [such that the output of this step in the last pass through the measurement loop is $\delta\hat{\underline{s}}(k|k)$].
   g. End-of-loop processing for the ith pass.

5. Measurement updating of state vector, i.e., computation of

$$\underline{\hat{s}}(k)^{+} = \underline{\hat{s}}(k|k) = \underline{\hat{s}}(k|k - 1) - \delta\underline{\hat{s}}(k|k).$$

In the following text, the preceding tasks (4a-d, f, and g) will be collectively referred to as *measurement incorporation*; the preceding tasks (2 and 4e, [supplemented with modified forms of 4a, c, and g)], as *covariance/gain filtering*.

2. *Departure from Sequentially Structured Filters*

After decomposition of work load to the previously identified or similar processing tasks and after obtaining timing and sizing estimates for each task, these tasks can be recombined into concurrently executable processes in many different ways. With timing and sizing data for each constituent task available, it is easy to predict not only the processor time requirements for processes formed from these tasks but also the memory requirements for the programs and data sets implementing these processes.

This leads to candidate *filter structures*. The designer next faces the problem of selecting the most suitable structure (or set of structures) for the problem at hand. He may select a set of structures, each suitable to a particular mode or phase of his estimation problem, and then apply the process control facilities of the real-time executive outlined in Section III to have processes adaptively reconfigured in real time.

The price to be paid for solving the scheduling problem via structures of concurrent processes is poorer functional performance because it leads to algorithms that usually are less "optimal" than their original, sequentially executable forms. Thus one task that the designer now confronts is to determine by how much the performance actually degrades. This is normally done by means of simulations.

D. *PARALLEL STRUCTURES*

1. *Introductory Remarks*

Next we illustrate several solutions to the real-time constraint problem through work-load decomposition into concurrent processes. For this purpose, we outline several ways for parallel structuring of Kalman filters.

Figure 3 gives an illustration of how a slight restructuring of the procedure used in the sequential model of Section V.C changes a sequential scheme to a parallely structured estimator with two concurrent processes: one for propagation/update of state vector $\underline{s}$; the other for processing of measurements and covariance/gain computations. The outputs of the Kalman filter, $\tilde{\underline{s}}(j|j)$, identified as "user's estimates" in

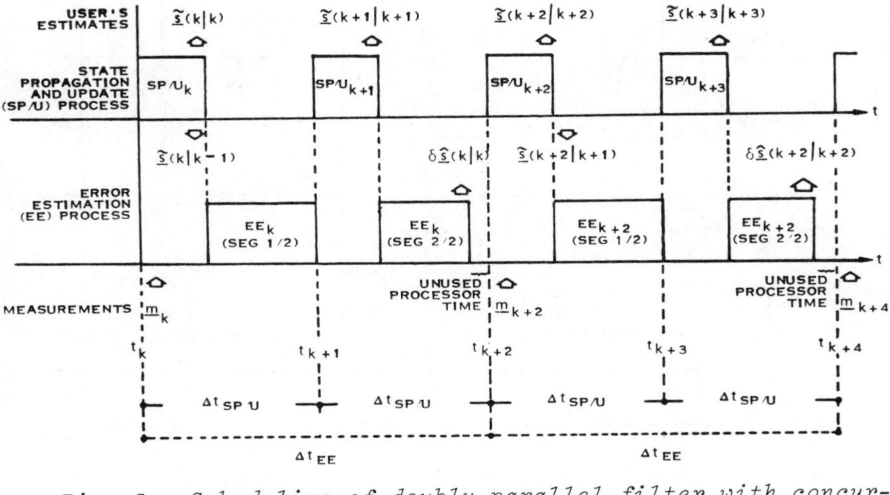

Fig. 3. Scheduling of doubly parallel filter with concurrent error estimation for special case $\Delta t_{EE} = 2\Delta t_{SP/U}$.

Fig. 3, are not "strictly Kalman" in the sense that every second time they are computed while using a time-propagated value of $\delta\underline{\hat{s}}$. For an indirectly formulated filter the second process estimates the error $\delta\underline{s}$ in state vector $\underline{s}$.

Further separation of measurement processing and covariance/gain computations by introduction of an additional concurrent process leads to a triply parallel filter structure consisting of three concurrently executable processes: one for state propagation/update, the second for measurement processing, and the third for covariance/gain computations. The resulting scheme is illustrated in Fig. 4.

If, instead of decomposing the work load to two processes as in Fig. 3, we allowed one process to propagate the state vector, process the measurements, and update the state vector (with the Kalman gains computed by the other process), while assigning to the other the processing of covariances and the

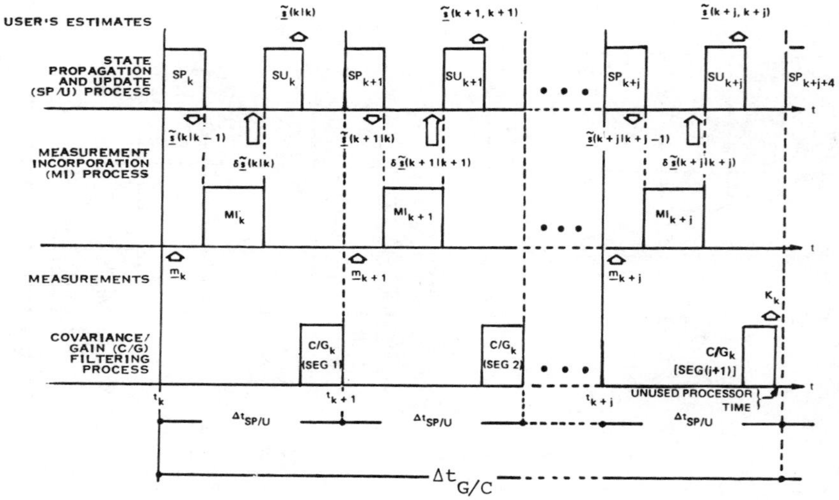

Fig. 4. Scheduling of triply parallel filter with concurrent measurement incorporation and covariance/gain filtering.

computation of Kalman gains, then we would obtain a doubly parallel estimation scheme with concurrent covariance/gain filtering, which is described in Subsection 4.

Next we examine the previously introduced three parallel filter structures in greater detail. We assume that only one processing element is available for filter functions. Hence concurrent processes resulting from filter decompositions must be executed in interleaved time fashion on a single processor.

2. *Parallel Estimation of State Error*

This is the doubly parallel structure shown in Fig. 3. For this structure we now assume indirect filter formulation. Hence, as mentioned previously, one process (called the *error estimation process*) estimates the error $\delta\underline{s}$ in state vector $\underline{s}$ (and actually performs all functions normally ascribed to a Kalman filter), while the other process (called the *state propagation/updating process*) propagates the state vector $\underline{s}$ and then updates $\underline{s}$ by subtracting from it the estimate of $\delta\underline{s}$ passed by the error estimation process.

Compared with the other two parallel filter structures discussed in the following text, this scheme yields high rate propagation/updating of the state vector. However, somewhat stale estimates of $\delta\underline{s}$ (although properly time-aligned by propagation) will in general be used for updating of $\underline{s}$.

This scheme may be the only recourse if it is required that the state vector $\underline{s}$ be propagated/updated at a rate much faster than that at which the whole filter can be executed. For example, this may be required in the navigation applications (where $\underline{s}$ represents the navigation solution) to computations of aerial cargo drops or of weapon deliveries. With this filter structure it is helpful to aid the propagation of

$\underline{s}$ with outputs from a measurement system (such as the velocity and acceleration inputs from an inertial subsystem) complementing the primary measurements on which the filter is operating.

This doubly parallel scheme is reduced to a sequentially structured filter when the execution rates of the state propagation/updating and error estimation processes are equal. In such a case (or when the rate of error estimation process is not significantly lower than that of the other process) this scheme, if properly handled, displays many good properties (such as robust initial convergence) of a Kalman filter.

The parallel error estimation scheme easily lends itself to measurement screening and nicely responds to real-time changes in the system model. Its chief disadvantage (in case the rate of error estimation process is relatively low) is a low rate of measurement incorporation, which may prohibit its use in dynamically lively applications. However, by *introduction of a third concurrent process for covariance/gain filtering* (and thus by separation of these functions from error estimation) the problem of low rate of measurement incorporation can be alleviated but at the cost of an additional increase in dissimilarity from the structure of canonical Kalman filter algorithms. Such a triply parallel scheme is discussed in Subsection 3.

If the state propagation/update and error estimation processes are the only two processes assigned to a processing element, they can be implemented by defining the first process as a cyclic process and the second as a background process. The latter will be given all free processor time remaining after execution of the cyclic process. Should there be other background processes assigned to the same processing element, the following two options are available: (a) define the error estimation process as one of several background processes but allow only one such process to be active at a time or (b) define the error estimation process as a deadline process.

3. Triply Parallel Estimation: Covariance/Gain Filtering Performed Concurrently with Error Estimation

This estimation scheme (summarized in Fig. 4 and constructed as indicated in the preceding subsection) processes measurements at a higher rate than the doubly parallel scheme with concurrent error estimation, but does it at the cost of performing the covariance filtering and the gain computations at a much lower rate. It should be used when a high rate of measurement incorporation is more essential to performance than optimal gains.

It is not difficult to see that this filtering scheme is awkward in screening and rejecting measurements and, at best, only sluggishly responds to changes in system model and poorly converges after initialization. All these poor properties are owing to low rate, autonomous processing of gains and covariances.

To implement a triply parallel estimation scheme on a processing element, three processes need to be defined: (a) a cyclic state propagation/update process, which can also be designed to serve as a logical controller of the entire Kalman filter; (b) a measurement incorporation process, which (depending on the measurement acquisition mechanism) may be implemented either as a cyclic process or an almost cyclically scheduled deadline process; and (c) a covariance/gain filtering process, defined as a background process, which will be given all free processor time remaining between repeated executions of the other two processes. However, should there be other background processes on the same processing element, then either one background process at most would be kept active at a time or the covariance/gain filtering process would have to be defined as a deadline process.

VI. SUMMARY AND CONCLUSIONS

In this chapter we addressed the control specialist who is facing the problem of having his estimation algorithms implemented as a working real-time system. We used the term "implemental design" to describe the activities concerned with adaptation and restructuring of algorithms for computer implementation.

From the start we assumed that distributed systems of microprocessors (or just of small computers) were the type of hardware on which implemental design was to be executed, but this did not rule out systems consisting of a single computer. With this assumption we narrowed the discussion to a generic class of real-time estimation/control systems considered to be suited to implementation on distributed microprocessors. We characterized them as small-to-medium-scale control systems, designed to be boundedly loadable, i.e., to accept a processing load not exceeding the bounds established at design time. To this category belong practically all real-time control systems that are equipped with estimators and that are to be implemented on hardware of the type considered here.

Next we introduced multiprogramming as a suitable processing environment and defined a structural model of software architecture for this environment. Such a model is needed for software timing and sizing, which was identified as an important task in implemental design of real-time software. It is also needed for design of a real-time operating system, called the real-time executive.

We also introduced process as a fundamental concept from theory of operating systems and used it to represent a program in execution but not necessarily executing at the moment. To simplify the processing environment model we also required preservation of one-to-one corresondence between programs and processes. Practically this requirement is not too restrictive for the following reasons: (a) each process needs only to be represented by a main program stub of minimal length and (b) the assumptions of bounded loading and finite reentrancy limit the number of processes that can exist.

The next topic was real-time executive. Selected issues of process management and resource allocation (such as deadlocks and their prevention, interprocess communications, and process synchronization) were reviewed. Thereafter our attention turned to two issues in real-time executive design that very much affect implemental design of estimation algorithms for real-time operations: process scheduling and interprocess communications.

At the start of the second part of this chapter we turned to the issues directly associated with estimators. In Section IV we reviewed several algorithmic and procedural aspects of estimator design, which must be considered if the resulting real-time estimator is to be numerically stable, computationally efficient, and robust to distrubances in measurements. Discussed were stable algorithms for covariance/gain processing in a Kalman filter and real-time system identification techniques. In Section V, by means of illustrations, we looked into practical schemes for decomposing estimators of the Kalman filter type into structures of concurrent processes. Two basic filter mechanization schemes were compared, underlying such parallel structures, were compared. They are direct and indirect filter formulations. Also, two modes of filter use, feedforward and feedback, were introduced.

APPENDIX I: KALMAN FILTER ALGORITHM FOR A DISCRETE LINEAR SYSTEM WITH SAMPLED MEASUREMENTS

In this appendix we summarize for reference purposes the standard form of Kalman filter algorithm, including the system model that this algorithm assumes, for a discrete linear system with sampled measurements.

A. SYSTEM MODEL

1. Propagation of the system state vector from $t = t_{k-1}$ to $t = t_k$:

$$\underline{s}(k) = F(k, k - 1)\underline{s}(k - 1) + G(k - 1)\underline{w}(k - 1). \tag{1}$$

2. Measurements at $t = t_k$:

$$\underline{m}(k) = H(k)\underline{s}(k) + \underline{u}(k). \tag{2}$$

3. Initial conditions at $t = t_0$:

$$E[\underline{s}(0)] = \hat{\underline{s}}(0), \quad \mathrm{Cov}[\underline{s}(0) - \hat{\underline{s}}(0)] = P(0). \tag{3}$$

4. Assumptions about system statistics:

   a. The processes $\{\underline{w}(k)\}$ and $\{\underline{u}(k)\}$ are zero-mean, mutually independent Gaussian processes with covariances

$$E[\underline{w}(k)\underline{w}(j)^T] = Q(k)\delta_{kj},$$

and

$$E[\underline{u}(k)\underline{u}(j)^T] = R(k)\delta_{kj}.$$

b. Furthermore, $\underline{s}(0)$ is independent of $\underline{w}(k)$ and $\underline{u}(k)$ for any k.

B. *ESTIMATION PROCEDURE*

1. Propagation of estimates from $t = t_{k-1}$ to $t = t_k$:

$$\hat{\underline{s}}(k)^- = F(k, k - 1)\hat{\underline{s}}(k - 1)^+, \tag{4}$$

$$P(k)^- = F(k, k - 1)P(k - 1)^+F(k, k - 1)^T + G(k - 1)Q(k - 1)G(k - 1)^T. \tag{5}$$

2. Updating of estimates at $t = t_k$:

$$K(k) = P(k)^-H(k)^T[H(k)P(k)^-H(k)^T + R(k)]^{-1}, \tag{6}$$

$$P(k)^+ = [I - K(k)H(k)]P(k)^-, \tag{7}$$

$$\hat{\underline{s}}(k)^+ = \hat{\underline{s}}(k)^- + K(k)[\underline{m}(k) - H(k)\hat{\underline{s}}(k)^-]. \tag{8}$$

C. *EXTENSIONS TO NONLINEAR MEASUREMENT EQUATIONS*

The measurement Eq. (2) are replaced with

$$\underline{m}(k) = \underline{h}[\underline{s}(k), t_k] + \underline{u}(k). \tag{9}$$

The linearized state-to-measurement transformation H appearing in Eqs. (6)-(8) are now obtained by means of vector differentiation of $\underline{h}[\underline{s}, t]$ with respect to $\underline{s}$:

$$H(k) = (\delta\underline{h}[\underline{s}(\tau), \tau]/\delta\underline{s})_{\tau=t_k}. \tag{10}$$

D. *NOTATION USED IN SECTIONS A-C*

Uppercase letters represent matrices.

Lowercase letters represent scalars or (if marked with bars underneath) column vectors.

$\underline{x}(k)$ represents the value of column vector $\underline{x}$ at $t = t_k$; similar notation is used to time-tag scalars and matrices.

A^T represents the transpose of matrix A; if $\underline{x}$ is a column vector, then $\underline{x}^T$ represents the transpose of $\underline{x}$ (a row vector),

$\delta_{kj} = 1$ if $k = j$; $= 0$, otherwise.

$\hat{\underline{s}}(k|i)$ denotes an estimate of $\underline{s}$ at time t_k that has been obtained by using a history of measurements up to and including the time $t_i (\leq t_k)$.

APPENDIX II: U-D FACTOR COVARIANCE/GAIN PROCESSING ALGORITHMS FOR KALMAN FILTERS

A. *INTRODUCTION*

Covariance and gain processing algorithms, operating on U and D factors of state error covariance matrix P, are a technique for implementing "square root filtering" without requiring computation of square roots. These algorithms offer a recommended approach for overcoming the numerical instability inherent in the standard (original) formulation of Kalman filter algorithms summarized in Appendix I. Numerical instability problems are caused by the repeated use of Eq. (7) in Appendix I for measurement updating of state error covariance matrix P. Examination of that equation shows that accumulation of roundoff errors may eventually cause matrix P to lose its positive definiteness. It should be noted that the U-D factor covariance filtering is just a numerically stable and computationally efficient method for implementing Kalman's estimation procedure (outlined in Appendix I), but is not an estimator of a type different from the Kalman filter.

The term "U-D covariance factorization" comes from a property of nonnegative definite symmetric matrices, according to which such a matrix P can be factored into $P = UDU^T$, where U is an upper triangular matrix with unit elements on its main diagonal and D is a diagonal matrix.

For convenience, we next summarize the basic U-D factor covariance filtering algorithms. For details the reader is referred to [11] and [10], the second being an updated review of the topic although narrower in scope than the first.

B. NOTATION

Suppose that the reference time of the current estimation cycle is t_k. To simplify the notation used in Appendix I (and to make it more compatible with the notation used in [10]), we drop explicit referencing to time and write $\underline{\tilde{s}}$ for $\underline{\hat{s}}(k|k - 1)$, $\underline{\hat{s}}$ for $\underline{\hat{s}}(k|k)$; similarly, $\tilde{P}$ for $P(k|k - 1) \triangleq P(k)^-$ and $\hat{P}$ for $P(k|k) \triangleq P(k)^+$. Otherwise, we use the same letters as in Appendix I to denote the quantities in terms in which the system model and the Kalman filter algorithms are formulated.

The following symbols are used to specify the size of the system model: n to denote the length of state vector $\underline{s}$; n_q, the length of process noise vector $\underline{w}$ (q here relates to process noise covariance matrix Q); and n_m, the length of measurement vector $\underline{m}$, although in the following text we consider only the sequential processing of scalar measurements.

C. U-D FACTOR MEASUREMENT-UPDATE ALGORITHM

Suppose that the following input quantities are given: H is a $1 \times n$ matrix (i.e., a row vector of length n) representing the linearized state-to-measurement transformation for the scalar measurement to be processed, R the noise variance ($\triangleq \alpha_0$) of the measurement to be processed, and $\tilde{U}$, $\tilde{D}$ the U- and

D-factors of P (time-propagated to t_k or measurement-updated at t_k for all measurements so far processed at t_k). Proceed as specified by the algorithm contained in Fig. 5 to perform covariance/gain update processing for a scalar measurement. To process a vector of n_m measurements, this algorithm would have to be embedded in a measurement processing loop (e.g., Section V.C) and then executed iteratively n_m times.

This algorithm uses a scalar λ and n-dimensional vector $\underline{f}$ and $\underline{g}$ as intermediate variables.

```
UDMUPD:  begin
         f^T := HŨ                      (where   f^T = [f_1, ..., f_n])
          g := Df̃;                      (where   g^T = [g_1, ..., g_n])
         for j = 1, ..., n do:
             α_j := α_{j-1} + f_j g_j;  (where   α_0 = R and α = α_n)
              if α_j = 0, then D̂_j := D̃_j;
                 else D̂_j := (α_{j-1}/α_j) D̃_j;
             ν_j := g_j;
             if j = 1, then go to ELj;
                if α_{j-1} = 0, then λ := 0;
                   else λ := -f_j/α_{j-1};
                for i = 1, ..., j - 1 do:
                   Û_ij := Ũ_ij + ν_j λ;
                   ν_i := ν_i + Ũ_ij ν_j;
                end                            (Recycle if i < j - 1)
   ELj:  end                                   (Recycle if j < n)
         k := (1/α_n) ν                        (k^T = [k_1, ..., k_n])
         end UDMUPD
```

Fig. 5. Executable (computational) part of U-D Measurement-Update Algorithm, defined by Thornton and Bierman ([10], pp. 198, 199). Inputs, outputs, and intermediate quantities are specified in Section C.

The outputs are as follows: $\underline{k}$ is a Kalman gain vector of length n or (by the notation of Appendix I) $n \times 1$ matrix K; $\hat{U}$, $\hat{D}$ are U- and D-factors of P, measurement-updated for all measurements so far processed at t_k. Instead of outputting $\underline{k}$, it is often preferable to output separately $\underline{\nu}$ as the normalized Kalman gain vector and the innovations variance α $(=\alpha_n)$, which, following the notation of Appendix I, can be expressed as $[H(k)P(k)^{-}H(k)^{T} + R(k)]$. This is because α is used in the measurement processing loop for screening a processed measurement by testing whether or not its residual lies within an acceptance interval of the form $(-b\alpha_n, b\alpha_n)$, where $b(> 0)$ is a scaling parameter.

D. COMPARISON WITH THE ORIGINAL FORM OF KALMAN FILTER

Next, we restate the covariance/gain filtering part of the original form of Kalman filter [defined in Appendix I by Eqs. (5)-(7)] for processing a single scalar measurement in terms of the notation introduced in the present appendix. We do it to facilitate comparison between the original algorithms and the U-D factor covariance/gain processing algorithms summarized in this appendix.

In terms of the simplified notation used in the present appendix, Eqs. (5)-(7) of Appendix I yield the following procedure:

<u>begin</u>

$\tilde{P} := F\hat{P}F^T + GQG^T$; (Covariance propagation to t_k)

$\underline{\nu} := \tilde{P}H^T$; (Normalized Kalman gain)

$\alpha := H\underline{\nu} + R$; (Innovations covariance)

$\underline{k} := \underline{\nu}\alpha^{-1}$; (Kalman gains at t_k)

$\hat{P} := \tilde{P} - \underline{k}\underline{\nu}^T$; (Covariance measurement update at t_k)

end

The preceding form of covariance measurement update [or equivalently Eq. (7) in Appendix I] is known to be computationally unstable in the sense that it may make P acquire negative characteristic roots as a result of roundoff errors and overconvergence of P. A stabler, and although computationally more expensive, version of that formula for a scalar measurement (with H being 1 × n matrix) is

$$\hat{P} := (I - \underline{k}H)\tilde{P}(I - \underline{k}H)^T + kRk^T.$$

Its vector measurement version is

$$\hat{P} := (I - KH)\tilde{P}(I - KH)^T + KRK^T,$$

where K now is an $n \times n_m$ matrix and H is an $n_m \times n$ matrix. Owing to the amount of processing required , this stabler form is rarely used in real-time applications.

E. PROPAGATION TIME-UPDATING OF STATE ERROR COVARIANCES

When the U-D factor filtering algorithms are used for measurement updating of state error covariance matrix P and computation of Kalman gains, the following two alternative approaches for performing the propagation of P are available: the Conventional Propagation-of Covariance Algorithm and the U-D Factor Propagation (Time-Update) Algorithm. In the following text these two approaches are outlined for propagation of P from time t_k to $t_{k+1} = t_k + \Delta t_K$, i.e., for computing $P(k+1)^- \triangleq P(k+1|k) \triangleq \tilde{P}$ from the measurement update of P obtained in the preceding estimation cycle.

F. THE CONVENTIONAL PROPAGATION-OF-COVARIANCE ALGORITHM

This algorithm for computing $\tilde{P}$, given $\hat{P}$ from the preceding cycle, in terms of factor matrices U and D is based on the following procedure:

a. Compute

$$\overline{P} := (FU)D(FU)^T, \quad (1)$$

which yields the canonical product representation of matrix $\overline{P}$. Here, $F \triangleq F(k + 1|k)$ is the state transition matrix for propagation of the state vector $\underline{s}$ from t_k to t_{k+1}.

b. Compute the process covariance matrix $Q = Q(k, \Delta t_k)$, which may be a function of time and of the propagation step size Δt_k.

c. Compute

$$\tilde{P} = \overline{P} + GQG^T, \quad (2)$$

where $G \triangleq G(k)$ is as defined by Eq. (1) in Appendix I.

d. Factor $\tilde{P}$ into $\tilde{U}$ and $\tilde{D}$ by means of the U-D Factorization Algorithm, specified in Fig. 6.

Although the computing implied by the above steps a through d is thought of as a stable process, it is noted on p. 188 of [10] that there exist important exceptions when F is large and/or P is ill-conditioned. In such situations, the resulting matrix P may have serious errors. Problems may also arise when, owing to roundoff errors, some characteristic values become slightly negative.

On the positive side the preceding covariance propagation algorithm yields (after Step c) $\tilde{P}$ expressed in the canonical product form, various parts of which (especially its main diagonal elements) are often used for both on-line and post-mission performance analysis. Also, the appearance of slightly

Input: $n \times n$ symmetric matrix $\tilde{P}$, with main-diagonal and upper-triangular elements stored in an $n \times n$ array P.

Output: $n \times n$ unit-diagonal, upper-triangular matrix $\tilde{U}$, with its upper triangular portion stored in $n \times n$ array U (which optionally can be "equivalenced" with array P so that the original $\tilde{P}$ is destroyed).

Output: the main-diagonal elements of $n \times n$ diagonal matrix $\tilde{D}$ stored in vector D (which optionally can be stored in locations of the main-diagonal elements of array P).

Remark: the algorithm does not explicitly generate the main-diagonal unit elements of $\tilde{U}$.

```
UDFTCTR: begin
         for j = n, n - 1, ..., 2 do:
             D̃_j := P_j,j;
              α := 1/D̃_j;
             for k = 1, ..., j - 1 do:
                    β := P_k,j;
                 Ũ_k,j := α*β
                 for i = 1, ..., k do:
                    P_i,k := P_i,k - β*Ũ_i,j;
                 end
             end
         end
         D_1 = P_1,1
         end UDFCTR
```

Fig. 6. U-D Factorization Algorithm.

negative characterisitic roots in $\tilde{P}$ can be avoided by keeping GQG^T sufficiently "large" compared with $\tilde{P}$ and/or by monitoring and then boosting, on the basis of need, the elements of diagonal matrix $\tilde{D}$. A related technique (in case G is not an identity matrix), borrowed from ridge regression, is to add to the right-hand side of Eq. (2) a positive definite diagonal matrix on detection of the need to boost $\tilde{P}$.

G. U-D FACTOR PROPAGATION (TIME-UPDATE) ALGORITHM

This algorithm is based on modified Gram-Schmidt orthogonolization. It is described on pp. 200-203 of [10].

To summarize it we first need to define a weighted inner product of two n-component vectors $\underline{a}$ and $\underline{c}$, weighted (normalized) by the main diagonal elements of an $n \times n$ matrix $B = \text{diag}[b_1, \ldots, b_n]$. We define this inner product as

$$(\underline{a}, \underline{c})_B = \underline{a}^T B \underline{c} = a_1 b_1 c_1 + \cdots + a_n b_n c_n. \tag{3}$$

Next we use two matrices from the system model introduced in Appendix I, the $n \times n$ state transition matrix $F = F(k+1, k)$ and the $n \times n_q$ process noise transformation matrix G, to define

$$W = [F\hat{U} \mid G]. \tag{4}$$

[Here, $\hat{U}$ and $\hat{D}$ denote the measurements updates (from the preceding estimation cycle) of U and D, respectively.] Thus, W is an $n \times N = n \times (n + n_q)$ matrix, the jth row of which will be denoted by $\underline{w}_j^T$.

Finally, we combine in the indicated order the main-diagonal elements of $n \times n$ diagonal matrix $\hat{D}$ with those of $n_q \times n_q$ process noise matrix Q to define an $N \times N$ diagonal matrix $\overline{D}$ (where again $N = n + n_q$) as

$$\begin{aligned} \overline{D} &\triangleq \text{diag}\,[\overline{D}_1, \ldots, \overline{D}_N] \\ &\triangleq \text{diag}\,[\hat{D}_1, \ldots, \hat{D}_n, Q_{1,1}, \ldots, Q_{n_q,n_q}]. \end{aligned} \tag{5}$$

With the needed definitions completed, we are ready to summarize the U-D Factor Propagation Algorithm, which we do in Fig. 7.

Input: n × N matrix W (with rows $\underline{w}_1^T, \ldots, \underline{w}_n^T$).

Input: N × N diagonal matrix $\overline{D}$ defined by Eq. (5).

Output: the upper triangular part $\tilde{U}$ of propagated n × n unit-diagonal, upper-triangular matrix U.

Output: the main diagonal elements, stored as a vector $\tilde{D}$, of n × n diagonal matrix D.

Define: $\underline{w}_j^{(0)} = \underline{w}_j$ for j = 1, ..., n.

UDFCTRPR: <u>begin</u>

<u>for</u> j = n, n - 1, ..., 2 <u>do</u>:

$\tilde{D}_j := (\underline{w}_j^{(n-j)}, \underline{w}_j^{(n-j)})_{\overline{D}}$;

<u>for</u> i = 1, ..., j - 1 <u>do</u>:

$\tilde{U}_{i,j} := (\underline{w}_j^{(n-j)}, \underline{w}_j^{(n-j)})_{\overline{D}}(1/\tilde{D}_j)$;

$\underline{w}_j^{(n-j+1)} := \underline{w}_j^{(n-j)} - (\tilde{U}_{i,j})\underline{w}_j^{(n-j)}$;

<u>end</u>

<u>end</u>

$\tilde{D}_1 = (\underline{w}_1^{(n-1)}, \underline{w}_1^{(n-1)})_{\overline{D}}$;

<u>end</u> UDFCTRPR

Fig. 7. U-D Factor Propagation (Time-Update) Algorithm.

H. CONCLUDING NOTES

Only the very basic forms (of "Bierman's method") of U-D factor covariance/gain processing algorithms have been summarized and compared here with the original form of Kalman's filter. For a more complete account of Bierman's approach refer to [11] or to [10]. For different approaches to "square root filtering" refer to Andrews [28] or Carlson [22]. Chapter 6 of [23] and Chapter 7 of [9] contain textbook introductions to this topic. Comparative timing and sizing of filtering algorithms are discussed in [11], [10], and [9].

As noted in Section IV, in implemental design of real-time Kalman filters for small computers, the value of "square-root filtering" algorithms is mainly due to (a) their numerical stability, (b) their suitability for implementation in single-precision floating-point arithmetic (except for computation of some dot products), and (c) their reasonable computational efficiency compared to Kalman's original formulation. Criterion (b) is important in implementations of real-time estimators on the microprocessors, for the disparity between the speeds of single and double precision forms of floating-point arithmetic worsens as one goes from hardware to software (i.e., interpretive) implementation of this arithmetic.

Limitations in the available processing resources and the existing real-time constraints usually motivate the exploitation of problem structure (see [10]) to reduce the processing load. There are several areas that should always be carefully examined and possibly exploited. The first is avoidance of floating-point operations on zero-valued operands. This can be attained via careful programming of algorithms. The second is structuring of vectors and matrices in the system model so as to introduce zero subvectors and submatrices, which would in turn yield an estimation problem of smaller size. This can often be accomplished through careful structuring of system model and mechanization of estimation algorithms. Next all matrix symmetries should be utilized to save both processing time and memory space. Finally, all kernel algorithms, operating on or producing matrices, should be almost always designed to handle matrices as single dimension arrays. The last feature allows efficient application of the same algorithm implementation (subprogram) to system models of varying dimensions and decompositions. In some applications considered here dimensions of the system model (such as the length of state vector) may change in real time.

APPENDIX III: ESTIMATION PROBLEM IN GPS USER'S NAVIGATION

A. *INTRODUCTION*

This appendix summarizes the GPS estimation problem and defines a system model for it. This problem is cited as an illustration several times in the main body of this chapter.

User of GPS navigation equipment is assumed to be either moving or staying stationary close to the surface of the earth. Several different types of GPS user's navigation equipment for various classes of users (e.g., a stationary user, a land vehicle, an aircraft, or a ship) have been developed or are still under development. [29] discusses integration of GPS with inertial systems; [30] describes GPS messages. Discussions by [12], [13], and [15] are samples of literature describing GPS user's navigation and/or its equipment. The estimation problem of GPS navigation and its system model actually depend on the particular type of equipment under consideration. For pedagogical reasons we overlook many technical details in this estimation problem and define a simplified system model for it.

B. *COORDINATE SYSTEM*

An earth-centered earth-fixed (ECEF) coordinate system (with coordinate axes denoted by x, y, and z) is used in all GPS navigation processing described here. The z-axis of such a coordinate frame coincides with the polar axis of the reference ellipsoid; x and y lie in the equatorial plane. The particular version of ECEF frame assumed here has its x-axis pointing toward the Greenwich meridian; the y-axis 90°, east of the x-axis.

C. NAVIGATION STATE VECTOR

The navigation state vector (which, in general, is a function of time) is defined by

$$\underline{s}^T = (b, f, x, y, z, v_x, v_y, v_z) \triangleq (b, f, \underline{p}^T, \underline{v}^T),$$

where b is the range bias in range measurements, owing to a bias in the clock of user's navigation equipment set relative to the GPS time; f = db/dt, the frequency drift rate of user's navigation equipment clock; $\underline{p}^T = (x, y, z)$, the ECEF coordinates of the antenna phase center (PC) in user's navigation set; and $\underline{v}^T = (v_x, v_y, v_z)$, which are the ECEF velocity components of the antenna PC. In GPS navigation, even for moderate dynamics users, one usually models acceleration. For simplicity, acceleration is not modeled in the present case.

D. DISCRETE-TIME MODEL

The discrete-time model of state vector dynamics is

$$\underline{s}(k) = F(k, k - 1)\underline{s}(k - 1) + \underline{w}(k - 1).$$

Let

$$\Delta t_k = t_k - t_{k-1},$$

and ideally one would like to assume that $\underline{w}(k)$ is a zero-mean Gaussian white noise process with

$$E[\underline{w}(k)\underline{w}^T(k)] = Q(k, \Delta t_k),$$

$$E(\underline{s}(0)] = \hat{\underline{s}}(0),$$

and

$$E([\underline{s}(0) - \hat{\underline{s}}(0)][\underline{s}(0) - \hat{\underline{s}}(0)]^T) = P(0).$$

The state transition matrix F is defined by the following transformations:

$$b(k) = b(k - 1) + \Delta t_k f(k - 1),$$

$$f(k) = f(k - 1) \exp[-\Delta t_k/\tau_b],$$

with the range bias correlation time τ_b assumed to be a constant or a slowly changing parameter, and

$$\underline{p}(k) = \underline{p}(k - 1) + \Delta t_k \underline{v}(k - 1),$$

$$\underline{v}(k) = \underline{v}(k - 1).$$

NAVSTAR-GPS satellites (on the pseudorange and delta pseudorange measurements of which the navigation filter operates) will be referred to as space vehicles (SVs).

For each tracked SV, the navigation filter during a measurement processing cycle receives (via the GPS receiver in the navigation set) a pair of pseudorange and delta pseudorange (an observed change in pseudorange over a count period of fixed length) measurements. For the jth SV, SV_j, these two measurements will be denoted by $PR_j(t)$ and $DPR_j(t)$, respectively. A pseudorange roughly is a range that has been synthesized from the readings of two distinct clocks (SV clock and user's navigation set clock) and that has not been corrected for the bias of user's navigation set clock with respect to the SV clock. In the following text it will be assumed that incoming pseudorange measurements are already corrected (actually they are not) for other errors, such as the SV clock errors with respect to GPS system time or the atmospheric signal delays. Thus if b(t) denotes the true but unknown range bias at time t and if $PR_j(t)$ is the corrected pseudorange from SV_j received at time t, then the transit range of the signal received from SV_j by user's navigation set at the same time t is represented by

$$R_j(t) = PR_j(t) - b(t).$$

Hence the predicted pseudorange measurement for SV_j at time t can be written as

$$P\hat{R}_j(t) = \hat{R}_j(t) + \hat{b}(t).$$

Similarly, the delta pseudorange measurement $DPR_j(t)$ for SV_j at time t is defined by

$$DPR_j(t) = PR_j(t+\delta t) - PR_j(t-\delta t),$$

where $\delta t_{DPR} \triangleq 2\delta t$ is the duration of delta range count, which is a design characteristic of the receiver. Hence the measurement DPR_j is predicted at time t by means of

$$\begin{aligned} DP\hat{R}_j(t) &= P\hat{R}_j(t+\delta t) - P\hat{R}_j(t-\delta t) \\ &= \hat{R}_j(t+\delta t) - \hat{R}_j(t-\delta t) + \hat{b}(t+\delta t) - \hat{b}(t-\delta t) \\ &\cong \hat{R}_j(t+\delta t) - \hat{R}_j(t-\delta t) + \hat{f}(t)\,\delta t_{DPR}. \end{aligned}$$

In a measurement processing cycle, a (PR, DPR) measurement pair is received from each of four (or occasionally fewer) tracked SVs and subsequently processed by the navigation filter.

To complete the system model, the measurement equation at t_k is written as

$$\underline{m}(k) = h[\underline{s}(k), t_k] + \underline{u}(k),$$

where we assume that

(a) the transpose of vector $\underline{m}(k)$ is of the form $[PR_1(k), \ldots, PR_{n_k}(k), DPR_1(k), \ldots, PR_{n_k}(k)]$, with n_k (≤ 4) being the number of distinct SVs from which measurements are available at time t_k;

(b) $\underline{u}(k)$ is a zero-mean Gaussian white noise process with $E[\underline{u}(k)\underline{u}^T(k)] = \mathrm{diag}\left[\sigma^2_{PR1}, \ldots, \sigma^2_{PRnk}, \sigma^2_{DPR1}, \ldots, \sigma^2_{DPRnk}\right]$; and

(c) $\{\underline{w}(k)\}$ and $\{\underline{u}(k)\}$ are mutually independent stochastic processes, which are also independent of $\underline{s}(0)$.

It is assumed that the GPS receiver, which acquires and preprocesses for the estimator pseudorange and delta pseudorange measurements, is designed to furnish extra observables from which the estimator directly computes σ^2_{PRj} and σ^2_{DPRj}. Such a receiver is described in [26].

E. EQUATIONS FOR PREDICTION OF RANGES AND DELTA PSEUDORANGES

The transit range $R_j(t)$ from SV_j of the signal received at time t is computed by means of range equation

$$R_j(t) = \left([x_j + \alpha y_j - x]^2 + [y_j - \alpha x_j - y]^2 + [z_j - z]^2\right)^{1/2}$$

$$= \left[(\Delta x_j)^2 + (\Delta y_j)^2 + (\Delta z_j)^2\right]^{1/2}, \tag{1}$$

where

(a) $\alpha = (\Omega)(\Delta t_{T(j)})$ is the angle by which the ECEF coordinate frame is rotated during the signal transit time from SV_j, with Ω representing earth's sidereal rate and $\Delta t_{T(j)}$ being the duration of signal transit from SV_j, a quantity that is unknown and must be estimated.

(b) (x_j, y_j, z_j) represent the ECEF position coordinates of SV_j at time $t_j = t - \Delta t_{T(j)}$; they must be computed by means of an extended form of Kepler's two-body problem algorithm while using the transmitted orbital parameters (called ephemeris data) of SV_j. The best approach is to recompute periodically (at a relatively low rate) the least-squares polynomials for predicting, as a function of time, the position coordinates of SV_j, (x_j, y_j, z_j). This approach saves processor time and yields, by means of analytic differentiation of polynomials, approximations to the time derivatives $(\dot{x}_j, \dot{y}_j, \dot{z}_j)$ of (x_j, y_j, z_j). These time derivatives are useful in obtaining the time derivatives $(\Delta\dot{x}_j, \Delta\dot{y}_j, \Delta\dot{z}_j)$ of $(\Delta x_j, \Delta y_j, \Delta z_j)$.

(c) (x, y, z) are the ECEF coordinates of the position at time t of the antenna phase center in user's navigation set. To predict $R_j(t)$ [i.e., to obtain $\hat{R}_j(t)$], the quantities (x, y, z) in Eq. (1) are replaced with their estimates at time t. The expression

$$R_j(t+\delta t) - R_j(t-\delta t), \tag{2}$$

needed in computing of the predicted value of $DPR_j(t)$ at time t, can be efficiently and with sufficient accuracy approximated by means of

$$([dR(\tau)/d\tau]_{\tau=t})\delta t_{DPR} = [\Delta x_j \Delta\dot{x}_j + \Delta y_j \Delta\dot{y}_j + \Delta z_j \Delta\dot{z}_j]/R_j(t), \tag{3}$$

where, as earlier stated, δt_{DPR} is the duration of delta pseudorange count. To predict the value of expression in Eq. (2), one substitutes in Eq. (3) the estimates of Δx_j, Δy_j, Δz_j, $\Delta\dot{x}_j$, $\Delta\dot{y}_j$, and $\Delta\dot{z}_j$ at time t.

F. MODELING OF PROCESS NOISE COVARIANCES

Suppose that the process noise manifests itself only through the unmodeled acceleration and through the range bias and bias rate of change components of state. Let Δt_k be the effective time step used for propagating the state error covariances P from t_{k-1} to t_k. Then the process noise covariance at time t_k is of the form

$$Q(k, \Delta t_k) = \left[\begin{array}{c|c} Q_b(\Delta t_k) & 0_{2\times 6} \\ \hline 0_{6\times 2} & Q_d(k, \Delta t_k) \end{array}\right],$$

where subscript b refers to range bias and its rate of change and subscript d to user's dynamics.

The 6 × 6 user's dynamics process noise submatrix Q_d is of the form

$$Q_d(k, \Delta t) = \left[\begin{array}{c|c} q_{pp}I_3 & q_{pv}I_3 \\ \hline q_{pv}I_3 & q_{vv}I_3 \end{array}\right].$$

Hence Q_d is constructed from three generating scalar parameters q_{pp}, q_{pv}, and q_{vv}. Obtain an auxiliary 2 × 2 matrix $\overline{Q}_d(k, t_k)$, constructed from these three parameters from

$$\overline{Q}_d(k, \Delta t_k) = \begin{bmatrix} q_{pp} & q_{pv} \\ q_{pv} & q_{vv} \end{bmatrix} = \int_0^{\Delta t_k} [F_d(\tau)]N[F_d(\tau)]^T d\tau,$$

where

$$F_d(\tau) = \begin{bmatrix} 1 & \tau \\ 0 & 1 \end{bmatrix}, \qquad N = \begin{bmatrix} 0 & 0 \\ 0 & n_{vv} \end{bmatrix},$$

$n_{vv} = 2\sigma_v^2/\tau_v^2$ represents the power spectrum density of velocity owing to unmodeled acceleration, σ_v^2 is the variance of velocity noise, and τ_v is the velocity correlation time constant. In general, σ_v^2 and τ_v are not time invariant.

Submatrix Q_b of Q is of the form

$$Q_b(\Delta t) = \begin{bmatrix} q_{bb} & q_{bf} \\ q_{bf} & q_{ff} \end{bmatrix},$$

where, assuming that the range bias rate correlation time τ_b is much greater than Δt,

$$q_{bb} \cong (n_{bb})\Delta t + (n_{ff}/3)(\Delta t)^3,$$

$$q_{bf} \cong (n_{ff}/2)(\Delta t)^2,$$

and

$$q_{ff} \cong (n_{ff})(\Delta t).$$

In the preceding expressions, parameters n_{bb} and n_{ff} characterize the clock of user's navigation set.

ACKNOWLEDGMENTS

The author wishes to express his gratitude to the staff of Texas Instruments Incorporated for the support received during the preparation of this chapter. He is particularly indebted to Phillip W. Ward for many years of opportunity to test in practice some of the ideas presented here, to Srini Raghavan for advice and criticism during preparation of this chapter, and to Beverly Littlejohn and Alice Dunbar for editing and typing expertise. He is also indebted to the editorial staff of Academic Press.

REFERENCES

1. R. K. SMYTH, *Astron. Aeron.* *18*(4), 40-52 (1980).
2. E. G. COFFMAN, Jr. and P. J. DENNING, "Operating Systems Theory," Prentice-Hall, Englewood Cliffs, New Jersey, 1973.
3. P. FREEMAN, "Software Systems Principles — A Survey," Science Research Associates, Chicago, 1975.
4. R. M. GRAHAM, "Principles of Systems Programming," Wiley, New York, 1975.
5. P. B. HANSEN, "Operating System Principles," Prentice-Hall, Englewood Cliffs, New Jersey, 1973.

6. P. W. WEGNER, "Programming with ADA – An Introduction by Means of Graduated Examples," Prentice-Hall, Englewood Cliffs, New Jersey, 1980.

7. V. B. GYLYS and J. A. EDWARDS, "COMPCON 76," Digest of Papers, IEEE Computer Society, pp. 353-356, 1976.

8. E. D. JENSEN and W. E. BOEBERT, "COMPCON 76," Digest of Papers, IEEE Computer Society, pp. 348-352, 1976.

9. P. S. MAYBECK, "Stochastic Models, Estimation, and Control," Vol. 1, Academic Press, New York, 1979.

10. C. L. THORNTON and G. J. BIERMAN, "Control and Dynamic Systems," Vol. 16 (C. T. Leondes, ed.), Academic Press, New York, 1980.

11. G. J. BIERMAN, "Factorization Methods for Discrete Sequential Estimation," Academic Press, New York, 1977.

12. J. N. DAMOULAKIS, V. GYLYS, and T. N. UPADHYAY, *Rec. IEEE 1978 Pos. Loc. and Nav. Symp.*, 388-395 (1978).

13. V. B. GYLYS and P. W. WARD, "Design and Performance of the Missile-Borne Receiver Set," Pres. at NAECON 1979. Reprinted in *Texas Inst. Equipm Group Eng. J. 3*(3) (1980).

14. S. E. MADNICK and J. J. DONOVAN, "Operating Systems," McGraw-Hill, New York, 1974.

15. T. N. UPADHYAY and J. N. DAMOULAKIS, *IEEE Trans. Aero. and Elect. Syst. AES-16*(4), 481-491 (1980).

16. E. G. COFFMAN, Jr. (ed.), "Computer and Job-Shop Scheduling Theory," Wiley, New York, 1976.

17. L. J. BASS, *SIAM J. Comput 2*(4), 273-280 (1973).

18. R. O. BERG and K. J. THURBER, *Proc. Natl. Elec. Conf. 27*, 275-280 (1972).

19. J. W. JORDAN, "Task Scheduling for a Real Time Multiprocessor," NASA TN-D-5786 (1970).

20. G. K. MANACHER, *J. Assoc. Comput. Mach. 14*(3), 439-465 (1967).

21. C. L. LIU and J. W. LAYLAND, "Scheduling Algorithms for Multiprogramming in a Hard Real-Time Environment," *J. Assoc. Comput. Mach. 20*(1), 46-61 (1973).

22. N. A. CARLSON, *AIAAJ 11*(9), 1259-1265 (1973).

23. B. D. O. ANDERSON and J. B. MOORE, "Optimal Filtering," Prentice-Hall, Englewood Cliffs, New Jersey, 1979.

24. H. W. BREWER, "Control and Dynamic Systems," Vol. 12 (C. T. Leondes, ed.), Academic Press, New York, 1976.

25. R. F. OHAP and A. R. STUBBERUD, "Control and Dynamic Systems," Vol. 12 (C. T. Leondes, ed.), Academic Press, New York, 1976).

26. P. W. WARD, *Proc. 3rd Internat. Geodetic Symp. Satellite Doppler Position* (1982).

27. G. T. SCHMIDT, "Control and Dynamic Systems," Vol. 12 (C. T. Leondes, ed.), Academic Press, New York, 1976.

28. A. ANDREWS, *AIAAJ 6*, 1165-1166 (1968).

29. D. B. COX, Jr., *Navigation 25*(2), 236-245 (1978).

30. A. J. VAN DIERENDONCK, S. S. RUSSELL, E. R. KOPITZKE, and M. BRINBAUM, *Navigation (J. Inst. Navig.) 25*(2), 147-165 (1978).

Global Approximation for Nonlinear Filtering with Application to Spreading Spectrum Ranging

W. MICHAEL BOWLES

Space Communications Group
Hughes Aircraft Co.
Los Angeles, California

JOHN A. CARTELLI

Technical Staff
ESL
Sunnyvale, California

I. INTRODUCTION

This chapter is a discussion of some global approximation procedures for nonlinear filtering. These procedures yield algorithms for recovering a signal from a measurement

ISBN 0-12-012719-9

containing signal plus noise. The celebrated Kalman filter solves linear Gaussian problems. For problems where linear Gaussian conditions are weakly violated, the Kalman filter serves as a good approximation. In many interesting problems, however, these conditions are not satisfied. For example, one of the random variables may have a multimodal density function or the signal may enter nonlinearly into the measurement. The techniques discussed here give the designer some tools to use when the Kalman filter is no longer a reasonable approximate solution to this problem.

II. ORGANIZATION

The first section is devoted to a brief statement of the general problem addressed here, and a discussion is presented, by means of an example, of the difference between global and local approximations. The extended Kalman filter will be seen to be a local approximation, and the hope is that the example chosen will illustrate the inherent difference between the extended Kalman filter and approximations to be developed later. The example problem chosen to illustrate the difference between local and global approximation is that of analyzing a feedback loop with a nonlinearity in the forward path. The local approximation for this problem is a small signal analysis or linearization. The global approximation chosen is a describing function analysis. The difference between these two is that the global approach predicts fundamentally nonlinear phenomena like limit cycles, whereas the small signal gain approach cannot. The particular example chosen is also useful in that it will recur when filtering is discussed in the section.

In Section III some global nonlinear filtering approximations are developed and their use with a radar ranging example is illustrated. The first part of the section is devoted to the introduction of this radar example. A radio ranging problem, similar to the radar problem discussed here, provided the authors with motivation to explore global approximation. The problem is one that cannot be solved satisfactorily by an extended Kalman filter. The remainder of Section III is devoted to the introduction of particular approximation methods and their application to the radar problem. The applications are developed and compared and their performance demonstrated.

A. PROBLEM STATEMENT

The object of this chapter will be to give some approximate filtering algorithms for the problem of recovering the signal from a measurement containing signal plus noise. It will be assumed throughout this chapter that the signal to be estimated is a random process that satisfies

$$\dot{x} = f(x, t) + g(x, t)n(t), \tag{1}$$

where f and g are known functions and n(t) is an m vector white noise with spectral matrix Q(t). The signal x(t) is an n vector. It is further assumed that the measurement from which the signal is to be extracted is of the form

$$z(t) = h(x, t) + v(t), \tag{2}$$

where h is a known function v(t) a white noise with spectral matrix R(t) and is independent of n(t). In Section II.B a radar tracking problem that has this form is presented, and many other physical problems can be modeled by this set of equations. The vector x is called the state vector or the message, depending on the situation. The vector z is called the measurement. The objective is to present some algorithms that process the measurements z(t) to determine the state x(t) with the smallest possible errors.

Some of the approaches to be used for extricating the signal from a noisy measurement require the equations to be in discrete-time form. Discrete-Time state and measurement equations have the form

$$x(i + 1) = f(x(i), i) + g(x(i), i)n(i) \tag{3}$$

and

$$z(i + 1) = h(x(i), i) + v(i), \tag{4}$$

where x and z are the discrete-time state and measurement, respectively. The functions f, g, and h are assumed to be known. The noise sequences h(i) and v(i) are white, independent, and Gaussian.

B. THE DIFFERENCE BETWEEN LOCAL AND GLOBAL APPROXIMATION

In this section an example problem illustrates the differences between global and local approximations. The problem chosen is to analyze the behavior of a nonlinear feedback loop. The loop to be analyzed is diagrammed in Fig. 1.

This tracking loop is first order. It has a nonlinearity in the forward loop that is linear for errors smaller than one in magnitude and goes to zero for errors larger in magnitude than two. The input to be tracked by the loop is a Brownian

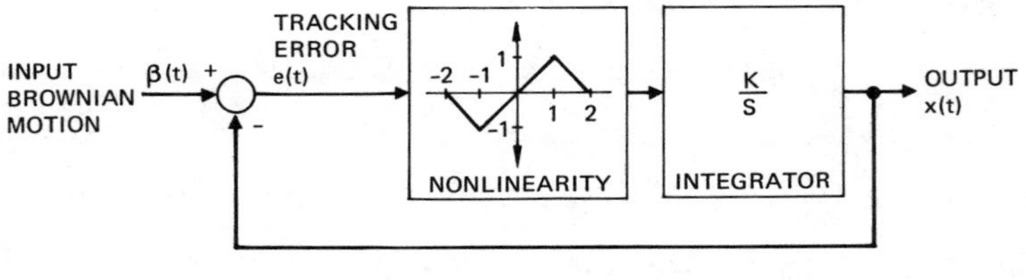

Fig. 1. A nonlinear feedback loop.

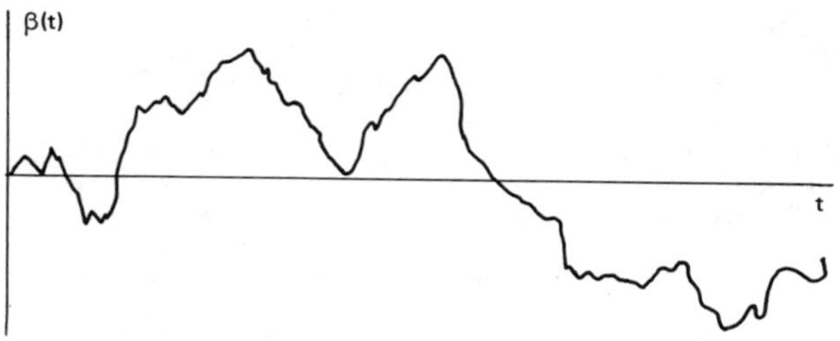

Fig. 2. Possible trajectory for a Brownian motion.

motion. A Brownian motion is a Gaussian random process. A typical time history might look like the trajectory in Fig. 2.

The Brownian motion can be thought of as the integral of a white noise. It will be assumed that the spectral level of this white noise is q. The magnitude of q determines how difficult the input is to track.

The form of the forward loop nonlinearity is an obvious source of difficulty for this tracking loop. Because errors larger than two result in zero restorative force, it is expected that there is some level of q for which the loop will be unable to follow the input with a finite error. If the input were a ramp and q its slope, then it would be clear that above some magnitude of q the input would be untrackable by the loop in Fig. 1. This would be clear because the tracking loop is first order and follows a ramp with a steady-state error. For a ramp input to a first-order loop, the magnitude of the steady-state error is proportional to the ramp's slope. When the slope becomes large enough that the steady-state error is greater than one, the loop in Fig. 1 will no longer follow it with a finite steady-state error. The object is now to demonstrate the same kind of dependence of the loop following error on q for the given Brownian motion input.

Two approaches will be taken. First, the loop will be linearized and analyzed statistically, and second, a describing function approach will be taken. The linearization approach is a local approximation and is directly analogous to an extended Kalman filter. The describing function approach is a global approach and is directly analogous to some of the approaches that will be taken to the nonlinear filtering problem in Section III.

To begin analyzing this loop, consider the differential equation that the loop error satisfies

$$\frac{d}{dt} e(t) = -Kf(e) + n(t). \tag{5}$$

In this equation f(e) is the forward loop nonlinearity shown in Fig. 1, K is the forward loop gain, and n(t) is the white noise, which is the derivative of the Brownian motion input. The first approach to analyzing this loop is to assume small error and linearize f(e) about zero. This yields the equation

$$\frac{d}{dt} e(t) = -Ke + n(t). \tag{6}$$

This linear equation is easy enough to analyze. The mean square tracking error is defined by

$$p(t) = E[e^2(t)], \tag{7}$$

and if it is assumed that E[e(0)] = 0 (that is, that the loop is initialized without any intentional error), then [1] p(t) satisfies the differential equation

$$\dot{p}(t) = -2Kp(t) + q. \tag{8}$$

The steady-state mean squared error p_s satisfies $\dot{p}_s(t) = 0$ and is easily found to be $p_s = q/2K$. Large input dynamics (large q) result in large tracking errors. Large forward loop gain (large K means a fast tracking loop) results in small tracking error. If q is small enough and K large enough that the errors stay small, then this linearized analysis is a sufficient characterization of the loop's behavior. The problem with linearization is that it gives no indication of the loop's behavior as the errors become large. As the one sigma error predicted by linearized analysis becomes large, only a small part of the error trajectories stay inside the range where the linearization is valid.

A second approach to analyze this loop is to use a describing function. The describing function procedure in this instance [2] is to assume that the error is Gaussian and to replace the nonlinear block with the linear block whose output best matches in a mean square error sense that of the true nonlinearity. The gain of the linear block is called the describing function gain.

Assume that the error has a Gaussian density with variance p, then the describing function gain G(p) is

$$G(p) = \frac{1}{(2\pi p)^{1/2}} \int_{-\infty}^{\infty} e f(e) \exp\left(-\frac{e^2}{2p}\right) de. \tag{9}$$

Some manipulation yields the describing function gain to be

$$G(p) = \frac{2}{(2\pi p)^{1/2}} \left[\int_0^1 \exp\left(-\frac{e^2}{2p}\right) de - \int_1^2 \exp\left(-\frac{e^2}{2p}\right) de \right]. \tag{10}$$

This gain depends on p, the mean square tracking error and can be thought of as the gain an average error trajectory sees. As p, the error variance, becomes small, G(p) approaches one, which is the linearized gain. As p becomes large, the describing function gain G(p) approaches zero -- a reflection of the fact that most of the error trajectories are outside the range to which the forward loop nonlinearity responds.

The differential equation for the tracking error, when written using the describing function gain, is

$$\frac{d}{dt} e(t) = -KG(p)e(t) + n(t). \tag{11}$$

The same approach as used for the linearized approach yields the variance equation

$$\dot{p} = -2KG(p)p + q. \tag{12}$$

Dependence of the describing function gain on the variance complicates the variance equation. Finding the steady-state variance requires solving the algebraic equation

$$G(p)p = q/2K.$$

Closed form solution of this equation is not possible, but a graphical solution demonstrates its qualitative properties. The function $G(p)p$ vs p is graphed in Fig. 3. It is clear from the form of the graph that if $q/2K$ is larger than about 0.42, then no steady-state solution exists.

The describing function approach has provided two pieces of information that the linearization approach did not. First, it anticipates some forward loop gain reduction as the variance grows and correspondingly predicts worse tracking errors. It

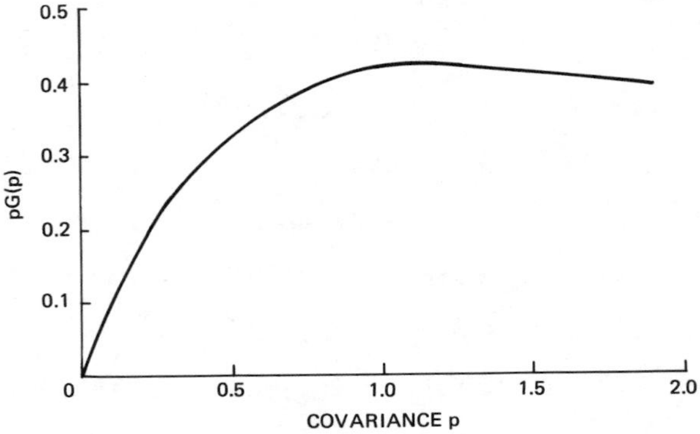

Fig. 3. Left-hand side of steady-state variance equation.

also predicts a combination of q and K for which the loop will be unable to track. The reason for the difference in the type of information these procedures give is that the describing function approximation depends on the global character of the nonlinearity. That is, it depends on the response of the nonlinearity to all different input magnitudes. The linearization approach, in contrast, depends on the character (derivative) of the nonlinearity near zero. The describing function approach is therefore called a global approximation, and the linearization approach is called a local approximation. In Section III these same ideas will be seen to apply to the nonlinear filtering problem. The extended Kalman filter will be shown to be a local approximation, and global approximations will be given. The difference in the type of information obtained from these two approaches will be of the same character as in the example just studied.

III. SOME GLOBAL APPROXIMATIONS FOR NONLINEAR FILTERING AND THEIR APPLICATION

In this section some global approximations are given. They have proved useful in nonlinear filtering. Some of these approximations are applied to some radio navigation and target tracking problems. The intent is to introduce some global approximations and to make clear how they are used by applying them.

The reader will observe that these global approximations are more burdensome to derive and implement than the extended Kalman filter. The global approximations will, as a reward, give filters that outperform the extended Kalman filter, particularly when the errors are large compared to the range for which linearization is valid. Additionally, these filters will offer more complete insight into the effect of the system nonlinearities on the filtering process. The describing function example in Section II.B illustrates the benefits of a global approximation. The global approximation gives a more accurate description of the error covariance when the errors are larger than the linear range of the forward loop nonlinearity. As the errors grow, the describing function analysis predicts gain reduction not predicted by the small signal approximation. In addition, the describing function approximation predicts a level of input that the tracking loop will no longer follow. Global filtering approximations will give improved fidelity and an analytical description of fundamentally nonlinear phenomena just as the describing function approach did.

The next items in this section are a brief discussion of nonlinear filtering and a description of the physical problem, which serves as an example. A radar tracking problem is chosen as an example problem. Several different approaches are taken to this problem. Each approach leads to a different mathematical formulation of a nonlinear filtering problem. Some of the mathematical problems that stem from this radar problem are very similar to those arising in other physical situations. Among these others are optical target tracking and laser communications.

The extended Kalman filter approach is demonstrated to be utterly unsuited for application to some of the formulations and inadequate in the others. The failure of the extended Kalman filter in this radar tracking problem makes it a good example problem for heralding the benefits of a global approach.

The last part of this section is devoted to some global approximations and to their application to the radar problem. The global approaches will prove to be quite effective. They will give filtering algorithms that are valid over a wide range of operating conditions, and they will provide an analytic description of the effect of the system nonlinearities. This description will be intuitively right and useful in understanding the filter's operation.

A. BACKGROUND FOR NONLINEAR FILTERING THEORY

As indicated in a preceding discussion, the problem addressed here is that of extracting the signal from a noisy measurement. It is supposed that the signal evolves as the solution to a differential equation driven by noise. The signal will be denoted by the n vector x(t) and is assumed to satisfy

$$\dot{x}(t) = f(x(t), t) + g(x(t), t)n(t). \tag{13}$$

The functions f and g are assumed to be known as is the initial probability density of x(0). The measurement z(t) is assumed to satisfy

$$z(t) = h(x(t), t) + v(t), \tag{14}$$

where h[x(t), t] is a known function. The time functions n(t) and v(t) are white noises. They are assumed to be independent and to have spectral density matrices

$$E[n(t)n^T(t + \tau)] = Q(t)\delta(\tau) \tag{15}$$

and

$$E[v(t)v^T(t + \tau)] = R(t)\delta(\tau). \tag{16}$$

The approach taken here to extract the signal from the noisy measurement of Eq. (14) is to compute at each point in time the conditional expectation of the signal x, given all the measurements taken up to that time. Throughout what follows this conditional expectation will be denoted by a hat. Thus $\hat{x}(t)$ is the conditional expectation of x(t), given all measurements collected up to time t.

The measurements themselves are processed to yield the conditional mean $\hat{x}(t)$. The measurements may be processed in other ways that might reasonably estimate the state vector. The conditional mean, however, is the estimator that minimizes the mean square error and is, therefore, a highly desirable one.

In this section the conditional mean is computed by propagating the solution to a differential equation. Kushner [3] first derived differential equations for the conditional mean. In fact he gave a differential equation for the conditional expectation of any twice continuously differentiable function of the state. Suppose $\phi(\ )$ is such a function, then

$$\frac{d}{dt}\,\hat{\phi}(x(t)) = \left[\widehat{\phi_x^T f} + \frac{1}{2}\,\mathrm{tr}\left(\widehat{gQg^T\phi_{xx}}\right)\right] + (\widehat{\phi h} - \hat{\phi}\hat{h})^T R^{-1}[z(t) - \hat{h}], \tag{17}$$

where f, g, and h are the functions appearing in the problem description given in Eqs. (13) and (14). In Eq. (17) ϕ_x is the partial derivative of ϕ with respect to x and ϕ_{xx} is the second partial. The symbol tr stands for the trace of a matrix, that is, the sum of its diagonal entries. To obtain a differential equation for the conditional mean $\phi(x) = x$ is substituted into Eq. (17).

In general Eq. (17) cannot be solved in closed form. The reason is that on the right-hand side appear hats (^) denoting conditional expectation. Taking the conditional expectation requires having the conditional probability density function. Propagating the conditional mean using Eq. (17) is generally not enough to propagate the conditional probability density function.

In the case where the Kalman filter applies, the conditional density is Gaussian and can be characterized by its mean and variance. In this case propagating

$$\hat{x} \quad \text{and} \quad \widehat{(x - \hat{x})(x - \hat{x})^T}$$

is all that is required to propagate the conditional probability density. Differential equations for the foregoing can be derived from Eq. (17). In the more general case the mean and covariance are insufficient to characterize the conditional density. Generally an infinite number of moments are required. It is not possible to propagate solutions to an infinite (or even large) number of differential equations, so some type of approximation is required. Such approximations are the subject of this chapter.

B. DESCRIPTION OF A RADAR TRACKING PROBLEM

A radar tracking problem serves throughout this chapter as an example. This section introduces the radar tracking problem to be used. The problem is described and posed mathematically.

The basic task for a radar is to determine the distance, or range, from itself to some maneuvering target. A radar accomplishes this by transmitting a signal and measuring the time required for the signal to travel to the target, be reflected, and return to the radar transmitter. Often the same antenna that transmits the signal is used to receive the return. The return signal is then processed to estimate the two-way transit time. The range to the target is inferred from this transit time. In this chapter global approximations will be used to arrive at algorithms for processing the radar return.

Many different types of signal waveforms find use in radars. The algorithms to be developed here will apply directly, or with minor modification, to many of the different waveforms. To be specific, however, a particular waveform is chosen for this example. The basic waveform considered here is built from a pseudorandom number (PRN) code.

The pseudorandom number code is a piecewise constant waveform built from a sequence of pseudorandom numbers. A pseudorandom number sequence is a sequence of numbers that can be generated systematically but has some of the desired properties of a sequence of random numbers. A familiar example of such a sequence is computer generated noise. The method for building a PRN code from a PRN sequence is as follows. Suppose $\{a_i\}_{i\geq 0}$ is a sequence of pseudorandom numbers. Choose a length of time T and define a PRN code S(t) by

$$S(t) = a_i, \qquad iT \leq t < (i + 1)T. \tag{18}$$

A possible PRN code S(t) is shown in Fig. 4. The length of time T is usually called the chipping rate. For example, for a particular code with a chipping rate of 10 MHz, $T = 10^{-7}$ sec.

A particularly useful class of the PRN codes is the class of linear feedback shift register codes. In practice such a code is generated by a pseudorandom number sequence in which

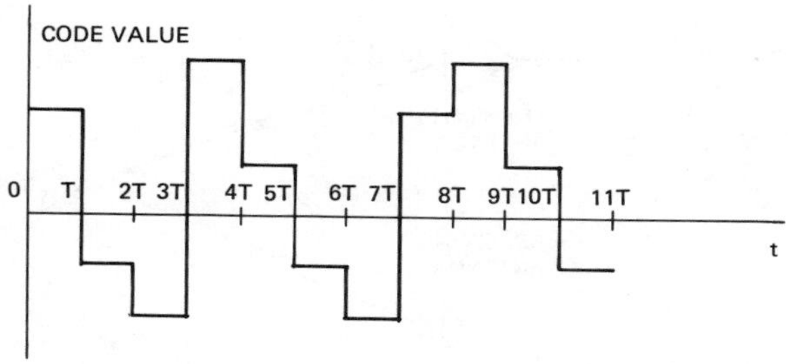

Fig. 4. Graph of possible PRN code.

the numbers are binary. These sequences look like coin toss sequences except that they repeat at some low frequency. Binary sequences are useful in practice because they can be generated by simple digital circuits.

A PRN code is used to build a signal waveform by multiplying a sinusoidal carrier wave by the PRN code. The result is then transmitted. If the PRN code is a ±1 binary code, then multiplying this code by the carrier sinusoid simply introduces a 180° phase shift when the PRN code equals -1 or leaves the sinusoid unchanged when the code is +1.

After being reflected and received at the radar, the signal first has its carrier wave removed. What is left is a PRN code that is delayed by comparison to the code on the transmitted signal. The object is to determine how much this received code is delayed. There are several different approaches to the problem of determining the delay between the transmitted and received waveforms. Suppose that $S(t + \theta(t))$ is the received PRN code and $\theta(t)$ is the delay in that code. The delay $\theta(t)$ is a function of time because the target is moving and the two-way transit time changing. Besides the delayed code $S(t + \theta(t))$ the received signal contains some noise. In some cases this noise is thermal. In other cases

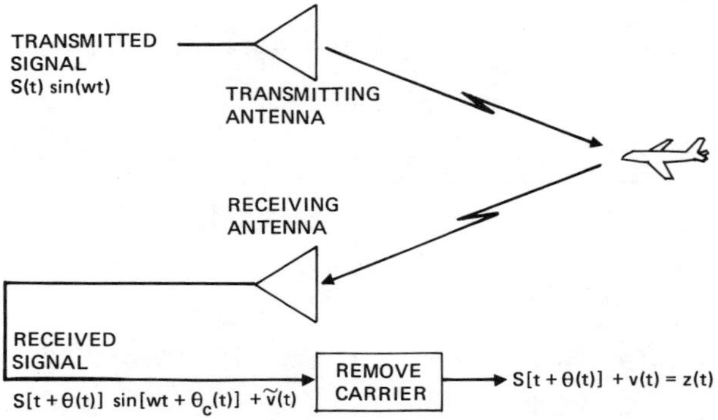

Fig. 5. Sketch of radar tracking system.

the noise is predominantly owing to other radio transmissions close in frequency to the radar's. A military target, for example, might transmit signals to confuse the radar. These signals would look like noise to the radar receiver.

The signal to be processed is a combination of the delayed PRN code $S[t + \theta(t)]$ and noise. If $z(t)$ is used to denote the signal to be processed, then mathematically

$$z(t) = S[t + \theta(t)] + v(t). \tag{19}$$

The sequence of events leading to this measurement is depicted in Fig. 5. The measurement $z(t)$ is scalar, and the measurement noise $v(t)$ is white with spectral density $r(t)$.

This radar tracking problem is now very nearly in the form of a nonlinear filtering problem. A state variable model for $\theta(t)$ is all that is required to complete the mathematical formulation of the problem. Suppose that the radar antenna is at the origin of a three-dimensional Cartesian coordinate system. The target has coordinates $(x_1(t), x_2(t), x_3(t))$ in this system. The target coordinates evolve according to the equations of motion for the target. There is some uncertainty in the evolution of the target location because the control inputs to the target (thrust level or changes in aerodynamic control surfaces) are unknown to the radar. The coordinates of the target can be aggregated into a vector $x(t)$ that has n elements, the first three of which are the coordinates x_1, x_2, and x_3. Other elements in the vector might be, for example, the target velocity or pitch angle. The target equation of motion can be put in the form

$$\dot{x}(t) = f(x(t)) + g(x(t))n(t).$$

The difficulty and importance of developing this state variable model is not to be minimized. The state model is the starting point for the filter designs that will be presented. The effectiveness of the filter will depend on the quality of the state variable model. A high dimension state vector leads to a computationally difficult design. It is necessary, therefore, to find a state model that captures the important features of the target motion in as short a state vector as possible. To be able to do this the designer needs to understand both the physics of the target motion and the requirements of the filter not yet designed. Arriving at a state model is in itself a difficult problem.

For purposes of this chapter a simple target motion model will be used. It will be assumed that the delay $\theta(t)$ is a Brownian motion. That is,

$$\dot{\theta} = n(t) \tag{20}$$

where $n(t)$ is a white noise with spectral density q. This target motion model is the simplest that still has some randomness. Even though it is a gross oversimplification of any real target's motion, it turns out to yield a filter that is useful for some problems. Part of the justification for using this model is that it keeps focus on the filter design problem instead of shifting it to the problem of modeling a particular target.

Mathematically the radar signal processing problem can be posed as

$$\dot{\theta} = n(t) \tag{21}$$

$$z = S[t + \theta(t)] + v(t). \tag{22}$$

The extended Kalman filter (EKF) is inapproapriate to apply to this problem. The EKF procedure requires differentiating $S[t + \theta(t)]$ with respect to $\theta(t)$. Because $S[t + \theta(t)]$ is piecewise constant, the derivative with respect to $\theta(t)$ is either zero or undefined (infinity). One could overcome this difficulty by using a finite difference instead of a derivative, but there is really no justification for a finite difference. The global approximations shown later apply directly to this problem. The fact that $S[t + \theta(t)]$ is not continuous (much less differentiable) does not cause them any difficulty.

There is another way to pose this radar signal processing problem. It is not so fundamental as the problem just posed. Some structure is imposed on the processor to arrive at a different formulation. There are two main reasons for considering this other formulation. First, this second formulation is mathematically the same as the problem of target tracking with a narrow field-of-view optical device (a telescope perhaps). This is an interesting and useful problem in its own right and a problem that appeals directly to most people's intuitions. Second, this second formulation is traditionally used to design radar signal processors. It is enlightening to see how traditional solutions compare to what global approximation yields and to compare the solutions obtained for these diffrent formulations.

The second formulation of this radar tracking problem a assumes that the received signal, after having the carrier signal removed, is multiplied by a code $S[t + \hat{\theta}(t)]$. This code is the same as the received code except that it is delayed by $\hat{\theta}(t)$ instead of $\theta(t)$. The delay $\hat{\theta}(t)$ can be though of as the delay that the radar expects for the received code to have.

The expected result of multiplying the received signal by $S[t + \hat{\theta}(t)]$ is the autocorrelation of the PRN code at time shift $\theta(t) - \hat{\theta}(t)$ corrupted by some noise.

The code autocorrelation $R_{ss}(\tau)$ defined by

$$R_{ss}(\tau) = \lim_{u\to\infty} (1/2u) \int_{-u}^{u} S(t)S(t + \tau)dt \tag{23}$$

has the form

$$R_{ss}(\tau) = \begin{cases} 1 - |\tau/T| & \text{for } |\tau - NT_R| \leq T \\ & \text{where } N \text{ is any integer,} \\ \varepsilon(\tau) & \text{otherwise,} \end{cases} \tag{24}$$

where T_R is the code repeat time and $\varepsilon(\tau)$ is a function that is small compared to one. Figure 6 shows how $R_{ss}(\tau)$ might look. It will be assumed in what follows that the code autocorrelation $R_{ss}(\tau)$ has the form

$$R_{ss}(\tau) = \begin{cases} 1 - |\tau/T|, & |\tau| < 1 \\ 0 & \text{otherwise.} \end{cases} \tag{25}$$

This assumption is justified, as far as the consequent estimation procedure is concerned, if the a priori probability of the state (range) is concentrated on an interval $<T_R$ wide.

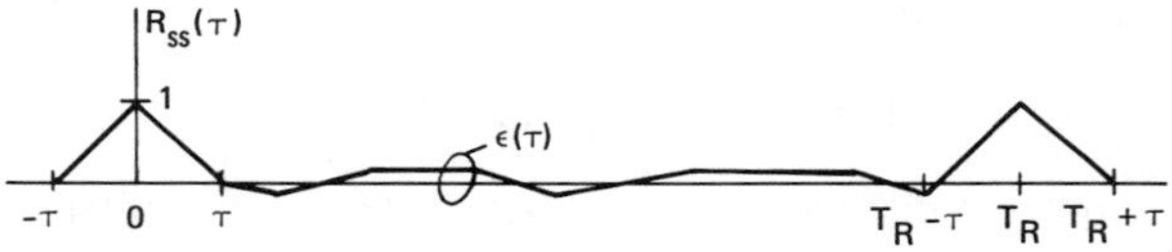

Fig. 6. Picture of PRN code autocorrelation.

In many practical systems the repeat time T_R may be very much larger than a priori timing uncertainties. For example, one ranging system in current operation has a repeat time $T_R = 200$ days, while initial timing uncertainties might be a few microseconds.

Mathematically the result of multiplying the measurement by a code with the expected delay is

$$z(t)S[t + \hat{\theta}(t)] = \{S[t + \theta(t)] + v(t)\}S[t + \hat{\theta}(t)]$$
$$= S[t + \theta(t)]S[t + \hat{\theta}(t)] + \tilde{v}(t). \qquad (26)$$

In Eq. (26) $\tilde{v}(t) = S[t + \hat{\theta}(t)]v(t)$ and is a white noise with spectral density $r(t)$ just like $v(t)$. The first term on the right-hand side of Eq. (26) displays a similarity to the integrand in the definition of the autocorrelation function. It seems reasonable to expect (and can be demonstrated) that the RHS of Eq. (26) and $R_{ss}[\theta(t) - \hat{\theta}(t)] + n(t)$ have equal time integrals, or, equivalently, that the outputs of the circuits shown in Fig. 7(a,b) have equal time integrals. If these two outputs have equal time integrals, then a measurement processor that acts as a low pass filter will have the same response to one as to the other. The processors proposed later will act as low pass filters, so modeling the physical situation in Fig. 7a by the block diagram of Fig. 7b will be valid.

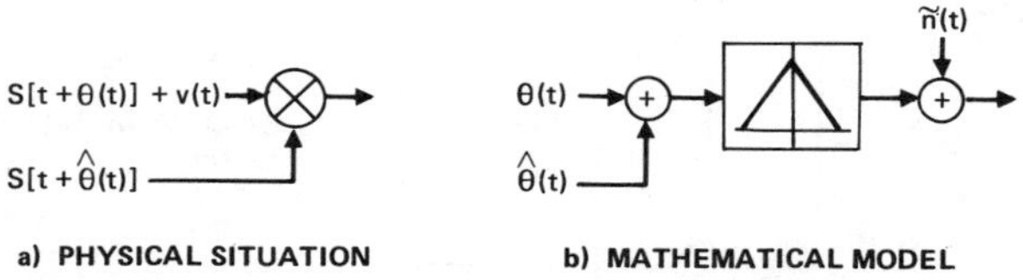

Fig. 7. Model for code correlator.

The essence of the preceding arguments is that, after some multiplications by known signals, the input signal may be taken to be a function $\tilde{z}(t)$ satisfying

$$\tilde{z}(t) = R_{ss}[\theta(t) - \hat{\theta}(t)] + \tilde{v}(t). \qquad (27)$$

The input signal was correlated with a single known code to produce the measurement $\tilde{z}(t)$. Several such correlations of the input can be performed against several shifts of the known code (i.e., against codes $S[t + d_1(t)]$, $S[t + d_2(t)]$, ...). This produces several measurements $\tilde{z}_i(t)$

$$\tilde{z}_i(t) = R_{ss}[\theta(t) - d_i(t)] + \tilde{v}_i(t), \qquad (28)$$

where $d_i(t)$ is the time shift used to generate the ith shift of the known code and the noises $\tilde{v}_i$ are independent of one another.

This measurement model is very similar in form to one that arises in optical target tracking. The measurement $\tilde{z}_i$ in Eq. (28) has two components. First, it contains noise. Second, it has a component owing to signal. If the ith delay d_i is equal to the delay on the received code, then the signal component is one. If the ith delay is grossly different than the received delay, then the signal component is zero. A typical optical sensor has the image plane (television screen, for example) divided into a matrix of small squares. Each small square has a component of its output owing to noise. It also

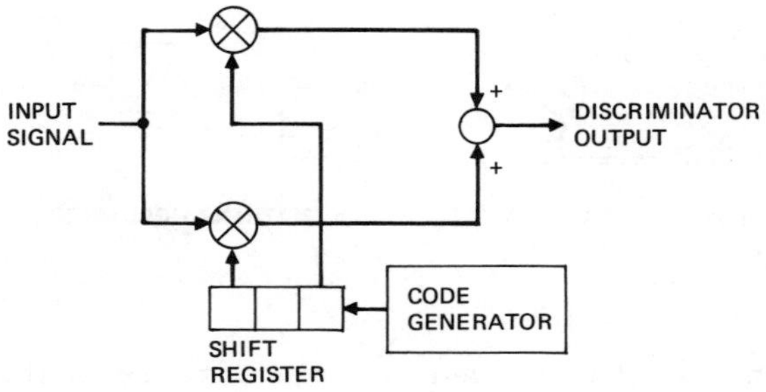

Fig. 8. Code loop discriminator.

has a component owing to the target. The target component is one if the target is in the small square and zero if it is outside. The code tracking problem can then be visualized as a one-dimensional optical tracking problem.

It is worthwhile at this point to describe briefly how the delay of a PRN code has traditionally been tracked. Figure 8 shows a block diagram of the circuitry typically used to develop an error signal. The two multipliers shown in Fig. 8 provide two correlations. The common input to these two multipliers is the received signal. The known code inputs to the correlators are time shifted by a fixed amount relative to one another. These time shifted codes are obtained by putting the code, out of the code generator, into a tapped delay line (shift register).

Suppose that the code in the center position of the shift register in Fig. 8 is believed to be in synchronism with the input code. That is, the code $S[t + \hat{\theta}(t)]$ is in the center of the shift register. The code one shift to the right is then $S(t + \hat{\theta} - 1)$, and that one shift to the left is $S(t + \hat{\theta} + 1)$. The results of multiplying each of these with the code (disregarding input noise) on the input signal are modeled, according

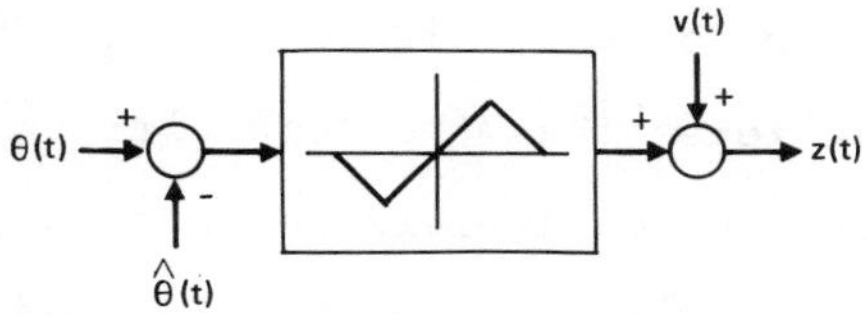

Fig. 9. Mathematical model of code loop early-late detector.

to a previous analysis, by $R_{ss}(\theta - \hat{\theta} + 1)$ and $R_{ss}(\theta - \hat{\theta} - 1)$, respectively. The difference between the two correlations with the input signal yields a measurement z(t) that satisfies

$$z(t) = R(\theta - \hat{\theta} - 1) - R(\theta - \hat{\theta} + 1) + v(t). \qquad (29)$$

The device shown in Fig. 8 is called an early-late detector. Early-late refers to the fact that the correlations are with local codes that are earlier and later than the expected input. Figure 9 shows the mathematical model of the device in Fig. 8. The early-late detector then gives an error measurement over a limited range. The circuit can be enclosed in a feedback loop and used to continuously track the input code delay. The resulting tracking loop is called a delay lock loop. In optical tracking problems there is an analogous error measuring circuit called a quadcell detector. This circuit has four optical sensors located in a square array -- one sensor at each corner of the square. Imagine that the square is oriented so that its sides are either vertical or horizontal. The difference between the sum of the outputs of the two right cells and the sum of the outputs of the two left cells gives an azimuth error indication. The difference between the top and bottom gives an elevation error indication.

The problems of using a nonlinearity of this sort in a feedback loop are fairly obvious. Because the forward loop nonlinearity gives no output for errors greater than two, it cannot sustain errors of that size. This limits the input dynamics and noise level that the loop will track.

In constructing the early-late detector only two multiplier outputs were used. If it appears to offer some advantage, many multiplier outputs can be provided. The object of the work that inspired the authors' interest in global approximation was to see if extra correlator outputs could be used to extend the range of delay dynamics and noise through which the delay can be tracked.

One approach to extending the range of operation is depicted in Fig. 10. Figure 10a shows on a single graph the outputs of several early and several late multipliers. Adding all the early correlations and subtracting all the late correlations yields a broadened forward loop nonlinearity as shown in Fig. 10b. This method is suggested, for example, in [4] and in [5]. The difficulty with adding these extra multiplier outputs in this manner is that each additional correlation brings with it additional noise. The measurement resulting from adding more than two multiplier outputs is then noisier than the traditional early-late measurement. This means that in the cases where the traditional scheme is able to track with small errors, the extended range scheme will experience relatively larger errors. Because of this the traditional wisdom

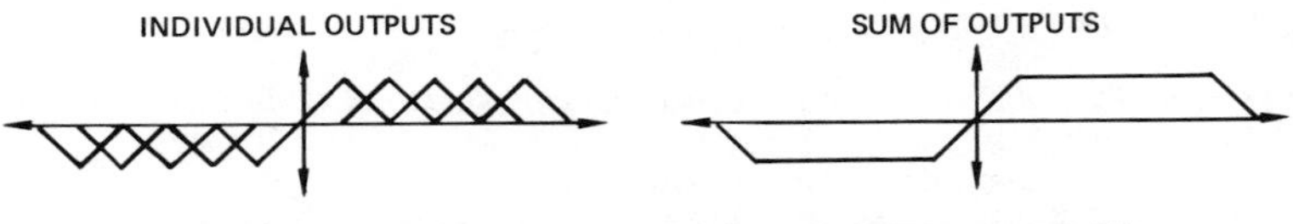

a) OUTPUTS OF INDIVIDUAL MULTIPLIERS

b) NONLINEARITY OBTAINED BY SUBTRACTING ALL EARLY MULTIPLIERS FROM ALL LATE MULTIPLIERS

Fig. 10. One method for employing multiple correlator outputs.

is that extra multipliers are not useful for tracking. The fallacy with this is that the reasoning only applies in benign conditions where the traditional scheme can track with small errors. That is, the reasoning is based on a small signal analysis. Use of global approximation will indicate how this reasoning should be modified. If conditions are severe enough to cause the failure of the traditional scheme, benefit can be derived by including extra multiplier outputs. This will be demonstrated in Section III.C.

Two starting points will be used to learn how to benefit from extra multiplier outputs. One approach starts by modeling the output of each multiplier as a separate measurement. The second approach starts by assuming that the multiplier outputs are weighted and added together to yield a single nonlinear error measurement. This measurement nonlinearity might, for example, look like the one graphed in Fig. 10b. In this second approach the shape of the nonlinearity is not specified. An optimum shape is determined by using global approximation techniques. This last approach is analogous to feedback communication wherein the modulation or measurement nonlinearity can be modified.

Altogether three starting points have been suggested. The different approaches use the same model for the delay dynamics but differ in that they use different models for the measurement. The first approach is to call the received code and noise in Eq. (22) the measurement. The second and third approaches assume that the received code has been multiplied by various shifts of a code generated in the receiver. The second approach considers the array of multiplier outputs to be the measurement. The third considers a single weighted sum of multiplier outputs to be the measurement.

None of these approaches is amenable to extended Kalman filtering. The extended Kalman filtering uses the partial derivative of the measurement nonlinearity with respect to the state variable evaluated at the expected state. As previously mentioned, the first measurement model where the received code is the measurement is not amenable to this approach because the code either has zero derivative or is not differentiable. The second approach where the multiplier outputs are considered measurements is not amenable because the derivative of the code autocorrelation is zero further than one away from its peak. This causes the extended Kalman filter to ignore outputs of correlators further than two away from the expected delay. The third approach wherein the measurement is modeled as a single adjustable nonlinear function of the state is not amenable to extended Kalman filtering either. Because the extended Kalman filter characterizes the nonlinearity by its slope evaluated at the expected value of the state, it considers the nonlinearities in Figs. 9 and 10b to be equivalent. In terms of small signal behavior they are equivalent, but in terms of large error behavior they certainly are not. These approaches are all amenable to global approximation as will be seen in Section III.C.

C. GAUSSIAN APPROXIMATION

The radar tracking problem described in Section III.B has been mathematically described in several different ways. All of the mathematical problems that have arisen from the radar problem fit within the general framework of the nonlinear filtering problem previously introduced. In this section an approximate solution for the nonlinear filtering problem will be used to arrive at solutions for the radar tracking problem. First, the approximation will be described generally. Next, the approximation will be applied to each of the mathematical problems that have arisen from the radar tracking problem. The inability of the extended Kalman filter to accomplish these design tasks will be pointed out, and the designs that result from the different mathematical formulations of the same radar problem will be compared.

In Section III.A Kushner's equations for propagating the mean and variance of the conditional density were presented. It was pointed out that the problem with these equations was that each equation required on its right-hand side the entire conditional density, whereas propagating the equation's left-hand side only yielded one moment of the conditional density. Because an infinite number of moments of the conditional density are required to reconstruct it, an infinite number of equations must be solved to propagate the conditional density. To circumvent this difficulty an approximation will be used.

Suppose that the plant equation is

$$\dot{x} = f(x(t), t) + g(x(t), t)n(t) \tag{30}$$

and that an observation of the form

$$z(t) = h(x(t), t) + v(t) \tag{31}$$

is made. Differential equations for the conditional mean and covariance can be derived directly from Eq. (17) presented in Section III.A. The differential equation for the mean is

$$\dot{\hat{x}} = \hat{f}(x, t) + \widehat{(x - \hat{x})h^T}R^{-1}(t)[z(t) - \hat{h}]. \tag{32}$$

Denote the covariance matrix by P, that is

$$P = \widehat{(x - \hat{x})(x - \hat{x})^T}. \tag{33}$$

The differential equation for the covariance is

$$P_{ij} = \widehat{(x_i - \hat{x}_i)f_j} + \widehat{(x_j - \hat{x}_j)f_i} + \widehat{(gQg^T)}_{ij}$$

$$- \widehat{(x_i - \hat{x}_i)h^T}R^{-1}\widehat{(x_j - \hat{x}_j)h}$$

$$+ \widehat{[(x_i - \hat{x}_i)(x_j - \hat{x}_j)(h - \hat{h})]}R^{-1}[z(t) - \hat{h}]/ \tag{34}$$

In this equation P_{ij} is the ijth element of the covariance matrix P. The initial conditions for the conditional mean and covariance equations, Eqs. (33) and (34), come from the known initial density of the state. Specifically,

$$\hat{x}(0) = E[x(0)] \tag{35}$$

and

$$P(0) = E\{[x(0) - \hat{x}(0)][x(0) - \hat{x}(0)]^T\}. \tag{36}$$

The approximation to be used here is best explained by an intuitive inspection of the right-hand side of the mean and covariance equations. Notice that the conditional density is required on the right-hand side of these equations in order to carry out the expectation operations. These expectation operations are the integral of the indicated quantities against the conditional density. For example, the quantity $\hat{f}(x, t)$ appears on the right-hand side of the mean equation. This quantity can be expressed in terms of the conditional probability density. Suppose that the conditional density of the state at time t, given measurements up to time t, is $p_t(x|A)$. The quantity $\hat{f}(x, t)$ is then given by

$$\hat{f}(x(t), t) = \int f(r, t)p_t(r\ Z)dr. \tag{37}$$

Because the conditional density appears in an integral like this, perhaps its precise shape is not critical to the accurate propagation of the conditional mean. The supposition is made that, in fact, as far as the quantities in the mean and variance equations are concerned, only the mean and variance of the conditional density are significant. If this is true the expectations on the right-hand side of the mean and variance equations can be carried out using any density that has the right mean and variance.

A density that is conveniently characterized by its mean and density is the Gaussian density and that is the one that will be used here. For example, using Gaussian approximation $\hat{f}(x, t)$ becomes

$$\hat{f}(x, t) = \int f(r, t) p_t(r|Z)\, dr$$

$$\cong \int f(r, t) \frac{1}{(2\pi \mathrm{de}P)^{n/2}} \exp\left\{\frac{1}{2}(r - \hat{x})^T P^{-1} (r - \hat{x})\right\} dr. \tag{38}$$

That is, all the conditional expectations on the right-hand side of the mean and variance equations are carried out by assuming that the conditional density is Gaussian in form with mean value $\hat{x}$ and covariance P. The derivatives of $\hat{x}$ and P appear on the left-hand side of the mean and covariance equations. What results is a coupled set of differential equations that can be solved by ordinary numerical methods. The effect of this approximation is then to truncate the number of equations required to propagate the conditional density. Because the density has been supposed to depend only on its mean and variance, only the mean and variance equations need to be propagated. The procedure leads to equations that are much like the familiar Kalman filtering equations in form but that, as will be seen, depend on the global character of the measurement and system nonlinearities.

D. *USE OF GAUSSIAN APPROXIMATION TO DETERMINE OPTIMUM MEASUREMENT NONLINEARITY*

The first mathematical problem on which Gaussian approximation will be used is the deformable detector problem. Suppose that the input delay process $\theta(t)$ satisfies

$$\dot{\theta}(t) = n(t) \tag{39}$$

and that the nonlinear measurement, built from weighted correlator outputs, satisfies

$$z(t) = h[\theta(t) - \hat{\theta}(t)] + v(t). \tag{40}$$

The noise processes $n(t)$ and $v(t)$ have spectral densities $r(t)$ and $q(t)$, respectively. The shape of the measurement nonlinearity $h(e)$ depends on what weights the correlator outputs are multiplied by before being added together. Either one of the nonlinearities shown in Fig. 9 and 10b could be achieved by some selection of weights. More generally, suppose that weight w_i is applied to the correlator shifted by i increments with respect to the expected on-time code. The result of this is a nonlinearity composed of straight line segments connecting the points $(-(n + 1), 0)$, $(-n, w_{-n})$, $(-(n - 1), w_{-(n-1)}, \ldots,$ $(-1, w_{-1})$, $(0, w_0)$, $\ldots$, $(m, w_m)(m + 1, 0)$ where the w_i are the arbitrary weights. This nonlinearity, shown in Fig. 11, will be denoted by $h(e)$. Notice that for an integer i, $h(i) = w_i$. The detector drawn in Fig. 11 would probably not be a useful one. The point is, however, that very general shapes are obtainable.

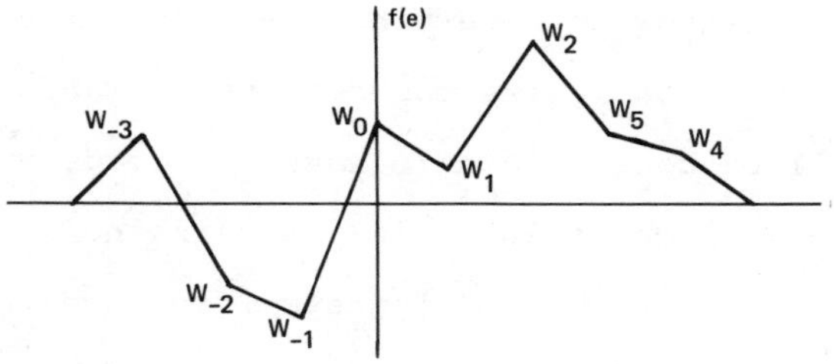

Fig. 11. Hypothetical detector obtainable by using weights w_i.

Noise is an essential consideration in determining the optimum detector shape. The noises present on the different correlator outputs are independent, zero mean, and white with equal covariances. Let $n_i(t)$ be the noise present on the output of the ith correlator and let $E(n_i(t)n_i(\tau)) = r\delta(t - \tau)$. The spectral density of the noise on the weighted sum of the correlator outputs is then

$$E\left[\sum_{i=-n} w_i n_i(t) \sum_{i=-n} w_i n_i(\tau)\right] = r \sum_{i=-n} w_i^2 \delta(t - \tau). \qquad (41)$$

The postdetection noise variance is then proportional to

$$\sum_{i=-n}^{m} w_i^2.$$

The w_i must be chosen so that their signal detection assets outweigh their noise liabilities.

It will be assumed that the function h( ) is such that

$$\sum_{i=-n}^{m} w_i^2 \cong \int h^2(e)\,de. \qquad (42)$$

For the nonlinearities that will arise in this design, this condition will be satisfied.

The object is now to determine the measurement nonlinearity h( ) (weights w_i) that gives the best performance. The nonlinearity will be constrained to have $\int h^2(e)de = 1$ and to be antisymmetric. Beyond that it is unconstrained. The procedure is to design a filter with h( ) unspecified and then to choose h( ) to optimize the filter's performance. The conditional moments [6] and [7] satisfy

$$\dot{\hat{\theta}} = \widehat{(\theta - \hat{\theta})h}(1/r)[z(t) - \hat{h}] \tag{43}$$

and

$$\dot{p} = -\left[\widehat{(\theta - \hat{\theta})h}\right]^2(1/r) + q$$
$$+ \widehat{(\theta - \hat{\theta})^2(h - \hat{h})}(1/r)[z(t) - \hat{h}]. \tag{44}$$

These equations result from specializing Eqs. (32) and (34) to the present situation. A lowercase p is used to represent the covariance to emphasize the fact that it is a scalar. Applying Gaussian approximation to this problem yields

$$d\hat{\theta} = \frac{G(p)}{r}dz \tag{45}$$

$$\frac{dp}{dt} = -\frac{G^2(p)}{r} + q \tag{46}$$

where

$$G(p) = \frac{1}{(2\pi p)^{1/2}}\int_{-\infty}^{\infty} eh(e)\ \exp\left(-\frac{e^2}{2p}\right)de. \tag{47}$$

This can be changed into a more recognizable form by defining (p) to be

$$H(p) = \frac{G(p)}{p} \tag{48}$$

$$= \frac{1}{p}\frac{1}{(2\pi p)^{1/2}}\int_{-\infty}^{\infty} eh(e)\ \exp\left(-\frac{e^2}{2p}\right)de. \tag{49}$$

The function H(p) is then the describing function gain for the nonlinearity h( ). If pH(p) is substituted for G(p), the filter equations become

$$d\hat{\theta} = \frac{pH(p)}{r}\,dz \tag{50}$$

$$\frac{dp}{dt} = -\frac{p^2 H(p)^2}{r} + q. \tag{51}$$

These equations can be recognized as the Kalman filter linearized with the describing function gains. Gaussian approximation can generally be interpreted as a Kalman filter linearized using a describing function. In general, there will usually be a data dependence in the covariance equation. Two elements of the problem under consideration combine to remove data dependence in the covariance equation. The measurement nonlinearity is a function of the estimation error, not of the state alone, and it is an antisymmetric function.

The mean and covariance equations represent an approximate solution to the filtering problem for an arbitrary nonlinearity h. The complete problem will be solved when the nonlinearity is selected to yield optimum filter performance. Inspection of the covariance reveals that only one term is affected by the choice of the nonlinearity. That term corresponds to the quadratic term in the usual Kalman filter. To minimize the covariance then, the best strategy is to maximize $h^2(p)$. Doing this makes the derivative of the covariance as small as possible. The optimum detector h^* then satisfies, subject to the constraint $||h||_2 = 1$,

$$\max\left[\int_{-\infty}^{\infty} eh(e)\,\exp\left(-\frac{e^2}{2p}\right)de\right] = \left[\int_{-\infty}^{\infty} eh^*(e)\,\exp\left(-\frac{e^2}{2p}\right)de\right]^2. \tag{52}$$

This is equivalent to solving the unconstrained problem

$$\max_{\Gamma} \frac{\left[\int_{-\infty}^{\infty} e\Gamma(e)\ \exp\left(-\frac{e^2}{2p}\right)de\right]^2}{\int_{-\infty}^{\infty} \Gamma^2(e)\,de} \tag{53}$$

and setting

$$h^*(e) = \Gamma^*(e)\left[\int_{-\infty}^{\infty} \Gamma^{*2}(e)\,de\right]^{-1/2}.$$

The Schwartz inequality may be used to solve for Γ^*.

$$\left[\int_{-\infty}^{\infty} e\Gamma(e)\ \exp\left(-\frac{e^2}{2p}\right)^2 de\right]^2 \leq \int_{-\infty}^{\infty} \Gamma^2(e)\,de \int_{-\infty}^{\infty} e^2\ \exp\left(-\frac{e^2}{p}\right)de. \tag{54}$$

Then

$$\frac{\left[\int_{-\infty}^{\infty} e\Gamma(e)\ \exp\left(-\frac{e^2}{2p}\right)de\right]}{\int_{-\infty}^{\infty} \Gamma^2(e)\,de} \leq \int_{-\infty}^{\infty} e\ \exp\left(-\frac{e^2}{p}\right)de, \tag{55}$$

and equality holds if

$$\Gamma^*(e) = e\ \exp\left(-\frac{e^2}{2p}\right). \tag{56}$$

Because

$$\int_{-\infty}^{\infty} \Gamma^{*2}(e)\,de = \int_{-\infty}^{\infty} e^2\left(-\frac{e^2}{p}\right)de \tag{57}$$

$$= (\pi p)^{1/2}\ \frac{p}{2} \tag{58}$$

then it follows that

$$h^*(e) = \left(\frac{p}{2}\right)^{-1/2} (\pi p)^{-1/4} e\ \exp\left(-\frac{e^2}{2p}\right). \tag{59}$$

Some discussion of this nonlinearity is in order. The optimal forward loop nonlinearity is graphed in Fig. 12.

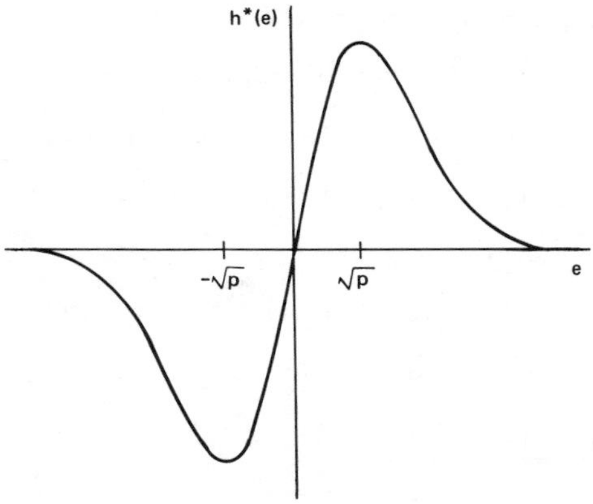

Fig. 12. Optimum measurement nonlinearity.

It is more or less linear over a range $(-(p)^{1/2}, +(p)^{1/2})$. An interesting feature of the design is that the nonlinearity is not fixed but changes in time. The nonlinearity depends directly on the tracking error variance p. Because p changes in time, then so does the nonlinearity. The variance, for example, might start out large when the radar is first turned on. As the signal is processed the radar becomes more certain of the target whereabouts and the variance decreases. As the variance decreases the linear range of the nonlinearity shrinks. The linear range of the nonlinearity is always between plus and minus one sigma of the predicted tracking error.

This general sequence of operations is more or less like those used in many optical and radio signal acquisition systems. A narrow field of view is required for final tracking so that the final tracking accuracy is good, but a broad field is required during initialization because the initial uncertainties are usually large. The standard procedure then is to begin operation with a broad field device and, after the errors have been reduced, to switch over to a narrow field device.

The procedure that has resulted from this nonlinear filtering approach agrees generally with standard practice and with intuition. This procedure offers the additional benefit that it provides an analytical framework for deciding when to switch between sensors.

Using the optimal detector gives mean and variance equations

$$\dot{\hat{\theta}}(t) = p\,\frac{H^*(p)}{r}\,z(t), \tag{60}$$

$$\frac{dp}{dt} = q - p^2\,\frac{H^{*2}(p)}{r}, \tag{61}$$

where

$$H^* = \frac{1}{(2\pi p)^{1/2}} \int_{-\infty}^{\infty} e h^*(e)\, \exp\left(-\frac{e^2}{2p}\right) de, \tag{62}$$

and

$$h^*(e) = \left(\frac{p}{2}\right)^{-1/2} (\pi p)^{-1/4} e\, \exp\left(-\frac{e^2}{2p}\right).$$

Integrating yields

$$H^*(p) = \frac{\pi}{2}^{-1/4} p^{-3/4}. \tag{63}$$

Thus

$$\dot{\hat{\theta}}(t) = \frac{\pi}{2}^{-1/4}\,\frac{p}{r}^{1/4}\,z(t), \tag{64}$$

$$\frac{dp}{dt} = q - \frac{\pi}{4}^{-1/2}\,\frac{p}{r}^{1/2}. \tag{65}$$

The steady-state covariance is then given by $\dot{p} = 0$ or

$$p^{1/2} = 4\pi^{1/2} qr \tag{66}$$

$$= 7.0898qr. \tag{67}$$

Figure 13 shows results of Monte Carlo simulation of this tracking loop. One hundred runs were made, and the predicted and actual mean square tracking errors, as functions of time,

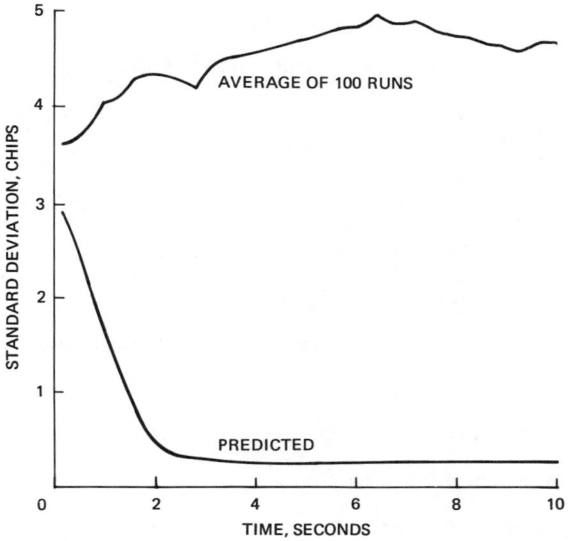

Fig. 13. Acquisition performance of Gaussian approximation.

are plotted in Fig. 13. The conditions for these runs are as follows. The error at the start is Gaussian with expected value zero and variance 10.0. The spectral density of the noise in the state equation (called q) is 1.0. The spectral density of the measurement noise (called r) is 0.354. This spectral level is chosen so that the predicted steady-state one sigma error is 0.25.

Figure 13 shows that for this problem Gaussian approximation does not work as well as one might hope. The covariance does not behave as it was predicted to behave. Figure 13 is a little misleading, however. The tendency is to believe that a particular trajectory will behave roughly like the one sigma trajectory. This is not the case, however. A sampling of the error trajectories indicates that for about 80% of the runs the errors behave as predicted. For the remaining 20% the errors are much worse than predicted. An average computed on the basis of these errors falls somewhere between the trajectories that are not captured and those that are. A given error trajectory, then, looks either somewhat worse or much better than the experimental one sigma plot that is shown.

The problem with the system as it is now configured is that the actual errors do not affect the covariance. Even when the actual errors are very large, the predicted covariance as plotted in Fig. 13 is quite small. Somehow the actual errors must factor into the covariance computation. The reason that the measurement does not affect the covariance is that the measurement nonlinearity is antisymmetric. In the covariance equation, Eq. (44) for example, the coefficient on the measurement is

$$(1/r)\,\overline{(\theta - \hat{\theta})^2 (h - \hat{h})} = 0. \tag{68}$$

If a Gaussian density is assumed, then any antisymmetric function of $\theta - \hat{\theta}$ has expected value zero. For this reason the data dependence drops out of the covariance equation and the covariance equation runs open loop. That is, the covariance is not responsive to actual errors.

This situation can perhaps be corrected by taking another measurement. The antisymmetric nonlinearity was constructed by adding weighted correlations, and a symmetric nonlinearity may be constructed by the same technique. In Section III.E it will be seen that this type of structure will follow naturally from posing the radar tracking problem differently. If multiplier outputs are treated as measurements then using the Gaussian approximation procedure will result in a mean equation just like the one here but a significantly different covariance equation. The difference will be that the covariance equation will have an adaptive term. This term will be seen to drive the covariance, so that it agrees with the actual tracking error. Thus the covariance estimation will be closed loop instead of open loop.

E. USE OF GAUSSIAN APPROXIMATION FOR PROCESSING MANY CORRELATOR OUTPUTS

The next problem formulation to be considered is the one wherein the output of each multiplier is itself considered a measurement. This formulation imposes less structure on the problem than the last one did. In the last formulation it was assumed at the outset that multiplier outputs were to be weighted and summed together. The filter design was thus not allowed the option of processing each multiplier output individually and then combining them nonlinearly. The only degree of freedom the filter design was allowed to resolve was the shape of the weighting function. The approach taken there can be justified because it is parallel to the approach normally taken to design this type of signal processing hardware and because the problem of determining an optimal measurement nonlinearity has application elsewhere. For radar signal processing, however, it will be seen that a more complete and better performing design can be achieved by removing some of the constraints. In Sections III.F and G less constrained formulations will be pursued.

Recall that when the outputs of the individual multipliers are considered as measurements, the system and measurement models become

$$\dot{\theta} = n(t) \tag{69}$$

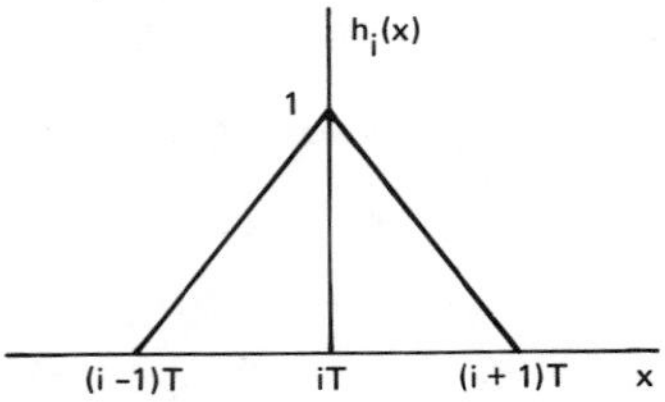

Fig. 14. Output of ith measurement nonlinearity versus tracking error.

and

$$z_i(t) = h_i(\theta - \hat{\theta}) + v(t), \tag{70}$$

where the measurement z_i is the output of the ith multiplier. The function $h_i(x)$ is the code autocorrelation function at shift x as graphed in Fig. 14. Kushner's equation can be used to find the mean and covariance equation for this formulation just as it was for the last one. In this case the equations become

$$\dot{\hat{\theta}} = \sum_i \widehat{(\theta - \hat{\theta})h_i}(1/r)(z_i - \hat{h}_i) \tag{71}$$

and

$$\dot{p} = q - \left[\sum_i \widehat{(\theta - \hat{\theta})h_i}\right]^2 (1/r)$$

$$+ \sum_i \widehat{(\theta - \hat{\theta})^2(h_i - \hat{h}_i)(1/r)(z_i - \hat{h}_i)}. \tag{72}$$

These are still unsolvable, but Gaussian approximation can be used to arrive at approximate mean and covariance equations just as in the previous section. Applying Gaussian approximation to this problem yields the mean equation

$$\dot{\hat{\theta}} = (1/r) \sum w_i z_i \tag{73}$$

and covariance equation

$$\dot{p} = q - (1/r)\left(\sum w_i\right)^2 + \left(\sum \alpha_i z_i - c\right). \tag{74}$$

In these equations the quantities h_i, w_i, α_i, and c are given by the following:

$$h_i = \frac{1}{(2\pi p)^{1/2}} \int_{-\infty}^{\infty} h_i(u) \exp\left(-\frac{u^2}{2p}\right) du, \tag{75}$$

$$w_i = \frac{1}{(2\pi p)^{1/2}} \int_{-\infty}^{\infty} u h_i(u) \exp\left(-\frac{u^2}{2p}\right) du, \tag{76}$$

$$\alpha_i = \frac{1}{(2\pi p)^{1/2}} \int_{-\infty}^{\infty} u^2 h_i(u) \exp\left(-\frac{u^2}{2p}\right) du, \tag{77}$$

$$c = \sum \alpha_i h_i. \tag{78}$$

The mean equation in this case is somewhat different in appearance than the mean equation derived in Section III.D. In reality, however, the two equations are strikingly similar. In the previous section the individual correlator outputs were weighted and summed to form a single measurement that entered the mean equation. The optimum weighting for the ith correlator was determined to within a multiplicative function of p to be of the form $iT \exp[-(iT)^2/2p]$. The mean equation in this case is also driven by a weighted sum of correlator outputs. If p, the error covariance, is large compared with T, then the weight w_i is approximately

$$w_i \cong \frac{1}{(2\pi p)^{1/2}}\, iT \exp\left(-\frac{iT}{2p}\right).$$

The filter starting with a less structured formulation has chosen to estimate the conditional mean with a structure quite similar to the one imposed during the formulation of the problem in the last section.

The covariance equation that has developed from the less structured formulation in this section is different than the covariance equation of the last section. The important difference is that measurements enter the covariance equation in this case. The effect of these measurements can be explained intuitively as follows.

The measurements are weighted and summed, and the result used to drive the covariance equation. Each measurement is some nonlinear function of the error (plus noise) and the weighted sum is also a nonlinear function of the error (plus noise). Thus in this case the error affects the covariance directly. The weight applied to the ith correlator output, when p is large, is

$$\alpha_i = \frac{1}{(2\pi p)^{1/2}}[(iT)^2 - p] \exp\left[-\frac{(iT)^2}{2p}\right].$$

This function is graphed in Fig. 16. These weights are applied to the correlator outputs and the weighted outputs summed. Thus some function of the tracking error $h_2(e)$ enters the covariance equation. For integer argument $ih_2(i) = \alpha_i$. It is also true that when the error covariance p is large compared to one, the function $h_2(i)$ is the same as the function graphed in Fig. 15. There is then a symmetric function of the tracking error that drives the covariance. The scalar c, which is subtracted on the right-hand side of the covariance equation (Eq. 74), is equal to the expected value of $h_2(e)$. Expected value means integration against a Gaussian density with covariance p. The predicted covariance p then influences the value of c. If the predicted error covariance is on the average equal to the actual error covariance, then $h_2(e)$ and $-c$ cancel. When these terms cancel, the covariance equation reverts to the open-loop equation derived in the last section. When these two terms do not agree, a correction term is introduced to the covariance equation. This correction drives the covariance so as to bring the scalar c, the expected value of $h_2(e)$, and the average value of $h_2(e)$ into coincidence. The covariance equation is enclosed in a feedback loop and driven to match the actual errors.

Monte Carlo simulation of this tracking system was performed. The conditions for this simulation were identical to those leading to the results of the last section. Two changes have occurred due to the approach used in this section. The actual errors are smaller and the predicted errors are larger than those shown in Fig. 13. There is a good match between the actual and predicted errors.

The approach taken in this section has been successful. It has yielded the qualitative information of the approach in the last section and has added a feedback term to the covariance equation. This addition has resulted in improved performance. The approach is still based on a formulation wherein structure is imposed. It is still the case that correlation of the received code with codes generated in the receiver is assumed. In the next section this structure will be removed, and what will result will be similar to the tracking loop derived here but will show improved performance.

F. APPLICATION OF GAUSSIAN APPROXIMATION TO ESTIMATION OF PN-CODE DELAY

In the third formulation of the radar tracking problem the delayed PN code waveform is taken to be the measurement. This approach is the least structured of all those taken here. In addition a more general model for the delay process (target motion) will be assumed. It will be assumed that the delay is the first element in a vector whose elements are necessary to describe the target's motion.

Let $x_1(t)$ denote the varying PN-code delay due to target motion and $\underline{x}(t)$ equal the n-dimensional state vector whose first component equals $x_1(t)$. We interpret the preceding system as the two equations

$$\begin{aligned} \dot{\underline{x}}(t) &= F\underline{x}(t) + Gn(t), \\ z(t) &= h(\underline{x}(t), t) + v(t), \end{aligned} \tag{79}$$

where F is the state feedback matrix, possibly time varying, G the input matrix, possibly time varying, n(t) the scalar white Gaussian noise (WGN) of spectral height Q, which models the unknown target dynamics

$$h(\underline{x}(t), t) = S[t - x_1(t)] = \text{the received code}, \tag{80}$$

v(t) the received noise (WGN) of spectral height r(t), and S(t) the reference PN-code waveform (±1 valued). The extended Kalman filter cannot be applied to this system because the measurement nonlinearity cannot be linearized about a reference trajectory. Attempting to linearize $h[\underline{x}(t), t]$ around a reference trajectory $\underline{x}_r(t)$ fails because

$$\begin{aligned} \left.\frac{\partial h[\underline{x}(t), t]}{\partial \underline{x}}\right|_{\underline{x}=\underline{x}_r} &= \left.\left[\frac{\partial h}{\partial x_1}\, \frac{\partial h}{\partial x_2} \cdots \frac{\partial h}{\partial x_n}\right]\right|_{\underline{x}=\underline{x}_r} \\ &= \left.\left[\frac{\partial h}{\partial x_1}\; 0 \cdots 0\right]\right|_{\underline{x}=\underline{x}_r}, \end{aligned} \tag{81}$$

but

$$\frac{\partial h}{\partial x_1} = \frac{\partial}{\partial x_1} S(t - x_1) = -S'(t - x_1) \tag{82}$$

and $S'(t)$ is very badly behaved because of the switching discontinuities in the code. Extended Kalman filtering is hence ruled out at the start because of the sharpness of the nonlinearities in the observation equation. We shall have to resort to global approximation of the exact nonlinear filtering equations.

Let $\underline{\hat{x}}(t)$ denote the conditional mean of $\underline{x}(t)$ given the measurements; and we have by [1], formulas for the evolution of the first and second moments of the conditional probability density function of $\underline{x}(t)$

$$\dot{\underline{\hat{x}}}(t) = F\underline{\hat{x}}(t) + (1/r)\left[\widehat{\underline{x}(t)h} - \hat{x}(t)\hat{h}\right][z(t) - \hat{h}], \tag{83}$$

$$\frac{dP_{ij}(t)}{dt} = [FP(t) + P(t)F^T + GQG^T]_{ij}$$

$$-(1/r)\left[\widehat{x_i(t)h} - \hat{x}_i(t)\hat{h}\right]\left[\widehat{x_j(t)h} - \hat{x}_j(t)\hat{h}\right]$$

$$+ (1/r)\widehat{\left[(x_i - x_i)(x_j - x_j) - \widehat{(x_i - x_j)(x_j - x_j)}\right]h}$$

$$\cdot [z(t) - \hat{h}]. \tag{84}$$

These equations are unsolvable, but a practical processing algorithm can be developed using Gaussian approximation. After applying Gaussian approximation several simplifications can be made to the resulting equations.

The first simplification that can be performed on these equations is the elimination of the subtractive portion $(-\hat{h})$ of the innovations process $z(t) - \hat{h}$ in the mean equation. This follows from two hypotheses: (a) the symmetry properties of the joint Gaussian distribution and (b) the assumption of high code frequency and lowpass processor. Explicitly, we assume "instantaneous averaging" of the product of two codes by the lowpass filter

$$S(t - x)S(t) \approx R(x). \tag{85}$$

From Eq. (82) the term under examination is

$$-(1/r)\left[\widehat{\underline{x}(t)h} - \underline{\hat{x}}(t)\hat{h}\right]\hat{h}, \tag{86}$$

which can be rewritten

$$-(1/r)\left\{\overline{[\underline{x}(t) - \underline{\hat{x}}(t)]h[\underline{x}(t), t]}\right\}\overline{h[\underline{x}(t), t]}. \tag{87}$$

Using Gaussian approximation on Eq. (87) and merging the multiplied expectations yields

$$-(1/r)\int_{-\infty}^{\infty}\int_{-\infty}^{\infty}[\underline{X} - \underline{\hat{x}}(t)]h(\underline{X}, t)h(\underline{Y}, t)N_{\underline{X}} \cdot [\underline{\hat{x}}(t), P(t)]N_{\underline{Y}}[\underline{\hat{x}}(t), P(t)]d\underline{X}d\underline{Y}, \tag{88}$$

where $N_{\underline{X}}(\hat{x}, P)$ means $\underline{X}$ is normally distributed with mean $\underline{\hat{x}}$ and covariance P. In these equations the integrals are over multidimensional Euclidean spaces. The limits on the integrals are $\pm\infty$. This is to indicate that the integral is over the entire space. Employing Eqs. (80) and (85) yields the useful identity

$$h(\underline{X}, t)h(\underline{Y}, t) = R(X_1 - Y_1). \tag{89}$$

Thus Eq. (88) becomes

$$\frac{1}{r}\int_{-\infty}^{\infty}\int_{-\infty}^{\infty}[\underline{X} - \hat{x}(t)]R(X_1 - Y_1)N_{\underline{X}} \cdot [\underline{\hat{x}}(t), P(t)]N_{\underline{Y}}[\underline{\hat{x}}(t), P(t)]d\underline{X}d\underline{Y}. \tag{90}$$

Define the error vector $\underline{e}(t)$ and associated dummy variables as such

$$\underline{e}(t) = \underline{x}(t) - \underline{\hat{x}}(t); \qquad \underline{V} = \underline{X} - \underline{\hat{x}}(t); \qquad \underline{W} = \underline{Y} - \underline{\hat{x}}(t), \tag{91}$$

and translate Eq. (90) from ($\underline{X}$, $\underline{Y}$) to $\underline{V}$, $\underline{W}$) coordinates to obtain an expression for the ith component of Eq. (90)

$$-(1/r) \int_{-\infty}^{\infty} \int_{-\infty}^{\infty} V_i R(V_1 - W_1) N_{\underline{V}}[\underline{O}, P(t)] N_{\underline{W}}[\underline{O}, P(t)] d\underline{V} d\underline{W}. \quad (92)$$

This expression equals zero for all i because the function V_i is odd in the argument ($\underline{V}$, $\underline{W}$), whereas R, $N_{\underline{V}}$, and $N_{\underline{W}}$ are even in the same argument. Hence, the product is odd and the integral is zero.

The second simplification occurs in the covariance equation. First, the subtractive portion of the third term of Eq. (84) is isolated.

$$-(1/r)\left\{\left[\overline{(x_i(t) - \hat{x}_i(t))(\hat{x}_j(t) - x_j(t))}\right.\right.$$
$$\left.\left. - \overline{\overline{(x_i(t) - \hat{x}_i(t))(x_j(t) - \hat{x}_j(j))}}\right] h(\underline{x}(t), t)\right\} \widehat{h(\underline{x}(t), t)}. \quad (93)$$

Employing the Gaussian assumption and instantaneous averaging we find that Eq. (93), after translation, equals

$$-(1/r) \int_{-\infty}^{\infty} \int_{-\infty}^{\infty} [V_i V_j - P_{ij}(t)] R(V_1 - W_1) N_{\underline{V}}[\underline{O}, P(t)] N_{\underline{W}}$$
$$\cdot [\underline{O}, P(t)] d\underline{V} d\underline{W}. \quad (94)$$

Second, the second term of Eq. (84) can be written

$$-(1/r)\left[\overline{[x_i(t) - \hat{x}_i(t)] h[\underline{x}(t), t]}\right]\left[\overline{[x_j(t) - \hat{x}_j(t)] h[\underline{x}(t), t]}\right]. \quad (95)$$

Again, combining integrals under the Gaussian assumption, using instantaneous averaging, and translating the integration domain yields for Eq. (95)

$$-(1/r) \int_{-\infty}^{\infty} \int_{-\infty}^{\infty} V_i W_i R(V_1 - W_1) N_{\underline{V}}[\underline{O}, P(t)] N_{\underline{W}}[\underline{O}, P(t)] d\underline{V} d\underline{W}. \quad (96)$$

The contention is that terms [Eqs. (94) and (96)] sum to zero. The calculation of these two integrals is detailed in the Appendix. They are

$$\text{Eq. (94)} = -\frac{1}{r}\left(\frac{P_{i1}P_{j1}}{P_{11}^2}\right)\left(\frac{P_{11}^3}{\pi}\right)^{1/2}\left[\exp\left(\frac{-1}{4P_{11}}\right) - 1\right], \tag{97}$$

$$\text{Eq. (96)} = +\frac{1}{r}\left(\frac{P_{i1}P_{j1}}{P_{11}^2}\right)\left(\frac{P_{11}^3}{\pi}\right)^{1/2}\left[\exp\left(\frac{-1}{4P_{11}}\right) - 1\right], \tag{98}$$

which negate each other, making receiver implementation much simpler.

Writing the remaining integral terms of Eqs. (83) and (84) in terms of the translated variable $\underline{V} = \underline{X} - \hat{\underline{x}}(t)$ we obtain the final result for the receiver

$$\dot{\hat{\underline{x}}}(t) = F\hat{\underline{x}}(t) + (1/r)\int_{-\infty}^{\infty} \underline{V}N_{\underline{V}}[\underline{O}, P(t)]S[t - \hat{x}_1(t) - V_1] \cdot dV_1 z(t), \tag{99}$$

$$\frac{dP_{ij}(t)}{dt} = [FP(t) + P(t)F^T + GQG^T]_{ij} + (1/r)\int_{-\infty}^{\infty} (V_iV_j - P_{ij})N_{\underline{V}} \cdot [\underline{O}, P(t)]S(t - \hat{x}_1 - V_1)dV_1 z(t). \tag{100}$$

The receiver has the following notable features: (a) the first term of each equation is dynamics dependent and accounts for propagation of the estimated diffusion in accordance with the given dynamic model, (b) the second term updates the estimates continuously using the received signal. Both employ locally generated PN-code waveforms, $S[t - \hat{x}_1(t) + V_1]$, (c) because of the use of the centered variable $\underline{e}(t)$ (or $\underline{V}$) in the two equations, there is feedback in the receiver from the present estimate $x_1(t)$ to the phase of the local codes, and Eq. (100) drives itself and also drives Eq. (99) through adjusting the value of $P(t)$.

The correspondence between this processor and those given previously can be illuminated by assuming $\underline{x} = x_1$ and that $F = 0$ and $G = 1$ in Eqs. (99) and (98). The receiver is specified by

$$\dot{\hat{x}}_1(t) = \frac{1}{r}\int_{-\infty}^{\infty} \frac{V_1}{(2\pi P_{11}(t))^{1/2}} \exp\left(\frac{-V_1^2}{2P_{11}(t)}\right) S \cdot [t - x_1(t) - V_1] dV_1 z(t), \qquad (101)$$

$$\dot{P}_{11}(t) = Q + \frac{1}{r}\int_{-\infty}^{\infty} \frac{V_1^2 - P_{11}^2(t)}{(2\pi P_{11}(t))^{1/2}} \exp\left(\frac{-V_1^2}{2P_{11}(t)}\right) S \cdot [t - x_1(t) - V_1] dV_1 z(t). \qquad (102)$$

These equations can be interpreted in two ways. (a) The integrals in Eqs. (101) and (102) are convolutions, and thus prescribe linear filters through which the feedback corrected local code $S[t - \hat{x}_1(t)]$ should be sent and subsequently multiplied by $z(t)$. The covariance $P_{11}(t)$ is to be treated as a slowly varying filter parameter. (b) Moving $z(t)$ inside the integral, the equations instruct us to form all correlations, $S[t - \hat{x}_1(t) - V_1) z(t)]$, for all V_1 in $(-\infty, +\infty)$, and then use the specified weighting pattern to sum them. If we approximate the continuous domain integral by a grid with spacing of one chip we shall have derived the structure discussed previously. Because of the difficulty of implemnting interpretation (a), we shall use this second approach here.

Approximating Eqs. (101) and (102) by discretization of V_1, we obtain

$$\dot{\hat{x}}_1(t) = \frac{1}{r} \sum_{i=-\infty}^{\infty} \left\{ \frac{i}{(2\pi P_{11}(t))^{1/2}} \exp\left[\frac{-i^2}{2P_{11}(t)}\right] \right\} \cdot \{S[t - \hat{x}_1(t) - i]z(t)\}, \quad (103)$$

$$\dot{P}_{11}(t) = Q + \frac{1}{r} \sum_{i=-\infty}^{\infty} \left\{ \frac{i^2 - P_{11}(t)}{(2\pi P_{11}(t))^{1/2}} \exp\left[\frac{-i^2}{2P_{11}(t)}\right] \right\} \cdot \{S[t - \hat{x}_1(t) - i]z(t)\}, \quad (104)$$

$S[t - \hat{x}_1(t) - i]$ is the local code that lags behind the on-time code $S[t - \hat{x}_1(t)]$, by i chips. The infinite sums in Eqs. (103) and (104) must be truncated for physical realizability. We shall assume that i goes from $-N_e$ to $+N_e$, and that the weights are small near those edge values. The weights in Eq. (103) are the same as those derived by [8,9] provided the values of $P_{11}(t)$ are the same. However, an auxiliary set of weights has been derived to drive the detector width, $2(P_{11}(t))^{1/2}$, making it a data dependent processor. The weighting patterns for the mean and variance equations are derived in Figs. 15 and 16.

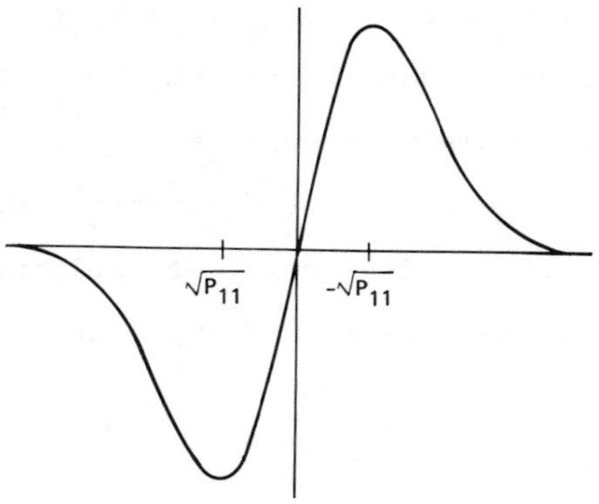

Fig. 15. Weighting pattern in mean equation.

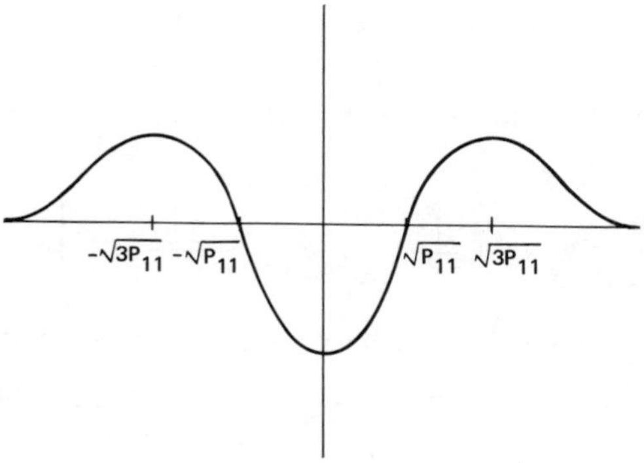

Fig. 16. Weighting pattern in covariance equation.

Figure 15 is the extended detector characteristic, which provides the feedback signal constantly to null the error $e_1(t) = x_1(t) - \hat{x}_1(t)$. Figure 16 is interpretable as such: if $z(t)$ should produce high correlation with codes $S[t - \hat{x}_1(t) - i]$ for $|i| < (P_{11}(t))^{1/2}$, then $P_{11}(t)$ is driven lower in order to produce a tighter mean detector weighting pattern for higher accuracy tracking; if $z(t)$ correlates with $S[t - \hat{x}_1(t) - i]$ for $|i| > (P_{11}(t))^{1/2}$, then $P_{11}(t)$ is increased to guard against losing lock. This data dependency helps guard against modeling errors and the inaccuracies of the Gaussian assumption.

A useful quality of this processor is that it is easily extensible to higher-dimension state variables. The two weighting patterns derived are the *only* two necessary regardless of the dynamics order. This is seen from Eqs. (99) and (100). The ith component of the second term of Eq. (99) equals

$$(1/r) \int_{-\infty}^{\infty} V_i N_{\underline{V}}[0,\ P(t)]S[t - \hat{x}_1(t) - V_1]dV_1 z(t). \qquad (105)$$

Eliminating all integrations except those with respect to V_1 and V_i, and factoring the jointly-normal density of V_1 and V_i

to a conditional times a marginal density, Eq. (105) becomes

$$\frac{1}{r}\int_{-\infty}^{\infty} N_{V_1}[0,\ P_{11}(t)]S[t - \hat{x}_1(t) - V_1]$$

$$\cdot\left[\int_{-\infty}^{\infty} V_i N_{V_i}\left(\frac{P_{i1}}{P_{11}} V_1,\ P_{ii} - \frac{P_{i1}^2}{P_{11}}\right)dV_i\right]dV_1 z(t). \qquad (106)$$

The integral enclosed in brackets equals the conditional mean of V_i given V_1, which is $P_{i1}V_1P_{11}$; hence Eq. (106) becomes

$$(1/r)(P_{i1}/P_{11})$$

$$\int_{-\infty}^{\infty} V_1 N_{V_1}[0,\ P_{11}(t)]S[t - \hat{x}_1(t) - V_1]dV_1 z(t). \qquad (107)$$

This tells us that $\hat{x}_i(t)$ is to be driven by the output of the corresponding expression in the $\hat{x}_1(t)$ equation, scaled by $P_{i1}(t)/P_{11}(t)$.

Likewise, the second term of Eq. (100) is computable as

$$\frac{1}{r}\,\frac{P_{i1}P_{j1}}{P_{11}^2}\int_{-\infty}^{\infty} |V_1^2 - P_{11}(t)|N_{V_1}[0,\ P_{11}(t)]$$

$$\cdot\ S[t - \hat{x}_1(t) - V_1]dV_1 z(t), \qquad (108)$$

which specifies a scaling factor of $P_{i1}P_{j1}/P_{11}^2$ to be applied to the $P_{11}(t)$ equation's output to drive the corresponding term of the $P_{ij}(t)$ equation.

G. DISCRETE-TIME POINT-MASS APPROXIMATION METHOD FOR PDF REPRESENTATION

The Point-Mass Approximation

We shall now concern ourselves with an approximate method of solving for the conditional probability density function (PDF) of discrete-time systems. Here, a useful technique is to propagate the PDF only at a set of points (grid) that

support most of the PDF. To begin, we specify the system and its *exact* recursive solution. The system is

$$\underline{x}(t + 1) = \underline{f}[\underline{x}(t), t] + \underline{g}[\underline{x}(t), t]\underline{n}(t), \tag{109}$$

$$\underline{z}(t) = \underline{h}[\underline{x}(t), t] + \underline{v}(t), \tag{110}$$

$$\underline{x}(0) = \underline{\xi}. \tag{111}$$

where $\underline{x}(t)$ is an n-dimensional state vector, $\underline{z}(t)$ a p-dimensional observation vector, $\underline{n}(t)$ a zero-mean m-dimensional WGN sequence of covariance matrix $Q(t)$, $\underline{v}(t)$ a zero-mean p-dimensional WGN sequence of covariance matrix $R(t)$, $\underline{g}$ a function that is matrix-valued $(n \times m)$, $\underline{f}$ and $\underline{h}$ are nonlinear functions, and $\underline{\xi}$ is a zero-mean Gaussian random vector of covariance matrix $P(0|-1)$ and mean $\hat{\underline{x}}(0|-1)$, which provides the initial PDF for the filter. Letting $p_{t/\tau}(\underline{\gamma})$ denote the probability density of $\underline{x}(t)$ given the observations

$$Z_0^{\tau} \equiv \{\underline{z}(0), \underline{z}(1), \ldots, \underline{z}(\tau)\}, \tag{112}$$

it is necessary for the filter to produce two functions (a) the *filtered* PDF $p_{t/t}(\underline{\gamma})$ of the state $\underline{x}(t)$, and (b) the *predicted* PDF $p_{t+1/t}(\underline{\gamma})$ of the state $\underline{x}(t + 1)$. Once the PDF has been constructed, any type of estimate $\hat{\underline{x}}(t/t)$ or $\hat{\underline{x}}(t + 1/t)$ can be generated, such as

(a) $\hat{\underline{x}}(t/t) = \int_{-\infty}^{\infty} \underline{\gamma} p_{t/t}(\underline{\gamma}) d\underline{\gamma}$ = conditional mean, for a minimum-variance approach;

(b) $\hat{\underline{x}}(t/t) = \underline{\gamma}$ where $p_{t/t}(\underline{\gamma}) \geq p_{t/t}(\underline{\beta})$ for $\underline{\gamma} \neq \underline{\beta}$ for a maximum likelihood estimate.

The filtering equation is simply an application of Bayes' law. Assuming that $p_{t/t-1}(\underline{\gamma})$ is available, and that z(t) has just been observed, then

$$p_{t/t}(\underline{\gamma}) = \frac{\Pr[\underline{z}(t)|\underline{x}(t) = \underline{\gamma}]p_{t/t-1}(\underline{\gamma})}{\int_{-\infty}^{\infty} \Pr[z(t)|\underline{x}(t) = \underline{\gamma}]p_{t/t-1}(\underline{\gamma})d\underline{\gamma}}. \tag{113}$$

Where $\Pr[\underline{z}(t)|\underline{x}(t) = \gamma]$ is the conditional density of the measurement $\underline{z}(t)$ given the state $\underline{x}(t)$. Given normal distribution of $\underline{v}(t)$, which we shall abbreviate as $N[\underline{O}, R(t)]$, we can deduce that

$$\Pr[\underline{z}(t)|\underline{x}(t) = \underline{\gamma}] = N[\underline{z}(t) - \underline{h}(\underline{\gamma}, t), R(t)]; \tag{114}$$

thus the filtered update is recursively given by

$$p_{t/t}(\underline{\gamma}) = \frac{N[\underline{z}(t) - \underline{h}(\underline{\gamma}, t), R(t)]p_{t/t-1}(\underline{\gamma})}{\int_{-\infty}^{\infty} N[\underline{z}(t) - \underline{h}(\underline{\gamma}, t), R(t)]p_{t/t-1}(\underline{\gamma})d\underline{\gamma}}. \tag{115}$$

To derive the predicted PDF $p_{t+1/t}(\underline{\gamma})$ in terms of $p_{t/t}(\underline{\gamma})$, one must weigh and summ all the possible ways that $\underline{x}(t + 1)$ can equal $\underline{\gamma}$. If we let $T_{t+1/t}(\underline{\gamma}|\underline{\beta})$ denote the transition probability, i.e., the probability that $\underline{x}(t + 1) = \underline{\gamma}$ given that $\underline{x}(t) = \underline{\beta}$, then

$$p_{t+1/t}(\underline{\gamma}) = \int_{-\infty}^{\infty} T_{t+1/t}(\underline{\gamma}|\underline{\beta})p_{t/t}(\underline{\beta})d\underline{\beta}. \tag{116}$$

The function T is easily ascertained by knowledge of the distribution of $\underline{n}(t)$. Then we have

$$T_{t+1/t}(\underline{\gamma}|\underline{\beta}) = N[\underline{\gamma} - \underline{f}(\underline{\beta}, t), \underline{g}(\beta, t)Q(t)\underline{g}^T(\underline{\beta}, t)]. \tag{117}$$

Hence the predicted density is recursively given by

$$p_{t+1/t}(\underline{\gamma}) = \int_{-\infty}^{\infty} N[\underline{\gamma} - \underline{f}(\underline{\beta}, t), \underline{g}(\underline{\beta}, t)Q(t)\underline{g}^T(\underline{\beta}, t)]p_{t/t}(\underline{\beta})d\underline{\beta}. \tag{118}$$

Equations (115) and (118) allow recursive propagation of the conditional PDF. However, for general $\underline{f}$, $\underline{g}$, and $\underline{h}$, it is rare that closed-form solutions will be available. Hence [10] and [11] developed the point-mass PDF representation.

The point-mass representation approximates $p_{t/t}$ and $p_{t+1/t}$ by a set of impulses

$$p_{t/\cdot}(\underline{\gamma}) \approx \sum_{l_1, l_2, \ldots, l_n = 1}^{2N+1} p_{t/\cdot}[\underline{b}(l_1, \ldots, l_n)]\,\delta[\underline{\gamma} - \underline{b}(l_1, \ldots, l_n)],$$

where $\underline{b}(l_1, \ldots, l_n)$ is a grid, taking values in $\mathbb{R}^n$. The simpler scheme is to keep the grid fixed in time. A more advanced scheme, developed by [10], is to translate the grid to maintain its center on the conditional mean and rotate the grid to align its axes with the principle axes of the error ellipsoid. The simpler version turns the filtering and prediction Eqs. (115) and (118), respectively, into

$$\begin{aligned} &p_{t/t}(\underline{b}(l_1, \ldots, l_n)) \\ &\quad = N\{\underline{z}(t) - \underline{h}[\underline{b}(l_1, \ldots, l_n)t], R(t)\}p_{t/t-1}[\underline{b}(l_1, \ldots, l_n)] \\ &\quad\quad \cdot \left\{ \sum_{m_1, \ldots, m_n = 1}^{2N+1} N\{\underline{z}(t) - \underline{h}[\underline{b}(m_1, \ldots, m_n), t], R(t)\} \right. \\ &\quad\quad\quad \left. \cdot\, p_{t/t-1}[\underline{b}(m_1, \ldots, m_n)] \right\}^{-1}, \end{aligned} \tag{119}$$

and

$$\begin{aligned} &p_{t+1/t}[\underline{b}(l_1, \ldots, l_n)] \\ &\quad = \sum_{m_1, \ldots, m_n = 1}^{2N+1} N\Big\{\underline{b}(l_1, \ldots, l_n) - \underline{f}[\underline{b}(m_1, \ldots, m_n), t], \\ &\quad\quad\quad \underline{g}[\underline{b}(m_1, \ldots, m_n), t]Q(t)\underline{g}^T[\underline{b}(m_1, \ldots, m_n), t]\Big\} \\ &\quad\quad\quad \cdot\, p_{t/t}[\underline{b}(m_1, \ldots, m_n)]. \end{aligned} \tag{120}$$

Equation (120) may, however, require a slight normalization to compensate for numerical inaccuracies that cause the total probability mass to deviate from 1. Alternatively, Eqs. (119) and (120) may be combined and a single renormalization performed to account for the denominator of Eq. (119) and numerical inaccuracies.

This basic point-mass solution is not immediately useful to the problem of spread-spectrum ranging because that problem is naturally continuous-time. However, a close variant of the Bucy point-mass technique can be used to solve this system by approximating the exact continuous-time solution (Kushner's Equation) by point masses. Furthermore, the point-mass solution is very natural for PN-code tracking because of the discrete-time nature of the code.

Tracking the conditional mean $\underline{x}(t)$ requires computing the PDF of $\underline{x}(t)$, $p_{\underline{x}}$. This further requires an on-line computation of Kushner's Equation, from which Eqs. (83) and (84) stem. The full PDF-propagation equation is

$$\frac{\partial p_{\underline{x}}\left(\underline{X},\ t \mid z_0^t\right)}{\partial t} = L[p_{\underline{x}}] + \frac{1}{r}\, p_{\underline{x}}\left(\underline{X},\ t \mid z_0^t\right) \cdot \left\{h(\underline{X},\ t) - \widehat{h[\underline{x}(t),\ t]}\right\}[z(t) - \hat{h}], \tag{121}$$

where L is the Fokker-Planck operator for our dynamics equation, (79), which is given by

$$L[p_{\underline{x}}] = -\sum_{i=1}^{n} \left(F_{ii} p_{\underline{x}} + F_i \underline{X}\, \frac{\partial p_{\underline{x}}}{\partial X_i}\right) + \frac{1}{2} \sum_{i=1}^{n} \sum_{j=1}^{n} g_i Q g_j\, \frac{\partial^2 p_{\underline{x}}}{\partial X_i \partial X_j} \tag{122}$$

where F_i is the ith row of F, F_{ij} the (i, j)th element of F, and g_i the ith element of g = G. Implementing this equation directly is impossible because of the continuous-valued domain over which p_x is defined, thus requiring infinite computer memory. This problem can be treated by Bucy's method of sampling $p_{\underline{x}}$ at a convenient spacing, and propagating $p_{\underline{x}}$ only at the chosen grid values of $\underline{X}$. Furthermore, this is natural for our system in particular because of the code waveforms, wherein a good spacing for the X_1 grid is 1 (chip).

Owing to computational overhead of implementing higher-order dynamics processes, we shall limit the discussion to the first-order process specified by $\dot{x}_1(t) = \xi(t)$. Then the discretized PDF is supported only by the natural unit-spaced grid selected for the x_1 axis. The following development is extensible to any n-dimensional process with its respective n-dimensional grid support. However, two important considerations must be borne in mind. (a) For the derivative of $x_1(t)$, e.g., $x_2 = \dot{x}_1$ = velocity (chips/sec), there is no natural grid spacing as for x_1. (b) Implementing an order-n process estimator will generally result in a different detector weighting pattern for each component of the state-variable update. This results because the marginal and conditional densities of an arbitrary joint density are not necessarily of the same family, as was the case with the jointly Gaussian density.

Kushner's Equation exhibits the same dynamics/predictor, measurement/update type of structure as evinced by the first and second terms of Eq. (121). Equation (121) for our first-order case becomes

$$\frac{\partial p_{x_1}\left(X_1,\ t|Z_0^t\right)}{\partial t} = \frac{1}{2} Q \frac{\partial^2 p_{x_1}}{\partial X_1^2} + \frac{1}{r} p_{x_1}\left\{h(X_1,\ t) - \widehat{h[x_1(t),\ t]}\right\}[z(t) - \hat{h}]. \tag{123}$$

Discretization of the dynamics term is best treated by approximating the second derivative by a three-point method. Letting Γ_1 denote the integer-separated values of X_1 that will support the sampled PDF, we may substitute

$$\frac{1}{2} Q\left[p_{x_1}\left(\Gamma_1 + 1,\ t|Z_0^t\right) - 2p_{x_1}\left(\Gamma_1,\ t|Z_0^t\right) + p_{x_1}\left(\Gamma_1 - 1,\ t|Z_0^t\right)\right] \tag{124}$$

for the second derivative of p_{x_1} at Γ_1.

The observation term of Eq. (123) is best handled by deriving an equivalent term that is directly obtained from discrete-*time* and discrete PDF-space (Γ_1) probabilistic considerations. Handling this term directly in discrete time is justified by practical considerations. Given the continuous-time formulation of Eq. (123), a receiver would normally only approximate that calculation by discretizing all functions and derivatives with respect to time. (This is simply because analog processing of the signals would be technically too difficult.) Hence the associated approximations would be possible sources of inaccuracy. A rederivation of the observation term of Eq. (123) proved to be simpler and more robust to point-mass approximations than direct discretization of the same under computer simulation.

Letting Δt denote the sampling period of the receiver, the correlations $S(t - \Gamma_1)z(t)$ will be discretized with respect to time and indexed by the integer n for n = 1, 2. 3, ... Hence our observed information is a sequence of $(2N_e + 1)$-dimensional random vectors parameterized by the discrete-time index n:

$$\underline{v}(n) = \begin{bmatrix} v_{-N_e}(n) \\ \vdots \\ v_i(n) \\ \vdots \\ v_{+N_e}(n) \end{bmatrix} \quad \text{for} \quad n = 1, 2, 3, \ldots, \tag{125}$$

where

$$v_i(n) = \int_{(n-1)\Delta t}^{n\Delta t} z(\tau) S\left\{\tau - \overbrace{[x_1((n - 1)\Delta t) + i]}^{\Gamma_1}\right\} d\tau. \tag{126}$$

N_e is the number of local-code phases ahead and behind the on-time code that are correlated with z(t). The estimate is also a discrete-time sequence; Δt is assumed to be small enough so that quantization error is acceptable. Notice that we shall let the Γ_1 grid move rigidly as the estimate $\hat{x}_1(n\Delta t)$ moves, so that the center value of Γ_1 equals $\hat{x}_1(n\Delta t)$:

$$\Gamma_1 = \hat{x}_1(n\ t) + i, \qquad i = -N_e, -N_e + 1, \ldots, +N_e. \tag{127}$$

This vector sequence of observations allows us to propagate the sampled PDF through Bayes' Law. Specifically, assume we have generated $p_{x_1}[\Gamma_1, (n - 1)\Delta t | Z_0^{(n-1)\Delta t}]$ for $\Gamma_1 = \hat{x}_1[(n - 1)\Delta t] - N_e$ to $\hat{x}_1[(n - 1)\Delta t] + N_e$ in unit steps and that

$$\hat{x}_1[(n - 1)\Delta t] = \sum_{\Gamma_1} \Gamma_1 p_{x_1}\left[\Gamma_1, (n - 1)\Delta t | Z_0^{(n-1)\Delta t}\right]. \tag{128a}$$

Then we must generate $p_{x_1}\left(\Gamma_1, n\ t|Z_0^{n\Delta t}\right)$ for the same Γ_1, and compute the new estimate

$$\hat{x}_1(n\Delta t) = \sum_{\Gamma_1} \Gamma_1 p_{x_1}\left(\Gamma_1, n\Delta t|Z_0^{n\Delta t}\right). \tag{128b}$$

Lastly, the set of points, $p_{x_1}\left(\Gamma_1, n\Delta t, Z_0^{n\Delta t}\right)$, for the current Γ_1 grid (which is centered on $\hat{x}_1[(n - 1)\Delta t)]$ must be interpolated to correspond to the values on the new Γ_1 grid centered on the new estimate $x_1(n\Delta t)$.

To begin this task we must first apply the Fokker-Planck operator of Eq. (124) to obtain the predicted PDF values:

$$\begin{aligned} p_{x_1}\ \Gamma_1, n\Delta t|Z_0^{(n-1)\Delta t} &= p_{x_1}\left[\Gamma_1, (n - 1)\Delta t|Z_0^{(n-1)\Delta t}\right] \\ &+ \frac{1}{2}\ Q\Delta t\Big\{p_{x_1}\left[\Gamma_1 + 1, (n - 1)\Delta t|Z_0^{(n-1)\Delta t}\right] \\ &- 2p_{x_1}\left[\Gamma_1, (n - 1)\Delta t|Z_0^{(n-1)\Delta t}\right] \\ &+ p_{x_1}\left[\Gamma_1 - 1, (n - 1)\Delta t|Z_0^{(n-1)\Delta t}\right]\Big\} \end{aligned} \tag{129}$$

for all Γ_1 in the current grid. The incoming vector $\underline{v}(n)$ then allows us to update these values to $p_{x_1}\left(\Gamma_1, n\Delta t|Z_0^{n\Delta t}\right)$ by Bayes' Law:

$$p_{x_1}\left(\Gamma_1, n\Delta t|Z_0^{n\Delta t}\right) = \frac{\Pr\ \underline{v}(n)|x_1(n\Delta t) = \Gamma_1, Z_0^{(n-1)\Delta t}\ p_{x_1}\left(\Gamma_1, n\ t|Z_0^{(n-1)\Delta t}\right)}{\sum_{\Gamma_1}[\text{numerator}]}. \tag{130}$$

Because $x_1(t)$ and $n(t)$ are Markov processes and $z(t)$ depends in a memoryless fashion on them, we have

$$\Pr\left[\underline{v}(n)\,|\,x_1(n\Delta t) = \Gamma_1,\ z_0^{(n-1)\Delta t}\right]$$
$$= \Pr[\underline{v}(n)\,|\,x_1(n\Delta t) = \Gamma_1]. \tag{131}$$

This likelihood function is easily computed by noting that the components of $\underline{v}(n)$ are distributed as

$$v_i(n)\,|\,x_1 = \Gamma_1 \approx N(\Delta t,\ r\Delta t), \qquad \text{for} \quad i = \Gamma_1 - \hat{x}_1[(n-1)\Delta t];$$
$$v_i(n)\,|\,x_1 = \Gamma_1 \approx N(0,\ r\Delta t), \qquad \text{for all other } i. \tag{132}$$

All $v_i(n)$ are independent because the correlations of white noise with the orthogonal local-code phases produce independent random variables. The single-chip grid spacing is very important in this respect for computational simplicity. Thus the likelihood function is given by

$$\Pr[\underline{v}(n)\,|\,x_1(n\Delta t) = \Gamma_1]$$
$$= \frac{1}{(2\pi\Delta t r)^{1/2}} \exp\left\{\frac{-[v_{\Gamma_1-\hat{x}_1}(n) - \Delta t]^2}{2\Delta t r}\right\}$$
$$\cdot \prod_{\substack{i=-N_e \\ i\neq\Gamma_1-\hat{x}_1}}^{+N_e} \frac{1}{(2\pi\Delta t r)^{1/2}} \exp\left\{\frac{-[v_i(n)]^2}{2\Delta t r}\right\}, \tag{133}$$

where $\hat{x}_1$ means $\hat{x}_1[(n-1)\Delta t]$. Equation (133) equals

$$\left(\frac{1}{(2\pi\Delta t r)^{1/2}}\right)^{2N_e+1} \exp\left[\sum_{i=-N_e}^{+N_e} \frac{-v_i^2(n)}{2\Delta t r}\right] \exp\left[\frac{2v_{\Gamma_1-\hat{x}_1}(n)\Delta t - (\Delta t)^2}{2\Delta t r}\right]. \tag{134}$$

Using Eq. (134) in Eq. (130) yields the measurement-update formula

$$p_{x_1}\left(\Gamma_1,\ n\Delta t \mid Z_0^{n\Delta t}\right)$$

$$= \frac{\exp\left[(1/r)v_{\Gamma_1 - \hat{x}_1}(n)\right] p_{x_1}\left(\Gamma_1,\ n\Delta t \mid Z_0^{(n-1)\Delta t}\right)}{\sum_{i=-N_e}^{N_e} \exp[(1/r)v_i(n)] p_{x_1}\left(\hat{x}_1 + i,\ n\Delta t \mid Z_0^{(n-1)\Delta t}\right)}, \qquad (135)$$

where $\hat{x}_1$ means $\hat{x}_1[(n - 1)\Delta t]$ and $\Gamma_1 = \hat{x}_1 + i$. A simple way to implement Eq. (133) is to scale the predicted probabilities $p_{x_1}\left(\Gamma_1,\ n\Delta t \mid Z_0^{(n-1)\Delta t}\right)$ by the factors $\exp(V_{\Gamma_1} - \hat{x}_1(n)/r)$ for each Γ_1. The scaled samples should then be normalized for unit sum, and Eq. (128b) is employed to generate the new estimate. Lastly, the grid should be shifted to the new values,

$$i = \Gamma_1 - \hat{x}_1(n\Delta t), \qquad i = -N_e, \quad -N_e + 1, \ldots, +N_e. \qquad (136)$$

An initial PDF assumption starts this recursive estimator/tracker.

Equations (129) and (135), which specify the receiver for the Brownian-motion case, are comparable in computer overhead to the DDAG detector. These equations dictate the minimum-variance estimator for our state-space system with only the approximations of finite PDF grid and discrete time. Notice, however, that the grid spacing was crucial to obtaining the measurement update formula for the Bayesian Detector, whereas in the DDAG detector, smaller spacing only implies sampling the weighting patterns at more points.

H. SIMULATION OF PN-CODE DELAY ESTIMATORS

Simulations of the first-order DDAG and Bayesian tracking loops were performed on an Amdahl 470V8 high-speed processor. The intent of these simulations was to determine the steady-state tracking variances of the two schemes within the two regimes: [low dynamics, high receiver noise] and [high dynamics, low receiver-noise]. Single-chip spacing of the correlators was employed in both cases, and the sampling interval Δt was fixed at 0.001 sec. A total of 41 correlators used ($N_e = 20$). Four runs of length 25,000 msec were performed in the low-dynamics regime; and four 10,000 msec runs were done with high dynamics. The theory to be demonstrated is that the Gaussian assumption is less accurate in the high-dynamics regime because the state variable enters the observation equation through the nonlinearity of code delay modulation, whereas the noise enters additively. For the eight simulations, the following sets of parameters (Table I) were chosen. The Gaussian Detector of Section III.D* was also run for comparison. The traditional early-late detector was not run because it quickly loses lock.

The mean-square error (MSE) is observed for each run. This parameter is computed every millisecond and averaged over the steady-state portion of the simulation (excludes an initial number of milliseconds). Tabulation of the tracking is in Table II. Even though the expected tracking variances are smaller for the four high-dynamics runs, the Gaussian loops

**This detector will herein be referred to as the Adaptive Gaussian (AG) detector, because it adapts to measured changes in noise and dynamics. The phrase "data-dependent" will be used to denote adaptivity by responding to measured errors.*

TABLE I. Listing of the Characteristics of the Four Low-Dynamics and Four High-Dynamics Runs

Run No.	Detector parameters: Q $\frac{\text{chips}^2}{\text{sec}}$	Detector parameters: r $\left(\frac{\text{chips}^2}{\text{Hz}}\right)_{dB}$	Tracking variance $P_{11_{ss}}$ computed by Eq. (66)	Length of simulation (msec)
L1[a]	15	-17	4.502	25,000
L2[a]	15	-15	11.31	25,000
L3[a]	15	-13	28.41	25,000
L4[a]	15	-11	71.36	25,000
H1[b]	100	-30	0.503	10,000
H2[b]	200	-30	2.011	10,000
H3[b]	400	-30	8.042	10,000
H4[b]	800	-30	32.17	10,000

[a] *L1-L4 are designations for low-dynamics runs;*
[b] *H1-H4 are designations for high-dynamics runs.*

clearly showed difficulty tracking these scenarios. This supports the theory that the Gaussian assumption is overly optimistic where the dynamics dominates the noise. The Bayesian Detector is an excellent tracking scheme for runs H1, H2, and H3. It was the only one that tracked H1 and H3 without loss of lock. In H4 only one protracted loss-of-lock event accounted for the poor final MSE. Though the other loops show better MSEs for this run, they did lose lock on multiple occasions. Similarly, the DDAG detector outperforms the AG detector in MSE for these four runs because it can widen itself to reacquire a signal near the edge of the correlator bank.

The four low-dynamics runs showed no loss-of-lock problems; hence these data are a more reliable indicator of steady-state tracking ability. Averaging the MSE/$P_{11_{ss}}$ ratios for the 4 25-sec runs, we can obtain a rough indicator of comparative

TABLE II. Tracking History

Run No.	Initial msec excluded	Tracking variance $P_{11_{ss}}$ computed by Eq. (66)	AG			DDAG			Bayesian		
			MSE	$\frac{MSE}{P_{11_{ss}}}$	Msec out of lock	MSE	$\frac{MSE}{P_{11_{ss}}}$	Msec out of lock	MSE	$\frac{MSE}{P_{11_{ss}}}$	Msec out of lock
L1	1250	4.502	8.421	1.871	0	3.266	0.7255	0	5.325	1.183	0
L2	1250	11.31	16.05	1.419	0	13.03	1.152	0	7.467	0.6602	0
L3	2500	28.41	24.74	0.8708	0	17.33	0.6100	0	7.199	0.2534	0
L4	5000	71.36	50.51	0.7078	0	41.13	0.5764	0	43.55	0.6103	0
H1	0	0.503	2768	5503	9620	4442	8831	9624	1.217	2.419	0
H2	0	2.011	20.08	9.985	0	5.288	2.630	0	2.820	1.402	0
H3	0	8.042	199.8	24.84	1333	30.23	3.759	37	5.522	0.6866	0
H4	0	32.17	96.04	2.985	653	50.08	1.557	173	137.1	4.262	963

TABLE III. Comparative MSE Performance in the Low-Dynamics Regime

Loop type	*Average:* $\frac{MSE}{P_{11_{ss}}}$	*Ratios*		
AG	*1.2172*	*1*	*1.589*	*1.800*
DDAG	*0.7660*	*0.629*	*1*	*1.132*
Bayesian	*0.6767*	*0.556*	*0.883*	*1*

tracking performance for the three loops (Table III). The three detectors still hold their relative performance, but the differences are less extreme. The Bayesian detector outperforms the AG detector in MSE by about 1.8:1. The same ratio for AG versus DDAG is about 1.6:1. Hence, the Gaussian assumption does not seriously degrade the tracking performance of a minimum-variance receiver in this regime.

The point-mass approximation is probably most useful where computing power is available and where the extended Kalman filter is known to fail because of poor linearizability of f or h. Other global approximations are available that require less computation but are not quite as general as point-mass and have their own associated problems. The most popular are

(a) Gaussian sums: derived by [12], this method is good for multimodal PDFs. It consists of representing the PDF as a sum of weighted Gaussian distributions (a nonorthogonal series) and propagating the weights essentially as a Kalman filter would.

(b) Other orthogonal series expansions: these include Edgeworth expansion [13] Gram Chalier series [14], Gauss-Hermite Polynomials [15], and Least Squares Polynomial Approximations [16]. Generally two problems occur with these methods: (1) truncation of the series may result in some points of the PDF being negative, (2) truncation may result in an unnormalized PDF.

Owing to the nature of the code-tracking problem (unimodality and the discrete-time nature of codes), the point-mass approximation was a natural choice for global nonlinear estimation.

APPENDIX

First, the computation of

$$-\int_{-\infty}^{\infty}\int_{-\infty}^{\infty} V_1W_1R(V_1 - W_1)N_{V_1}[O, P_{11}(t)] \cdot N_{W_1}[O, P_{11}(t)]dV_1dW_1 \tag{137}$$

will be detailed. Inserting the multivariant Gaussian density function, this becomes

$$\frac{-1}{2\pi P_{11}(t)}\int_{-\infty}^{\infty}\int_{-\infty}^{\infty} V_1W_1R(V_1 - W_1)\ \exp\left[\frac{-\ V_1^2 + W_1^2}{2P_{11}(t)}\right]dV_1dW_1. \tag{138}$$

Consider a rotation of the (V_1, W_1) axes by 45°, specified by

$$\begin{bmatrix} g \\ f \end{bmatrix} = \frac{1}{(2)^{1/2}}\begin{bmatrix} 1 & 1 \\ 1 & -1 \end{bmatrix}\begin{bmatrix} V_1 \\ W_1 \end{bmatrix} \quad \text{or} \quad \begin{bmatrix} V_1 \\ W_1 \end{bmatrix} = \frac{1}{(2)^{1/2}}\begin{bmatrix} 1 & 1 \\ 1 & -1 \end{bmatrix}\begin{bmatrix} g \\ f \end{bmatrix}. \tag{139}$$

Then we can write

$$V_1^2 + W_1^2 = f^2 + g^2, \qquad R(V_1 - W_1) = R((2)^{1/2}f)$$

$$V_1W_1 = \tfrac{1}{2}(g + f)(g - f). \tag{140}$$

The function $R((2)^{1/2}f)$ is given by $1 - (2)^{1/2}|f|$ for $|f| < 1/(2)^{1/2}$, and 0 otherwise. Hence the full region of integration is a vertical strip $(2)^{1/2}$ wide in the fg plane (Fig. 17).

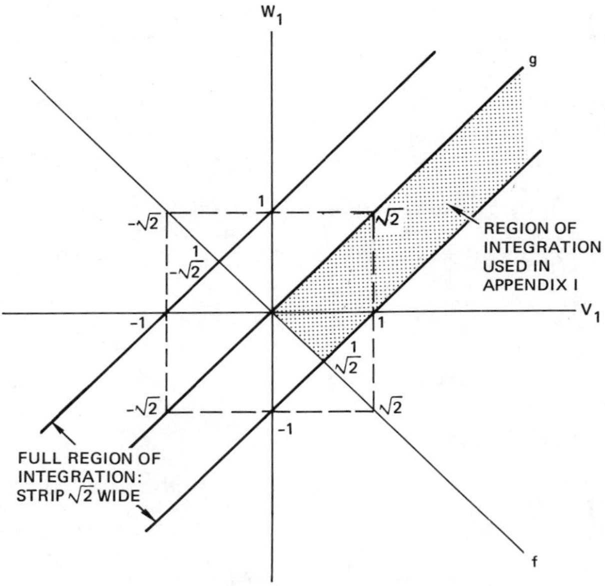

Fig. 17. Rotation used in the appendix.

Because our three functions in Eq. (140) are even, we may limit the integration to the shaded area indicated in Fig. 17, and multiply by 4. Thus expression (138) becomes

$$\frac{-4}{2\pi P_{11}(t)} \int_0^{\frac{1}{(2)^{1/2}}} \int_0^{\infty} \exp\left[\frac{-(f^2 + g^2)}{2P_{11}(t)}\right] \cdot \frac{(g + f)(g - f)}{2}(1 - (2)^{1/2}f)\,df\,dg, \quad (141)$$

which becomes

$$(-2)\frac{1}{2\pi P_{11}(t)} \int_0^{\frac{1}{(2)^{1/2}}} \int_0^{\infty} \exp\left[\frac{-(f^2 + g^2)}{2P_{11}(t)}\right] \cdot (g^2 - (2)^{1/2}fg^2 - f^2 + (2)^{1/2}f^3)\,df\,dg, \quad (142)$$

a sum of four integrals over rectangular supports, and separable. Computation of the integrals and addition of the results yields the final value of

$$+\left(\frac{P_{11}^{3}(t)}{\pi}\right)^{1/2}\left\{\exp\left[\frac{-1}{4P_{11}(t)}\right]-1\right\} \tag{143}$$

as the value of expression (137).

Next, the value of

$$-\int_{-\infty}^{\infty}\int_{-\infty}^{\infty}\left[V_1^2-P_{11}(t)\right]R(V_1-W_1)N_{V_1}[0,\ P_{11}(t)]$$
$$\cdot\ N_{W_1}[0,\ P_{11}(t)]\,dV_1\,dW_1 \tag{144}$$

will be shown exactly to cancel expression (137). This insures that a receiver with a one-dimensional state vector can safely drop the middle term in the variance equation. Expression (144) equals

$$\frac{-1}{2\pi P_{11}(t)}\int_{-\infty}^{\infty}\int_{-\infty}^{\infty}\left[V_1^2-P_{11}(t)\right]R(V_1-W_1)$$
$$\cdot\ \exp\left[\frac{-\left(V_1^2+W_1^2\right)}{2P_{11}(t)}\right]dV_1\,dW_1. \tag{145}$$

Again, we shall align our new coordinate system with Eq. (139) and integrate over the region indicated in Fig. 17. Using

$$V_1^2-P_{11}(t)=\tfrac{1}{2}(g+f)^2-P_{11}(t);\qquad R(V_1-W_1)=1-(2)^{1/2}f$$
$$V_1^2+W_1^2=f^2+g^2, \tag{146}$$

we obtain separable integrals, which all sum out to:

$$-\left(\frac{P_{11}^{3}(t)}{\pi}\right)^{1/2}\exp\left\{\left[\frac{-1}{4P_{11}(t)}\right]-1\right\}, \tag{147}$$

which is the desired result.

To generalize this computation to the (i, j)th component of the covariance matrix requires first dealing with the term

$$-\int_{-\infty}^{\infty}\int_{-\infty}^{\infty} V_i W_j R(V_1 - W_1) N_{\underline{V}}[\underline{O}, P(t)] N_{\underline{W}}[\underline{O}, P(t)]\, d\underline{V} d\underline{W}. \tag{148}$$

Eliminating all variables of integration except for V_1, V_i, W_1, and W_j allows us to write this as

$$-\int_{-\infty}^{\infty}\int_{-\infty}^{\infty}\int_{-\infty}^{\infty}\int_{-\infty}^{\infty} V_i W_j R(V_1 - W_1) \cdot N_{V_1, V_i}\left(\begin{bmatrix}0\\0\end{bmatrix}, \begin{bmatrix}P_{11} & P_{1i}\\ P_{i1} & P_{ii}\end{bmatrix}\right) \cdot N_{W_1, W_j}\left(\begin{bmatrix}0\\0\end{bmatrix}, \begin{bmatrix}P_{11} & P_{1j}\\ P_{j1} & P_{jj}\end{bmatrix}\right) dV_1 dV_i dW_1 dW_j. \tag{149}$$

Rearranging the remaining integrations,

$$-\int_{-\infty}^{\infty}\int_{-\infty}^{\infty} R(V_1 - W_1)\left[\int_{-\infty}^{\infty} V_i N_{V_1, V_i}\left(\begin{bmatrix}0\\0\end{bmatrix}, \begin{bmatrix}P_{11} & P_{1i}\\ P_{11} & P_{ii}\end{bmatrix}\right) dV_i\right] \cdot \left[\int_{-\infty}^{\infty} W_j N_{W_1, W_j}\left(\begin{bmatrix}0\\0\end{bmatrix}, \begin{bmatrix}P_{11} & P_{1j}\\ P_{j1} & P_{jj}\end{bmatrix}\right) dW_j\right] dV_1 dW_1. \tag{150}$$

The bracketed integrals are computed using the properties of jointly Gaussian density function and recognizing conditional means and covariances. The two integrals are, respectively, computed to be

$$\frac{P_{i1}}{P_{11}} V_1 N_{V_1}(O, P_{11}); \qquad \frac{P_{j1}}{P_{11}} W_1 N_{W_1}[O, P_{11}(t)], \tag{151}$$

which turns expression (150) into:

$$-\left(\frac{P_{i1}P_{j1}}{P_{11}^2}\right)\int_{-\infty}^{\infty}\int_{-\infty}^{\infty} V_1 W_1 R(V_1 - W_1) N_{V_1}[O, P_{11}(t)] \cdot N_{W_1}[O, P_{11}(t)]\, dV_1 dW_1. \tag{152}$$

This is the same as expression (137) scaled by $P_{i1}P_{j1}/P_{11}^2$. A similar computation shows that

$$-\int_{-\infty}^{\infty}\int_{-\infty}^{\infty} (V_iV_j - P_{ij})R(V_1 - W_1)N_{\underline{V}}[\underline{O}, P(t)]N_{\underline{W}}[\underline{O}, P(t)]d\underline{V}d\underline{W} \tag{153}$$

equals (144) scaled by the same factor. Thus as expressions (137) and (144) add to zero, so do (148) and (153).

REFERENCES

1. A. H. JAZWINSKI, "Stochastic Processes and Filtering Theory," Academic Press, New York, 1970.

2. A. GELB and W. E. VANDER VELDE, "Multiple-Input Describing Functions and Nonlinear System Design," McGraw-Hill, New York, 1968.

3. H. J. KUSHNER, *J. SIAM Control Ser. A 2*(1), 1106-1109 (1964).

4. J. J. SPILKER, "Digital Communications by Satellite," Prentice-Hall, Englewood Cliffs, New Jersey, 1977.

5. M. L. SCHIFF, International Telemetry Conference, June, 1977.

6. M. FUJISAKI, G. KALLIANPUR, and H. KUNITA, *Osaka J. Math. 9*(1), 19-40 (1972).

7. J. M. C. CLARK, "Recent Mathematical Developments in Control," D. J. Bell, ed., Academic Press, New York, 1973.

8. W. M. BOWLES, "Correlation Tracking," PhD. Thesis, MIT, Cambridge, Mass., June 1980.

9. W. M. BOWLES, "Extended Range Delay Lock Loop," presented at *1979 NAECON Conf.*

10. R. S. BUCY, *J. Astro. Sci. 17*, 80-94 (1969).

11. R. S. BUCY and K. D. SENNE, *Automatica 7*, 287-298 (1971).

12. D. L. ALSPACH and H. W. SORENSON, *IEEE Trans. Automatic Control 17*, 439-448 (1972).

13. H. W. SORENSON and A. R. STUBBERUD, *Int. J. Control 8*, 33-51 (1968).

14. K. SRINIVASAN, *IEEE Trans. Automatic Control 15*, 3-10 (1970).

15. C. HECHT, "Proceedings of the Second Sumposium on Nonlinear Estimation Theory and Its Applications," San Diego, CA, pp. 152-158, September 1971.

16. F. B. HILDEBRAND, "Introduction to Numerical Analysis," McGraw Hill, New York, 1956.

INDEX

D

E

F

G